T0320119

# The Chinese Strategic Mind

*In loving memory of Liu Wanjie and Dong Ming, whose love has inspired and guided me throughout my journey.*

# The Chinese Strategic Mind

SECOND EDITION

Hong Liu

*Alliance Manchester Business School, University of Manchester, UK*

Edward Elgar PUBLISHING

Cheltenham, UK • Northampton, MA, USA

© Hong Liu 2024

All rights reserved. No part of this publication may be reproduced, stored in a
retrieval system or transmitted in any form or by any means, electronic, mechanical or
photocopying, recording, or otherwise without the prior permission of the publisher.

Published by
Edward Elgar Publishing Limited
The Lypiatts
15 Lansdown Road
Cheltenham
Glos GL50 2JA
UK

Edward Elgar Publishing, Inc.
William Pratt House
9 Dewey Court
Northampton
Massachusetts 01060
USA

A catalogue record for this book
is available from the British Library

Library of Congress Control Number: 2024934619

This book is available electronically in the **Elgar**online
Business subject collection
http://dx.doi.org/10.4337/9781803927305

ISBN 978 1 80392 729 9 (cased)
ISBN 978 1 80392 730 5 (eBook)

Printed and bound by CPI Group (UK) Ltd, Croydon, CR0 4YY

# Contents

# Figures

# About the author

As Founding Director of the China Business Centre at Manchester Business School, Hong Liu earned a bachelor's degree in engineering from Beijing University of Science and Technology, a master's degree in economics from People's University of China, and a doctorate in business administration from Warwick Business School.

Governments worldwide, including those of China, Britain, Poland, and Brunei, have sought Hong Liu's expertise and advice in global business. He has provided counsel to these governments and engaged in consulting activities with senior executives of multinational corporations (MNCs). His cooperations with MNCs such as European Aeronautic Defence and Space Company (EADS), Volvo Trucks, and AstraZeneca have involved formulating effective strategies for success in China.

Hong Liu is a sought-after speaker at conferences and events attended by senior executives from both MNCs and public organisations. He has authored numerous journal papers on global business and is the author of the acclaimed book *Chinese Business: Landscapes and Strategies*.

# Author's experience and mindset

The central theme of the book, which aims to unravel the mysteries surrounding the differences in mindset between individuals from China and Western nations, lies in the concept of 'holism' or 'holistic cognition'. My previous academic experiences, including earning a PhD and interacting with over 700 Chinese senior officials and executives, have provided valuable insights, but they alone would not suffice to fully validate my objective viewpoint. To demonstrate the evolution of my impartial mindset, I feel compelled to share some relevant aspects of my background, despite the risk of appearing self-promotional.

Raised in an intellectually inclined family, my formative years coincided with the tumultuous era of the Cultural Revolution. During this period, formal education was discouraged, as the government advocated for students to glean knowledge from workers, farmers, and soldiers. Consequently, I engaged in a diverse array of non-traditional educational experiences.

One significant classroom practice involved students reading and studying Mao Zedong's select works at the beginning of each day. Moreover, students were required to participate in hands-on activities involving the care of pigs and sheep, as well as agricultural tasks like crop planting and harvesting in rural areas. Additionally, students were assigned to work at the school's blacksmith forge and at external factories, where they interacted with workers and operated various machine tools.

I devoted myself to a range of sports, such as table tennis, martial arts, badminton, and athletics. Additionally, I explored the intricacies of Chinese musical instruments and traditional folk dances, and I played Chinese chess. To showcase my dedication, I achieved the title of table tennis champion in a third-tier Chinese city for three consecutive years. This legacy enabled me to claim the men's table tennis championship at the 2006 Tournament of European Business Schools. Moreover, I excelled as a regional junior champion in Chinese chess and earned championship titles in badminton and various athletic pursuits during my high school tenure.

Due to limited formal educational opportunities, I immersed myself reading classics, including Chinese literary masterpieces such as the *Romance of the Three Kingdoms*, *Water Margin*, and the *Journey to the West*, as well as translated global treasures, such as Arthur Conan Doyle's *Sherlock Holmes* series, Alexandre Duma's *The Three Musketeers*, Charlotte Bronte's *Jane Eyre*, and

Charles Dickens' *Great Expectations*. A particular book that piqued my curiosity was *One Hundred Thousand Whys?*

Towards the end of the 1970s, the Chinese government reintroduced the college entrance examination system. Through my personal dedication and accumulated knowledge, I found myself among a fortunate few in my generation to secure a place in one of China's esteemed science and technology universities.

Upon graduating, I joined an engineering institute based in Tianjin, where I was assigned to the office of 'Chief Engineering' in the institute. Over a span of two years, among other projects, I was tasked with designing a material supply system for one of the city's largest steel manufacturing plants. I acted as the coordinator as part of the chief engineering function, bringing together a diverse group of team members from various functional departments within the institute.

The early 1980s witnessed China's economic reforms, leading to a significant demand for individuals with expertise in economics. I became one of the successful applicants for a master's degree in economics at the People's University of China. This esteemed institution had a specialised focus on nurturing individuals for government positions, which were considered the most desirable career path at that time.

The master's degree programme in economics in China spanned three years and encompassed various aspects beyond traditional classroom lectures and dissertation writing. We actively participated in consulting services for regional government reform initiatives and conducted research on the progress of economic reforms.

It is worth noting that, during that period, China did not have a dedicated business school. However, as economic reforms continued to deepen, the process of marketisation gained momentum. Consequently, there arose a demand for individuals equipped with professional knowledge in business administration, which was absent within the Chinese educational system.

During that period, an influential Hong Kong education foundation initiated a programme, which aimed to identify and sponsor suitable candidates through a selection process conducted in Greater China, including mainland China, Taiwan, and Hong Kong. The selected individuals would be sent to universities in Europe and North America to pursue advanced doctoral education. There were 54 specialised areas available for candidates to choose from, including disciplines such as sociology, algebraic geometry, immunology, pharmacology, agricultural microbiology, American literature, international economics, and more.

Among these areas of specialisation was 'industrial trade', which stood out as the only field involving micro business operations and management. The subjects tested for this field covered economics, international trade laws, marketing, and English. Notably, at that time, Chinese universities did not offer comprehensive and systematic training in all these areas within any of their colleges or departments.

Out of the numerous areas of specialisation, I was fortunate to be awarded the scholarship in the sole field associated with business. It was revealed later that more than 8000 individuals from Greater China took part in the examinations, and out of the 54 specialised fields, only 36 were selected and granted scholarships.

In this concise opening, it is worth highlighting that a 'holistic' outlook has been a fundamental aspect of my education, life, and career. I have had the privilege of living through and being actively involved during a significant period in China's history, witnessing first-hand the transformation under the influential guidance of both Mao Zedong and Deng Xiaoping. In addition, I have observed the dynamic shifts in leadership, experiencing the governance of subsequent generations including Jiang Zemin, Hu Jintao, and Xi Jinping.

What sets me apart from my peers is my commitment to maintaining an impartial perspective. I have embraced an open-minded approach that enables me to explore various perspectives without constraints. From the beginning of my academic journey at a prestigious British university, my holistic approach has continued to shape my career trajectory.

Diverging from the path of most of my Western colleagues, my research and publications have spanned a broader range of areas, including strategy, international business, marketing, and technology management. While a holistic approach to research may not always be favoured, I firmly believe that it holds immense value in unravelling the strategic mysteries specific to China. In this regard, I bring a unique advantage in bridging the Chinese and Western strategic mindsets, offering insights that stem from my comprehensive understanding of both perspectives.

# Preface

*Everyone thinks of changing the world, but no one thinks of changing himself.*
—Leo Tolstoy

*It is not necessary to change. Survival is not mandatory.*
—W. Edwards Deming

Over the past three decades, China has ascended as a prominent global player while the influence of the US-led Western world has notably waned. Throughout this period, Western nations have either misconstrued or consciously disregarded Chinese strategic thinking. The academic world has witnessed a scarcity of scholarly works aimed at unravelling this puzzle and offering practical counsel to Western leaders.

Noteworthy is the more assertive and confrontational stance adopted by US-led Western governments towards China. Starting with Donald Trump's presidency, successive US administrations have pursued policies focused on imposing trade sanctions, reducing engagement, restricting Chinese high-tech industries and businesses, and taking positions on various political issues concerning China. Notably, there has been a substantial dearth of consideration for the perspectives and responses of the Chinese government and businesses.

These US policies have failed to achieve their intended objectives, particularly in terms of reducing trade deficits, revitalising US manufacturing, bringing back jobs by cutting down on imports from China, and limiting China's access to high-tech chips. Western strategic thinking can be identified as one of the fundamental causes behind the failure of these policies. US economic performance has worsened significantly as a result.

China has witnessed a steady rise in various aspects, including areas of business and industry, economy, political influence, and military affairs, while its Western counterparts have experienced a significant decline. In 2022, the trade deficit between China and the US soared to $1.18 trillion, reaching the highest level in the past three decades. This stands in contrast to the situation in 1981, when China's GDP represented less than 10% of that of the United States, whereas in 2022, it exceeded 70%.

Moreover, according to the International Monetary Fund, China's share of world GDP in 2022, based on purchasing power parity, was 18.9%, surpassing the United States' share of 15.4%.[1] In 2007, China held the title of the largest trading partner with 70 countries while the United States was the leading trading nation with 130 countries. However, by 2017, China had emerged as the largest trading partner with 135 countries, while the United States' position shifted to being the top trader with 70 nations.[2]

China's dominance in global supply chains is now widely acknowledged, encompassing both critical and everyday goods. It has emerged as the world's leading producer of steel, solar panels, electronics, coal, plastics, buttons, car batteries, and many more. In addition, China's influence in the automotive sector has surged, with its car exports quadrupling since 2021, catapulting it into the position of the world's largest auto exporter, particularly in the realm of electric vehicles.

In terms of military capabilities, China has made significant strides. In 2019, it boasted a larger naval fleet than the United States and possessed a vast military personnel count of 2.5 million. While the United States still outpaces other nations by a substantial margin in defence expenditure, spending $877 billion in 2022, China's defence budget of $292 billion secured second place.[3] Notably, the United States and China are the only two countries to have launched over 140 satellites into orbit.[4]

As of September 2023, the China National Intellectual Property Administration (CNIPA) reports that the country's valid invention patents had reached 4.805 million, while the number of trademarks stands at 45.122 million. In 2022, the annual registered volume of copyrights amounted to 6.353 million. China has maintained its position as the world leader in PCT international patent applications for four consecutive years.[5]

In 2023, China emerged as the leader in the science and technology (S&T) clusters, according to the Global Innovation Index released by the World Intellectual Property Organization (WIPO). Out of the top 100 S&T clusters, China secured a ranking of 24, surpassing the United States, which maintained its count of 21 from the previous year. Notably, among the top five S&T clusters, China dominated, with three prominent positions.[6]

Just three decades ago, China was heavily dependent on foreign companies for its communication technologies and capabilities. At that time, Huawei functioned merely as a reseller, and China's most advanced communications satellites were manufactured in the United States. The global market for subsea fibre-optic cable providers was dominated exclusively by companies from the United States, Europe, and Japan. China not only lacked the infrastructure but also the capability to product such systems. In fact, China's initial connection to the worldwide internet was established through a Sprint satellite network in 1994. However, since then, China has undergone a tremendous evolution. It has transitioned from being a customer to becoming a supplier, from imitating existing technologies to driving innovation, and from being a network subsidiary to becoming an operator in its own right.[7]

The Chinese government has displayed an increased sense of confidence, assertiveness, and willingness in engaging in a reciprocal manner in international political affairs. This has resulted in a significant expansion of its influence in global relations, with a more active role in African, Middle Eastern, Latin American, and ASEAN countries.[8] A notable example of China's growing role occurred in 2023 when China surprised the world by successfully mediating the rapprochement of Saudi-Iran relations. This diplomatic breakthrough, which came after a prolonged period of animosity between the two nations, demonstrated China's entry into the realm of Middle East intermediation – a sphere traditionally dominated by the United States.

President Xi Jinping's official statements have demonstrated China's increasing assertiveness and evolving ambition over the past five years. During his meetings with Presidents Obama and Trump, five years ago, President Xi expressed his vision, stating that 'the Pacific Ocean is big enough to accommodate China and the United States'. However, in a recent meeting with President Joe Biden in San Francisco on 15 November 2023, President Xi adopted a different tone, highlighting that 'the Earth is big enough to accommodate both countries'.[9]

As of September 2023, the One Belt and One Road (B&R) initiative has attracted 154 members, which includes approximately 80% of the 193 member states of the United Nations. In terms of international development finance, China has surpassed the United States by a 2-to-1 ratio since the launch of the B&R. While the growth of the B&R may be seen as more symbolic than substantive, it paints a picture of countries whose aspirations for their relationships with China outweigh their concerns. This suggests that most of the global community is not inclined towards 'decoupling' from China,[10] which is an objective pursued by the United States.

These changes and trends indicate that the Western academic world has struggled to effectively tackle the challenges posed by the Chinese strategic mindset. As a result, Western leaders have not received the necessary clear and insightful theoretical guidance. In addition, it is apparent that Western governmental policies towards China and international strategies involving China by Western companies have proven ineffective. This calls for comprehensive strategic evaluations, reflections, and adjustments.

Sun Tzu, an ancient Chinese strategist, expresses the view that, with the comprehension of the foe and thyself, in countless battles, danger will never encircle you.[11] Due to Western governments' tendency to view Chinese players through their own lenses, they have often failed to truly understand their counterparts. Consequently, their policies have largely been shaped by their own preconceptions, resulting in a self-fulfilling prophecy.

This situation can be attributed, in part, to the West's historical dominance in academia, particularly in the humanities, which has fostered elites educated within a shared cognitive framework.[12] Chinese cognition has remained relatively obscure and unfamiliar to them. Hence, in various domains, Western participants often find themselves at a disadvantage due to a relative lack of understanding about their adversaries, where their Chinese counterparts excel in this regard.

Given the trajectory of China's ascent to a central position in the global arena, it is imperative for Western leaders to thoroughly comprehend this development. This understanding will enable them to make informed decisions regarding whether China should be regarded as a formidable adversary, a potentially ally, or somewhere in between, all from a Chinese perspective. Regardless of the strategic choice to be made, recognising the importance of comprehending China is of the utmost significance.

In this book, the terms 'strategic thinking' and 'the strategic mind' are used interchangeably to refer to a cognitive process. It involves decision makers gathering and analysing information related to a strategic problem and subsequently developing a solution to that problem.

The book aims to explore the root causes of global dynamics and present alternative solutions to navigate the current trend. The fundamental question it addresses derives logically from pressing practical phenomena, particularly the contrasting developmental paths of China and the United States and its allies. The central premise of this book posits that different mindsets between the West and China have exerted a substantial influence on the trajectories of political, economic, and military development. The book seeks to answer to the following logical questions:

1.  Why has China steadily ascended to global prominence while the United States and its allies have experienced a gradual decline over the past three decades?
2.  What are the key factors contributing to the divergent mindsets between China and Western nations?
3.  What are the unique characteristics of the Chinese strategic mind?
4.  How do the distinct mindsets between China and the West impact their strategic decision-making in both theory and practice?
5.  What are the strategic implications of these mindset differences for policymakers and decision-makers?

If the current global economic trajectory continues, and China remains politically and economically stable, it is highly probable that China will surpass the United States and emerge as the world's largest economy in the foreseeable future. It is anticipated that prominent European and American business schools will introduce academic courses focusing on Chinese strategic thinking or strategy when the time comes. These courses would emphasise the development and implementation of strategies from a Chinese standpoint, as well as encourage research conducted from a Chinese perspective.

Given that China has emerged as the global industrial power and a key driver of economic growth, it has become crucial for major economies to engage in business with China, regardless of the political or ideological differences that may exist. Consequently, Western decision-makers must recognise the significance of considering a Chinese perspective and incorporating it into their strategic choices. This necessitates a cognitive adaptation or shift, which should be viewed as an ongoing and evolving process.

The question of whether individuals from different cultures exhibit variations in their cognitive processes has long been widely discussed as a general topic.[13] In the field of social psychology, extensive research suggests that there are significant distinctions in the cognitive processes between individuals from Asian and European backgrounds.[14] At its core, Chinese cognition is distinguished by holistic thinking, which encompasses perceiving the context as a unified whole and emphasising the interconnections between objects and their contexts. Conversely, Western cognition is characterised by analytical thinking, which directs attention towards individual objects and categorising them based on their attributes.[15]

The significance and urgency of comprehending the strategic thinking or mindset of another culture cannot be overstated, as it is underscored by the inherent link between strategic thinking and strategy formation. Strategy lies at the heart of an organisation, as it asserts that the strategic decisions made by a firm directly impact its performance.[16]

Strategy in the military field encompasses the art of harmonising objectives, approaches, and resources, with the aim of achieving a delicate equilibrium. It involves the discernment of desired outcomes, as well as the identification of the tools and techniques at one's disposal to attain those outcomes.[17] Although the term 'strategy' traces its roots back to ancient times, its essence remains relevant in contemporary contexts.

Sun Tzu is widely recognised as a pioneer of strategy, thanks to his influential work, *The Art of War*.[18] However, in the Western world, the origins of strategic thought can be traced back to various ancient strategists. Among them are Aeneas Tacticus (450–400 BC), who authored the earliest surviving treatise on the art of war,[19] and notable figures like Alexander the Great (356–323 BC)[20] and the Byzantine Emperor Leo VI (around AD 900). It was Leo VI who introduced the term *stratēgia* (στρατηγία), referring to 'the art of the general' or 'the art of command'.[21] Interestingly, the word 'strategy' itself only gained widespread usage in the English language during the early 19th century.[22]

The concept of strategy emerged in the field of organisational studies during the 1950s, initially by scholars from Harvard Business School.[23] Over the years, it evolved into a well-established management discipline by the 1980s.[24]

Despite its recognised significance, often referred to as 'strategic manage-ment' since 1979[25] to reflect its establishment as an academic field,[26] there remains a lack of consensus among both strategy researchers and practitioners regarding its definition.[27]

After conducting a comprehensive review of the literature on strategic man-agement, researchers have identified eleven distinct definitions that represent various aspects of the field.[28] Each of these definitions focuses on a different facet, such as business policy,[29] organisational performance,[30] the external environment,[31] internal resources,[32] and strategy implementation.[33]

To assist individuals in accomplishing their objectives, three distinct forms of thinking can be employed: decision or action-orientated thinking, belief-focused thinking, and personal goal-orientated thinking.[34] Within the realm of strategic management, this implies that strategic thinking is a pre-requisite for, or occurs simultaneously with, the formulation of a strategy.[35] Strategic thinking involves mental and reasoning processes, while strategy represents the tangible result of engaging in strategic thinking.

The importance of strategic thinking in shaping firm strategies and perfor-mance is widely acknowledged in the literature.[36] However, there is a lack of consensus regarding the precise definition of 'strategic thinking'.[37] Numerous studies have predominantly focused on the characteristics of Western stra-tegic thinking, which encompasses various aspects.[38] It is understood as the cognitive process employed by strategists,[39] involving the identification of alternative viable strategies or business models that cater to customer values.[40] Strategic thinking is often described as a synthesising process that incorporates intuition and creativity,[41] as well as a mode of thought that is both creative and divergent.[42] It encompasses strategic reasoning,[43] and 'thinking strategically,[44] and the ability to think strategically.[45]

The primary objective of this book is to capture the interest of Western academics and practitioners by highlighting the often-overlooked aspect of Chinese strategic thinking. By doing so, it aims to serve as a bridge, facilitating Western readers' understanding and entry into the realm of Chinese cognitive perspectives on strategy formulation. Furthermore, the book seeks to generate a broader curiosity among Western audiences, encouraging research and edu-cational endeavours focusing on comprehending the intricacies of the Chinese strategic mind.

Western elites can gain significant benefits from acquainting themselves with Chinese thinking:

(a) Avoidance of misunderstanding or misjudgement: familiarising oneself with Chinese thinking helps prevent misunderstandings and misjudge-ments when interacting with Chinese competitors or colleagues. By grasping the intricacies of Chinese culture and mindset, Western elites can navigate cross-cultural exchanges with greater sensitivity and efficiency.

(b)  Enhanced comprehension of Chinese strategic intentions or motivations: By comprehending Chinese strategic thinking, Western decision-makers can better grasp Chinese strategic intentions, underlying motivations, aspirations, and contextual factors that shape strategic choices. This understanding enables them to navigate cross-cultural complexities and adapt their strategies accordingly.

(c)  Expansion of strategic horizons: Embracing Chinese strategic thinking broadens the strategic horizons of Western elites, facilitating their own strategic development. By integrating diverse perspectives, they can gain fresh insights, innovative approaches, and alternative solutions to complex challenges.

This book intends to generate a profound impact, akin to 'throwing out a minnow to catch a whale'. It aspires to ignite a surge of insightful research and inspire talented researchers to actively engage in the development and dissemination of knowledge pertaining to Chinese strategic thinking.

China achieved the remarkable feat of becoming the world's second-largest manufacturer in 2006, surpassing Japan, and further solidified its position by emerging as the world's largest manufacturer in 2010, overtaking the United States. This exceptional growth propelled China to be acknowledged as the second-largest economy globally in 2010, and by December 2014, it became the largest economy in terms of purchasing power parity (PPP).[46] Notably, China's economy, when measured in US dollars, is expected to surpass that of the United States in the foreseeable future,[47] underscoring its continued upward trajectory.

Foreign direct investment has played a significant role in driving the early period of rapid economic growth in China.[48] This growth can largely be attributed to the competition and cooperation between Chinese and Western businesses. The competitive advantage of nations lies in their industrial competitiveness, which, in turn, depends on the competitive advantages of individual firms.[49]

To effectively compete against or collaborate with Chinese players, foreign participants must have a thorough understanding of their strategic thinking. Knowledge of strategic thinking is vital for organisational leadership and strategy, enabling foreign players to gain an advantageous position in their engagements with Chinese counterparts.[50]

In Chinese philosophy, the marketplace is commonly likened to a battlefield, and strategic thinking in Chinese business is closely intertwined with traditional military thought. It is crucial to emphasise the profound impact of Mao Zedong, a renowned Chinese leader and strategist, who skilfully harnessed the essence of Chinese strategic thinking to establish himself as an 'invincible general' in both military and political realms. Mao's strategic principles and methodologies continue to prove effective in the realm of Chinese business.

Since the early 1980s, numerous firms led by entrepreneurs have risen in China, establishing themselves as industry forerunners. Among them, companies like Huawei, Haier, and Alibaba have achieved prominent positions not only domestically but also on the international stage. These entrepreneurs embarked on their ventures with scarce resources and limited access to Western strategic knowledge and techniques. Instead, they relied on ethos and experiences deeply rooted in Chinese culture and values to drive their success.

Chinese mental processes stem from a cultural root that differs significantly from those found in the West. This cultural divergence has given rise to a distinctive Chinese philosophy and a holistic way of thinking. China's rich and unique history, coupled with its philosophical and holistic outlook, has gradually shaped distinct approaches to strategic thinking in various domains, such as warfare, political and social conflict, and business dealings.

This book aims to highlight the contrasting aspects of strategic thinking between China and the West without asserting any inherent superiority or inferiority. Andrew Roberts expresses the view that it is utterly absurd to assert that Homer surpasses Shakespeare, or that Shakespeare outshines Goethe.[51] Nevertheless, if individuals or entities from one culture possess a deeper understanding of the cognitive processes of another culture compared to vice versa, it could potentially provide them with a competitive advantage over their adversaries.

The foundation of the Chinese mindset lies in Chinese tradition, which has shaped its strategic thinking throughout history. Notable individuals such as *Lu Shang, Sun Tzu, Zhuge Liang, Liu Bowen, Mao Zedong*, and many others have significantly contributed to the development and refinement of Chinese strategic thought. Their contributions have not only absorbed and applied existing knowledge but enriched and advanced the reservoir of Chinese strategic thinking.

Until today, Mao Zedong's ideas and theories have continued to serve as a significant source of inspiration for decision makers in China's politics, military, and business sectors. Research has revealed that the strategies employed by numerous Chinese business leaders have been greatly influenced by Mao Zedong's ideology.[52] It is widely acknowledged that Xi Jinping, the leader of China, is a devoted follower of Mao Zedong, having wholeheartedly embraced Mao's approaches when dealing with both domestic and international affairs.[53] The understanding of Mao Zedong's thinking style, which represents the essence of Chinese strategic thought, remains of utmost importance and should not be underestimated.

China's historical legacy surpasses that of all other major empires in Eurasia, including the Egyptian, Roman, Byzantine, Arabian, Ottoman, and Tsarist-Soviet empires.[54] From a historical perspective, China's economic development has gone through a transformative journey. At its zenith, China held the position of the world's largest economy until 1840, commanding an impressive 32.9% share of global GDP,[55] while the entirety of Europe accounted for approximately 20%.[56] However, from the mid-1800s to the early 1950s, China experienced a significant economic decline and downturn.

The turning point came with the establishment of the People's Republic of China under the leadership of Mao Zedong in 1949. This marked the cessation of China's economic decline, and during the period from 1952 to 1978, the country witnessed an annual per capita GDP growth of 3%.[57]

In 1978, China stood among the world's most impoverished nations. With a real per capita GDP that was merely one-fortieth of the United States' and one-tenth of Brazil's. China faced significant economic challenges. However, since then, China has experienced remarkable economic growth, with its real per capita GDP expanding at an average rate surpassing 8% per year for many years. As a result of this exceptional progress, China's real per capita GDP stood at nearly one-fifth of the US level and was on par with that of Brazil in 2012.[58] China's per capita GDP crossed the significant threshold of $10 000 in 2019, with the precise value of being $10 276. By 2022, this indicator had further surged to $11 560.

The significant transformation in modern China has mainly been shaped by two influential Chinese leaders: Mao Zedong, who played a pivotal role in securing China's independence and establishing the People's Republic of China, and Deng Xiaoping, who spearheaded the nation's economic revolution through his visionary reform policies and strategic frameworks. It is often said: without Mao Zedong, China would not have achieved its independence, and without Deng Xiaoping, the Chinese people would not enjoy the prosperous lives they have today.

Mao Zedong's ideological framework is deeply rooted in Chinese tradition, as pointed out by Kissinger, who highlighted Mao's reliance on Sun Tzu rather than Lenin when it came to his foreign policy pursuits.[59] In contrast to Marxist principles, Mao was the first communist leader to advocate that revolution should originate from the peasantry rather than the urban proletariat.[60] Mao's theories have demonstrated their efficacy in navigating conflicts, battles, and warfare, both internally and externally. Consequently, Mao emerged predominantly as the victor in both internal and external military operations and political confrontations.

In contrast, Deng Xiaoping's remarkable ability to transform the Chinese economy stemmed from his adept fusion of Chinese thinking with Western economic theories and experience. By incorporating Western theories and practices that had demonstrated effectiveness, Deng's ideology proved highly receptive to these external influences.

The nature of strategic thinking is deeply influenced by cultural context, and Western approaches often prove impractical when applied in China, and vice versa. This cultural disparity was evident even during the early stages of the Communist Party of China (CPC), where conflicts arose between domestic members and those affiliated with the Communist International (Comintern), also known as the Third International.

Notably, military campaigns conducted under the guidance of the Comintern yielded unfavourable outcomes. One such example is Otto Braun, who adopted the name of Li De and was a graduate of the Frunze Military Academy. He was dispatched to China as a representative from the Comintern to provide guidance to the CPC. By late 1934, the CPC army was mainly led by Braun, alongside Zhou Enlai and Bo Gu, who collectively made all military decisions.

By employing a conventional Western strategy, Braun encouraged the CPC to directly confront the larger and better equipped KMT forces. This decision proved detrimental, as the CPC army suffered a severe setback, resulting in a significant reduction in its battle forces from 86 000 to about 25 000 within a year.

Braun enjoyed the backing of the Comintern and received support from the 'Bolsheviks', who held dominance over the CPC. Under their rule, the CPC governed the 'Soviet Republic of China'. However, as the autumn of 1933 transitioned into winter 1934, Chiang Kai-Shek's Fifth Campaign began to encroach upon CPC controlled regions. The Soviet Republic of China experienced successive contractions, shrinking in size. By 1934, the CPC had relinquished 58% of their territory holdings.[61]

In 1936, Braun conceded to Edgar Snow that Western strategic approaches did not always prove effective in China. To make a sound decision regarding military tactics, it was crucial to consider Chinese psychology, traditions, and their unique military experiences. He acknowledged that Chinese comrades possessed superior knowledge compared to Western military advisors when it came to employing the correct tactics in engaging in the Chinese civil war.[62]

Following Mao Zedong's ascent to the CPC leadership, a significant shift began to unfold in the fate of the party. This transformation signalled a departure from the effect of 'foreign thinking' within the Chinese context.

Most of the leaders of the CPC, except for Mao Zedong, possessed overseas experience. A significant number among them had spent time in Russia. Additionally, there were those who pursued studies and work in Europe, including Zhou Enlai, Zhu De, and Deng Xiaoping.[63] Nevertheless, despite their exposure to Western cultures and ideologies, they could not match Mao's profound understanding of China's unique context and his exceptional skills.

Mao's knowledge and abilities were deeply rooted in his experiences within his homeland.

Under Mao's visionary theories and leadership, the CPC experienced remarkable growth and development. His understanding of China's socio-political landscape and his ability to effectively navigate its complexities were instrumental in the party's progress. Mao's insights and directives propelled the CPC from strength to strength, shaping its trajectory and positioning it as a prominent force in Chinese history.

This book embraces a comprehensive perspective on the analysis of Chinese strategic thinking, incorporating various fields such as literature, military studies, political science, history, sociology, psychology, philosophy, linguistics, and business strategy, including the sources of both the Chinese and English languages. By integrating a thorough examination of these disciplines with two case studies, it sheds light on the development, characteristics, and significant strategic implications of the distinct Chinese strategic mindset.

The recognition of the influence of strategic thinking on business and international affairs originated from a notable observation: the occurrence of numerous instances in which Western and Chinese politicians and business leaders have experienced misunderstandings despite substantial efforts made by Western academics and practitioners to bridge the cultural or communicational gaps. Consequently, the question has arisen: what would be the fundamental factors that contribute to these misunderstandings or disconnections between the two sides?

The concept of 'mindset' or 'thinking' has taken centre stage as the pivotal factor primarily due to its cultural specificity and inflexibility, making it resistant to quick-fix approaches. As the Director of China Business Centre, I have had extensive engagements with Chinese senior executives and officials, and Western multinational leaders, providing ample opportunities to explore this subject matter. These interactions have laid the foundation for the insights shared in this book.

This book presents a comprehensive portrayal of the Chinese strategic mindset, offering Western readers a framework to enhance their understanding of the intentions and motivations of Chinese decision-makers. Written from a Chinese perspective, it incorporates Western methodologies, bridging the gap between East and West. With its multidisciplinary approach, the book serves as an ideal textbook or reference book for students of all levels at universities, professionals, and practitioners, catering to the needs of business studies, international relations, politics, and security, war, and defence studies.

## NOTES

1.    Swanson, A. (2023). The Contentious U.S.–China Relationship, by the Numbers. *The New York Times*, July 7, 2023. https://www.nytimes.com/2023/07/07/business/economy/us-china-relationship-facts.html. Retrieved on 23 October 2023.
2.    Jin, Y.N. (2022). *Weishenme Shi Zhongguo (The Rise of China)*, Beijing United Publishing Co. Ltd., p. 240.
3.    Swanson (n 1).
4.    Jin (n 2) p. 240.
5.    The China National Intellectual Property Administration (CNIPA). https://news.cctv.com/2023/11/08/ARTIhPpWUE9NGIgXwo1dzjs9231108.shtml. Retrieved on 9 September 2023.
6.    Dutta, S., Lanvin, B., León, L.R., and Wunsch-Vincent, S. (2023). *Global Innovation Index 2023 Innovation in the Face of Uncertainty*. World Intellectual Property Organization. https://www.wipo.int/edocs/pubdocs/en/wipo-pub-2000-2023-en-main-report-global-innovation-index-2023-16th-edition.pdf. Retrieved on 14 October 2023.
7.    Hillman, Jonathan E. (2021), *The Digital Silk Road: China's Quest to Wire the World and Win the Future*, Profile Books, pp. xi–xii.
8.    Feigenbaum, E.A. (2017). China and the World: Dealing with a Reluctant Power. *Foreign Affairs*, 96(1), pp. 33–40.
      Mulvad, A.M. (2019). Xiism as a Hegemonic Project in the Making: Sino-communist Ideology and the Political Economy of China's Rise. *Review of International Studies*, 45(3), pp. 449–70.
      Smith, S. (2021). China's 'Major Country Diplomacy': Legitimation and Foreign Policy Change. *Foreign Policy Analysis*, 17 (2), pp. 1–18.
      Pu, X.Y. and Myers, M. (2022). Overstretching or Overreaction? China's Rise in Latin America and the US Response. *Journal of Current Chinese Affairs*, 51(1), pp. 40–59.
9.    Wang, V. and Pierson, D. (2023). In Talks With Biden, Xi Seeks to Assure and Assert at the Same Time. *The New York Times*, November 16, 2023. https://www.nytimes.com/2023/11/16/world/asia/china-biden-xi-summit.html. Retrieved on 17 November 2023.
      Hawkins, A. (2023). 'Planet Earth is Big Enough for Two': Biden and Xi meet for first time in a year. *The Guardian*, 15 November 2023. https://www.theguardian.com/us-news/2023/nov/15/joe-biden-xi-jinping-san-francisco-china-apec. Retrieved on 16 November 2023.
10.   Tiezzi, Shannon (2023). How China's Belt and Road Took Over the World. *The Diplomat*, September 12, 2023. https://thediplomat.com/2023/09/how-chinas-belt-and-road-took-over-the-world/. Retrieved on 27 October 2023.
11.   Griffith, S.B. (1963). *Sun Tzu: The Art of War*, Translated and with an Introduction by Samuel B. Griffith and a Foreword by B.H. Liddell Hart, Oxford University Press, p. 125.

12. Nisbett, R.E. (2003). *The Geography of Thought: How Asians and Westerners Think Differently . . . and Why*. New York: Free Press, p. xx.
13. Cole, M. and Scribner, S. (1974). *Culture and Thought*. John Wiley & Sons, Inc.
14. Nisbett (n 12).
15. Detailed descriptions and analyses will be given in Chapter 3.
16. Porter, M.E. (1980). *Competitive Strategy*. New York: Free Press.
    Porter, M.E. (1985). *Competitive Advantage*. New York: Free Press.
    Porter, M.E (1991). Towards a Dynamic Theory of Strategy. *Harvard Business Review*, Winter, 12, pp. 95–117.
    Wernerfelt, B. (1984). A Resource-based View of the Firm. *Strategic Management Journal*, 5, pp. 171–80.
    Barney, J.B. (1991) Firm Resources and Sustained Competitive Advantages. *Journal of Management* 17, pp. 99–120.
    Peteraf, M.A. (1993). The Cornerstones of Competitive Advantages: A Resource-based View. *Strategic Management Journal*, 14, pp. 179–91.
17. Freedman, L. (2013). *Strategy: A History*. Oxford University Press, p. xi.
18. Collins, J.M. (1973). *Grand Strategy: Principles and Practices*. Naval Institute Press, p. xx.
19. Cummings, S. (1993) Brief Case: The First Strategists. *Long Range Planning*, 26(3), pp. 133–5.
20. Collins (n 18).
21. Heuser, B. (2010). *The Strategy Maker: Thoughts on War and Society from Machiavelli to Clausewitz*. Praeger, pp. 1–2.
22. Freedman, L. (2013). *Strategy: A History*. Oxford University Press, p. 72.
23. Snow, C.C. and Hambrick, D.C. (1980). Measuring Organizational Strategies: Some Theoretical and Methodological Problems. *Academy of Management Review*, 5(4), 527–38.
24. Montgomery, C.A. and Porter, M. (1991). *Strategy: Seeking and Securing Competitive Advantage*. Harvard Business Review Book Series.
25. Schendel, D. and Hofer, C.W. (1979). *Strategic Management: A New View of Business Policy and Planning*. Boston, MA: Little Brown.
26. Nag, R., Hambrick, D.C. and Chen, M.J. (2007). What is Strategic Management, Really? Inductive Derivation of a Consensus Definition of the Field. *Strategic Management Journal*, 28(9), pp. 935–55.
27. Bourgeois, L.J. III (1980). Strategy and Environment: A Conceptual Integration. *Academy of Management Review*, 5, pp. 25–40.
    Gluck, F., Kaufman, S. & Walleck, A. S. (1982). The Four Phases of Strategic Management. *Journal of Business Strategy*, 2(3), pp. 9–21.
    Chaffee, E.E. (1985). Three Models of Strategy. *Academy of Management Review*, 10(1), pp. 89–98.
    Mintzberg, H., Ahlstrand, B. and Lampel, J. (2009). *Strategy Safari: Your Complete Guide through the Wilds of Strategic Management*. FT Prentice Hall.
    Freedman (n 22) p. 72.

Nag et al. (n 26) p. 935–55.

28.    Ibid.

29.    Learned, E.P., Christensen, C.R. and Andrews, K.D. (1965). *Business Policy: Text and Cases*. Homewood, IL: Richard D. Irwin.

30.    Schendel, D. and Hofer, C.W. (1979). *Strategic Management: A New View of Business Policy and Planning.* Boston, MA: Little Brown.

31.    Bracker, J. (1980). The Historical Development of the Strategic Management Concept. *Academy of Management Review,* 5(2), pp. 219–24.

32.    Jemison, D.B. (1981). The Contributions of Administrative Behavior to Strategic Management. *Academy of Management Review*, 6(4), pp. 633–42.

33.    Van Cauwenbergh, A. and Cool, K. (1982). Strategic Management in a New Framework. *Strategic Management Journal*, 3(3), pp. 245–64.

34.    Baron, J. (2008). *Thinking and Deciding* (4th ed.). Cambridge University Press, pp. 5–6.

35.    Isenberg, D.J. (1984). How Senior Managers Think. *Harvard Business Review*, November-December, pp. 81–90.
       Gavetti, G. & Rivkin, J.W. (2005). How Strategists Really Think: Tapping the Power of Analogy. *Harvard Business Review*, April, pp. 1–10.

36.    Porter, M.E. (1987). Corporate Strategy – The State of Strategic Thinking. *The Economist*, May 23, pp. 19–22.
       De Wit, B. and Meyer, R. (2010). *Strategy Process, Content, Context: An International Perspective*, Fourth Edition. South-Western, p. 53.
       Goldman, E.F. (2007). Strategic Thinking At the Top. *Sloan Management Review*, 48(4), pp. 74–81.

37.    Heracleous, L. (1998). Strategic Thinking or Strategic Planning? *Long Range Planning*, 31(3), pp. 481–7.

38.    Srivastva, S. and Associates (1983). *The Executive Mind*. Jossey-Bass Publishers.
       Zabriskie, N.B. and Huellmantel, A.B. (1991). Developing Strategic Thinking in Senior Management. *Long Range Planning*, 24(6), pp. 25–32.
       Heracleous (n 37) pp. 481–7.
       Goldman (n 36) pp. 74–81.

39.    Hellgren, B. and Helin, L. (1993). The Role of Strategists' Ways-of-thinking in Strategic Change Processes. In J. Hendry and G. Johnson with J. Newton (Eds.) *Strategic Thinking: Leadership and the Management of Change*, John Wiley & Sons.

40.    Abraham, S. (2005). Stretching Strategic Thinking. *Strategy & Leadership*, 33(5), pp. 5–12.

41.    Mintzberg, H. (1994). The Fall and Rise of Strategic Planning. *Harvard Business Review*, January-February, pp. 107–14.

42.    Heracleous (n 37) p. 481–7.

43.    De Wit and Meyer (n 36).

44.    Zabriskie and Huellmantel (n 38) pp. 25–32.

45.    Goldman (n 36) pp. 74–81.

Moon, B.J. (2013). Antecedents and Outcomes of Strategic Thinking. *Journal of Business Research*, 66, pp. 1698–708.

46.  Tung, R.L. (2016). Opportunities and Challenges Ahead of China's 'New Normal'. *Long Range Planning*, 49, pp. 632–40.

47.  In 2014, officially announced in *The Financial Times*, the IMF estimated the size of the US economy would be $17.4 trillion, whilst the size of China's economy would be $17.6 trillion.
Giles, C. (2014). China Poised to Pass US as World's Leading Economic Power this Year. *The Financial Times*, 30 April 2014.
Giles, C. (2014). Money Supply: The New World Economy in Four Charts. *The Financial Times*, 7 October 2014.

48.  Liu, X., Burridge, P. and Sinclair, P.J.N. (2002). Relationships between Economic Growth, Foreign Direct Investment and Trade: Evidence from China. *Applied Economics*, 34, pp. 1433–40.
Li, X.Y. and Liu, X.M. (2005). Foreign Direct Investment and Economic Growth: An Increasingly Endogenous Relationship. *World Development*, 33(3), pp. 393–407.
Whalley, J. and Xin, X. (2010). China's FDI and non-FDI Economies and the Sustainability of Future High Chinese Growth. *China Economic Review*, 21(1), pp. 123–35.

49.  Porter, M.E. (1990). The Competitive Advantage of Nations. *Harvard Business Review*, March-April, pp. 73–91.

50.  See Porter, M.E. (1987). Corporate Strategy – The State of Strategic Thinking. *The Economist*, May 23, pp. 19–22.
Zabriskie and Huellmantel (n 44) pp. 25–32.
Hendry, J., Johnson, G. and Newton, J. (1993). *Strategic Thinking: Leadership and the Management of Change*. John Wiley & Sons.
Cusumano, M.A. and Markides, C.C. (2001). *Strategic Thinking for the Next Economy*. Jossey-Bass.
Bonn, I. (2001). Developing Strategic Thinking as a Core Competency. *Management Decision* 39(1), pp. 63–71.
Goldman, E.F. (2012). Leadership Practices that Encourage Strategic Thinking. *Journal of Strategy and Management*, 5(1), pp. 25–40.

51.  Roberts, A. (2011). *The Art of War: Great Commanders of the Ancient World*. Quercus.

52.  Li, S. and Yeh, K. (2007). Mao's Pervasive Influence on Chinese CEOs. *Harvard Business Review*, 85, pp. 16–17.

53.  Lee, T.C. (2018). Can Xi Jinping be the Next Mao Zedong? Using the Big Five Model to Study Political Leadership. *Journal of Chinese Political Science*, 23, 473–97.
Mulvad (n 8) pp. 449–70.

54.  Deng, K.G. (2000). A Critical Survey of Recent Research in Chinese Economic History. *Economic History Review*, 53(1), pp. 1–28.

55.   Maddison, A. (2007). *Chinese Economic Performance in the Long Run, 960–2030*, The Organisation for Economic Co-operation and Development (OECD).

56.   Kennedy, P. (1988). *The Rise and Fall of the Great Powers*. Fontana Press, p. 189.

57.   Zhu, X. (2012). Understanding China's Growth: Past, Present, and Future. *The Journal of Economic Perspectives*, 26 (4), pp. 103–24.

58.   Ibid.

59.   Kissinger, H.A. (2011). *On China*. Allen Lane, p. 102.

60.   Woodruff, W. (2005). *A Concise History of the Modern World*. Abacus, p. 213.

61.   Salisbury, H. (1985). *The Long March: The Untold Story*. Macmillan, p. 42.

62.   Jin, Y.N. (2015). *Ku Nan Hui Huang* (*Misery and Glory*). The Writers Publishing House Co. Ltd, p. 472.

63.   Ren, Z.G. (2013). *Wei Shen Mo Shi Mao Zedong?* (*Why Is Mao Zedong?*). Guang Ming Daily Publisher, p. 218.

# Acknowledgements

I extend my heartfelt appreciation to Edward Elgar Publishing for their support throughout the publication process of this book. Special thanks to Ms Francine O'Sullivan and her team for their valuable feedback, editorial expertise, and dedication to ensuring the quality and coherence of this work.

I am thankful to the individuals listed below for their encouragement and support: Robin Wensley, Stephen Perry, Nigel Campbell, Lars-Uno Roos, Clement Feng, Richard Hua, Rui Ying, Ian Lafferty, Paul Morris, and Andrew Leung.

I own an immeasurable debt of gratitude to my wife, Xu Ying, and my daughter, Angela, for their patience, understanding, and belief in my pursuits.

Lastly, I deeply appreciate the support, whether direct or indirect, from the organisations listed below for my endeavour:

Hong Kong K.C. Wong Education Foundation

Volvo Trucks Global

European Aeronautic Defence and Space Company (EADS)

People's University of China

Warwick Business School

University of Otago Business School

# 1. Knowledge lacuna and consequences

*Science is organised knowledge. Wisdom is organised life.*
– Immanuel Kant

*Believe you can and you are halfway there.*
– Theodore Roosevelt

## CAUSAL EFFECT IN REALITY

It continues to be an astonishing revelation that only a few Western policy-makers and business leaders have recognised that many conflicts and disagreements with their Chinese counterparts stem from misunderstandings or misjudgements arising from differing strategic perspectives.

Michael Pillsbury, a senior fellow at the Hudson Institute and a consultant to the US Defense Department, highlighted the ongoing enigma surrounding the Middle Kingdom. He argued that China, potentially the most formidable adversary Western nations have ever encountered, continues to elude their understanding, despite six decades of study, collaboration, and conflict. The root of the problem, Pillsbury suggests, lies not with China itself, but with these nations' own perspective. Throughout these six decades, Westerners have consistently viewed China through the lens of their own self-interests.[1]

Recently, it has been suggested that the primary hurdle hindering American comprehension of China is Washington's persistent determination to misconstrue China's intentions and strategic objectives. Rather than granting credibility and legitimacy to China's perspective, Washington's approach has been marked by a steadfast refusal to acknowledge and understand China's strategic outlook and goals.[2]

Mindset differences play a crucial role in shaping the strategies of nations and firms within an international context, ultimately leading to strategic outcomes that range from mildly detrimental to highly destructive. This influence stems from two distinct pathways:

1.  Opponent-orientated strategies, which revolve around direct conflict and competition, wherein one or both parties strive to outperform the other. These strategies can yield two possible outcomes:

a.  Prevailing without extensive conflict: In some instances, one party can achieve victory over the other without significant fighting by surpassing the adversary's strategy. The conflict between the United States and the Soviet Union during the first cold war serves as an apt example.

The Cold War can be described as a prolonged period of neither war nor peace between the United States and the Soviet Union following World War Two. After their victories in 1945 over Germany and Japan, these two countries emerged as the dominant global powers. However, their subsequent rivalry and tense relationship had the potential to escalate into a devastating 'hot' war involving nuclear weapons, capable of wiping out entire regions and leaving no survivors anywhere on Earth.[3]

The outcome of the Cold War has established the United State as an unrivalled victor, making a triumph as complete and definitive as any conflict in history. The adversary, the formidable Soviet Union, has been erased from the geographical landscape, leaving no trace of its former might. The foundation of its ideological warfare against the United States, the Communist ideology, lies in utter disarray and disgrace. In contrast, the democratic capitalist way of life championed by the United States stands gloriously vindicated.[4]

The Soviet Union collapsed in 1991, leading to its disintegration into 15 independent republics. Between 1980 and 1991, the United States embarked on a new transformative strategy in its engagement with the Cold War. This strategy encompassed a comprehensive assault, including ideological, economic, technological, and military fronts, aimed at eroding the foundation of the Soviet system. Remarkably, this multifaceted approach yielded resounding success,[5] showcasing the superiority of the United States' strategy and ultimately leading to the downfall of the Soviet Union without the need for extensive military confrontation.

b.  Engaging in battles or wars: Alternatively, opponent-orientated strategies may lead to bloody or bloodless conflicts, resulting in losses on both sides. Although one party might emerge as the victor, such a victory can be considered pyrrhic due to the significant costs incurred. These strategies often involve intense competition and can result in long-lasting conflicts. The outcome of such battles may leave both parties significantly weakened, highlighting the high price paid for victory.

In the case of the US–China trade war, which was initiated by the Trump administration in 2018, the United States has not been successful in achieving its objectives. Instead, it has experienced an increase in trade deficits with China. Albeit US consumers have primarily borne the burden of tariffs imposed on Chinese goods, China has also faced losses due to reduced exports to the United States. However, the magnitude of China's losses has been significantly smaller compared to that of the United States. While China's dominance may experience a decline, it is still anticipated to maintain a significant role as one of the key participants in global trade.[6]

The decision by the United States to restrict and ban the sale of advanced computer chips to China has had significant consequences, which some perceive as an aggressive act.[7] China's high-tech companies, especially Huawei, have suffered a major setback as a result,[8] albeit temporarily. However, this decision has not come without its own costs, as US chip companies have also faced heavy financial losses.

On the one hand, China has been the largest chip market globally, accounting for approximately 40% of annual chip demand. This has led to substantial losses for US chip manufacturers. On the other hand, China's retaliatory measures, such as imposing export restrictions on two crucial metals, gallium and germanium, which are heavily relied upon by Western countries for semiconductor production, have caused significant harm to Western high-tech companies.[9]

A rational analysis indicates that the United States has encountered difficulties in the chip war against China.[10] The introduction of Huawei's Mate 60 Pro on 29 August 2023 serves as evidence that the United States' aspirations to limit and control the company's vital technology have not been realised.

From a long-term perspective, the actions taken by the United States would exert significant pressure on the Chinese government and high-tech companies to advance their chip manufacturing technologies.[11] Throughout history, whenever Western governments have prohibited the export of certain technologies to China, it has consistently prompted China to develop these technologies swiftly and sometimes surpassingly. Notable examples include high-speed trains, tunnel-boring machines (TBM), thin 'hand-torn steel', photovoltaic solar panels, aero-engines, atomic and hydrogen bombs, as well as military and aerospace technologies.

2.  Non-opponent-orientated strategies, which focus on indirect competition, aiming to foster the growth of businesses, industries, or economies without the explicit goal of surpassing specific opponents. These strategies contribute to strengthening competitiveness by developing and con-

solidating the company, industry, or government's own interests. Their strategic intent is to nurture and expand their businesses or industries. Over time, the successful implementation of these strategies would significantly enhance player's international competitiveness and proficiency. Examples of such strategies include China's One Belt and One Road initiative, high-speed trains, solar panels, and electric auto industries. Despite entering these sectors relatively late, China has managed to dominate the global markets.

It is important to note that the United States has chosen an opponent-orientated strategy to define its economic policy, while China has prioritised a non-opponent-orientated or an economy-orientated approach. These two distinct strategies have led to entirely different paths in their economic development.

## (I)

Dr Henry Kissinger was instrumental in fostering reconciliation between the United States and China. In his book *On China* he offers valuable insights into the historical development of significant political and military events in China, as well as the potential misinterpretation of strategic intentions between American and Chinese politicians and military leaders.[12] Thanks to Kissinger's deep understanding of Chinese culture and his counsel to politicians, the United States government enjoyed a prolonged period of harmonious and mutually beneficial relations with China.

As a highly knowledgeable historian, Dr Kissinger promptly advised the US government that fostering a positive relationship with China would require achieving a balance with both the USSR and China. This approach would allow both the United States and China to identify shared interests and cooperate in jointly safeguarding against Russia threats to both China and Europe.[13] Additionally, such a relationship would alleviate the challenges faced by the United States in the Vietnam War.[14]

It is important to acknowledge the present political landscape, which features China and Russia aligned on one side, whilst the United States stands alongside its key allies, including Britain, Japan, South Korea, Australia, and other European nations, on the other.

After the Soviet Union dissolved, the new Russian government under Yeltsin and later Putin actively sought to strengthen relations with Western countries. While Yeltsin pursued pro-Western policies,[15] Putin even explored the idea of Russia joining NATO. However, Putin faced insurmountable challenges in this pursuit, viewing NATO as a primary adversary and desiring a position of equality with the United States in shaping NATO's decisions,[16] a goal that proved unattainable. Despite efforts to foster close ties, Russia continued to be perceived as a potential threat, leading to the rejection of its overtures and ultimately resulting in Russia's complete isolation from the West.[17]

Simultaneously, the relationship between China and the West grew strained and confrontational, primarily due to the United States' policy of containing and curbing China's development. Consequently, China and Russia gradually transformed into strategic allies,[18] leveraging their complementary resources. China emerged as a global industrial powerhouse, possessing unparalleled manufacturing capabilities, while Russia boasted abundant natural resources such as oil, natural gas, and extensive arable land for food production.

The entente between Russia and China can be primarily attributed to the actions of Western nations. There has been a sentiment that US policymakers should consider the statecraft employed by Richard Nixon, the former US president, and his chief foreign policy adviser Henry Kissinger. Their approach involved leveraging divisions between Soviet Russia and China to counter Soviet expansionism. Given the challenges faced by the United States in the 21st century, their diplomatic strategies and understanding geopolitics are worth emulating.[19]

Examining the impact of strategic thinking in the military domain would be relevant for understanding its influence on business strategies.[20] The connection between military and corporate strategy is well-established, as corporate strategy draws heavily from its origins in military strategy.[21] The application of military strategic principles in contemporary warfare has demonstrated its viability in the business landscape.[22]

The exploration of warfare, along with the quest for a comprehensive theory of war, has served as a focal point for scrutinising the Western pursuit of strategic theories.[23] As far back as 1967, it was recognised that Mao Zedong's strategic thought demonstrated the ability to surpass mere materialistic and hardware considerations.

In October 1950, during the Korean War, an event unfolded where the Chinese launched a decisive attack on the approaching United Nations forces near the River Yalu. Surprisingly, despite lacking key elements of warfare such as firepower, air support, and armour, the Chinese inflicted a resounding defeat on the United Nations forces.[24] The failure to grasp the significance of Mao Zedong's theories led to the French defeat in Indochina and contributed later to the American failure in South Vietnam.[25]

The Korean War, a conflict that unfolded on the Korean Peninsula seven decades ago, stands as poignant example of miscommunication and misinterpretation between US and Chinese leaders, leading to catastrophic consequences. Despite a persistent endeavour of the Western academic community to explore the reasons and methods behind China's intervention in the Korean conflict, a consensus on this matter has remained elusive.[26]

On 25 June 1950, an unexpected assault was launched by the North Korean People's Army (KPA) against South Korea, breaching the 38th parallel that marked the border between the two sides. Within three days, the KPA successfully seized control of Seoul, thereby occupying South Korean for a period of three months. In response to the aggression, the United Nations (UN) swiftly authorised member nations to employ military force in a counteroffensive.

Consequently, the KPA was gradually pushed back towards the 38th parallel, prompting the Chinese government to take notice. China vehemently opposed any UN forces crossing the 38th parallel and issued a warning to the United States government through the Indian Ambassador to China. The essence of the warning was that if the UN forces were to breach the parallel, China would intervene in the conflict.

General Douglas MacArthur, the Commander-in-Chief of the UN Command at the time, misinterpreted the intentions and motivations of China. His reassurance to President Harry Truman that 'the Chinese would not attack' and that victory was close at hand[27] proved to be inaccurate. In the event of a hypothetical Chinese intervention, General MacArthur expressed his confidence that the newly established air force bases in Korea would inflict heavy causalities upon Chinese forces attempting to advance towards Pyongyang.[28]

The Chinese warning was disregarded. The UN forces repelled KPA forces, pushing them beyond the 38th parallel and towards the Yalu River, which marks the border with China.

If China had a democratic leadership system, General MacArthur's perspective on the matter would be apt and to the point, considering China's comparatively limited military capabilities compared to the United States. Furthermore, notably, a significant number of Chinese generals expressed opposition to their country's intervention in the Korean War.[29]

During the period, Mao Zedong held a position of paramount authority within the Chinese leadership structure. However, General MacArthur largely overlooked Mao's motives, logic, and strategic theories when making his decisions.

Western scholars have observed notable disparities in the decision-making processes between Chinese and Western strategic choices at the national level. Mao's authoritative position within the politburo played a vital role. While other members may have appeared as equals, Mao held a distinct position of primacy among them. He personified the emerging Chinese leadership, and his peers acknowledged and respected his authority by deferring to his judgement.[30]

Mao Zedong had a different interpretation of the US involvement in the Korean War. According to Kissinger, Mao Zedong perceived the United States' actions as a re-entry into the Chinese Civil War.[31] The deployment of troops to Korea and the positioning of the fleet in the Taiwan Strait were seen by China as strategic moves that threatened their security, akin to placing two stones on the Wei Qi board. These actions were interpreted as an encirclement strategy China feared would have detrimental consequences.[32]

Throughout his military career, Mao Zedong skilfully commanded Chinese Red Armies in confrontation against adversaries who possessed superior strength and better resources. It has been observed that, despite initially having meagre resources, Mao Zedong displayed exceptional success throughout the extensive years of the Civil War. Astonishingly, the majority of his decisions, albeit often accompanied by bloodshed and challenges, proved to be accurate and fruitful.[33]

From Mao Zedong's perspective, intervention in the Korean War was not a matter of choice, but a necessity to protect China's national interests. Mao recognised that, if the West controlled Korea, it would pose significant threats to China. Bevin Alexander observed that the primary motivation of Communist China was not to save the North Korean leaders, but rather to safeguard China from potential American aggression.[34]

The UN forces in the Korean War faced another significant challenge in the form of their unfamiliarity with Chinese methods of warfare. The Chinese employed highly effective mobile and guerrilla tactics,[35] as well as the strategic manoeuvres of detour and interposition. These tactics, derived from ancient military strategies, had been extensively utilised during the anti-Japanese and Chinese Civil Wars.

In essence, if there had been a better understanding of Chinese strategic thinking, the outcomes of various conflicts between the West and the East might have been altered, subsequently shaping a distinct international political and economic landscape.

On 19 October 1950, the Chinese People's Volunteer Army made their way across the Yalu and entered the battlefields of Korea. China's official engagement in battles began on 25 October 1950. The conflict eventually concluded when the United Nations forces returned to the 38th parallel and a cease-fire agreement was signed on 27 July 1953. Chinese leaders and the public firmly believed that China emerged victorious in the war.

During the initial stage of the Korean War, US decision-makers viewed the conflict primarily through the lens of military engagements, assuming that Moscow held the ultimate decision-making power.[36] Meanwhile, it was believed that Moscow viewed Europe as the primary theatre of conflict between the Communist and Western worlds, with reluctance to support China to engage in the Korean War.[37]

The US administration was entirely blind to the possibility of unilateral action by Beijing. They simply did not contemplate the prospect that the Chinese might intervene in Korea for their own reasons, regardless of Soviet wishes or policies.[38]

In neglecting to acknowledge China's deep involvement, US leaders greatly underestimated the determination of Chinese armies and the effectiveness of their strategies, despite their inferior weaponry and limited resources in battle.

The Korean War had significant implications for China's international relations, leading to a complex situation. The legacy of the war, including the memory of Chinese intervention, coupled with China's domestic politics, allowed the United States to effectively isolate the People's Republic of China from the international system until the 1970s.[39]

Numerous books in the Chinese language extensively portray and depict most of the battles and military campaigns of the Korean War, typically presenting them in a positive manner that highlights China's political and military advantages. From China's perspective, the war signifies a notable triumph over imperialism, despite daunting challenges. It served as a powerful catalyst, introducing the People's Republic of China to the international arena with a resounding impact.[40]

Chinese leaders held the belief that the intervention had bolstered the security of a reformed China. Additionally, Chinese leaders were of the opinion that the Chinese People's Volunteers had inflicted severe damage upon the military capabilities of the United States, thereby postponing the possibility of a full-scale conflict between China and the United States.[41]

The Sino-US conflict in the Korean War, devoid of any positive outcomes, including the so-called 'peace' that followed, holds no redeeming qualities. This war, largely forgotten by both nations, should serve as a sombre reminder for policymakers in Washington and Beijing alike. The Korean War was far from being an accidental event; rather, it was a result of miscalculations and miscommunications that not only prolonged the conflict but also expanded its scope beyond what was necessary.[42]

Numerous conflicts between China and the United States have arisen from a flawed beginning, with both sides making decisions rooted in mistaken assumptions about each other's strategic mindset. According to Kissinger, from the perspective of Western strategic analysis, many of Beijing's military endeavours during the initial three decades of the Cold War appeared implausible and, on the surface, unachievable.[43] China and the United States were heading towards a confrontation due to their failure to comprehend each other's strategic intentions.[44]

The United States prioritised the accumulation of overwhelming military might, whereas China emphasised the importance of achieving decisive psychological impact. It was only a matter of time before either side would make a misjudgement.[45]

In a Bloomberg interview back in 2011, Elon Musk, the CEO and co-founder of Tesla, dismissed BYD, a Chinese auto company, as a significant competitor and even chuckled at the idea. He remarked, 'Have you seen their car? I don't think they make a good product'. However, during a subsequent Bloomberg interview in May 2023, Musk demonstrated a newfound respect for BYD and refrained from making any dismissive remarks.

The first of quarter of 2023 witnessed an amazing surge in BYD's profits, surpassing 400% compared to the same period the previous year. In the last quarter of 2023, BYD overtook Tesla as the world's largest electric vehicle manufacturer, selling 526 000 units compared to the American firm's 484 000.[46] Additionally, BYD surpassed Volkswagen to become the top-selling brand among all auto companies in China. The company captured nearly 40% of the Chinese new energy vehicle market, while Tesla's share remained just over 10%.[47]

Differing culture mindsets have been noted by a business consultant and executive. As per the consultant, throughout my career as a representative for Western companies engaged in Asian business ventures, I have consistently encountered the challenge of bridging the gap between Eastern and Western ways of thinking. The root cause of this misunderstanding lies not solely in language but rather in the fundamental differences in our thought processes. Asian and Westerners possess distinct ways of thinking that are as divergent as their spoken languages. I vividly remember a statement made by Donald Frisbee, CEO and Chairman of PacifiCorp, who once expressed, 'If I could just understand how the Asian thinks, I would know how to deal with him'.[48]

During the London 2010 Olympics, the badminton event became embroiled in a controversy of extraordinary scale for a sport known for its peaceful nature. To the surprise of a Western audience, Chinese and other Asian players were intentionally losing matches. This perplexing behaviour left Western spectators bewildered, struggling to comprehend the situation. However, this unconventional approach stemmed from a calculated strategy devised by a Chinese coach who, devoid of any sense of wrongdoing, considered it merely a means to increase the likelihood of securing gold medals.

In the year 2000, I found myself in a remarkable position as a consultant accompanying the President, International of a renowned European automobile multinational. Our mission was clear: travel to China and explore the potential for establishing a joint venture with a prominent Chinese counterpart.

However, our endeavour had to be carried out discreetly as any joint venture involving major Chinese companies in 'strategic sectors' required government approval or allocation. Our hope was to discover common ground between the European and Chinese companies, which would allow us to pursue a potential joint venture from the companies' perspective. If successful, our next step would involve lobbying the government to grant our proposal.

In terms of the negotiation teams involved, the European company was represented by two individuals: the president and myself. In contrast, the Chinese company had a team consisting of at least six to eight members. To prevent the emergence of sensitive issues that could potentially lead to political embarrassment, the president of the Chinese company chose not to directly participate in the negotiation at the table.

The negotiation setting was carefully arranged, with the European president and myself on one side of the table, facing the team members of the Chinese company on the other side. However, what caught our attention was the presence of a grey-haired 'old man' sitting in the back row of the Chinese team. He appeared to be a mere bystander or listener, rather than an active participant.

As it turned out, the old man sitting in the back row held a significant role as the true representative of the president of the Chinese company. His purpose was to relay the key messages and convey the intentions of the Chinese president. The negotiation team, on the other hand, was entrusted with the task of engaging in discussions without being equipped with specific terms and conditions, as such decisions fell outside their jurisdiction. This approach, although unfamiliar to foreign counterparts, is not uncommon in Chinese business practices.

## (II)

The sustained development of China's economy in the past four decades can be attributed to a combination of factors, including its ability to avoid direct conflicts with Western countries, skilfully negotiating for developmental opportunities leveraging Western technological inputs, and mostly importantly, the government's policies and strategies that have centred around industrial and infrastructure development. These policies and strategies have been guided by unique Chinese thinking or philosophy.

One Belt and One Road (B&R), China's developmental strategy, has sparked intense debate in both media and the academic sphere.[49] Introduced in 2013, the initiative aims to create connections among numerous economies across Eurasia and East Africa through a series of infrastructure investments.

The Chinese government asserts that the primary objective of the B&R is to foster prosperity in developing countries that lack the capability to undertake large-scale infrastructure projects independently. This goal is to be achieved by establishing an extensive network of airports, deep-water ports, fibre-optic networks, highways, railways, and oil and gas pipelines. Moreover, the B&R harbours an implicit ambition: to safeguard China from the economic decline that may ensue due to its slowing growth rate and high debt levels.[50]

However, the US government has primarily viewed the B&R as a strategic manoeuvre by China aimed at challenging US global power. They perceive it as an attempt by China to establish alternative international institutions that align with Chinese values and diminish US influence. Furthermore, they interpret it as a step towards a Sinocentric world order[51] and a challenge to US maritime supremacy.[52]

This initiative, born from the vision of President Xi Jinping,[53] draws inspiration from Chinese tradition and builds up two historical B&R initiatives. The first occurred during the Han Dynasty in the 2nd century BC, while the second took place in the 15th century AD during the Ming Dynasty.[54] Reflecting on an old Chinese proverb that emphasises the importance of roadbuilding for prosperity, this initiative emerges as China's market and resources reach saturation. A parallel can be drawn to traditional Chinese medicine, which underscores the need for unobstructed meridians in the human body for good health. In essence, the B&R strategy embodies a holistic approach, mirroring Chinese tradition and values.

For the past four decades, China's domestic economic growth has been guided consistently by the same philosophy. A key driver of its rapid economic development has been the substantial investment in infrastructure.[55]

While the primary objective of the B&R is not to surpass rival competitors, its outcomes can nevertheless influence China's competitiveness. The initiative aims to foster a win-win situation by promoting interdependence and mutual benefits between China and the economies participating in the project, should it prove successful. The successful implementation of the B&R strategy relies on two key factors.

1. It requires a leader or coordinator who possesses a holistic mindset, embracing a vision of common prosperity and demonstrating a long-term perspective. The initiative encompasses a broad spectrum of goods and services, including infrastructure, supply chain integration, transportation, technology, and financial integration. This comprehensive approach incorporates the utilisation of China's credit information system and currency.

   The projects in the energy sector, ICT, manufacturing, and transportation aim to establish vertical integration within China's production supply chain, technology and service infrastructure, and transportation networks. The comprehensive initiative is designed to achieve several objectives, including expanding the presence of Chinese state firms in foreign markets, creating new opportunities for the export of Chinese goods and services, and ensuring reliable access to foreign agricultural resources, energy supplies, and strategic commodities essential for China's economic growth and policy implementation.[56] By strategically integrating these sectors, China seeks to strengthen its global economic influence and enhance its self-sufficiency in vital industries.

   As of September 2023, the B&R initiative witnessed the participation of 154 countries through signing Memoranda of Understanding with

China.[57] Extensive research has revealed that the initiative has proven to be economically advantageous for participating countries, leading to a notable increase in export revenues.[58]

From 2013 to 2021, China's cumulative trade in goods with countries along the Belt and Road route (B&RCs) amounted to $10.4 trillion. The average annual growth rate exceeded that of China's overall foreign trade growth during this period and represented 27.4% of China's total goods trade. In 2021, China's total import and export of goods with BRACs reached US$1.8 trillion, reflecting a 23.6% yearly increase.[59]

In addition to investments, Chinese enterprises also established trade and economic cooperation zones in B&R countries. These zones have served as platforms for fostering local economies and promoting industrial consolidation. From 2013 to 2018, the B&R has resulted in the creation of 420 000 jobs and has successfully lifted 40 million people out of poverty.[60]

2. In order to actively engage in and reap the rewards of the B&R initiative, China, as the host of the B&R initiative, must possess specific economic prerequisites, including surplus industrial capacity and finance flexibility. Over time, it has become evident that China's resources and capabilities align remarkably well with the requirements and resources of participating countries. China has long been recognised as an 'infrastructure powerhouse', showcasing unparalleled expertise in constructing intricate and highly sophisticated infrastructure projects. The subsequent examples serve to illustrate this remarkable prowess:

   • High-speed rail networks: As of the conclusion of 2022, China had successfully constructed an extensive high-speed rail (HSR) network spanning over 42 000 kilometres, effectively connecting nearly every region within the country. This remarkable achievement positions China as the predominant global contributor, accounting for two-thirds of the world's HSR infrastructure. Notably, China also boasts the fastest scheduled train in the world.

     Research demonstrates that the implementation of HSR has significantly contributed to industrial transformation within China. It has facilitated the transition from the primary to secondary and tertiary industry sectors, thereby upgrading the over industrial structure of the nation. Moreover, the influence of HSR extends the promotion of tertiary industry aggregation in densely populated urban centres, fostering economic growth and development. This effect is particularly pronounced in large cities with high population density, as it reduces the concentration of transportation, warehousing, and postal sectors. Furthermore, the positive impact of HSR on neighbouring cities is evident, as it generates a noticeable spill-over effect, encouraging economic progress in these areas as well.[61]

- Bridge and tunnel infrastructure: China boasts an impressive record when it comes to bridge and tunnel infrastructure, particularly evident in its ownership of a staggering 80 of the world's 100 highest bridges. Among these remarkable feats of engineering is the Hong Kong-Zhuhai-Macau Bridge. Spanning the vast expanse of the Pearl River Delta, this bridge stretches more than 55km (34 miles), solidifying its reputation as an unrivalled engineering accomplishment.

  The bridge, as depicted by *The Wall Street Journal*, is an impressive structure that surpasses California's iconic Golden Gate Bridge in length by a factor of 20. This six-lane bridge serves as a vital link connecting a dynamic regional economic zone encompassing 70 million individuals. The combined annual GDP of this zone amounts to $1.51 trillion, exceeding the economic output of the San Francisco Bay Area by nearly twofold. Furthermore, this economic zone's GDP is larger than the entire national economies of prominent countries such as Australia, Spain, or Mexico.[62]

- High-tech projects: China is at the forefront of numerous cutting-edge endeavours, and among them stands the Five hundred-meter Aperture Spherical Telescope (FAST). The remarkable technological feat was successfully launched in Guizhou province in 2020, solidifying its status as the largest radio telescope on the planet. Boasting a surface area equivalent to 30 football courts, FAST serves as a prime example of China's extraordinary high-tech infrastructure initiatives.

- Digital connectivity: China has emerged as the leading global provider of communications technology, with Huawei operating in over 170 countries. However, China boasts more than just Huawei as a digital giant. Two Chinese companies, Hikvision and Dahua, deliver 40% of the world's surveillance cameras. In addition, Hengyang Group supplies 15% of the world's premium optics and is one of the four major suppliers of submarine cables, which are responsible for carrying 95% of international data traffic. China's Beidou, a global navigation satellite system, covers a larger number of capital cities worldwide (165) compared to US GPS system.

  These diverse connections, spanning from space to the ocean floor, are integral to China's Digital Silk Road (DSR). The DSR represents a strategic convergence of Chinese President Xi Jinping's signature policies and initiatives. It was first mentioned in 2015 as an essential component of China's One Belt and One Road Initiative.[63]

## THE INERTIA OF THE ACADEMIC SPHERE

The events unfolding in the West can largely be traced back to the realm of academia. It is evident that there has been a significant lack of comprehensive research, knowledge, and instruction on Chinese strategic thinking, which has ultimately hindered the ability of Western leaders to make informed choices.

In the field of strategy and management as general disciplines of social sciences, scholars typically closely examine the best or worst practices found in various industries and economies. They then develop theories, principles, and guidelines that can be shared with practitioners and students in various academic settings. As an example, three consultants from the Boston Consulting Group (BCG) have dedicated their efforts to identifying multitudes of strategy frameworks and theories over the course of the past six decades. From their research, they have formulated five distinct strategic approaches: classical, adaptive, renewal, visionary, and shaping. Each of these approaches is designed to address different types of strategy environments.[64]

The academic world's apparent indifference towards the events unfolding in China, and the lack of sufficient efforts to address strategic issues from a Chinese perspective, has raised questions. Despite the widespread recognition that a comprehensive understanding of Chinese strategy requires Western decision-makers to adopt a Chinese lens, there seems to be a prevailing tendency to overlook this imperative. The tendency can mainly be attributed to Western cognitive rigidity, which has been shaped by centuries of Western dominance in the humanities.

In the realm of both social and natural sciences, Western theory and methodology have held sway. It has been acknowledged that North American and European scholars have dominated research on management and organisation in the West. The domain of Chinese management studies has witnessed remarkable growth over the past four decades. Management theories originating from the United States have continued to maintain their dominance in the analysis of Chinese firms.[65] This trend has resulted in a dearth of local indigenous research, both on a global scale and notably within China.[66]

Chinese management research, including context-sensitive studies, often tends to adopt a Western viewpoint. Given the substantial economic influence of the West, particularly North America and Europe, Chinese management research has gravitated towards Western outlook.[67] In many cases, this is driven by a desire to align with established paradigms and benefit from the credibility and recognition associated with Western scholarship.

When it comes to natural sciences, there is little doubt that they have emerged from the Western world, rooted in Western logical thinking. The Western worldview is characterised by the formulation of theories and subsequent practical applications, which has led to significant advancement in science and technology since the 17th century. However, this approach has often encountered challenges and limitations when applied to social studies, especially within the context of China.[68] In contrast, the domain of social sciences in China has a rich tradition that spans over two thousand years, influenced by distinctively Chinese philosophical and military thought.

The distinct characteristics of Chinese and Western cultures, when viewed through a philosophical lens, have been eloquently portrayed and emphasised. Chinese culture, at its core, has been deeply rooted in the humanities, while modern Western culture has predominantly focused on advancements in science. Scientific pursuits prioritise the latest developments, with a dictum that states 'the more up-to-date, the more acceptable'. However, this dictum no longer holds true in the realm of humanities, where the notion of 'the more recent, the more acceptable' no longer applies.[69]

Mao Zedong held a vision wherein Western and Chinese traditions would coexist and equally shape the future global landscape. In his perspective, both traditions would play a crucial role, each contributing half to the world's progress.[70]

In the area of philosophy, certain systems, such as the *I Ching*, Confucianism, Taoism, and Mohism, have predominantly remained overlooked by mainstream research interests. Instead, they have been relegated to the status of a narrowly confined domain, limited to specialised inquiries in the Western scholarly sphere.

Furthermore, Western philosophers have employed reason to diminish the philosophical significance of classic Chinese texts, primarily due to their departure from Western expectations regarding the intellectual depth and content of philosophical writings. Chinese philosophical texts often appear to lack the theoretical underpinnings of ontology, epistemology, and formal logic that are customary in Western philosophical works. Consequently, they have been regarded as deficient in terms of philosophical discourse.[71]

Due to its classification as 'unphilosophical' by Western philosophers, the perception of Chinese philosophy would lead to two noticeable outcomes. Firstly, it would be regarded as having limited worth in terms of scholarly investigation, as evidenced by the minimum attention dedicated to the study of distinctively Chinese mode of reasoning.[72] Secondly, Chinese philosophy would remain relatively obscure or challenging to fully grasp, resulting in only a small number of individuals outside the specialised realm of philosophy gaining a genuine understanding of it.

Notably, management theories originating from the United States may not be universally embraced by European and Asian countries.[73] It has been observed that modern Chinese business leaders draw influence from a diverse range of philosophical and ideological traditions, such as Confucianism,

Taoism, Mohism, Legalism, and Communism.[74] Throughout history, the Chinese people have shown a keen interest in studying social phenomena and engaging in social studies, driven by their deep rooted belief in the interconnectedness of human and nature.[75]

The disparities in values between Chinese and Western cultures have been widely acknowledged. Europeans, in their attempts to 'civilise' China through a combination of gunboat diplomacy, trade, and missionary efforts over the past century or so, have been perplexed and frustrated by Chinese people's strong attachment to their own culture. Particularly noteworthy is the traditional Chinese attitude that regards their civilisation as the only genuine one, with the Chinese empire considered coextensive with the civilised world.[76]

Gordon Redding has perceptively discerned significant disparities between Oriental and Occidental modes of thinking. It is often a source of astonishment for Western individuals to witness the notable variations in cognitive processes among Oriental people, and vice versa. This issue stems from an inherent difficulty in transcending one's own worldview and recognising the potential for an alternative perspective. Nonetheless, the fields of psychology, philosophy, and anthropology, which extensively explore the Chinese culture, abound with references that consistently acknowledge and describe such differences.[77]

In the sphere of psychology, it was widely accepted until recently that fundamental reasoning processes were universally identical across all cultures.[78] Similarly, in the fields of strategy and management, there has been a prevailing tendency towards a 'Western cognition or logic', characterised by analytical thinking. This stands in contrast to the dominant cognitive mode in China, which favours holistic thinking.[79] It is worth noting that much of strategy research, due to its inherent nature, tends to be more atomistic than holistic, concentrating on only a handful of variables at a time.[80]

The dearth of cross-cultural research on strategic thinking likely stems from the widespread belief that theories on strategic thinking possess universal applicability.[81] This inclination within the Western social-science domain has inadvertently hindered the advancement of cross-cultural comprehension between the West and China at its core.

If Western and Chinese societies were to exist in complete isolation from each other, the challenges of cross-cultural understanding would be largely non-existent. However, when individuals from these two cultures come into contact and engage in communication, collaboration, and/or competition, it becomes crucial for them to align their perspectives in order to avoid misunderstandings and misinterpretations. Extensive research in the fields of military and political studies has thrown light on the fact that the Chinese strategic mindset is heavily influenced by China's ancient military doctrines and cultural heritage, setting it apart from Western approaches.[82]

There is evidence indicating that Chinese businesses have incurred significant costs as a result of their failure to grasp Western strategic thinking in international mergers and acquisitions.[83]

Overall, there is a noticeable lack of literature and scholarly discourse addressing the intricacies of Chinese strategic thinking. This deficiency is particularly evident in top academic journals where articles on the subject are scarce and widely dispersed.

It is worth highlighting that comprehensive investigations into military strategic thought have been limited in scope.[84] The scant attention given to the topic within the community of Sinologists has resulted in minimal direct debate concerning the Sun Tzu text. Moreover, the research conducted during the 1980s and 1990s has generally overlooked the intellectual and philosophical aspects inherent in ancient Chinese military thought.[85]

During the 1960s, there was a noticeable lack of attention and understanding of Chinese strategic thinking within the field of military studies. This oversight was highlighted when the French defeat in Vietnam during the 1950s was attributed to this very factor. It is important to note that Vietminh regular troops were receiving training in China during this period. The subsequent war in Vietnam loosely adhered to the patterns elucidated in Mao Zedong's speeches and communiques, which were readily available in the West. Consequently, it should not have posed significant difficulty for the French to recognise this situation and proactively address the emerging challenges by undertaking a comprehensive study of Mao's warfare tactics, as demonstrated during conflicts against both Jiang Kai-Shek and the Japanese.[86]

Elliot-Bateman posed a thought-provoking inquiry and offered his own interpretation, questioning why Mao's doctrines have not yet been comprehended despite the considerable attention given to this imperative in various books and articles in the past. It is undeniable that numerous individuals have perused Mao's works, as well as those of Giap, with both volumes often adorning the bookcases of many esteemed military officers as a symbolic representation of their profession. However, it is disheartening to observe that these works are seldom read beyond the initial twenty pages or so, resulting in Mao remaining an enigmatic figure.[87]

Henry Kissinger has observed the significant pertinence of Sun Tzu's treatise in today's world. He asserts that, even in the present day, Sun Tzu's writings possess an immediacy and profound understanding that position him alongside the most distinguished strategic thinkers in history. It could be argued that the neglect of Sun Tzu's principles played a crucial role in the frustration experienced by the United States in its Asian Wars.[88]

In China, the examination of warfare is fundamentally an exploration of society. It recognises that war is not a solitary military endeavour, but rather a societal occurrence shaped by the distinctive attributes and intricacies inherent in human social and economic nature, as well as historical context.[89] To really comprehend Chinese strategic thought, it is imperative to adopt an all-encompassing perspective.

In Western societies, the progress made in the natural sciences has played a pivotal role in the rapid advancement of technology and industry. This, in turn, has led to the flourishing and rejuvenation of various industries, contributing to the prosperity of Western economies. Consequently, the field of academic business research has felt compelled to adopt a more 'scientific' approach, placing greater emphasis on analytical, quantitative, and mathematical methodologies. However, this growing inclination has resulted in a widening disparity between the research conducted and the practical needs of professionals in the field.

The West has witnessed a notable shift towards the prominence of rationality and scientific inquiry. This trend can be attributed to the influence of positivism, a philosophical perspective that emerged in the 19th century and gained prominence in the 20th century. Positivism asserts that scientific knowledge, based on empirical evidence and logical reasoning, is the only valid form of knowledge. It places a strong emphasis on objectivity, quantification, and the use of mathematical models to understand and explain phenomena. These ideas and ideals gained momentum and greatly influenced various fields. Fast-forward to the 1950s, there has since been a growing impact of scientific thinking on the academic discipline of management.

Morgen Witzel's observation highlights a trend where there has been a renewed emphasis on scientific thinking and rigour in the realm of management, leading to a desire to reduce uncertainty. Thus, people have increasingly applied scientific thinking and calculation to a wide range of subjects. In this pursuit, there has been a tendency to consider knowledge as 'proper' only if it can be scientifically proven and expressed in mathematical form.[90] Relying solely on managing by numbers stifles innovation as it forces managers to prioritise short-term predictability over long-term potential.[91]

The application of scientific thinking and calculation to various domains, such as those in natural science and economics, has undoubtedly yielded significant advancements and insights. Mathematics provides a powerful language for modelling and analysing complex systems, allowing for precise predictions and optimisation.

However, it is important to recognise that not all forms of knowledge can be easily quantified or expressed in mathematical terms. There are domains, such as humanities, including the sub-fields of strategy and management, and ethics, where the complexity and diversity of human behaviour and experiences make it challenging to reduce everything to mathematical equations. These fields often require qualitative research methods, interpretive frameworks, and holistic approaches to capture the richness and nuances of human phenomena.

Game theory, a widely recognised mathematical and scientific framework, serves as a standard tool for decision making in economics.[92] However, when confronted with intricate scenarios characterised by numerous choices spanning indefinite time horizons and involving extensive social groups, these methods may fall short in comprehensively elucidating the underlying factors influencing agent behaviour.

In such complex settings, the limitations of game theory become apparent. While game theory assumes rationality and strategic thinking on the part of individuals, it fails to account for various psychological, sociological, and contextual aspects that shape decision-making processes. Moreover, the assumptions of complete information and perfect rationality often do not hold in real-world scenarios, thus limiting the applicability of game theory in capturing the intricacies of agent behaviour.[93]

Clausewitz was among the first to recognise the limitations of the Enlightenment approach in developing Western theories of warfare and military strategy. The focus of warfare during that time had primarily shifted towards the production of weapons, the construction of fortifications, and the organisation of armies, as well as finding ways to effectively manoeuvre them. This shift led to greater emphasis on mechanics rather than siege strategy and military tactics. In attempting to systematise the material aspects of warfare, the prevailing approach either reduced superiority in warfare to mere numerical data, thus making it depend solely on mathematical laws, or became fixated on geometric factors as a crucial determinant.

Given the prevailing pattern, Clausewitz firmly asserted that these methods of conduct yielded merely geometrical outcomes devoid of any worth. With a unidirectional perspective that neglected variability and solely focused on material factors, such theoretical approaches proved insufficient in mastering actual existence.[94]

The Korean War witnessed a notable military operation known as 'Showdown', which was led by General James Van Fleet, the then commander of the US Eighth Army and United Nations forces. The operation serves as a compelling example of strategic emphasis on mechanical factors in warfare and its limitations.

Spanning from 14 October to 24 November 1952, General Fleet's mission revolved around capturing three strategically vital hills – Pike's Peak, Sandy Ridge, and Jane Russell Hill – collectively referred to as the 'Triangle Hill'. The success or failure of this operation would have a significant impact on the outcome of the Korean War.

In order to achieve his objective, General Fleet relied on the notion of the mechanical determinant in military operations. He insisted that his troops be provided with five times the normal ammunition ration, leading to the term of 'the Van Fleet load' among the soldiers, indicating an exceptional load of rations. His underlying belief was that victory would be determined by the expenditure of firepower and military resources. General Fleet and his forces witnessed firepower rations that surpassed anything seen during the Second World War, causing the hilltops to be reduced by over two metres due to relentless bombardment. Yet, despite the scrupulous planning and the extravagant consumption of firepower, the operation ultimately ended in a woeful failure. The objective of capturing the Triangle Hill remained elusive to General Fleet and his troops, resulting in significant setbacks.[95]

From a methodological perspective, quantitative research primarily focuses on issues related to 'what' and 'how many/much', while leaving 'how' or 'why' inquiries to qualitative research.[96] Although quantitative research is undeniably valuable for comprehending the business realm and fulfilling broad macro objectives, it may not be suitable for offering specific recommendations on how to achieve positive performance.

The current overemphasis on quantitative research may inadvertently overlook other valuable research methodologies that provide a more holistic comprehension of intricate phenomena. Qualitative research approaches, for example, are capable of effectively examining the interactions among contextual factors, human behaviour, and organisational dynamics, which quantitative research alone may struggle to address. A de-emphasis on qualitative research can restrict the scope and profundity of knowledge, potentially impeding the development of comprehensive and pragmatic solutions to real-world problems.

In 2014, a research project was launched by the marketing department of a renowned European business school. The project aimed to investigate the publication distribution of faculty members from the United Kingdom in leading international journals. To everyone's astonishment, a researcher from a prestigious British business school rose to the top among academics, having an astonishingly high number of articles published in top-ranking journals. However, what was equally surprising was that very few staff members at the business school where the research was conducted were familiar with the researcher's name or any of his/her publications.

There exists a paradoxical phenomenon and trend: in order for research outcomes to exert a substantial influence on managerial practices, they must be published in prestigious academic journals. However, to have a paper accepted by such journals, the research tends to require a high degree of quantitativeness or academic rigour, often rendering it impractical in real-world scenarios. Curiously, the more mathematical formalism an author employs in addressing a problem, the more difficult it becomes for the audience to comprehend.

Consequently, exceptionally talented and remarkable young researchers are compelled to pursue 'academic', quantitative, and tightly focused research in order to progress in their academic career. Consequently, only a limited number of brilliant minds are dedicated to publishing papers that cater to a practical audience.

The inclination towards narrowness and overstated viewpoints is a natural consequence of analytical thinking-based research prevalent in the field. Researchers often probe deep into specific aspects of strategy, exploring them in detail. While this approach yields valuable insights, it is crucial to recognise that it represents only one facet of the broader strategy landscape.

Considering analytical thinking-based research, we may draw a parallel to the health condition of an individual. Using an anatomical analogy, we may associate different areas of research on strategy with specific organs. For instance, strategy research can be compared to the 'brain', marketing research to the 'heart', human resources research to the 'lung', and organisational behaviour research to the 'liver', among the others.

If we envision a person in a state of complete health, we can attribute this to various healthy factors associated with each healthy organ. A healthy brain is linked to the right business strategy, a healthy heart to a well-executed marketing strategy, a healthy lung to an effective human-resource strategy. It is important to know that a healthy person possess a range of properly functional organs, even though one may function better than another.

While functional organs play a crucial role in our wellbeing, *thinking* in an appropriate way about how to lead a healthy lifestyle serves as the foundation for good health. Moreover, the proper functioning of each organ is interdependent with others. For instance, a person's lung relies on their heart to distribute the oxygen it collects, just as their heart muscle depends on the oxygen it receives from their lungs. Simultaneously, the heart supplies the brain with a steady stream of oxygen-rich blood, while the brain regulates the heart rate and blood pressure. Should any organ fail, it would have a detrimental impact on the person's overall health. Likewise, in the event that any significant functions within an organisation fail to meet expected standards, the overall performance of the organisation would suffer.

The purpose of the preceding discussion on research methodological patterns and trends in academia is not to diminish the significance and validity of quantitative or analytical business research, as it continues to serve as a strong foundation for business studies. Instead, it proposes that the academic community should strive for a more balanced approach, shifting from an excessive emphasis on quantitative research to a combination of quantitative and qualitative research. This shift would foster, within the community, a holistic research outlook, which is better suited to address matters in the realms of international business and relations, where cross-cultural elements hold significant importance.

In order to gain a comprehensive understanding of Chinese social issues, it is necessary to approach them from a holistic perspective, which often entails conducting multidisciplinary and qualitative studies. While certain Chinese academics who have received education in the United States and Europe have attempted to address this by designing and collaborating with US and European professors on research projects related to decision-making in Chinese enterprises or by Chinese entrepreneurs, these endeavours have not yielded desired outcomes. This is largely due to their reliance on Western strategic frameworks to analyse Chinese strategic decisions. Consequently, the field of business education and understanding on Chinese strategy and management continues to be dominated by Western perspectives.

A compelling argument has been put forth regarding the necessity for the West to adapt its perspectives in order to comprehend China. It posits that attempting to understand or interpret China solely through a Western lens is an insurmountable task. As China ascends to the status of a great power and gradually surpasses America as the world's dominant force within the next two decades, it will become imperative for us to relinquish our Western-centric attitudes and strive to comprehend China on its own unique terms. However, the magnitude of the mindset shift that awaits us is truly colossal.[97]

Social psychologist Richard Nisbett has shared a comparable observation, highlighting that individuals in Eastern countries hold a valid belief that the West's intellectual and moral arrogance has been fostered by its military, political, and economic dominance over the past five centuries.[98]

US state officials and army officers have actively sought to gain insights into the Chinese strategic mindset by engaging in the study of the ancient Chinese board game Wei Qi, more commonly known as 'Go' in the West. This initiative arises from their recognition of the significance of understanding Chinese strategic thinking in effectively engaging with Chinese counterparts in global affairs. It is acknowledged that numerous Chinese political and military decisions on the international stage have been influenced by a Wei Qi perspective, which has often been misinterpreted or misconstrued by Western political and military leaders.

Kissinger offered perceptive insights into the influence of Wei Qi on Chinese strategic thinking. He noted that, in China's conflicts with both the United States and the Soviet Union, Mao and his top associates approached the threat through the lens of Wei Qi, specifically the concept of averting strategic encirclement. It was precisely in these deeply rooted elements that the superpowers encountered the greatest challenge in understanding Mao's strategic manoeuvre.[99]

Understanding the Chinese strategic mind solely through the reading of Sun Tzu's *Art of War* or Mao Zedong's military works would remain a formidable challenge, as previously mentioned. This is primarily due to the fact that the strategic thinking that underpins these strategies is heavily influenced by cultural factors.

# NOTES

1. Pillsbury, M. (2014). Misunderstanding China: How did Western Policy Makers and Academics Repeatedly get China So Wrong? *The Wall Street Journal*, 17 September 2014.
2. Heer, P. (2023). Washington's Wilful Blind Spot on China. The National Interest. October 31, 2023. https://nationalinterest.org/feature/washington%E2%80%99s-willful-blind-spot-china-207120. Retrieved on 2 November 2023.
3. Service, R. (2015). *The End of the Cold War: 1985–1991*. Macmillan, p. 1.
4. Shattan, Joseph (1999). *Architects of Victory: Six Heroes of the Cold War*. The Heritage Foundation, p. 1.
5. Ibid., p. 2.
6. Gopalakrishnan, B.N. et al. (2022). Isolating China: Deglobalisation and its Impact on Global Value Chains. *Foreign Trade Review*, 57(4), pp. 390–407.
7. Palmer, A.W. (2023). 'An Act of War': Inside America's Silicon Blockade Against China. *The New York Times Magazine*, 17 July 2023.
8. Miller, C. (2022). *Chip War: The Fight for The World's Most Critical Technology*. Simon & Schuster, p. 317.
9. The measures of restricting, curbing, and banning exports of technology adopted by the US government reflect a typical 'analytical' approach to strategy, resulting in a limited effect on Chinese high-tech firms and industry. If a 'holistic' approach had been adopted from 2018, the blow to China would have been devastating. This will be further analysed in Chapter 7.
10. Goldman, D.P. (2023). Why America is Losing the Tech War with China. *The National Interest*, 23 July 2023.
11. Miller (n 8) p. 320.
12. Kissinger, H.A. (2011). *On China*. Allen Lane.
13. Cohen, W.I. (2007). Chinese Lessons: Nixon, Mao, and the Course of U.S.-Chinese Relations. *Foreign Affairs*, 86(2), pp. 148–54.
14. Kissinger, H.A. (1979). *Henry Kissinger: The White House Years*. George Weidenfeld & Nicolson Ltd, pp. 167–94.
    Sempa, F.P. (2019). Nixonian Geopolitics and the U.S.-China Rivalry. *Competition Forum*, 17(2), pp. 252–7.
15. Stent, A. (2019). *Putin's World: Russia Against the West and with the Rest*. Twelve, p. 218.
16. Ibid., p. 126.
17. Krickovic, A. and Pellicciari, I. (2021). From 'Greater Europe' to 'Greater Eurasia': Status Concerns and the Evolution of Russia's Approach to Alignment and Regional Integration. *Journal of Eurasian Studies*, 12(1), pp. 86–99.
18. Stent (n 15) pp. 208–9.
19. Sempa (n 14) pp. 252–7.
20. Mintzberg, H., Quinn, J.B. and Ghoshal, S. (1995). *The Strategy Process (European Edition)*. Prentice Hall.

De Wit, B. and Meyer, R. (2010). *Strategy Process, Content, Context: An International Perspective* (4th ed.). South-Western.

Pars, Matthijs (2013). Six strategy lessons from Clausewitz and Sun Tzu. *Journal of Public Affairs*, 13(3), pp. 329–34.

21. Kim, W.C. and Mauborgne, R. (2004). Blue Ocean Strategy. *Harvard Business Review*, October, pp. 1–9.

22. Santamaria, J.A., Martino, V. and Clemons, E.K. (2004). *The Marine Corps Way: Using Maneuverer Warfare to Lead a Winning Organization*. McGraw-Hill.

    Cawood, D. (1984). Managing Innovation: Military Strategy in Business. *Business Horizons*, 27(6), pp. 62–6.

    McNeilly, M.R. (2011). *Sun Tzu and the Art of Business Six Strategic Principles for Managers*. Oxford University Press.

    Bungay, S. (2011). How to Make the Most of Your Company's Strategy. *Harvard Business Review*, January–February, pp. 132–42.

23. Jullien, F. (2004). *A Treatise on Efficacy: Between Western and Chinese Thinking* (J. Lloyd, trans.). Honolulu: University of Hawaii Press.

24. Elliott-Bateman, M. (1967). *Defeat in the East: The Mark of Mao Tse-tung on War*. London: Oxford University Press, p. xii.

25. Ibid., pp. xii–xiii.

26. West, Philip (1989). Interpreting the Korean War. *The American Historical Review*, 94(1), pp. 80–96.

    Guo, C. and Ren, R. (2003). Learning and Problem Representation in Foreign Policy Decision-making: China's Decision to Enter the Korean War Revisited. *Public Administration Quarterly*, 27(3/4), pp. 274–310.

    Hao, Y.F. and Zhai, Z.H. (1990). China's Decision to Enter the Korean War: History Revisited. *The China Quarterly*, 121 (March), pp. 94–115.

    Kim, D. (2016). China's Intervention in the Korean War Revisited. *Diplomatic History*, 40(5), pp. 1002–26.

27. Hastings, M. (1987). *The Korean War*. Pan Books, p. 172.

28. Ibid.

29. Mott IV, W.H. and Kim, J.C. (2006). *The Philosophy of Chinese Military Culture.* Palgrave Macmillan, p. 107.

30. Halberstam, D. (2007). *The Coldest Winter: America and the Korean War*. Macmillan, p. 341.

31. Kissinger (n 12) p. 130.

32. Ibid., p. 131.

33. Halberstam (n 30) p. 338.

34. Alexander, B. (2000). *Korea: The First War We Lost*. Hippocrene Books, p. 21.

35. Elliott-Bateman (n 24).
    Halberstam (n 30).

36. Foot, R. (1985). *The Wrong War: American Policy and the Dimensions of the Korean Conflict, 1950–1953*. Cornell University Press, p. 234.

37. Ibid., pp. 233 Mao Tse-tung 4.

38. Hastings (n 27) p. 170.
39. Farley, R. (2014). Deadly Lessons: The Last Time China and America Went to War. *The National Interest*, 24 October 2014.
40. Ibid.
41. Zhang, S.G. (1995). *Mao's Military Romanticism: China and the Korean War, 1950–1953*. University Press of Kansas, p. 248.
42. Farley (n 39).
43. Kissinger (n 12) p. 103.
44. Ibid, p. 132.
45. Ibid., p. 521.
46. The Economist (1996). The Overseas Chinese: Inheriting the Bamboo Network, *The Economist*, January 13–19 2024, p. 16.
47. White, E. (2023). BYD and Peers Make Their Marque as Chinese Car Sector Comes of Age: Electric-vehicle Models Win Growing Consumer Favour, Leaving Foreign Rivals Well Behind in the Race. *The Financial Times*. London (UK), 19 January 2023.
    White, Edward, Li, Gloria and Jung-A, Song. (2022). China's BYD Takes Electric Car Crown from Tesla: Automobiles. *The Financial Times*. London (UK), 6 July 2022.
    Mollman, Steve (2023). Elon Musk Admits BYD Cars 'are Highly Competitive these Days' After 2011 Clip Shows Him Laughing at the Rival Now Trouncing Tesla in China. *Fortune.com*, 5/28/2023. Retrieved on 08/06/2023.
48. Chu, C.N. (1991). *The Asian Mind Game*. New York: Rawson Associates, p. 5.
49. Li, J.T. et al. (2022). The Belt and Road Initiative and international business policy: A kaleidoscopic perspective. *Journal of International Business Policy*, 5 (2), pp. 135–51.
50. Luft, G. (2016). China's Infrastructure Play: Why Washington Should Accept the New Silk Road. *Foreign Affairs*, 95(5), pp. 68–75.
51. Feigenbaum, E.A. (2017). China and the World: Dealing With a Reluctant Power. *Foreign Affairs*, 96(1), pp. 33–40.
52. Sempa (n 14) pp. 252–7.
53. Mulvad, A.M. (2019). Xiism as a Hegemonic Project in the Making: Sino-communist Ideology and the Political Economy of China's Rise. *Review of International Studies*, 45(3), pp. 449–70.
54. Luft (n 50) pp. 68–75.
55. Liu, Z. and Liu, X. (2022). Is China's Infrastructure Development Experience Unique? *Journal of Chinese Economic and Business Studies,* DOI: 10.1080/14765284.2022.204007. Retrieved on 11/06/2023.
56. Sutter, K.M, Schwarzenberg, A.B. and Sutherland, M.D. (2022). China's 'One Belt, One Road' Initiative: Economic Issues. *Congressional Research Services*, 22 December 2022. https://crsreport.congress.gov/product/pdf/IF/ IF11735. Retrieved on 10/06/2023.

57. Tiezzi, Shannon (2023). How China's Belt and Road Took Over the World. *The Diplomat*, September 12, 2023. https://thediplomat.com/2023/09/how -chinas-belt-and-road-took-over-the-world/. Retrieved on 27 October 2023.
58. Mau, K. and Seurn, R. (2023). One Belt, One Road, One Way? Where European Exporters Benefit from the New Silkroad. *Review of World Economics*, 159(2), pp. 257–97.
59. Fan, S. (2023). Does the Belt and Road Initiative Promote Bilateral Trade? An Empirical Analysis of China and the Belt and Road Countries. *Global Journal of Emerging Market Economies*, 15(2) 190–214.
60. The Economist (2015). How China's Belt and Road Initiative is changing. *The Economist* (Online), October 17, 2023. https:// www .proquest .com/ docview/2877719312?accountid=162157. Retrieved on 27 October 2023.
61. Hu, M.Y. and Xu, J. (2022). How Does High-Speed Rail Impact the Industry Structure? Evidence from China. *Urban Rail Transit*, 8, 296–317. https://doi .org/10.1007/s40864-022-00175-w. Retrieved on 14/06/2023.
62. Khan, M. (2018). China's New 34-Mile Bridge Links Up 70 Million People in Planned Megalopolis. *The Wall Street Journal*, October 22, 2018. https:// www .wsj .com/ articles/ chinas -new -34 -mile -bridge -to -link -up -70 -million -people-in-planned-megalopolis-15402077. Retrieved on 1 November 2023.
63. Hillman, Jonathan E. (2021). *The Digital Silk Road: China's Quest to Wire the World and Win the Future*. Profile Books, pp. 2–3.
64. Reeves, M., Haanæs, K. and Sinha, J. (2015). *Your Strategy Needs a Strategy*. Harvard Business Review Press.
65. Liu, W. et al. (2022). Chinese Management Studies: A Matched-Samples Meta-Analysis and Focused Review of Indigenous Theories. *Journal of Management*, 48(6), pp. 1778–828.
66. Tsui, A.S. (2004). Contributing to Global Management Knowledge: A Case for High Quality Indigenous Research. *Asia Pacific Journal of Management*, 21, pp. 491–513.
    Tsui, A.S. (2007). From Homogenization to Pluralism: International Management Research in the Academy and Beyond. *Academy of Management Journal*, 50(6), pp. 1353–64.
    Leung, K. (2012). Indigenous Chinese Management Research: Like It or Not, We Need It. *Management and Organization Review*, 8(1), pp. 1–5.
67. Ibid.
68. Jullien (n 23).
    Henkel, J.E. (2006). A Treatise on Efficacy: Between Western and Chinese Thinking (review). *Philosophy East and West*, 56(2), pp. 347–451.
69. Wu, J. (1972). Western Philosophy and the Search for Chinese Wisdom. *Invitation to Chinese Philosophy*. Naess, A. and Hannay, A. (eds), Universitetsforlaget, p. 5.
70. Ren, Z.G. (2013). *Wei Shen Mo Shi Mao Zedong?* (*Why Is Mao Zedong?*). Guang Ming Daily Publisher, p. 81.
71. Čarnogurská, M. (1998). Original Ontological Roots of Ancient Chinese Philosophy. *Asian Philosophy*, 8 (3), pp. 203–13.

72. Reding, J.P. (2004). *Comparative Essays in Early Greek and Chinese Rational Thinking.* Ashgate, p. 101.
73. Hofstede, G. (1993). Cultural Constraints in Management Theories. *Academy of Management Executive*, 7, pp. 81–94.
74. Fernandez, J.A. (2004). The Gentleman's Code of Confucius: Leadership by Values. *Organizational Dynamics*, 33(1), pp. 21–31.
    McDonald, P. (2012). Confucian Foundations to Leadership: A Study of Chinese Business Leaders Across Greater China and South-East Asia. *Asia Pacific Business Review*, 18(4), pp. 465–87.
    Tsui, A.S., Wang, H., Xin, K., Zhang, L. and Fu, P.P. (2004). 'Let a Thousand Flowers Bloom': Variation of Leadership Styles Among Chinese CEOs. *Organizational Dynamics*, 33, pp. 5–20.
75. Schwartz, B. (1985). *The World of Thought in Ancient China.* Harvard University Press, pp. 350–82.
76. Schram, Stuart (1967). *Political Leaders of the Twentieth Century: Mao Tse-tung.* Penguin Books, p. 16.
77. Redding, G.S. (1980). Cognition as an Aspect of Culture and Its Relation to Management Processes: An Exploratory View of the Chinese Case. *Journal of Management Studies*, 17(2), pp. 127–48.
78. Gardner, H. (1985). *The Mind's New Science.* New York: Basic Books.
    Nisbett, R.E. (2003). *The geography of thought: How Asians and Westerners think differently . . . and why.* New York: Free Press.
79. Nisbett, R.E., Peng, K., Choi, I. and Norenzayan, A. (2001). Culture and Systems of Thought: Holistic Versus Analytic Cognition. *Psychological Review*, 108(2), pp. 291–310.
    Peng, K. and Nisbett, R.E. (1999). Culture, Dialectics, and Reasoning About Contradiction. *American Psychologist*, 54, pp. 741–54.
    Norenzayan, A. and Nisbett, R.E. (2000). Culture and Causal Cognition. *Current Directions in Psychological Science*, 9(4), pp. 132–5.
80. De Wit and Meyer (n 20).
81. Ibid.
82. Thomas, T. L. (2007). The Chinese Military's Strategic Mind-Set. *Military Review*, 87(6), pp. 47–55.
    Pye, L.W. and Leites, N. (1982). Nuances in Chinese Political Culture. *Asian Survey*, 22(12), pp. 1147–65.
83. E.g., see Williamson, P.J. and Raman, A.P. (2011). How China Reset its Global Acquisition Agenda. *Harvard Business Review*, April, pp. 109–14.
84. Sawyer, R.D. (1993). *The Seven Military Classics of Ancient China.* Westview Press, Inc.
    Johnston, A.I. (1995). *Cultural Realism: Strategic Culture and Grand Strategy in Chinese History.* Princeton University Press.
85. A statement by Johnston (1995) quoted by Kane, T.M. (2007). *Ancient China on Postmodern War.* Routledge, p. 10.
86. Elliott-Bateman (n 24) p. 5.
87. Ibid., p. 16.

88.   Kissinger (n 12) pp. 25–6.
89.   Elliott-Bateman (n 24) p. 6.
90.   Witzel, Morgen (2012). *A History of Management Thought*, London and New York: Routledge, p. 184.
91.   Greenspan, A. and Wooldridge, A. (2018). *Capitalism in America: A History*. Allen Lane, p. 319.
92.   Samuelson, L. (2016). Game Theory in Economics and Beyond. *The Journal of Economic Perspectives*, 30(4), pp. 107–30.
93.   Harre, M.S. (2022). What Can Game Theory Tell Us about an AI 'Theory of Mind'? *Games*, 13(3), p. 46.
94.   Jullien (n 23) p. 10.
95.   Catchpole, Brian (2010). *The Korean War: 1950–1953*. Constable & Robinson Ltd, pp. 171–2.
96.   Yin R.K. (2003). *Case Study Research: Design and Methods (3rd Edition)*. Sage, London, pp. 4–9.
      Hakim, C. (1987). *Research design*. London: Unwin Hyman, p. 28.
97.   Jacques, M. (2012). Why do We Continue to Ignore China's Rise? Arrogance. *The Observer*, Sunday 25 March 2012.
98.   Nisbett (n 78) p. xx.
99.   Kissinger (n 12) p. 103.

# 2. Language and thinking: the root of divergence

> *The limits of my language mean the limits of my world.*
> – Ludwig Wittgenstein

> *By words the mind is winged.*
> – Aristophanes

## A MISSING LINK IN BUSINESS RESEARCH

One of the fundamental premises of this book asserts that the cognitive modes of diverse cultures exhibit variations, and it is crucial to comprehend these dissimilarities in order to facilitate clear and effective cross-cultural communication and interactions. In addition, understanding the true intentions and motivations of the other party is vital for formulating an effective strategic response. Why then do cognitive differences exist among different cultures? What are the potential roots of these variations?

China boasts a remarkable uninterrupted history that surpasses that of any other great empires in Eurasia, including renowned civilisations such as the Egyptian, Roman, Byzantine, Arabian, Ottoman, and Tsarist-Soviet empires.[1] The Chinese language, which dates back millennia, stands as one of the oldest languages globally and is deeply ingrained in the country's culture. Its creation and evolution mark the genesis of Chinese civilisation, exerting a profound influence on Chinese thought. While Egyptian hieroglyphic writing, Mesopotamian cuneiform, and Mayan glyphs also rank among the world's oldest languages, they have unfortunately faded into extinction. The invention of writing, widely recognised as a pivotal achievement, serves as the foundation that supports and empowers modern society, a notion well-founded and justified.[2]

The concept that language shapes human thought has been a topic of interest among scholars in the Western world since 1836, when German philosopher Wilhelm von Humboldt began to explore this idea.[3] Among those who have contributed to the extensive studies of the relationship between language and thought include linguists,[4] philosophers,[5] anthropologists,[6] and psychologists.[7] Notably, Harold Innis is recognised as one of the pioneering thinkers who examined the potential impact of writing on human cognitive patterns.[8] Despite the considerable body of literature on this subject,[9] a consensus regarding the nature of the language-thought relationship has remained elusive to this day.[10]

Benjamin Lee Whorf, an American linguist, and Edward Sapir, an American anthropologist-linguist, put forth the idea that language influences thought.[11] This concept, commonly referred to as the 'Sapir-Whorf hypothesis' or 'Whorfian hypothesis', encompasses several key points. Firstly, languages differ in how they categorise and partition the world semantically. Secondly, the structure of one's language shapes the way one perceives and comprehends the world. Thirdly, consequently, speakers of different languages may have distinct perspectives on reality.[12]

A milder interpretation of the Whorfian hypothesis suggests that the language an individual speaks predisposes, rather than determines, their perceptions of the world. This viewpoint, summarised by John Carroll, likens language structure to a lattice or screen that influences how we perceive and interpret our experience.[13]

Scholars like Gentner and Goldin-Meadow point out that the relationship between language and thought encompasses not just a single inquiry but a multitude of interconnected questions. Language serves as a powerful perspective through which we perceive and understand the world. It equips us with tools that expand our capabilities and enable us to comprehend aspects of reality that might have eluded us otherwise. To fully explore these potentials, it is essential to engage in comparison across languages and various fields of knowledge, as well as analyse the viewpoints of both linguistically influenced and non-linguistically influenced thinkers. By pursuing such an agenda, we can expect to uncover a nuanced understanding of the Whorfian hypothesis, rather than a simple binary affirmation or negation.[14]

The inquiry into the potential impact of linguistic variances between Chinese and Indo-European languages on the cognitive disparities between these two populations warrants a separate categorisation that merits particular consideration.

Chinese civilisation stands apart from other civilisations in terms of language development. Unlike Indo-European languages, the Chinese language has evolved independently and showcases a remarkable indigenous interest in various grammatical features. It is noteworthy that Chinese civilisation remains the sole non-Indo-European civilisation worldwide to have cultivated a distinct and robust lexicographic tradition and a sustained systematic pursuit of term definitions, devoid of significant external influences.[15]

Sinologists have long been captivated by the enigma of correlating Chinese thought with the intricate structure of the Chinese language. However, thus far, they have managed to discern very few sufficiently clear issues that lend themselves to fruitful debate.[16]

When examining the Eastern and Western writing systems in a comparative context, scholars widely agree that spoken language has exerted the most significant influence on human thought processes and is fundamental to its very inception. Following closely behind the impact of speech is the role of writing; Chinese and Western alphabetic literacy, in particular, embody two contrasting extremes of written communication. Notably, the divergent thought patterns found in Eastern and Western cultures correspond to the distinctive characteristics of their respective writing systems.[17]

Inspired by his initial experiences in Hong Kong, Alfred Bloom embarked on a captivating journey, looking into the impact of language on thinking in China and the West. The culmination of his research efforts resulted in the publication of a book entitled *The Linguistic Shaping of Thought: A Study of the Impact of Language on Thinking in China and the West.*[18] Within the book, Bloom lends support to the Whorfian hypothesis, asserting that Chinese individuals possess a distinct manner of thinking compared to their Western counterparts because of the fundamental structure of their language. Specifically, he argues that the Chinese language's characteristics contribute to a deficiency in counterfactuals and the conceptualisation of universal concepts.

It is claimed that the Chinese language is more suited for conveying poetic insights rather than facilitating logical thinking.[19] In his book *Language and Logic in Ancient China*, Chad Hansen firmly asserts the grammatical structure of the Chinese language hinders logical reasoning among the Chinese people,[20] and this claim is supported by studies in psychology.[21]

The current discourse in the West may be summarised as follows: Language is a complex and multifaceted phenomenon that is intrinsically linked to culture, social cognition, and abstract thinking. While it is intertwined with these aspects of human experience, language is also recognised as a unique and specialised adaptation that plays a vital role in shaping culture, cognition, and social behaviour.[22] However, studies exploring the customary mode of reasoning in Chinese culture have hitherto been constrained in their extent and breadth.[23]

When it comes to examining the relationship between the Chinese language and thought in Western studies, certain limitations become apparent. In the Western context, there may not be a strong motivation to conduct a comparative study on the language–thought relationship between the West and China.[24] There is often a prevailing preconception that the alphabet is the defining feature that shapes the Western world.[25]

Until now, the majority of investigations into the Chinese language–thought relationship have approached the subject from a static standpoint. Typically, these studies concentrate on analysing the established language structure such as 'mass noun' or 'count noun' or interpreting specific texts.[26]

In Chad Hansen's study, the Chinese language is described as follows: It is not naturally or intuitively readable. Written Chinese adheres to a conventional grammar. Characters in Chinese are not self-explanatory, universally understood, or inherently meaningful symbols. Numerous characters are phonetic compounds composed of an ideographic radical. Additionally, some characters function as rebus characters, meaning they are borrowed from another context solely to represent a word with a similar sound. Furthermore, Chinese characters do not strongly resemble pictures, and synonyms are not identical.[27]

Christoph Harbsmeier explores the intricate relationship between language and logic. He takes such an approach focusing on the Chinese language, particularly written classic Chinese, providing detailed descriptions of its logical and linguistic features.[28] This perspective reveals a limitation in the existing body of research, which has predominantly examined the language–thought relationship from a Western analytical standpoint. By shifting our vantage point to a Chinese perspective, new insights and understandings of this relationship can be gained.

To explore the language–thought relationship from a Chinese perspective, a holistic or dynamic approach should be employed. This entails examining the origins and evolution of the Chinese language, seeking to comprehend how language has influenced and shaped thought processes.

The Chinese language stands out markedly from Indo-European languages in its formation and structure. The global business landscape is significantly shaped by the business environment, where national culture plays a pivotal role, with language serving as a fundamental element of national culture.[29] From a Chinese standpoint, the Chinese language system not only impacts Chinese thought patterns but also extends its influence to other cultural aspects, including ideological and philosophical reasoning, patriarchal clan rules and regulations, poetry, music and dance, the penal code, customs, and traditional medicine.[30] Understandably, little attention has been given thus far to examining the implications of the Chinese language in realms of business or military studies because of its holistic nature.

## FORMATION OF THE CHINESE LANGUAGE

Language has played a pivotal role in the development of civilisation, marking meaningful milestones throughout history. The Chinese and English languages have distinct origins and foundations. English, belonging to the Germanic group, is part of the Indo-European language family and utilises the Roman alphabet for written communication.

On the other hand, tracing the precise origin of Chinese characters poses a challenge.[31] According to Chinese tradition, the concepts of characters can be attributed to Fu Xi, the first mythical emperor of China, while the visual development of characters is credited to Cang Jie. The systematisation of the Chinese writing is said to have been accomplished by Huang Di, also known as the 'Yellow Emperor', the third legendary emperor of China, around the 25th century BC.[32] However, extensive research suggests that Chinese writing emerged around 1200 BC, during the late Shang Dynasty. This conclusion is supported by archaeological evidence, such as oracle bone inscriptions found on ancient artefacts.[33]

Chinese writing is believed to have originated in the context of ancient divination practices. Rather than being ritualistic communications with spirits, the inscriptions that have been discovered are considered the records created by diviners for the benefit of future generations. In many ways, the development of Chinese script followed a similar path to that of writing systems in Mesopotamia and Egypt.[34]

It is believed that Cang Jie, serving as the official historian to Huang Di, the earliest known ruler in Chinese prehistory (around 2600 BC), played a vital role in the creation of the earliest form of the Chinese pictographic writing system.[35] Faced with the challenge of documenting significant events without a suitable writing system, Cang Jie conceived the idea of constructing written 'words'.

Cang Jie's inspiration stemmed from observing the tracks left by birds and animals. He proceeded to depict simplified pictures of various common animals and presented them to unfamiliar individuals, requesting them to identify the depicted animals. As these strangers successfully associated the drawings with their corresponding animals, Cang Jie introduced this method to others. Over time, this innovative approach gained acceptance among the populace, leading to the birth of the Chinese pictographic language system.

Cang Jie, as an esteemed official historian, held the crucial responsibility of gathering and employing all original characters, thus contributing to the compilation of pictographs created by ordinary individuals. Among the literature treasures of China stands the earliest Chinese dictionary '*Shuowen Jiezi*' (*Discussing Writing and Explaining Characters*), written by Xu Shen, a renowned scholar of the Eastern Han Dynasty.[36] In this literary work, Xu Shen recounts the legendary tale of Cang Jie's creation of Chinese characters.[37] It becomes evident that the Chinese writing system has undergone numerous developments by different individuals throughout its long history since Cang Jie is said to have invented the fundamental technique of constructing pictographic characters. Nevertheless, pictography has remained the foundation of the Chinese writing system.[38]

The earliest discovered form of written Chinese, known as the 'oracle bone inscriptions', consists of characters or inscriptions on flat cattle bones or tortoise shells. These inscriptions primarily documented various aspects of state governance, agriculture, husbandry, as well as divination practices, battles, and hunting expeditions, providing details such as dates, activities, and outcomes. Archaeologists have unearthed over 100 000 pieces of oracle bones, containing more than 4500 distinct characters, of which approximately 1700 have been deciphered. While the oracle bone inscriptions date back around 3500 years, it is likely that the development of the Chinese writing system had already begun much earlier, as the system had already been conventionalised by that time. The exact timing of this development, however, remains unresolved.

The '*Shuowen Jiezi*' provides a systematic categorisation and analysis Chinese characters based on six graphical structural types, commonly referred to as *Liu Shu* in Chinese.[39]

### Pictographs

A pictograph is a symbol that has been conventionally stylised to represent an object, such as the Sun or the Moon, as a picture-symbol, based on its resemblance to the actual object. It represents the earliest and most fundamental stage of word formation. The characters formed using this method are single words, primarily nouns that depict flowers, plants, birds, animals, and natural phenomena. Figure 2.1 presents some examples.

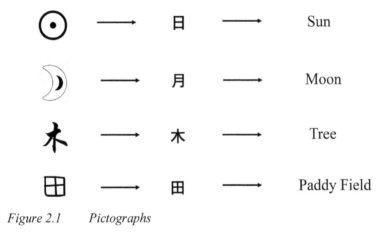

*Figure 2.1       Pictographs*

As depicted in the figure, the original forms or structures of characters, such as the Sun, the Moon, a tree, and a paddy field, closely resemble the actual objects, making them easily recognisable based on their visual representations. However, over time, the resemblance between the characters and the objects gradually diminishes.

## Simple Ideograms

Simple ideograms are pictographs that have additional symbols added to represent new words. Pictographs, on their own, have limitations in expressing positional relationships, specific parts of objects or creatures, and complex or abstract concepts. However, by combining simple symbols with pictographs, it becomes possible to create words for such concepts that are both easily memorable and comprehensible. Figure 2.2 provides illustrative examples.

| 一 | One | 二 | Two |
| 上 | Up | 下 | Down |
| 本 | Root | 末 | Tip |

*Figure 2.2*　　*Simple ideograms*

In the figure, directional and positional concepts like 'up', 'down', 'above', and 'below' can be conveyed by incorporating a horizontal line positioned above or below an element within an existing pictogram. For instance, by adding a short line underneath the horizontal stroke of '木', which means 'tree' in Chinese, produces '本' meaning 'root'. Conversely, if the additional line is placed above the original horizontal stroke, making '末', the new meaning becomes 'tip' or 'end' (of a tree). Furthermore, when the pictograph '日' meaning the 'Sun' is combined with '本' denoting 'root', it makes the word '日本' indicating Japan, which directly translates to 'the root of the Sun'. This term signifies the geographical location where the Sun rises.

## Compound Ideograms

Compound ideograms are novel linguistic units created by merging two or more distinct pictographs. As exemplified in Figure 2.3, amalgamating three instances of the individual 'person' character (人) yields a fresh lexeme denoting 'many (individuals)' (众). Likewise, the combination of two depictions of trees (木) results in the semantic entity 'forest' (林). Furthermore, adopting a more abstract perspective, the concept of 'goodness' (好) emerges from the fusion of a 'woman' (女) and a 'child' (子), as visually represented in Figure 2.3.

人 (Human being) ⟶ 众 (Many)

木 (Tree) ⟶ 林 (Forest)

日 (Sun) + 月 (Moon) ⟶ 明 (Brightness)

田 (Paddy field) +力 (Power) ⟶ 男 (Man)

女 (Woman) + 子 (Child) ⟶ 好 (Goodness)

*Figure 2.3      Compound ideograms*

**Phonograms**

Phonograms are linguistic units composed of two components: one representing semantic meaning and the other representing pronunciation. These components combine to form eight distinct combinations, as exemplified below.

1.  In phonograms, the meaning of a word is conveyed by its left-hand component, while the right-hand component indicates its pronunciation. For instance, consider the characters 柯 (stalk) and 秧 (seedling). In these examples, the left-hand components (木 and 禾) represent 'tree' and 'grass', respectively, while their right-hand components (可 and 央) determine their respective pronunciations.
2.  Phonograms feature a relationship where the right-hand component corresponds to meaning, while the left-hand component pertains to pronunciation. For instance, consider the characters 颈 (neck) and 顶 (top or tip). In these cases, the left-hand components determine pronunciation, while the right-hand components convey meaning.
3.  In the third combination, the inner component of the character signifies meaning, while the outer component determines pronunciation. This can be observed in words like 问 (question) and 闷 (stuffiness).
4.  In the fourth combination, the outer component of the character is associated with meaning, while the inner component pertains to pronunciation. Examples of this combination can be found in characters such as 阀 (valve) and 阅 (reading).
5.  The fifth combination is characterised by the top component representing the meaning of the character, while the lower component pertaining to pronunciation. Examples of this combination can be seen in words like 苇 (reed) and 花 (flower).

6. The sixth combination is the opposite of the fifth, where the lower component signifies meaning, while the upper component determines pronunciation. Two illustrative characters are 忍 (tolerance) and 恐 (fear).
7. In the seventh combination, the upper left component specifies meaning, while the lower right component relates to pronunciation. Characters such as 俪 (married couple) and 旗 (flag) exemplify this pattern.
8. In the last combination, the upper right component indicates meaning, while the lower left component denotes pronunciation. This can be observed in characters like 颖 (husk) and 望 (observation).

The process of word formation using phonograms is characterised by a straightforward and easily comprehensible structure. Consequently, it is the most commonly employed method, accounting for 90% of Chinese characters. However, due to the extensive evolution of the Chinese writing system throughout millennia, identifying the role or meaning of each component can often be challenging. Thus, Chinese writing is not strictly classified as a purely pictographic system but rather as a mixed logographic or morpho-syllabic system.[40]

### Phonetic Loans

Phonetic loans refer to foreign words that do not have an equivalent in the Chinese language. To represent these words, Chinese uses characters that have the same pronunciation, known as homophones. However, it is important to note that phonetic loans make up only a small portion of the Chinese vocabulary and have a limited role in the creation of new words. Nevertheless, as the language continues to evolve, this method remains a convenient option for forming new words.

### Derivatives

Derivatives in Chinese refer to characters that are mutually explanatory or synonymous, like 老 (old age) and 考 (long life, aged). While derivatives may appear to be interchangeable synonyms, they actually expand the application of the original character to some extent, thereby implying the formation of new words. Thus, derivatives represent both the application and formation of characters, playing a role in extending their usage.

## THE ROLE OF LANGUAGE IN SHAPING THOUGHT

In alphabetic writing systems of Indo-European languages, the process of forming words is designed in a way that strongly promotes analytical thinking.

By utilising a finite set of letters, it becomes possible to express any word or sentence by arranging a specific combination of these letters. Consequently, this linguistic characteristic has led to the belief that reality itself is composed of a combination of fundamental 'elements'. When this logic approach is applied to the field of chemistry, scientists have successfully identified numerous essential chemical elements. These elements have been organised and classified within the periodic table of chemical elements, which was formulated in 1869 by the renowned Russian chemist Dmitri Mendeleev.

In contrast to Indo-European alphabetic systems, the formation of Chinese characters follows a process of synthesis and comprehensiveness, emphasising the holistic thinking of Chinese individuals. The evolution of Chinese characters, progressing from pictograph to simple ideogram, then to compound ideogram, and finally to phonogram, results in a word formation process that is more synthetic compared to languages like English. For instance, the Chinese character '说' (speak) is composed of a '口' (mouth) atop a '人' (man), while the character '羊' (sheep) is conceptually represented by a sheep's head.

To grasp and develop these characters, one must rely on synthetic or holistic thinking, which stands in contrast to the analytical thinking prevalent in the Western context. Phonograms, which constitute the majority of Chinese characters, consist of two elements, as mentioned earlier – one indicating meaning and the other representing sound. As a result, a logical notion has emerged, suggesting that the universe encompasses both natural and humanistic phenomena, and these two realms may constitute elements of a larger unity. This notion has fostered a distinct Chinese philosophical perspective, asserting that humanity is an interconnected part of nature. Consequently, it has further nurtured holistic thinking among Chinese speakers.[41] The inclination towards holistic thinking has in turn exerted a significant influence on various domains, including the development of military strategies and the conventional diagnostic and therapeutic methods employed in traditional Chinese medicine.

The theory of the 'alphabet effect' provides support for the significant role of language in society, particularly in relation to intellectual advancements. This theory highlights the intellectual consequences of the alphabet, including abstraction, analysis, rationality, and classification. These cognitive processes have formed the foundation for Western abstract scientific and logical thinking.[42] Furthermore, the alphabet effect is believed to have played a crucial role in the emergence of various fundamental aspects of Western civilisation, such as capitalism, nationalism, the Renaissance, the Industrial Revolution, the Reformation, and the modern theories of chemical elements and atomic structure.

According to Logan, the alphabet effect suggests that the first scientific literature, regardless of its Oriental or Occidental origins, was destined to be written using alphabetic script. This is due to the belief that the alphabet creates an environment conducive to the flourishing of abstract theoretical science.[43] While it may be debatable whether this theory holds true in its entirety, it sheds light on the impact of language on thought patterns.

The dissociation of elements in Western alphabetic languages from tangible objects contributes to a predisposition towards abstract thinking among their speakers, readers, and writers. This inclination towards abstraction is particularly relevant in the realm of science. Scientific ideas are initially conceived through logical reasoning in an abstract manner, and subsequently tested and explained to establish or validate scientific theories. The essence of science lies in acquiring knowledge about natural laws governing the world, and abstract thinking serves as a fundamental component of this process.

As a result, the Western tradition has produced numerous scientists who have formulated theorems, laws, and axioms grounded in logical inference and reasoning. Examples include Aristotelian philosophy, Euclidean geometry, Euler's theorem, Isaac Newton's laws of physics, Albert Einstein's theories of relativity, and many others. These achievements underscore the marked impact of abstract thinking on scientific advancement within Western civilisation.

Throughout its extensive and unbroken history, China can proudly claim credit for the invention of numerous materials, machines, and various other entities that can be categorised as 'techniques' or 'technology', such as gunpowder, the compass, printing, the seismograph, and more others. However, it should be noted that that these achievements primarily fall within the realm of technology rather than science. Chinese classic science and technology, in reality, predominantly encompass technological advancements rather than scientific discoveries. Notable areas of progress in ancient China include agronomy, military science, medicine, and arts and crafts. Conversely, the development of purely theoretical natural science, detached from practical applications, was largely absent.[44]

Christoph Harbsmeier acknowledges that ancient Chinese civilisation faced challenges when dealing with abstract concepts or properties. He attributes this phenomenon to the absence of morphemes akin to the English suffix '-ness' within the Classical Chinese language,[45] although this limitation is not intrinsically linked to language formation. Taking an alternative viewpoint, Chad Hansen arrives at a similar proposition by suggesting that the Chinese language's treatment of nouns resembles mass nouns in English. For instance, words like 'water' and 'hair' in English do not require the formation of abstract concepts. Similarly, Chinese nouns, functioning in a comparable manner, may not necessitate the need for abstract postulations.[46]

China's development has been significantly constrained by the absence of scientific advancement. The progress of science relies on two factors: motivation, which encompasses the desire for a fulfilling life and happiness,[47] and ability. Both factors are intricately linked to the Chinese language, directly and indirectly. As suggested by Nisbett, China's failure to foster scientific development can be partially attributed to lack of curiosity.[48] However, even if curiosity were present, the absence of a concept of nature would have hindered the advancement of science.

In a pictographic language like Chinese, the meaning of a word is closely tied to the visual representation of the actual object. Consequently, Chinese individuals tend to excel in 'imaginative' rather than 'abstract' thinking.[49] Despite China's numerous inventions and technological breakthroughs throughout Chinese history, the emergence of enduring scientific theories with abstractive characteristics has been scarce.

Linguistic scholars widely agree that the Chinese written language is better suited for the composition of poetry rather than abstract scientific thinking. In essence, Chinese is inherently an artistic language rather than a scientific one.[50] The inclination towards artistic expression has resulted in a lack of linguistic propensity for abstract thinking, which, in turn, led to the absence of a system for abstract time-keeping or a linear progressive calendar in ancient China.

The Chinese calendar, known as the *Gan* and *Zhi* system, derives its foundation from the concept of stem and branch, resembling the structure of a tree. It comprises ten Heavenly Stems (*Gan*) and twelve Earthly Branches (*Zhi*), forming a cycle of 60 years. However, this system proves inadequate for recording historical events, as Chinese history would encompass numerous cycles of 60 years. Consequently, China has been compelled to adopt the Western system, based on the dating of the Christian era, to accurately record its past.[51]

The structure of the Chinese language has played a pivotal role in generating a unique form of philosophy, including the likes of Confucianism, Taoism, and Dark Learning, which integrates elements of Confucianism and Taoism,[52] profoundly influencing Chinese culture. The Chinese language's structure is characterised by its remarkable ability to represent the complexity of concrete objects, as well as social and natural phenomena, with a high degree of simplicity. This linguistic characteristic has in turn fostered the emergence and evolution of Chinese philosophies, resulting in a culture that embodies great simplicity.[53]

In essence, Chinese philosophy stands out as the most human-centric and practical among various philosophical schools.[54] The emphasis on practicality and the human experience has contributed to the absence of a distinct scientific tradition in China. Instead, the focus has been on philosophical systems that deeply resonate with the human condition and offer practical wisdom for navigating life's challenges.

The Chinese language is intricately linked to certain aspects of Chinese philosophy, as evidenced by the following examples.

As per *Shuowen Jiezi*, an authoritative ancient compilation of Chinese etymology, 道 or '*Tao*' in English, denotes the path to walk on. Structurally, it comprises the components representing 'foot' and 'head', implying the act of following the footstep of the head. Thus, the original meaning of '*Tao*' is 'the path people walk', functioning as both a noun and an ideogram. Just as individuals must follow a specific path to reach their destinations when walking, the concept extends to complete tasks successfully by adhering to certain rules. Consequently, the significance of '*Tao*' expands to encompass 'principle' or 'doctrine', among other interpretations.

'*Tao*' represents a natural law or rule that governed the world before the advent of humans. Through the evolution of life, humans gradually acquired consciousness, leading to an understanding of '*Tao*' and the emergence of '*Te*' (morality or virtue). '*Te*' functions as a code that defines human behaviour, evolving over an extensive period after human came into existence. '*Tao*' comes before and surpasses '*Te*'.[55]

'One' (一) is one of the most frequently used characters in the Chinese language, boasting the fewest strokes, making it easily recognisable and convenient to write. However, this seemingly simple character contains incredibly profound meanings, earning it the moniker of a magical Chinese character.

In ancient Chinese belief, 'one' symbolises the supreme and the origin of all things. According to Laozi's '*Tao Te Ching*', *Tao* gives birth to 'one', 'one' gives birth to 'two', 'two' gives birth to 'three', and 'three' gives birth to all things. This insightful aphorism left a lasting impression on subsequent generations of scholars. All life in the universe is unified into one life force, sharing a common source. The great Way creates One (*Taiji*), and everything in life is part of the One (the One is everything). Therefore, it is conceivable that when everything reaches its conclusion, all things (Dharma) return to Oneness (*Taiji*), signifying the return of everything to Oneness (the One is everything). Consequently, all things belong to the One place.[56]

Through a comparative study of the linguistic structures of Chinese and English, it becomes evident that individual languages have an impact on the cognitive processes of their speakers. Specifically, in cognitive domains that involve the presentation of the world, the influence of language can be remarkably substantial.[57] As such, the Chinese language, with its concrete and tangible formation of characters, has fostered a practical mindset among the speakers.

It has been observed that the inclination towards abstraction, which is a defining characteristic of ancient Greek philosophy, finds no parallel in Chinese philosophy.[58] This disparity can be attributed to the influence of language on thought processes. The nature of Chinese characters, rooted in the physical and material aspects of the world, has cultivated a practical frame of mind among Chinese philosophers and scholars. Consequently, the emphasis on abstract reasoning and conceptual thinking, which is prevalent in ancient Greek philosophy, has not been a prominent feature of Chinese philosophical tradition.

Scholars such as Hansen and Bao have observed the features of the Chinese language that lead to the absence of logic in Chinese philosophy. Their analysis highlights two crucial points. Firstly, based on the grammatical structure of the ancient Chinese language, it is apparent that Chinese thought does not encompass abstract entities such as ideas and concepts. Secondly, this absence of abstract entities leads to a nominalistic nature within Chinese philosophy. Consequently, adopting a nominalistic interpretation of Chinese philosophy presents an elegant, simpler, and more coherent understanding.[59]

Social psychological research supports the assertion that Chinese philosophy exhibits a lack of logic. In fact, it has been suggested that that the Chinese not only lack formal logic but also a principle of contradiction.[60] This crucial observation sheds light on one of the primary factors contributing to challenges in cross-cultural communication and understanding. Westerners often make the assumption that the Chinese possess the same logical reasoning as themselves, or alternatively, that they lack logic altogether. However, Chinese logic operates on the basis of analogy and induction, rather than strict matching and deduction.[61]

The nature of pictographic word formation often leads to a thinking pattern where individuals interpret something without truly comprehending it. By observing a component of a Chinese character that represents its meaning, one may hastily deduce the word's significance. For example, when encountering a text containing a word with elements like '木' (tree) or '鸟' (bird), it is tempting to assume that it pertains to some form of tree or bird, which can encompass numerous variations. Consequently, even without fully grasping the precise meaning of the word, one can continue reading. However, the evolution of Chinese characters, including phonetic loans and derivatives, has resulted in many components of word formation becoming disconnected from their original meanings, leading to erroneous interpretations.

Hall and Ames also observed that Chinese individuals often exhibit cognitive processes characterised by ambiguity and indefiniteness that have been identified through an analysis of the character formation of the Chinese language by Chinese linguists.[62] According to Hall and Ames, Chinese dictionaries can give the impression that numerous crucial categories of cultural interpretation possess multiple meanings, necessitating the translator to carefully choose the most suitable one based on context. This particular approach to the Chinese language highlights the issue that we have consistently encountered when exploring the Chinese world.[63] These authors further draw a comparison to the Western cultural counterpart, which is starkly contrasting in nature.

They emphasised that, by considering the significant role that univocal definition played in shaping Western philosophy, we can better appreciate the unfamiliarity of a tradition like that of the Chinese, which never underwent such a development.[64] It is worth noting that many of the top-quality CNC lathes are manufactured by German companies, as the German language, belonging to the Indo-European language family, is known for its high degree of precision. In contrast, Chinese companies may face greater challenges in achieving a comparable level of precision in their manufacturing processes. However, in the realm of strategy, this cultural characteristic of the Chinese reflects a certain degree of flexibility in their strategic positioning, allowing for manoeuvrability.

National languages exhibit a dynamic and developmental nature. They undergo evolution and incorporate new vocabulary through cultural exchanges and interactions with other linguistic traditions. Alphabetic languages, in particular, possess a remarkable capacity to assimilate words from nonstandard dialects or foreign languages, in terms of both pronunciation and orthography. English serves as a prime illustration of this phenomenon, as it has assimilated numerous terms from diverse languages such as French, German, Italian, and Spanish, and has further incorporated a multitude of neologisms stemming from contemporary societal and economic advancements. This inherent flexibility, adaptability, and openness associated with alphabetic languages have consequently endowed Western societies with these same characteristics. This linguistic versatility has played a significant role in shaping pivotal historical events and institutions, including the Magna Carta, the Industrial Revolution, the Glorious Revolution, and the establishment of parliamentary systems.

In contrast, Chinese characters prioritise ideography over pronunciation or phonetics, which tend to be dynamic, varying significantly across regions and over time. This emphasis on ideography has granted Chinese characters a remarkable stability that transcends temporal and spatial boundaries, making them resistant to linguistic evolution. Consequently, the Chinese writing system faces considerable challenges in incorporating neologisms from other spoken languages or dialects and integrating them into standard Chinese. Similarly, the system encounters difficulties when assimilating foreign words, due to phonetic incompatibility, often leading to the new word being associated with an existing morpheme, resulting in misunderstanding. Overall, the Chinese character system lacks the flexibility, adaptability, and openness found in alphabetic languages. Consequently, this characteristic has a notable impact on Chinese ideologies.

The inflexibility of Chinese written characters exerts influence over various social and ideological domains. For instance, in Chinese politics, there is a strong emphasis on adhering to the 'orthodox line' or the central party line. Similarly, Chinese literature often revolves around the 'orthodox school',

while trade guilds uphold the 'rules and disciplines' passed down by previous masters. Moreover, philosophy in China is heavily influenced by the
'Confucian orthodoxy'. In Chinese cultural and academic spheres, the promotion of multiple schools of thought is discouraged, with one particular school
typically designated as the prevailing paradigm. This is exemplified by the
dominance of Confucianism as the orthodox or national system of thought
since the Han Dynasty.

Consequently, the Chinese intellectual tradition is commonly characterised
by a strong commitment to continuity. To illustrate this, the dominant position
of Confucianism in Chinese thought systems serves as a good example. Prior
to its emergence during the Zhou Dynasty, Confucianism had undergone
adaptations to accommodate thinkers as diverse as Mencius and Hsun Tzu.
The inclusive nature of Han Confucians like Chia I and Tung Chung-shu,
who incorporated eclectic elements as well as the influence of the Buddhism
on neo-Confucians with its intricate metaphysics, all contribute to the organic
growth of the continuous Confucian tradition.

Even in contemporary times, scholars such as Tung Chun-I and Fung Yu-lan
can be seen as 'neo-neo-Confucian', reflecting the ongoing development and
relevance of Confucian ideas. In this traditional paradigm, a figure's prominence is not determined by how much they deviate from their historical inher-
itance, but rather by the extent to which they embody, express, and amplify
their tradition. Hence, throughout history, there has been an extraordinary
emphasis on historical records in China. These records serve as a repository of
the past cultural tradition from which the new ideas and insights can emerge.

In contrast to the development of Western thought, which is rooted in
a strong 'atomistic' and 'essentialistic' commitment that can be traced back
to the early Greeks, the prominence of a historical figure is often determined
by the extent to which they embody discontinuity with the past. Figures like
Descartes, Kepler, or Einstein stand out precisely because they challenge the
prevailing status quo and sharply deviate from it. Throughout history, these
individuals are recognised as catalysts that set their respective disciplines on
new trajectories.[65]

Since the establishment of the People's Republic of China, each generation's
leader of the Communist Party of China has set a central or priority policy line,
commonly known as the 'orthodox' line. During Mao Zedong's reign, the
priority was placed on class struggle, while during the era of Deng Xiaoping,
the central policy line shifted towards pragmatism, as evidenced by slogans
such as: 'Practice is the sole criterion for testing truth' or 'No matter black cats
or white cats, as long as they catch mice, they are good cats'. Similarly, under
Jiang Zemin's leadership, a policy line known as the 'Three Representations'
was introduced, highlighting that the Communist Party of China represents the
most productive force, culture, and the interests of the majority. Jiang's suc-

cessor, Hu Jintao, further altered the orthodox line by emphasising principles such as 'putting people first', adopting a 'scientific outlook on development', and striving to build a 'harmonious society'.

All in all, the Chinese writing system has played a significant role in shaping the ideological aspects of China's cultural and social domains.[66] The shifts in central policy and ideology reflect the influence of the Chinese character's stability and the importance placed on adhering to an established orthodoxy.

The linguistic characteristics of Chinese and Western languages contribute to several significant disparities in cognition. These distinctions can be summarised as follows:

1. Logic: Due to differences in language structure, Chinese individuals possess a distinct logic compared to their Western counterparts.[67] Unlike Western cultures, the Chinese did not develop a formal system of logic. There is a noticeable absence of discussions on forms of inference, such as Aristotelian or Nyaya syllogisms.[68] This divergence in logical frameworks creates a significant challenge for effective communication between Westerners and Chinese individuals, as there is no readily available bridge to connect the two modes of thinking. The disparity in logic alone indicates a fundamental gap between Western and Chinese thought processes.

2. Thinking styles: Chinese individuals tend to exhibit a predisposition towards imaginative, corporeal, or practical thinking, while Westerners display a greater inclination towards abstract thinking. The linguistic characteristics of the Chinese language, with its emphasis on pictography, contribute to a mode of thinking that is often more concrete and focused on practical applications. In contrast, Western languages, with their alphabet-based structures, facilitate abstract thinking and conceptualisation. These divergent thinking styles further contribute to differences in cognitive approaches between Chinese and Western cultures.

3. Thinking characteristics: Chinese individuals typically exhibit a holistic thinking style, focusing on the entirety of a phenomenon or object and placing less emphasis on specific details. In contrast, Western individuals tend to adopt a more analytical thinking approach, paying closer attention to finer details. These distinct thinking tendencies can be attributed to the linguistic characteristics that have shaped the Chinese and Western languages throughout their origin and evolution.

The Chinese written language, originating from pictography, comprises several components that fulfil distinct roles. These components come together in the formation of Chinese characters, fostering a thinking style that embraces the interconnectedness and interdependence of various aspects. The process of character formation nurtures a mindset that values a comprehensive perspective and encourages a holistic approach to comprehension and interpretation.

Conversely, the alphabet-based writing systems of Western languages facilitate a more analytical thinking process. The segmentation of words into individual letters encourages a focus on discrete units and enables precise analysis and examination of details. This linguistic structure fosters a thinking style that emphasises breaking down complex ideas into component parts, and thorough examination and understanding.

In alphabetic languages like English, each individual word possesses a unique and distinct identity, reflecting the analytical nature of cognition. In order to fully comprehend a newspaper, such as *The New York Times*, one would typically need to have command over approximately 20 000 words. Conversely, Chinese, characterised by a holistic cognition, embraces interconnectedness. By acquiring knowledge of around 3000 characters, one can navigate through countless combinations of phrases and meanings, enabling comfortable expression and understanding of Chinese media articles.

Essentially, Western languages, through their respective cultures, place importance on differentiation, with each word serving as a distinct unit. In contrast, the Chinese language seeks out and shares common characteristics. For instance, among words associated with water, their characters consistently incorporate a component representing water. This can be observed in words such as: 江 (a common name for rivers in Southern China), 河 (a common name for rivers in Northern China), 湖 (lake), 海 (sea), and 洋 (ocean), where the left part of all the characters signifies 'water'. Similarly, the objects related to metals feature a distinct 'metal' component within their characters, as seen in words like 银 (silver), 铜 (copper), 铁 (iron), and 锡 (tin).

A distinction between Western and Chinese languages lies in the fact that Western languages require a vast vocabulary with distinct words for each object, whereas Chinese relies on shared components to express meaning, resulting in a smaller set of characters for communication. This cultural difference can be seen as China's emphasis on 'commonality' as opposed to the Western focus on 'individuality'.

According to a Chinese scholar's comparison of various versions of the United Nations Constitution, including Chinese, English, French, Spanish, Russian, and Arabian, the Chinese version uses the fewest words, indicating that Chinese can convey sophisticated and comprehensive ideas in a simpler and more concise manner compared to other national languages.[69]

An example of this efficiency is found in the influential ancient Chinese text *Sun Tzu's Art of War*, which consists of only 6075 Chinese characters. Despite its brevity, it conveys profound military wisdom with both philosophical and practical insights. In contrast, Clausewitz's Western classic *On War* spans three volumes and contains 730 000 words. Judging solely by the size of their works, it is evident that Sun Tzu's treatise would have a much broader readership.

4. Impact on ideology and culture: Western languages based on alphabets are known for their flexibility, adaptability, and openness, which have influenced the development of Western culture. The inherent characteristics of alphabet systems allow for easy incorporation of new words and concepts, fostering a culture that embraces change and innovation.

On the other hand, the Chinese character writing system exhibits traits of stability, resistance to change, and a limited receptiveness to neologisms. The nature of the Chinese character writing system influences the ideological and cultural attributes of Chinese society. The stability of the characters and their conservative nature contribute to a cultural environment that values tradition, continuity, and a preference for established norms.

5. Impact on the development of Chinese philosophy: The creation and evolution of Chinese characters, deeply connected to the physical and material aspects of the world, have profoundly influenced Chinese philosophers and scholars, shaping a pragmatic outlook in Chinese philosophy. Furthermore, the structure of the Chinese language, renowned for its amazing capacity to convey the intricacies of tangible objects, social dynamics, and natural phenomena with remarkable simplicity, has given rise to a philosophy that values profound simplicity.

The differences identified in this chapter, stemming from linguistic characteristics, manifest at a fundamental level, giving rise to disparities across various domains of the humanities, including Chinese strategic thinking and traditional Chinese medicine. To illustrate the impact of these divergent mindsets on reality, a descriptive example is presented below.

In this scenario, the president of a large Chinese company is hosting a visit from a renowned Japanese company in order to negotiate a business deal. Following a series of meetings, discussions, and negotiations, both parties are satisfied with the agreed-upon terms and conditions, resulting in the successful conclusion of the deal. During a celebratory banquet, in line with cultural norms in Asia, the presidents of both the Chinese president are seated together, engaging in friendly and relaxed conversations.

During a spontaneous moment, the Japanese president, as a gesture of fostering a closer relationship, asked the Chinese president if he could use two pairs of square-sectioned wooden chopsticks to create the word '田', which denotes his surname in kanji, meaning 'paddy field'. After a brief moment of contemplation, the Chinese president successfully devised the pattern expected by the Japanese president, resulting in a more harmonious atmosphere.

If you, as a Western reader, would like to attempt to recreate the pattern using four chopsticks, resembling the character, please feel free to do so. Normally, six chopsticks would be required to accomplish the task. This is a moment that highlights the importance of problem-solving approaches. If you approach the challenge with a conventional Western mode of thinking, it may appear nearly impossible. In truth, many Western individuals have found the task to be daunting. Once you have either succeeded or given up, you may refer to the 'answer' provided in the note[70] if desired.

## NOTES

1.    Deng, K.G. (2000). A Critical Survey of Recent Research in Chinese Economic History. *Economic History Review*, 53(1), pp. 1–28.
2.    Houston, S., Baines, J. and Jerrold, C. (2003). Last Writing: Script Obsolescence in Egypt, Mesopotamia, and Mesoamerica. *Comparative Studies in Society and History*, 45(3), pp. 430–79.
3.    Gentner, D. and Goldin-Meadow, S. (2003). *Language in Mind: Advances in the Study of Language and Thought*. The MIT Press, p. 3.
      von Humboldt, W. (1999). *On Language: On the Diversity of Human Language Construction and its Influence on the Mental Development of the Human Species* (M. Losonsky, Ed.; P. Heath, Trans.). Cambridge University Press.
4.    Whorf, B.L. (1941). The Relation of Habitual Thought and Behavior to Language. In L. Spier (Ed.), *Language, Culture and Personality*. Salt Lake City, UT: University of Utah Press.
      Whorf, B.L. (1956). *Language, Thought & Reality*. The M.I.T. Press.
      Lardiere, D. (1992). On the Linguistic Shaping of Thought: Another Response to Alfred Bloom. *Language in Society*, 21(2), pp. 231–51.
      von Humboldt (n 3).
5.    Wu, J.S. (1969). Chinese Language and Chinese Thought. *Philosophy East and West*, 19(4), pp. 423–34.
      Wu, K.M. (1987). Counterfactuals, Universals, and Chinese Thinking – A Review of The Linguistic Shaping of Thought: A Study in the Impact of Language on Thinking in China and the West. A.H. Bloom (Book Review). *Philosophy East and West*, 37(1), pp. 84–94.
6.    Sapir, E. (1949). In D.G. Mandelbaum (Ed.), *Selected Writings of Edward Sapir*. University of California Press.
      Bloom, A.H. (1979). The Impact of Chinese Linguistic Structure on Cognitive Style. *Current Anthropology*, 20(3), pp. 585–6.
7.    Au, T.K. (1983). Chinese and English Counterfactuals: The Sapir-Wharf Hypothesis Revisited. *Cognition*, 15, pp. 155–87.
      Boroditsky, L. (2001). Does Language Shape Thought? Mandarin and English Speakers' Conceptions of Time. *Cognitive Psychology*, 43(1), pp. 1–22.
      Bloom, P. and Keil, F.C. (2001). Thinking Through Language. *Mind & Language*, 16(4), pp. 351–67.
      Tomasello, M. (1999). *The Cultural Origins of Human Cognition*. Harvard University Press.

8.  Logan, R.K. (1986). *The Alphabet effect: The impact of the phonetic alphabet on the development of Western civilization.* New York: St. Martin's Press, p. 46.
    Innis, H.A. (1951). *The Bias of Communication.* University of Toronto Press.
    Innis, H.A. (1950). *Empire and Communications.* Oxford University Press.

9.  Many studies are multidisciplinary in nature, e.g. Edward Sapir's writings involve linguistics, ethnology, anthropology, and psychology – see Greenberg. J.H. (1950). Selected Writings of Edward Sapir in Language, Culture, and Personality by David G. Mandelbaum (Book Review). *American Anthropologist*, 52(4), pp. 516–18.
    Crick, M. (1976). *Explorations in language and meaning: Towards a semantic anthropology.* London: Malaby Press.

10. Boroditsky (n 7) pp. 1–22.
    Gentner and Goldin-Meadow (n 3).

11. Sapir (n 6).
    Whorf (1941) (n 4).
    Whorf (1956) (n 4).

12. Gentner and Goldin-Meadow (n 3) p. 4.

13. Carroll, J.B. (Ed.) (1956; 1997). *Language, Thought, and Reality: Selected Writings of Benjamin Lee Whorf.* Cambridge, MA: Technology Press of Massachusetts Institute of Technology.

14. Gentner and Goldin-Meadow (n 3) p. 12.

15. Harbsmeier, C. (1998). *Science and Civilisation in China. Volume 7, Part 1: Language and logic.* K. Robinson (Ed.). Cambridge University Press, p. xxii.

16. Graham, A.C. (1985). 'Language and Logic in Ancient China by Chad Hansen (Book Review) by A.C. Graham', *Harvard Journal of Asiatic Studies*, 45(2), 692–703.

17. Logan (n 8) pp. 46–7.

18. Bloom, A.H. (1981). *The Linguistic Shaping of Thought: A Study in the Impact of Language on Thinking in China and the West.* Lawrence Erlbaum Associates.

19. Wu (n 5) pp. 423–34.

20. Hansen, C. (1983). *Language and Logic in Ancient China.* University of Michigan Press.

21. Nisbett, R.E. (2003). *The Geography of Thought: How Asians and Westerners Think Differently . . . and Why.* New York: Free Press, p. 27.

22. Bloom, P. (1998). Some Issues in the Evolution of Language and Thought. In D.D. Cummins and C. Allen (Eds.), *The Evolution of Mind.* Oxford University Press.

23. Reding, J.P. (2004). *Comparative Essays in Early Greek and Chinese Rational Thinking.* Ashgate.

24. Martin, M.R. (1987). Language and Logic in Ancient China by Chad Hansen: Reviewed by Michael R. Martin. *The Journal of Philosophy*, 84(1), pp. 37–42.

25.   Logan (n 8).
      Man, J. (2000). *Alpha Beta: How Our Alphabet Shaped the Western World.*
      Headline.
26.   Hansen (n 20).
      Ivanhoe, P.J. (1987). One View of the Language–Thought Debate: A Review
      of 'Language and Logic in Ancient China' by Chad Hansen Reviewed by:
      Philip J. Ivanhoe. *Chinese Literature: Essays, Articles, Reviews*, 9(1/2),
      pp. 115–23.
27.   Hansen, C. (1993). Chinese Ideographs and Western Ideas. *The Journal of
      Asian Studies*, 44(3), pp. 491–519.
28.   Kim, Y.S. (1999). Towards a 'Comparative History of the Foundations of
      Science': Language and Logic in Traditional China. *Annals of Science*, 56,
      pp. 451–60.
29.   Harris, P.R. and Moran, R.T. (1996). *Managing Cultural Differences*. Gulf
      Publishing Company.
      von Humboldt (n 3).
30.   He, J.Y., Hu, S.B. and Zhang, M. (2002). *Zhongguo Hanzi Wenhua Daguan
      (A Grand Exposition of Chinese Culture: Chinese Characters)*. Peking
      University Publishing House.
31.   Zheng, T.Z. (1997). Hanzixue Tonglun *(Generalities of Chinese Characters
      Science)*. Fujian People's Publisher, p. 52.
32.   Wieger, L. (1965). *Chinese Characters: Their Origin, Etymology, History,
      Classification, and Signification*. New York: Paragon Book Reprint Corp,
      p. 5.
33.   Harbsmeier (n 15) p. 36.
34.   Ibid.
35.   Major Chinese classics mention Cang Jie as the person who initially creates
      Chinese characters, e.g. Zhang, S.J. et al. (2007). Lushi Chunqiu *(Master
      Lu's Spring and Autumn Annals)*. China Book Bureau.
      Hutton, E.L. (2014). Xunzi*: The Complete Text Translated by and with an
      Introduction by Eric L. Hutton*. Princeton University Press.
      Han, Feizi (2003). *Han Feizi: Basic Writings*, translated by Burton Watson,
      New York: Columbia University Press.
36.   Boltz, William G. (1993). Shuo wen chieh tzu 說文解字. In Loewe, Michael
      (ed.), *Early Chinese Texts: A Bibliographical Guide.* Berkeley, CA: Society
      for the Study of Early China, and the Institute of East Asian Studies,
      University of California, pp. 429–42.
37.   He et al. (n 30) pp. 4–5.
38.   Western linguistic scholars generally describe the Chinese writing system as
      a 'logographic conception': see Harbsmeier (n 15) p. 34.
39.   Xu, H.Y. (1963). *Xu Shen's* Shuowen Jiezi *(Xu Shen's Explaining and
      Analysing Chinese Writing)*. China Book Bureau.
      Tang's explanations of Xu Shen's *Shuowen Jiezi* (*Discussing Writing and
      Explaining Characters*) (2014). *Shuowen Jiezi* (explained and edited by
      Tang Yi), Enterprise Management Publishing House.

40.   Fischer, S.R. (2001). *A History of Writing*. Reaktion Books.
      Hung, Y.N. (2011). How a Morphosyllabic Writing System Works in Chinese. *Reading in Asian Languages*, Routledge.
41.   He et al. (n 30) p. 190.
42.   Logan (n 8) p. 21.
43.   Ibid., p. 54.
44.   Zi, Z. (1987). The Relationship of Chinese Traditional Culture to the Modernization of China: An Introduction to the Current Discussion. *Asian Survey*, 27(4), pp. 442–58.
45.   Harbsmeier (n 15) p. 229.
46.   Gentner and Goldin-Meadow (n 14), p. 12.
47.   Fung, Y.L. (1922). Why China Has No Science – An Interpretation of the Chinese History and Consequences of Chinese Philosophy. *International Journal of Ethics*, 32(3), pp. 237–63.
48.   Nisbett (n 21) p. 21.
49.   He et al. (n 30) p. 189.
50.   Wu (n 19) pp. 423–34.
51.   Liu, S.H. (1974). Time and Temporality: The Chinese Perspective. *Philosophy East and West*, 24(2), pp. 145–53.
52.   Hansen, C. (1985). Chinese Language, Chinese Philosophy, and 'Truth'. *The Journal of Asian Studies*, 44(3), pp. 491–519.
      Wu (n 19) pp. 423–34.
53.   Ibid.
54.   Fung (n 47) pp. 237–63.
55.   Tang's explanations of Xu Shen's *Shuowen Jiezi* (*Discussing Writing and Explaining Characters*) (2014). *Shuowen Jiezi* (explained and edited by Tang Yi), Enterprise Management Publishing House, p. 295.
56.   Ibid., pp. 88–9.
57.   Bloom (n 6) pp. 585–6.
58.   Nisbett (n 21) p. 17.
59.   Bao, Z.-Ming (1985). Language and Logic in Ancient China by Chad Hansen: Review by Bao Zhi-Ming. *Philosophy East and West*, 35(2), pp. 203–12.
60.   Nisbett (n 21) p. 26.
61.   Logan (n 42) p. 48.
62.   He et al. (n 30) p. 189.
63.   Hall, D.L. & Ames, R.T. (1995). *Anticipating China: Thinking Through the Narratives of Chinese and Western Culture*. State University of New York Press, p. 225.
64.   Ibid., pp. 225–6.
65.   Ames, R.T. (1994). *The Art of Rulership*. State University of New York Press, p. xx.
66.   He et al. (n 62) p. 190.
67.   Wagner, R.G. (1999). *Science and Civilisation in China, Volume 7, Part 1: Language and Logic* by Christoph Harbsmeier; Kenneth Robinson

Reviewed by Rudolf G. Wagner. *The American Historical Review*, 104(5), pp. 1644–5.

Logan (n 25).

68.   Liu, S.H. (1974). The Use of Analogy and Symbolism in Traditional Chinese Philosophy. *Journal of Chinese Philosophy*, 1, pp. 313–38.

69.   Zhang, W.W. (2021). *Xin Bainian Xin Zhongguo* (*China in the New Era*). Eastern Publishing House, pp. 7–9.

70.   The four chopsticks are put together in a bundle (note the cross-sectional shape of the chopsticks), so that when viewed from the end, their square tips would form the word '田'.

# 3. A framework for the Chinese strategic mind

*Do not bite at the bait of pleasure, till you know there is no hook beneath it.*
— Thomas Jefferson

*In questions of science, the authority of a thousand is not worth the humble reasoning of a single individual.*
— Galileo Galilei

## THE STRUCTURE AND COMPONENTS OF FRAMEWORK

Figure 3.1 depicts a framework designed to facilitate the analysis and comprehension of the Chinese strategic mindset. The framework comprises three main sections:

(a) The lower section: This segment consists of Western strategic knowledge that can be potentially relevant to the Chinese context. It is represented as a scale ranging from zero to entirety. At one end of the scale, a Chinese decision-maker may possess no knowledge of Western strategic principles and theories. On the other end, another decision-maker may have acquired substantial knowledge on Western strategic management through reading, management training, or formal education.

In the domain of Chinese entrepreneurship, there exists a spectrum of familiarity with Western strategic theories. While some entrepreneurs may have no exposure to these theories, others may have gained extensive knowledge through their attendance at Western universities and their study of Western strategy literature. Certain concepts such as Porter's generic competitive strategy, competitive advantage, and the competitive advantage of nations are regarded as 'universal knowledge' that can assist Chinese decision-makers in contemplating generic strategic options and policy directions. However, relying solely on these theories without incorporating Chinese thinking or cultural adaptation would be insufficient for achieving business development or competitive advantage within the Chinese environment.

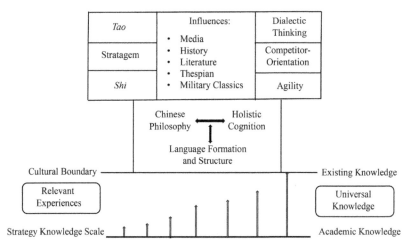

*Figure 3.1     A conceptual framework for the Chinese strategic mind*

It is rare to find instances where successful Chinese entrepreneurs or business leaders attribute their accomplishments in China solely to Western strategic theories or principles. On the other hand, numerous individuals have highlighted the influence of Chinese philosophical works, such as *I Ching*, Taoism, Sun Tzu, Buddhism, and Confucianism, which have significantly shaped their pursuits and achievements. An illustrative case is that of Deng Xiaoping, the former Chinese leader, who adeptly amalgamated Chinese traditions with Western theories and experiences, engendering a remarkable economic reform miracle in China.

(b) The upper section: This displays the architecture of the Chinese strategic mindset, which encompasses a unique set of components that shape its distinctive approach to strategic thinking. The components, which interact with one another, include *Tao*, stratagem, *Shi* (the potential of a situation), Chinese dialectic, competitor orientation, and agility. Furthermore, these idiosyncrasies are influenced by various cultural and technological factors, embracing media development, history, literature, performing arts, and military classics.

(c) The middle section: This section exhibits the fundamental elements that underpin the Chinese strategic mindset. It encompasses the Chinese language, philosophical system, and holistic thinking. As previously discussed, the structure and development of the Chinese language are intricately linked to Chinese philosophy and holistic thinking. These three components emerged simultaneously and cohesively influenced one another, collectively establishing the foundation of the architecture of the Chinese strategic mind.

## TAO

*Tao* or *Dao* represents a distinct Chinese concept that embodies a profound mode of thought, probing the fundamental essence and inherent nature of phenomena at large, including strategic quandaries. The term carries the literal meaning of 'way', 'route', or 'path', while simultaneously encompassing the notions of 'doctrine' and 'principle'. Its implications are intricate and elusive, and defy precise expression.

Lao Tzu describes *Tao* in such a way that the complete embodiment of the *Tao* is reflected in the pursuit of impeccable action, genuine virtue, supreme power.[1] Those who wholeheartedly adhere to the *Tao* become the living testament to its profound revelation. It is through the *Tao* that all things are infused with vitality, while the *Te*[2] grants a deep sense of fulfilment. Nature acts as the sculptor that moulds their essence, and it is through the act of living that they ultimately attain their truest state of wholeness and fulfilment.[3]

*Tao*, regarded as the law of nature, serves as the wellspring and bedrock from which all life on the planet emerges, making it the very essence of triumph. This belief finds unanimous acceptance among the thinkers and philosophers of ancient China. Both Confucians and Taoists shared a common understanding of an ultimate, indescribable, and all-encompassing reality that underpinned and harmonised everything observed by individuals and events they encountered.[4] This reality was known as the *Tao*, representing the cosmic path or course of the universe, the fundamental essence that governed all phenomena, the inherent order of nature or the moral foundation.[5]

At the core of *Tao* lies the notion that everything is composed of contradictions and embodies a harmony of opposites. These opposites include qualities such as large and small, beauty and ugliness, long and short, light and dark, strong and weak, victory and defeat, and more. The Chinese term *yang* symbolises 'sunshine' and represents active, hot, bright, masculine, dry, and hard attributes. Conversely, *yin* signifies the opposite of sunshine, representing passive, cold, dark, feminine, wet, soft characteristics, and so on.

The fundamental concept conveyed is that *Tao* serves as the origin of all existence in the universe. It is emphasised that *Tao* gives life to the concept of 'the one'. The one, in turn, gives life to the concept of 'the two'. The two then give life to the concept of 'the three'. Ultimately, this progression leads to the emergence of countless entities and phenomena in the world. It is explained that all beings in the universe harmonise with the passive and receptive energy of *yin* while also embracing the active and assertive energy of *yang*. The interplay between the two forces permeates and encompasses the entirety of the universe.[6]

The *yin* and *yang* exist as a contrasting duo, intricately intertwined to bring forth the entirety of existence within the cosmos. Yet, these opposing forces possess the potential to transform into their polar opposites. Deeply rooted within the *yin* lies the seed of the *yang*, just as within the *yang* resides the seed of the *yin*. As the *yin* approaches its zenith, it naturally transitions into the *yang*, while the *yang*, in turn, gravitates towards the *yin*, thus establishing the prime pattern of motion within the universe.

Continuous transformation occurred within the unchanging patterns of *Tao*, unveiling the unique essence of *Tao* to those who possessed the insight to perceive them. These individuals guided their actions and thoughts in harmony with the intricate fabric of these patterns. The ruler's *Tao* encompassed the art of governance, characterised by benevolence, inspiration, and compassionate indulgence. On the other hand, the people's *Tao* embodied the virtues of obedience, loyalty, and filial piety. When the ruler ruled in accordance with *Tao*, the people naturally followed suit, obeying the principles embedded within *Tao*.[7]

The essence of *Tao* is deeply intertwined with Chinese cosmology, ontology, and other general worldviews, making it a force that can exert both direct and indirect influence on the Chinese strategic mindset from multiple angles. The following section will explore several specific examples that are directly linked to Chinese strategic thinking.

To begin with, *Tao* delves into the essence of a matter, or a phenomenon, or an issue. Therefore, in order to comprehend the Chinese strategic mind, it becomes imperative to explore the following inquiry: what constitutes the fundamental nature of 'strategy'?

Lao Tzu expresses the idea, at the beginning of *Tao Te Ching*, that a path that can be easily followed is not the true path, and a name that can be easily labelled is not the true name. *Tao*, the principle he refers to, exists both as an unnamed essence and as a named concept. In its nameless form, *Tao* serves as the underlying essence that encompasses all things. In its named form, *Tao* take on the role of the nurturing source from which all things emerge.[8]

Liu An, a prince of the Han Dynasty, held the position of ruler over the Huainan Kingdom. During his reign, he undertook the task of editing a highly esteemed treatise known as the *Huainanzi*, which was completed in 139 BC. His goal was to provide guidance and support to his nephew, Emperor of Wu of Han. This influential work, often translated as the '*Book of the Master of Huainan*' or the '*Huainan Philosophers*', encompasses a wide range of philosophical and intellectual teachings.

In the book, Liu An explicates that everything possesses a weakness that can overcome it, except for the *Tao*, which remains invincible. Its invincibility arises from its lack of fixed form or rigid power. The *Tao* flows endlessly, akin to the perpetual motion of the sun and moon. Its pattern eludes all who seek to grasp it. It governs form while remaining formless, allowing its excellence to be fully realised. It encompasses all things without becoming an object itself, thus achieving victory without yielding.[9]

These teachings propose that if understanding and adhering to the *Tao* or the Way, the law of nature, grants invincibility, yet the *Tao* defies description, definition, or naming. When applying the concept of the *Tao* to strategic management, the 'best strategy' or the core of successful strategy cannot be named, described, or declared in advance. If it were, it would cease to be the 'best strategy'. Sun Tzu articulates his view that the victorious military strategist only seeks battle after victory has been won; they do not reveal themselves in advance.[10] If everyone is aware of and follows the so-called 'best strategy', they would all pursue the same course of action, eradicating any competitive advantage. However, by following the *Tao* of strategy or the 'right way' of formulating strategy, individuals can become unconquerable. Nevertheless, the strategy they employ would be unique and effective solely within that specific context.

Bin Hong, a Chinese scholar, proposes that the *Tao* can be perceived through 'heart'. Through his research, he has discovered that ancient Chinese generals who achieved victory in battles and Chinese entrepreneurs who attained success often relied on their 'sixth sense'. Hong believes that the profound understanding of *Tao*, felt within the heart, represents the pinnacle of strategy development. In practical terms, the perception and comprehension of *Tao* do not rely on certain fixed methods but are instead based on accumulated experience and knowledge.

Hong points out an intriguing example from the Western Han Dynasty, where a renowned Chinese general named Huo Qubing (140–117 BC) had never read Sun Tzu's *Art of War*. Nevertheless, General Huo applied strategies that were amazingly similar to those preached in the classic treatise. Hong attributes this phenomenon to General Huo's exceptional ability to sense *Tao* in military strategy.[11]

From a rational standpoint, I believe that an analysis of this phenomenon could suggest that General Huo shared a similar strategic mindset to Sun Tzu. This similarity may have arisen from their exposure to the same language and Chinese philosophies, which influenced their thinking in strategic matters.

For Westerners seeking to understand Chinese strategy, grasping the essence of the *Tao* of Chinese strategy is crucial. It serves as the foundation of the Chinese strategic mind and underlies the decision-making process of Chinese leaders. Although it is often difficult to explicitly discuss or model, its influence can be discerned through the factors that shape Chinese strategies. This understanding will enable a deeper insight into the mindset and decision-making processes of Chinese strategists, fostering more effective engagement and collaboration between Western and Chinese counterparts.

Many Western decision makers, particularly those who have received business education, tend to construct strategies based on established frameworks. Consequently, their approaches often lack distinctiveness or differentiation, limiting their competitive advantage. In contrast, their Chinese counterparts are not confined to a rigid model and exhibit a propensity for forward-looking in their strategy development.

Secondly, *Tao* is associated with the concept of 'greatness'. According to Lao Tzu, all greatness emanates from *Tao*. It bestows greatness upon Heaven, Earth, and humanity. The wellbeing of mankind relies on the harmonious order of the Earth, which, in turn, is governed by the laws of Heaven. Furthermore, Heaven's order is sustained by the principles of *Tao*. However, *Tao* is independent and self-sustaining. It possesses the ultimate freedom and tranquillity, finding solace within its own essence.[12]

A strategist who understands and embraces the *Tao* of strategy possesses a natural inclination towards envisioning the farthest horizon. The extent of one's vision determines the height one can reach. A limited vision relegates one to mediocrity, while a grand vision serves as the foundation for achieving greatness. A prime example of this is Mao Zedong, who, in his late twenties, articulated his vision as 'the transformation of China and the world'. He dedicated himself to realise his vision, which ultimately led to the transformation of both himself and China. This transformative journey culminated in the proclamation of the founding of the People's Republic of China in 1949, leaving a significant impact on the world.[13]

In the early stages of his entrepreneurial journey in 1999, Jack Ma, the founder of Alibaba, boldly declared his ambition: our aim is not to be the number one in China, but to become the global leader.[14] However, Jack Ma's ambition has remained breath-taking throughout years. He envisioned creating an Internet company that would endure for a remarkable eighty years, paralleling the average lifespan of a human being. As time progressed, Jack Ma further extended Alibaba's life expectancy to 102 years, aiming for the company to transcend three centuries starting from its founding in 1999. From the inception, he pledged to challenge and surpass the giants of Silicon Valley.[15]

In the Western world, Elon Musk stands as a prime example of an entrepreneur and multi-billionaire whose achievements in the business realm are primarily attributed to his vision and aspirations rather than conventional money-making strategies. Musk has gained renown for his ambitious and visionary goals, such as colonising Mars and revolutionising transportation.

Throughout his career, Musk has exhibited a steadfast determination to pursue his visionary goals, often pushing the boundaries of what is deemed achievable. His dreams and vision have served as the impetus behind a multitude of ventures, including Tesla Motors, SpaceX, Starlink, Neuralink, Tesla Energy, The Boring Company, and OpenAI and xAI. By thinking big and setting audacious objectives, Musk has successfully inspired others and attracted exceptionally talented individuals to work with him.

Contrary to a primary focus on financial gains, Musk's endeavours have frequently placed him on the brink of bankruptcy. However, his perseverance and relenting pursuit of grand visions and dreams have ultimately rewarded him with immense wealth, positioning him as one of the wealthiest individuals on the planet.

Lao Tzu proclaims that when a seeker of truth becomes aware of the *Tao*, they exert tremendous effort in their pursuit of understanding. An ancient proverb illuminates this path: clarity may initially appear obscured, the direct route may seem twisted, absolute certainty may appear unstable, immense power may seem feeble, pristine purity may appear tainted, abundance may seem empty, stability may seem uncertain, and apparent truth may be deceptive. The great square lacks sharp corners, while the vast vessel never reaches fullness. The *Tao*, though concealed, radiates as the luminous beacon that illuminates this world in all its glory.[16]

Similar to manoeuvring pieces in a game of chess, a great vision anticipates future moves, strategically advancing towards the objective with wisdom, deliberation, and confidence. In the context of Chinese culture, a vision is shaped by the idea of harmony between nature and humanity,[17] relying on a conceptual envisioning process rather than a purely visual one.

Thirdly, Chinese philosophy centres around the pursuit of the *Tao*, which represents the highest ideal. The philosophers of China consider it to be the pinnacle of human existence, characterised by 'sageness within and kingliness without'. This state of being serves as the ultimate moral standard, which a sage strives to achieve. Attaining this standard grants the sage a role of leadership and influence in society.

Fung Yulan, a renowned Chinese philosopher, explains that the essence of the sage's character is marked by sageness, while their outward behaviour manifests as kingliness. This means that, through inner tranquillity and self-cultivation, the sage achieves spiritual enlightenment, and through his noble and virtuous actions in society, he fulfils his role. Being the actual head of the government is not a prerequisite for a sage. Therefore, the philosophy being discussed is known as the *Tao* of 'sageness within and kingliness without', as described by the philosophers of China.[18]

Chinese philosophy, regardless of the specific school of thought, universally embraces the concept of *Tao*.[19] *Tao*, along with *Te*, which signifies ethics, conscience, or morality, are fundamental principles found in Lao Tzu's *Tao Te Ching*.[20]

The notion of *Te* originates from *Tao*, follows its path, and influences human behaviour by establishing moral standards. While having its own distinct teachings, Confucianism shares the Taoist ideals of *Tao* and *Te*. Confucian ethics encompasses the Five Constant Virtues, which are human-heartedness, righteousness, the observance of rituals, wisdom, and reliability (trustworthiness).[21] These virtues have served as a guiding framework for human thought and behaviour for over two millennia.

Because *Te* is guided and governed by the *Tao*, anything that deviates from the principles of proper *Te* is likely to be unsuccessful and meet with failure. Lao Tzu teaches that true virtue lies in selfless giving and assisting others without expecting anything in return. Such actions are considered virtuous, while keeping track of one's deeds or helping others solely for the purpose of gaining personal merit lacks true virtue. The ultimate virtue is to act without a sense of self, the greatest kindness is to give unconditionally, and the highest form of justice is to perceive without bias or preference.[22]

A Chinese proverb elegantly encapsulates the significance of *Te*, not only in military endeavours but also in the realm of business. It emphasises that achieving small victories necessitates diligence, medium victories require talent, and big victories demand wisdom. However, the ultimate key to achieving any victory, regardless of its scale, lies in *Te*, an amalgamation of virtue and alignment of the law of nature.

The *Te* perspective is frequently overlooked by individuals with unscrupulous intentions in military, political, or business realms. Due to historical factors, the Japanese population has a deep understanding of *Sun Tzu's Art of War* and other Chinese military classics. This has been evident in the knowledge and application demonstrated by Japanese military commanders and business leaders, who often display a higher level of comprehension when it comes to the tactical aspects of Sun Tzu's teachings. Unlike China, where there has not been a comparable social mandate, in Japan, these treatises have been considered essential reading.[23]

Despite their extensive knowledge of Chinese military classics, it is evident that Japanese readers have often chosen to neglect or disregard the *Te* principles emphasised in these works. This disregard has had detrimental consequences for Japanese military and business endeavours. A notable example can be found in Japan's strategies during World War II (WWII), where its initial victories in the battlefields of China and Southeast Asia were overshadowed by ultimate military defeat, largely due to the Japanese government and military commanders' disregard for the fundamental principles of *Te*.

A prominent illustration of this neglect can be seen in the Pearl Harbor attack conducted by Japan. This attack took place with no formal declaration of war, completely surprising the United States and leading to substantial loss of life and destruction. Numerous battleships, cruisers, and other vessels were either sunk or severely damaged. The attack resulted in the tragic death of 2340 individuals, while many more were left wounded or missing. The base itself was left in ruins, marking it as one of the most devastating military disasters in US history.

This act of aggression blatantly disregarded international norms and principles, as it deliberately targeted a military installation and a civilian population. Instances of such reprehensible behaviour that deliberately ignored international norms can be observed in Japan's cruel actions during WWII, particularly in China and Southeast Asia.

On 7 December 1941, the Japanese Embassy in the United States reached out to the US State Department in the morning, requesting an appointment with Secretary Hull at 1 pm. Subsequently, a follow-up phone message was received, pushing back the appointment to 1.45 pm. At 2.20 pm, Secretary Hull finally met with Japanese Ambassador Nomura and envoy Kurusu, engaging in what seemed to be peace negotiation.

However, unbeknownst to the US government, just forty-five minutes prior to this meeting, Japanese bombers launched a devastating attack on Pearl Harbor. It becomes evident that the Japanese government exploited diplomatic protocols to deceive the US government, thus maximising the effectiveness of their surprise attack.[24]

A significant number of companies that have engaged in immoral and illegal activities have faced downfall. The following are examples where the Chinese companies have committed flaws and illegal acts.

- In 2008, 22 major Chinese milk companies were found to have produced milk contaminated with melamine. Furthermore, a study focusing on the period from 1999 to 2011 identified 412 instances of corporate scandal in China.[25]
- In 2021, the Chinese Securities Regulatory Commission (CSRC) dealt with a total of 609 cases related to securities violations, including 163 major cases. These cases involved various illegal activities such as financial fraud, fund misappropriation, market manipulations disguised as market value management, insider trading, and failure of intermediary institutions to fulfil their duties diligently.[26]

Chinese philosophy demonstrates that companies engaging in unethical business may achieve temporary success but will ultimately face consequences. Considering that the Chinese market economy is relatively young in comparison with Western economies, and its legal system lacks religious foundations, it is gradually maturing.

## STRATAGEMS

The extensive usage of stratagems in China represents a cultural phenomenon and a significant aspect of the Chinese strategic mindset. Chinese military literature reveals a notable disparity in strategic thinking and approach between China and the West. In military conflicts and combat scenarios, the Chinese prioritise wisdom, whereas the Western approach centres around strengths and powers.[27]

The *Huainanzi* provides an insight into the principles, strategies, and significance of military affairs. It preaches that the commander's perception must be focused and comprehensive. Perceiving singularly entails observing the unseen. Knowing singularly means understanding the unknown. The ability to see what others fail to see is referred to as 'enlightenment', while the capacity to know what others are unaware of is known as a 'spirit-like' quality.[28]

In the influential military treatise, written in 750 CE, *Strategies for the Human Realm*, a compelling viewpoint is also presented, asserting that no ruler who has ever governed a state successfully achieved kingship without relying on wisdom and strategy. The text underscores the pivotal responsibility of the general in harmonising governing principles, employing astuteness to discern subtleties, and establishing affairs through strategic acumen. It emphasises that the general's wisdom and strategic prowess are crucial factors in perceiving opportunities amidst challenges and contemplating the potential misfortune concealed within the depth of darkness.[29]

In the realm of political, military, or commercial conflicts, the essence of Chinese wisdom, known as *zhi*, finds its expression primarily through the adoption of stratagems. Lawrence Freedman highlights the insightful observation made by Lisa Raphals, who drew parallels between *zhi* and the concept of métis discussed by Detienne and Vernant. *Zhi* encompasses a wide range of meanings, including wisdom, knowledge, intelligence, skill, craft, cleverness, and cunning. An individual who embodies *zhi* assumes the role of a sagacious general, leveraging the art of deception to triumph over adversaries possessing greater physical might, much like those endowed with métis.[30]

The concept of a stratagem is closely intertwined with that of strategy. Both *stratagem* and *strategy* originate from Greek roots and share the same family lineage headed by its noun στρατηγός (general, in the sense of military leader) and its verb στρατηγέω (to be a general).[31] *Strategy* encompasses several meanings across different contexts. It refers to the art of a general, including the generalship's skills and attributes. It contains the actions undertaken by a general with foresight, expediency, fame, and tenacity, specifically in relation to military affairs.

On the other hand, stratagem carries distinct connotations. It embraces military, diplomatic, and strategic trickery, utilising unseen and nonviolent psychological tactics to accomplish a general's strategic objectives. It involves the development of an ingenious plan, military ruse, and deception. Stratagem extends beyond the military realm and also include domestic political chicanery and deceit in everyday life.[32]

According to Frontinus, a Roman senator, strategy encompasses all accomplishments by a commander, characterised by foresight, advantage, enterprise, or resolution. On the other hand, stratagems, or *strategemata*, rely on skill and cleverness. These stratagems prove effective not only in situations where the enemy must be evaded but also where they must be overcome. Frontinus's stratagems include both elements of trickery and deception and practical considerations and endeavours to maintain the morale of troops.[33]

The significance and application of stratagems, known as *mou lue* in Chinese, hold a prominent position within Chinese literature; this concept has been extensively explored and widely embraced in various fields in China, including politics, military affairs, sports, and diplomacy. Notable figures and their works such as *Han Feizi*,[34] *Sun Tzu*, and *Gui Guzi*,[35] the bible of *mou lue*, have contributed to the understanding and implementation of stratagem. Moreover, classic literature like *The Analects, Tao Te Ching, Thirty-Six Stratagems, Tai Kung's Six Secret Teachings*, and *One Hundred Unorthodox Strategies* are replete with tales of intrigue and strategic manoeuvring. Thus, the use of stratagems has permeated Chinese society, forming a distinct subculture.

In the Chinese context, stratagem incorporates both tactical and strategic elements. It involves the art of understanding and navigating complex situations, employing cunning and resourcefulness to achieve desired outcomes. This multifaceted understanding of stratagem underscores its deep-rooted influence on Chinese thinking and behaviour, extending beyond specific domains to shape various aspects of life.

A successful stratagem embraces a comprehensive perspective of the situation, placing emphasis on the utilisation of the stratagem to neutralise or subdue the adversary. Sun Tzu's teachings emphasise that the utmost importance in warfare lies in attacking the enemy's strategy.[36] This implies that the most effective path to victory involves outsmarting the opponent's strategies, compelling them to retreat, avoid confrontation, or surrender. Such a stratagem requires a commander's foresight, which is based on a meticulous evaluation of the *Xing* – the specific circumstance or configuration – and *Shi* – potential, momentum, or prevailing trend.[37] By capitalising on the inherent advantage of the situation represented by *Shi*, victory can be achieved.

At the core of stratagem is the achievement of strategic objective through the application of '*qi*' or the unorthodox in battles or warfare. Sun Tzu elucidates that, typically, conventional methods are employed in combat, but triumph is achieved through unorthodox means. Consequently, those who excel in deploying unorthodox strategies are as boundless as the heavens and as limitless as the Yangtze and Yellow rivers.[38]

Ralph Sawyer has dedicated his research to the comprehensive study of significant military events and ancient writings in China. Through his meticulous analysis, Sawyer has drawn the conclusion that Chinese warfare operates on distinct principles separate from those guiding European military strategies. Central to this distinction is the concept of *qi* or the unorthodox.[39]

Sun Tzu's *Art of War* conveys a profound message: the pinnacle of excellence in warfare is not measured by a hundred victories in a hundred battles but by the ability to subjugate the enemy's army without engaging in direct combat.[40] This perspective defies traditional norms, and Sawyer regards it as a highly unorthodox concept. Sawyer explicates that, by employing diplomatic coercion, disrupting the enemy's plans and alliances, and frustrating their strategies, the idealised form of complete victory can be attained.[41]

The Chinese demonstrated remarkable strategic prowess during the Korean War, particularly evident in their adept utilisation of stratagems. A notable instance was their covert deployment of 300 000 troops into North Korea within a month, evading detection. Among them, approximately 180 000 positioned themselves discreetly along the western stretch of the extended front, while an additional 120 000 lay in wait to the east, ready to launch a surprise attack once UN forces were deployed.

This cunning manoeuvre exploited the fact that the advancing UN troops, burdened by a substantial amount of equipment, became highly visible targets. Meanwhile, the communist army, comprising around 30 Chinese divisions, remained virtually invisible, earning them the description by a military historian as a 'phantom which cast no shadow'.[42]

China's One Belt and One Road (B&R) initiative, introduced by the Chinese government in 2013, embodies a cooperative and inclusive approach to fostering economic development. With the potential for remarkable success, this ambitious programme aims to position China as a prominent economic and diplomatic influence in the integration of Eurasia. Often likened to China's version of the Marshall Plan, it symbolises a forward-looking strategy for regional/global collaboration and prosperity.[43]

Sun Tzu advises against engaging in direct confrontation during battles, advocating instead for victories achieved through covert battle plans. He asserts that the key to victory lies in the intricate design and formation of these plans, yet the majority fail to grasp the essence. While everyone can observe the surface-level manifestation of these strategies, the true methods behind Sun Tzu's triumphs remain elusive to all. Consequently, once a victory is attained, Sun Tzu refrains from replicating his tactics, opting instead to adapt and respond to ever-changing circumstances using an extensive repertoire of approaches.[44]

In contrast to the contemporary emphasis on clearly communicating the commander's intent to subordinate commanders, Sun Tzu advocated for the commanding general to remain enigmatic and inscrutable, not only to the enemy but also to his own troops.[45] For a considerable period, Western politicians have expressed their grievances regarding the limited military transparency exhibited by China's leadership, which hampers a clear understanding of its strategic intentions.[46] This behavioural inclination is ingrained with their strategic mindset, rather than being a deliberate and contemporary policy.

In reality, there is a notable pattern of Chinese deceptive behaviour aimed at concealing organisational ability. Rooted in Deng Xiaoping's national policy of 'hiding its brightness and biding its time', China has strategically maintained a low profile regarding its economic and military capabilities. Over time, China has gradually emerged as a formidable opponent in various domains, leading to a sudden realisation in the West about its prowess.

Within the business world, numerous MNCs have often overlooked seemingly insignificant Chinese competitors, who have clandestinely and skilfully risen to become major contenders to these MNCs. Notable examples include companies like Haier, BYD, SDLG, and many others.

Deception is emphasised in ancient Chinese literature. Sun Tzu elucidates that deception forms the foundation of all warfare. When possessing the ability, one should feign incapability; when engaged, display inactivity. When in close proximity, give the illusion of being far away; when distant, create the perception of being nearby.[47] Timing movements to gain advantage and introducing variations in the situation through the dispersion and concentration of forces become crucial tactics.[48]

According to Sun Bin, the art of luring the enemy into battle lies in the adept use of hidden plans and concealed deceptions. Deliberate tactical errors and minor losses as calculated missteps are orchestrated to create an illusion of vulnerability, enticing the opponent to believe they have discovered a weakness to exploit.[49] Sun Bin's perspective highlights the significance of psychological warfare and the power of manipulating perception to secure victory on the battlefield.

Sawyer elucidates the potential impact of deception, emphasising its evolution as a strategic tool aimed at beguiling the enemy. Whether the objective is to sow confusion or manipulate the opponent's response, deceptive acts have long been harnessed to achieve these ends. When crafted with ingenuity and executed with precision, the enemy finds themselves bewildered, unsure of where to strike or which formations to employ. Consequently, they become vulnerable to committing fatal errors, inadvertently presenting the opposing army with a tangible advantage ripe for exploitation.[50]

Deception, a concept of great importance in the military field, has been thoroughly studied and recognised as highly pertinent to modern warfare.[51] Surprisingly, however, the practice of deception has received limited attention in the world of business. In the realm of business competition, employing deception can yield significant advantages. By deceiving competitors, a firm can induce them to misallocate their resources or engage in unprepared competition, thereby causing them to waste valuable assets. Moreover, deception allows a company to conceal its own strengths and weaknesses, enabling it to gain a substantial edge in a specific market segment or niche. Furthermore, by utilising the same resources repeatedly for multiple tasks, a firm can create a deceptively threatening effect.

The importance of paying attention to the opponent's strategy becomes more pronounced when the relative strengths of the conflicting parties become closely matched. Sun Tzu's teachings offer a rationale for this approach. In general, when it comes to employing military strategy, the following guidelines apply: If your strength is 10 times that of the enemy, surround them; if it is five times, launch an attack; if it is double, divide your forces. If your strength is equal to that of the enemy, you may engage them with stratagems. If your strength is lesser, you may seek to bypass or circumvent the enemy. And if you are outmatched in strength, it may be wise to avoid direct confrontation altogether.[52]

During the 1970s and 1980s, Japanese companies were perceived as relatively weaker players compared to their American and European counterparts. However, they were able to gain a competitive edge by employing a competitive approach of stratagem nature. As a result, they gradually outperformed their American and European counterparts in various industries.[53] As Japanese companies gained strength globally, their focus shifted towards adopting a technology-led strategic orientation.[54]

Similarly, when Chinese companies found themselves in a relatively weaker position compared with Western counterparts, they often resorted to utilising strategic manoeuvres whenever feasible or appropriate. However, once a Chinese company emerges as the leader in a particular industry, the usefulness of stratagem diminishes. As a leader, the company no longer has direct competitors to outmanoeuvre, but instead must aim for high aspirations, particularly by fostering innovation and creativity. Chinese companies in the electric auto and solar panel industries, for instance, have undergone similar transitions.

Pye and Leites have observed significant differences between Chinese and Western approaches to deception, despite acknowledging that both sides employ it in military operations. Chinese deception focuses more on manipulating the enemy into making unwise decisions, rather than safeguarding the integrity of their own plans. On the other hand, other cultures, such as those in the West, primarily utilise deception to ensure that their forces can achieve their maximum offensive capabilities. For the Chinese, the main advantage of deception lies in the ability to achieve objectives without deploying their own forces.[55]

Sawyer has extensively explored the art of deception in Chinese literature, highlighting tactics such as employing disguises and projecting false appearances. On the other hand, embracing formlessness and remaining inscrutable compels the enemy to either anticipate the most probable tactics and respond accordingly or disperse their forces to cover all possibilities. This ultimately leads to fractures and localised imbalances in power.[56]

The strategic allocation of resources to focus on a particular point of vulnerability in the adversary has been frequently utilised as a form of stratagem in China. Through this approach, it becomes possible to overcome the opponent despite having fewer resources at one's disposal. Throughout Chinese history, numerous instances have occurred where a smaller force has triumphed over a significantly larger rival by employing this very principle. Sun Tzu states that by concentrating our forces while the enemy remains divided, we can attack with a strength tenfold greater than theirs. Consequently, we become the many while the enemy becomes few.[57] The subsequent examples serve as illustrations of this strategy in action.

Galanz (Guangdong Galanz Enterprises Co., Ltd.), a prominent manufacturer of electronic home appliances, was established in 1978. Headquartered in Foshan, Guangdong, the company has emerged as a leading global player in the microwave market. During the early 1990s, it gained recognition as a reputable Chinese microwave brand, capturing a substantial 25% market share in China. This significant market position drew the attention of international competitors including Panasonic, Sharp, Samsung, and LG. Recognising Galanz's growing influence, these competitors adopted a strategic approach to undermine its market dominance. Leveraging superior technology and abundant resources, they opted for lowering their prices, deliberately incurring losses in order to gain or restrict Galanz's market share. In response to this competitive manoeuvre, Galanz strategically reallocated its resources by divesting all other profitable business ventures at discounted prices.

In 1996, Galanz made a bold move to confront foreign brands directly. Taking a high-risk approach, the company slashed prices on its high-end product range by 40%. This disruptive action sent shockwaves through the competition, causing chaos and uncertainty among industry players. By 1998, Galanz had solidified its position as the dominant leader in the microwave market in China, with a market share exceeding 35%. Fast forward to January 2019, Galanz's influence had expanded on a global scale. The company had captured an astounding 50% share of the world's microwave market.[58]

An alternative approach to implementing *qi*, the unorthodox, involves catching one's opponent off guard and acting in ways that exceed their expectations. Sun Tzu advises targeting the unprepared enemy and launching a surprise assault when they least expect it. These tactics are essential for achieving victory as a strategist. They cannot be discussed in advance.[59]

The late US President Richard Nixon astutely observed that the communist system tends to reward those who excel in intrigue but often brings downfall to practitioners of compromise.[60] The emphasis on employing wisdom and stratagem in conflict inherently reflects a competitive orientation, utilising intelligence, ingenious plans, or unorthodox methods to outmanoeuvre rivals.

However, an excessive focus on the deployment of stratagems can lead decision-makers to overlook the 'big picture', engaging in clever tactics without considering the broader vision or attaining only minor, short-term advantage, at the expense of long-term yields.

Ren Zhengfei, the founder of Huawei, which is the world's largest telecom equipment manufacturer and a prominent Chinese high-tech company, fell victim to a trading company's deception in the 1980s. This incident resulted in a loss of 2 million RMB for his state-owned company, a significant amount of money at that time. As a consequence, he was compelled to resign from the company and established Huawei.[61]

## *SHI*

The Western strategising process draws its foundation from the European tradition, where an ideal form is established as the objective to be achieved. Subsequently, actions are planned and executed to transform this form into reality.[62] Initially rooted in scientific and production development, this process has gradually been applied to various fields within the humanities. At its core, this process involves the creation of models inspired by Platonism, where the model is determined on a 'theoretical' basis and then submitted to 'practice'.

The effectiveness of the model-making process has long raised a question: Does what works so well in terms of technical control over nature translate equally well into managing human situations and relationships? Aristotle was the first to recognise that, while science can bring rigour and understanding to the necessary aspects of things, thereby facilitating technical efficacy, the situations in which our actions take place are inherently indeterminate. Despite our efforts, our actions cannot eradicate their inherent contingency, and their unique characteristics cannot be fully covered by any universal law. Consequently, action cannot simply be categorised as an extension of science.

As Aristotle observed, matter possesses an indeterminate power of contraries that resist complete determination imposed by the ideal 'form'. Similarly, the world never fully aligns with the order we aspire to establish. As a result, there is inevitably a discrepancy between the planned model for our actions and what we manage to achieve. In essence, practice always falls somewhat short of theory.[63]

The Chinese term '*Shi*' holds significant importance in Chinese strategic thinking and culture. It is traditionally translated as 'situation', 'potential', 'power', or 'energy'. Unlike the Western theory–practice dichotomy, the concept of *Shi* offers an alternative approach. It does not construct an ideal world of forms, archetypes, or pure essences that exist independently from reality, but rather shapes and informs it. *Shi* perceives reality as a dynamic and interconnected process, continuously regulated and influenced by interacting factors. These factors, while opposing, are also complementary in nature, represented by the famous *yin* and *yang*.[64]

By embracing *Shi*, Chinese thought transcends the limitations of a rigid dichotomy and acknowledges the complexity and fluidity of situations. It emphasises the importance of comprehending the ever-changing context and adapting strategies accordingly. *Shi* provides an approach to understanding the multifaceted nature of reality and encourages a holistic approach to problem-solving and decision-making.

The significance of this notion in Chinese strategic thinking is evident in its frequent appearance in influential works such as Sun Tzu's *Art of War*, Sun Bin's *Military Methods*, and the *Book of Lord Shang*.[65] Its importance is underscored by Sun Tzu's emphasis on a proficient commander's ability to attain victory by adapting to the circumstances, rather than imposing it upon their subordinates.[66]

Jiang Ziya, also known as Jiang Taigong or Tai Kung, played a pivotal role as a military strategist and advisor to Kings Wen and Wu of Zhou during the 12th and 11th centuries BC in ancient China. His treatise, titled *Six Secret Teachings*, has been recognised as one of the *Seven Military Classics of Ancient China*.

In this treatise, Tai Kung imparts his wisdom to King Wu regarding the fundamental principles of military strategy. He emphasises that the ancient masters of warfare did not rely solely on physical means to achieve victory, but rather understood the importance of spiritual engagement and strategic power [*Shi*]. They recognised that success or failure on the battlefield was determined by their ability to harness these essential elements. Those who grasped this concept prospered, while those who overlooked it met their downfall. Tai Kung elucidates to King Wu that the true essence of employing an army lies in skilfully employing these spiritual and strategic forces, as opposed to seeking dominance beyond the celestial realm or beneath the earthly plane.[67]

Xue Juzheng, a renowned scholar-official and historian, emphasises the essentiality of perceiving, comprehending, adapting to, creating, utilising, riding, controlling, manipulating, borrowing, and following *Shi*. Authority devoid of an understanding of *Shi* would be rendered powerless. Moreover, failure to discern the shifting tides of *Shi* would inevitably lead to defeat.[68]

According to François Jullien, *Shi* represents a unique potentiality that does not arise from human agency but rather derives from the inherent disposition of objects and phenomena.[69] He notes that Sun Tzu introduces the concept of '*Shi*' as a crucial element in military strategy. Rather than relying on conceptualisation, Sun Tzu illustrates its meaning through the vivid imagery of a rushing mountain stream that possesses the ability to carry boulders along with it, generating a powerful and explosive force.

Jullien highlights that, while the term defies a singular interpretation and remains partially undefined in various contexts, we can discern its pivotal role in the expression of Chinese thought. In Chinese intellectual discourse, *Shi* typically operates discreetly, seldom codified or extensively commented upon. However, in fulfilling this role, the term appears to underpin and justify some of the most significant ideas within Chinese philosophy and culture.[70]

In the reinterpretation of Sun Tzu's *Art of War*, the term *Shi* takes on three dimensions of connotation, encompassing 'circumstances' or 'conditions', 'physical disposition' in association with the deployment of military forces, and the occupation of a superior position that grants access to potential advantages. Ames provides an interpretation of these connotations, suggesting that *Shi* can be understood collectively or individually, referring to the superior position itself, the inherent advantage derived from the position, and the skilful manipulation of this advantage.[71]

The effectiveness of *Shi* stems from the rationality that *Tao* serves as the origin and bedrock of all living entities, comprising the contradictory *yin* and *yang* pairs, which constantly intermingle and transform. Those who align their actions with the natural order will be invincible. Rather than attempting to conquer nature, human beings were meant to coexist harmoniously with the cyclic flux and the local surroundings, navigating the interplay of *yin* and *yang*. There was no need to adjust their conduct to align with the patterns and flow of *Tao*. Moving slowly in the correct direction was more favourable than rushing along the wrong path.[72]

As influential schools of Chinese philosophy, both Confucianism and Taoism share the belief that aligning one's actions and existence with nature grants significant power to individuals and entities. Consequently, this perspective has fostered a Chinese fascination with the unique power of *Shi* since approximately the 4th century BC.[73] In Chinese culture, adhering to *Shi* during times of conflict signifies an endeavour to act in harmony with *Tao*, leading to ultimate triumph.

In the field of military studies, embracing *Shi* entails making strategic decisions based on the advantageous or disadvantageous nature of a given situation, in order to adapt to or exploit it. Sun Tzu advises that the general, having recognised the advantage of their plan, should create circumstances that will contribute to its success. Here, the 'situation' refers to the need for the general to act promptly in accordance with what is advantageous, thereby controlling the balance of power.[74] *Shi* can be seen as the latent strategic potential that can be unleashed during battles. Different generals may harness this potential in diverse ways, leading to varying outcomes. An accomplished commander possesses the ability to swiftly adapt to the situation expediently and take proactive measures to achieve victory.

*Shi* can be understood as the potential of a situation that regulates the courage and cowardice displayed by combatants. While strength and weakness are influenced by the situation, courage and cowardice are inherent qualities of that situation. In other words, our response to a situation is shaped by its inherent potential rather than being predetermined by our personal qualities.[75]

For instance, in a battle, if the solders find themselves in a position where they have no option to retreat and are left only the choice of fighting or facing certain death, even those who are typically considered 'naturally' cowardly may display great courage in order to survive. The situation compels them to act bravely.

Furthermore, a strategically crafted situation can have a threatening and deterrent effect on the enemy. It influences the enemy's willingness to engage in battle, determines their disposition towards fighting, and shapes the display and enforcement of power. Sun Tzu provides further insights into this point. He illustrates it by stating that when torrential water forcefully propels boulders, it is due to the momentum it carries.[76]

Similarly, a commander who relies on the situation strategically deploys their troops, utilising them in combat as one would roll logs and stones. Just as the inherent nature of logs and stones is to roll, if they are round, the potential of well-directed troops in battle can be likened to that of round boulders descending from the heights of a mountain.[77] In both cases, the force and direction of the situation propel the object forward, highlighting the importance of leveraging the situation's potential to achieve desired outcomes in warfare.

Henry Kissinger provides his interpretation of the concept. In his view, the strategist's primary objective is not merely to analyse a specific situation but rather to understand its connection to the broader context in which it unfolds. He argues that no particular constellation or arrangement remains static; every pattern is temporary and fundamentally subject to change. Thus, the strategist's task is to discern the direction of this evolution and utilise it to achieve their desired objectives. To describe this quality, Kissinger refers to Sun Tzu's use of the term '*Shi*', which he identifies as a concept with no direct Western equivalent.[78]

Lau and Ames highlight that Western readers often tend to quickly categorise situations into one side of a conflict or the other. In contrast, *Shi* takes into account numerous factors from both sides of the conflict, such as numbers, terrain, logistics, morale, weaponry, and more, as they converge on the battlefield. This comprehensive assessment aims to determine which side possesses the advantage over the other. Ultimately, it is the interplay between surplus and deficiency, as these factors collide, that gives rise to 'force of circumstances' in the contest. *Shi* becomes the catalyst for the tide of battle. It encompasses the acquisition and utilisation of resources, which instil in troops the determination to engage in combat and emerge victorious.[79]

Liu An categorised 'strategic advantages' into three types: the advantage of morale or the force of *qi*, the advantage of terrain or the force of terrain, and the advantage of opportunity or the force of circumstance.[80]

During the Korean War, Mao Zedong's understanding of war extended beyond a mere clash of physical forces between two states. He recognised and embraced Sun Tzu's crucial concepts of *Tao* and *Shi*. Mao acknowledged Sun Tzu's teachings, which emphasised the ruler's capacity to shape favourable conditions (*Shi*) and the general's ability to effectively command a war. Through these principles, Mao believed that, even when faced with objective disadvantages, the skilful manipulation of subjective factors could ultimately lead to a decisive advantage.[81]

Deng Xiaoping, known as the driving force behind China's economic reform, played a pivotal role in modelling the country's transformation. Following the conclusion of the Cultural Revolution, in 1978, Deng formulated a strategic approach to reform that perplexed many Western economists and politicians due to its *Shi*-based principles.[82] The tumultuous period of the Cultural Revolution from 1966 to 1976 left the Chinese people yearning for economic growth, creating a potent desire for change. Concurrently, the active reform efforts witnessed in Eastern European nations served as a catalyst for China's own journey.

Deng's approach to reform was distinctive in that it unfolded gradually and progressively, avoiding the economic upheaval that characterised the reforms in Eastern Europe and the former Soviet Union. Lacking a predetermined end goal, the reforms were implemented in an evolutionary manner. Deng refrained from imposing his own vision on society, instead embracing a policy of non-intervention. This approach allowed economic development to unfold with minimal interference from the Communist Party or the government, although political reforms remained restricted.[83]

Wanxiang (Wanxiang Group Corporation) is a prominent Chinese conglomerate that was established in 1969 by Lu Guanqiu. The company has diverse operations spanning real estate, finance, automotive components manufacturing, and clean energy. With a global presence, Wanxiang operates through approximately 30 overseas subsidiaries, over 40 factories, and employs more than 20 000 individuals across the United States, the UK, Germany, and 10 other countries. As of 2020, Wanxiang held the 35th position among the top 500 Chinese companies.

Lu Guanqiu, born into a farming family, managed to pursue his entrepreneurial ambition despite limited formal education. Notably, he developed a reputation as a devoted reader, dedicating an average of five hours daily to perusing books, journals, magazines, and newspapers. This earned him the moniker of a 'farmer theorist or entrepreneur'. Lu's initial inspiration for venturing into the Chinese auto parts industry was influenced by his understanding of *Shi*, a concept that guided his entrepreneurial vision.

During the 1980s, Lu Guanqiu demonstrated remarkable foresight by astutely interpreting subtle cues and drawing inferences about China's future auto industry. Even though there was no explicit government policy or announcement indicating this direction, Lu perceived the imminent growth of the sector. Relying on his ability to read between the lines, he made the strategic decision to venture into the auto component industry. This choice was driven by a thorough appraisal of the company's available resources, competences, and untapped potential. Lu's insightful evaluation ultimately paved the way for the establishment of a colossal multinational enterprise.

In 1999, Jack Ma, the founder of Alibaba, embarked on a transformative business journey alongside a group of 17 friends. Recognising the immense potential of the Internet, Ma made a strategic decision to enter the e-commerce industry. Specifically, he identified the untapped opportunities in connecting Chinese small manufacturers with overseas buyers as a catalyst for substantial growth. Ma's astute assessment of this potential laid the foundation for a series of successes within Alibaba's family of internet-based businesses.

*Shi* represents the overall combat effectiveness, whether realised or potential, of a military unit, deployment, or strategic position. This assessment takes into account both the inherent qualities and external circumstances that influence the military formation at a given moment. Thus, assuming all other factors are equal, a group of 10 highly skilled archers would possess greater *Shi* than a group of 10 poorly trained archers. However, if the former were positioned in a valley while the latter were deployed on a hilltop, the balance of *Shi* might be reversed.[84]

According to Kissinger, Sun Tzu's most crucial insight lies in recognising that, in military or strategic engagement, everything is interconnected and relevant. Weather conditions, terrain features, diplomatic efforts, intelligence gathered from spies and double agents, supply chains and logistics, the balance of forces, historical perspectives, the intangible elements of surprise, and morale; all these factors are intertwined and mutually influential. Thus, subtle shifts in momentum and relative advantage occur due to the interplay between the interplays. In essence, there are no isolated events in strategic contests.[85]

In today's rapidly evolving business landscape, it is crucial to adapt and embrace leading trends in order to stay competitive. Failing to do so can have detrimental consequences, as one may be overshadowed by competitors who have embraced the changing dynamics.

For example, consider the impact of the internet on traditional brick and mortar supermarkets. With the rise of online businesses, supermarkets recognised the need to establish an online presence to counter the competitive threats posed by internet companies. This approach, known as the 'click and mortar' strategy, allowed them to leverage the advantages of both physical and online retail.

However, there have been instances where companies failed to adapt to the changing trends and suffered dire consequences. One such example is Wang Laboratories, the once-legendary computer company founded in 1951 by Dr An Wang, a Chinese American engineer, and Dr Ge-Yao Chu. During the 1980s, Wang Laboratories experienced remarkable success, boasting annual revenues of $3 billion and employing over 33 000 individuals. Dr Wang enjoyed a prominent position as the head of one of Massachusetts' leading and rapid-growing companies in the 1980s, recognised as one of the 12 eminent immigrants and esteemed innovators in the United States. However, in 1992, the company faced a significant setback when it was compelled to seek bankruptcy protection.

One of the primary factors contributing to the company's downfall was its rigid focus on its existing word processing business, particularly mini-computer and 'mid-frame' systems. Deplorably, the company failed to embrace the emergence of general-purpose personal computers accompanied by software, which represented a notable shift in the industry during the 1980s. This oversight can be attributed to their inability to acknowledge and respond to the changing trends and technologies that were reshaping the industry.

*Shi* can be consciously shaped or manipulated in one's favour in order to achieve strategic advantage. A specific case serves as an illustration of this approach.

An example involves a Chinese entrepreneur who acquired a piece of the land with the intention of building a marketplace and becoming its operator. Initially, the land was barren, hosting only a handful of small traders and peddlers. The buyer envisioned transforming it into a prominent furniture market within the region. Recognising the challenging circumstances and inherent risks, the entrepreneur devised a meticulous strategy to create favourable *Shi*.

The location was rebranded as the 'Red-Star Furniture City' and a statue of Lu Ban, a revered historical figure in Chinese carpentry, was erected at the entrance of the 'city'. A banner bearing the slogan: '*Customer is Emperor*' was prominently displayed on the walls. Furthermore, several reputable furniture companies were invited to exhibit and sell their products in the 'furniture city' at no cost.

Consequently, in the wake of these efforts, the dynamics of *Shi* began to unfold, fuelled by the increasing demand and supply of furniture. Soon enough, the Red-Star Furniture City garnered a formidable reputation as the foremost hub within the region.[86]

A significant instance where the *Shi* concept played a crucial role was during the last conflict between China and Vietnam. On 17 February 1979, China initiated a multipronged attack on Vietnam from its southern region, which later became known as the Third Vietnam War. Despite facing numerous unfavourable circumstances, such as the lingering aftermath of the Cultural Revolution, including challenges like outdated military equipment and troops lacking practical combat experience, the Chinese leadership carefully weighed all factors and determined it was necessary to engage in this war.

The key factor that influenced the decision was the Soviet Union's establishment of a strong *Shi*. The Soviet Union had deployed its troops around regions like Indochina, Africa, and the Middle East, with Vietnam serving as one of its influential allies in Indochina. According to Kissinger, in a broader context, the war arose from Beijing's interpretation of Sun Tzu's concept of *Shi*, which encompasses the trends and 'potential energy' of the strategic environment. Deng Xiaoping, with the objective of halting and, if possible, reversing what he perceived as an unfavourable momentum in Soviet strategy, aimed to act.[87]

Jack Ma, the founder of Alibaba, once employed an analogy to illustrate the competitive dynamics between Alibaba and its Western counterpart, eBay. He stated that, while eBay may be a shark in the vast ocean, he sees himself as a crocodile navigating the Yangtze River. In such a scenario, fighting in the ocean would lead to defeat, but contending in the river would result in victory for Alibaba.[88]

To gain a thorough understanding of the strategic intentions of their Chinese counterparts, Western decision-makers must adopt a perspective that allows them to examine the *Shi* surrounding a given situation. By putting themselves in their counterparts' shoes, they can effectively analyse the prevailing circumstances. This approach helps prevent potential misunderstandings and enables the development of a competitive advantage.

## DIALECTIC

Cross-cultural research in the field of social psychology has revealed notable and fundamental variations in cognitive reasoning between Chinese and Western perspectives.[89] These differences are ascribable to the influence of Chinese dialectic, which is deeply embedded in the *yin* and *yang* mode of thinking.

The concept of *yin* and *yang* forms the essential elements of the *I Ching,* also known as the *Book of Changes,* which is regarded as the first of all the Chinese classics. During the Zhou Dynasty (1046–771 BC), six classics were recognised, including the *I Ching, Classic of Poetry, Classic of History, Classic of Rites, Classic of Music,* and the *Spring and Autumn Annals.* Subsequently, during the Eastern Zhou Dynasty (770–221 BC), two additional classics were added to the collection, namely *The Analects* and *Classic of Filial Piety.* In the Tang Dynasty (618–907), five additional classics were incorporated into the existing compilation from the Eastern Zhou Dynasty.

The *I Ching* serves as the foundational source of Chinese culture, encompassing various philosophical traditions, such as Confucianism, Taoism, and the School of Mo Tzu. From ancient dynasties until the present era, the *I Ching* and *The Ten Wings* have undergone extensive interpretation, not only in the school of Confucianism but also those of Taoism and Buddhism.[90]

International scholars who have dedicated extensive study to the *I Ching* have ardently conveyed their perspectives on its profound nature and inherent complexity. Undoubtedly the *I Ching* stands as one of the most paramount literary works in the world. Its origins trace back to a mythical antiquity, captivating the minds of esteemed Chinese scholars throughout history up until the present day. Virtually all of the greatest and most momentous aspects of China's three-millennium cultural history has either drawn inspiration from this book or influenced the interpretation of its text. The philosophy, science, and statecraft of China, in particular, have continually drawn from the wellspring of insight contained within the *I Ching.*[91]

To gain insight into Chinese strategic thinking, a fundamental understanding of the *yin–yang* mode of thinking is essential. Sima Tan, a renowned Chinese historian and the father of Sima Qian, the author of the *Records of the Great Historian* (S*hiji*), wrote an influential essay that delves into six schools of thought. These schools include Confucianism, Taoism, Mohism, Legalism, the 'School of Names', and the 'School of *Yin* and *Yang*' (*yin–yang jia*).[92] Since its inception, the School of *Yin* and *Yang* has had a profound impact on the development of Chinese philosophy.

The creation of the *I Ching* is commonly attributed to three sources:

1.  Fu Xi: An ancient mythological ruler in China's early history, Fu Xi is believed to have originated the eight trigrams. These trigrams, as depicted in Figure 3.2, are based on the concepts of *yin* and *yang,* forming the foundation of the *I Ching.* Fu Xi envisioned the universe as a harmonious interplay between *yin* and *yang.*
2.  King Wen of the Zhou Dynasty (1111–721 BC): During the Zhou Dynasty, King Wen expanded upon Fu Xi's work by developing the 64 hexagrams. These hexagrams serve as a comprehensive system for under-

*Figure 3.2     An image of the eight trigrams*

standing and interpreting various aspects of human lives and the universe. King Wen's contributions provided deeper insights and explanations for the *I Ching*'s principles.

3.  Confucian disciples: The disciples of Confucius played a crucial role in developing the *I Ching*. They compiled a set of commentaries known as *The Ten Wings*, which provided detailed explanations and interpretations of the 64 hexagrams. By integrating these *Ten Wings* with the *I Ching*, they aimed to unlock the mysteries of the universe and foster harmony among humanity. It is believed that the composition of the *I Ching* was a collaborative effort spanning several centuries, involving numerous wise scholars.[93]

The *I Ching* proposes that the origin of all things can be traced back to the *Taiji*, which gives rise to *yin* and *yang*. This fundamental concept of complementary opposites forms the basis for understanding the dynamics and transformations within the universe. Figure 3.3 depicts the iconic symbol of *yin* and *yang*, which appositely illustrates potential interplays and changes inherent in this eternal contradictory pair. In the symbol, *yin* is represented by the dark half, while *yang* is symbolised by the white half. Notably, there exists no rigid boundary between *yin* and *yang*. Instead, a dot of *yin* resides within the *yang* side, symbolising the seed of growth, and likewise, a dot of *yang* resides within the *yin* side, representing the seed of growth. This interplay between *yin* and *yang* forms a continuous and ever-changing unity marked by contradiction and transformation.

*Figure 3.3      The yin yang symbol*

The first Chinese character of the *I Ching* (易经) is '易' (Yi), and it has been associated with three distinct meanings since the Han Dynasty (206 BC).[94] These meanings are 'simplicity', 'change', and 'constancy'.[95] The symbol of *yin* and *yang*, represented by a circular shape with a curved dividing line, signifies the potential interplay and transformation between *yin* and *yang*. It embodies the concept of 'you are part of me and I am part of you'. The second character of the *I Ching* is '经' (Jing), which translates to 'classic'. Therefore, the title of the *I Ching,* apart from denoting the 'book of changes', holds an additional layer of interpretation: it signifies that the *I Ching* is the founda-tional classic text, giving rise to other 'classics' in an ever-evolving manner. The original form of the Chinese character '易' (Yi) is a combination of the Sun (representing *Yang*) on top and the Moon (representing *Yin*) at bottom. This composition symbolises that one can gain an understanding of the uni-verse by delving into the principles of *yin* and *yang*.

The authors of the *I Ching*, wise sages from ancient China, observed that amidst the ever-changing phenomena, certain elements remained constant. For instance, they noted the constant rising of the Sun from the East and its setting in the West, as well as the predictable cycle of the Four Seasons. These observations inspired them to distil the enduring principles or unchanging rules into the *I Ching*. This Chinese classic serves as a profound representation of Chinese dialectic, encapsulating the dynamic interplay of opposing forces and the continuous pursuit of harmony and balance.

Peng and Nisbett have outlined three fundamental principles, from the viewpoint of social psychology, that characterise Chinese dialectic thinking,[96] derived from the teachings of the *I Ching* and Taoism.

The first principle is the 'Principle of Change', which suggests that the universe is constantly evolving, and objects, events, and states of being in the world consistently oscillate between two opposing extremes. Consequently, individuals from East Asian cultures, when compared to their Western counterparts, tend to anticipate a shift or transformation in various phenomena, departing from the existing status quo.[97]

Peng and Nisbett assert that the question of 'to be or not to be' is not a central concern. Instead, life is perceived as an ongoing transition from one state of being to another, where the notion of 'to be' does not equate to a static existence, and 'not to be' encompasses a state of being. This perspective arises from the understanding that reality is dynamic and adaptable, and therefore, the concepts that mirror reality are likewise active, mutable, and subjective rather than being objective, rigid, and clearly defined entities.[98]

The second principle embodies the 'Principle of Contradiction', which posits that reality lacks precise delineation and is teeming with contradictions. Given the perpetual nature of change, contradictions persist. Within everything, the existence of opposites such as old and new, good and bad, strong and weak, and so forth is observed.[99]

The traditional Chinese perspective of '*yin* and *yang*' incorporates the notion of contradictions or a unity of opposites, recognising the inherent value in both 'A' or 'not-A'. Lao Tzu emphasises that all entities uphold *yin* and embrace *yang*, and the interplay between these two forces permeates the entire universe. However, it is only at the serene juncture between inhaling and exhaling that one can truly apprehend their perfect harmony.[100]

In Chinese dialectic, contradictions are employed to comprehend the relationships between objects or events, to transcend or integrate apparent opposites, and even to embrace conflicting yet enlightening viewpoints. The ultimate goal of reasoning lies in the Middle Way,[101] differing from the Hegelian dialectic where a thesis is followed by an antithesis, eventually resolved through synthesis. Unlike the Hegelian approach, the Chinese dialectic is characterised by its nonaggressive nature, aiming to reconcile contradictions rather than merely resolving them.[102]

China's policy of 'One Country and Two Systems', as formulated by Deng Xiaoping and enshrined in the constitution, embodies a dialectical perspective. It is a unique manifestation of a country that combines socialist and capitalist systems, represented by mainland China and Hong Kong, respectively. This principle does not have a direct counterpart in Western countries.

Furthermore, the Chinese display remarkable dexterity in maintaining and deepening relations with countries that may have conflicting interests, such as Iran, Saudi Arabia, and Israel. This ability to navigate complex diplomatic landscapes demonstrates the seriousness with which China approaches the mission.[103]

Given that all phenomena consist of contradictory pairs, symbolised by the *yin* and *yang*, which represent the unity of opposites, and considering that these pairs have the potential to transform into their opposites, Chinese decision-makers exhibit a distinct approach when responding to 'adverse news or incidents' as compared to their Western counterparts. The Chinese tend to explore the potential for these negative occurrences to evolve into positive outcomes. The perspective is reflected in various Chinese sayings, such as 'failure is the mother of success' and 'a fall in the pit, a gain in your wit'.[104]

Lao Tzu offers valuable insights into this dialectical thinking by asserting that misfortune is intertwined with good fortune, and vice versa. The events that are bestowed upon us by the heavens remain mysterious in their ultimate purpose and their boundless possibilities. Today, those considered righteous may resort to cunning strategies, while tomorrow, those perceived as good may become enveloped in darkness.[105]

On the other hand, Western logic finds its roots in Aristotle and is characterised by a binary and precise mode of thinking influenced by mathematics. In this framework, two plus two always equals exactly four, without any alternative possibilities. Objects or concepts are categorised as either 'A' or 'not-A', with no room for overlap or contradiction. This is an all-or-nothing logic strictly adheres to principles of non-contradiction and the excluded middle.

Researchers specialising in social psychology offer concise explanations for this phenomenon. They suggest that Westerners, believing in the existence of a single truth, strive to reconcile apparent contradictions. Employing formal logic to evaluate propositions, Western thinkers tend to assess both sides of an opposing argument, rejecting the less plausible option in favour of the more convincing one. This approach can even lead to a polarisation of initial preferences, as Westerners seek synthesis and resolution in the face of seeming contradictions.[106]

The 'Principle of Holism' is a fundamental aspect of Chinese dialectic thinking, representing the third of the principle identified by Peng and Nisbett. It plays a central role in Chinese thought and provides a solid foundation for the Principle of Contradiction. Holism is marked by several distinguishing features, including thematic and family-resemblance-based categorisation of objects, a keen focus on contextual information and relationships during visual attention, a tendency to attribute causes based on the specific situation, and a strong inclination towards dialecticism.

In contrast, analytic cognition exhibits different characteristics. It involves taxonomic and rule-based categorisation of objects, a narrower focus during visual attention, a disposition towards attributing causes based on individual dispositions, and the use of formal logic in reasoning.[107]

Therefore, the Principle of Holism captures the essence of Chinese dialectic thinking, highlighting the holistic nature of cognition in Chinese culture. This holistic approach emphasises the interconnectedness of various elements, their contextual significance, and the recognition of contradictions and dialectical tensions within a given situation.

Another group of social psychologists offer explanations about its nature. Holistic thinking entails an inclination towards perceiving and comprehending the broader context or field as a cohesive unit. This encompasses paying attention to the relationships between a central or focal object and its surrounding field or environment. Moreover, individuals with a holistic thinking style tend to prioritise explaining and deducing events based on these contextual relationships.[108]

In order to obtain a comprehensive understanding of a particular phenomenon it is crucial to recognise its interplay with the context in which it unfolds. This involves recognising how the phenomenon both influences and is influenced by its surrounding context.[109]

The literature on culture and cognition has predominantly directed its attention towards exploring the distinctions in fundamental cognitive processes, such as thinking styles and belief systems, between individuals from Eastern and Western cultures. Notably, Eastern Asian thought has been strongly associated with holistic thinking, while Western thought has been characterised by analytical thinking.[110]

Analytical thinking in Western culture involves a tendency to detach the object from its surrounding context, focusing on the attributes of the object as a means to categorise it, and employing rules derived from these categories to explain and predict the object's behaviour.[111]

The utilisation of stratagem approaches lies at the heart of Chinese strategic thinking, and there is a notable alignment between the application of these approaches and Chinese dialectic. Due to their inclination towards holistic cognition, the Chinese mindset allows for a wider range of subtleties when implement a strategy; this includes options such as 'not-A', 'A', '1/2A', '1/3A', '1/4A', and '1/5A', among others.

On the other hand, the Western mindset tends to limit decision-makers to choosing between 'A' or 'not-A'. In essence, Chinese decision-makers have an advantage over their Western counterparts because they possess greater mental freedom to develop a scheme or plan. Theoretically, Western decision-makers only have two options at their disposal.

Another element contributing to the harmony between the Chinese mindset and dialectic originates from Taoist principles. Lao Tzu's teachings assert that, in order to diminish someone's power, they must first be allowed to grow. To weaken someone, they must initially be strengthened. To bring someone low, they must first be elevated to a position of power. To take something away from someone, it must first be given. This concept is referred to as the 'subtle light'.[112]

## COMPETITOR ORIENTATION

In all conflicts, whether they occur in military or business settings, and across various cultures, the consideration and analysis of competition are natural and often seen as necessary or even essential. However, responses to competitor actions can vary in terms of the degree of emphasis placed on them.

In Chinese culture, competition occupies a central position, both philosophically and at a higher level. Competitors often take the spotlight and are thoroughly studied, either to be imitated or dealt with, thereby influencing the core activities of organisations. This approach, characterised by a focus on competitors, is known as competitor orientation.

Under this orientation, the strategies, technologies, or products of the target competitor heavily influence the organisation's strategy and policies. The entire organisation is mobilised or coordinated to adopt this orientation, with the goal of matching or neutralising the target competitor. If the target competitor is effectively neutralised, the organisation shifts its focus to a new target competitor, initiating another cycle of endeavours.

If the organisation attains the leading position within the industry but fails to undergo a philosophical or strategic transformation and organisational change, it is highly probable that it will lose its sense of direction and encounter premature downfall. An illustration of this perspective can be found in Sun Tzu's *Art of War*, where a significant portion of the discussion revolves around the concept of the 'enemy' or 'opponent'. Sun Tzu emphasises the importance of conducting a thorough evaluation and understanding of the true nature of one's adversary. He advises asking critical questions such as: 'Which ruler possesses the Tao? Which general exhibits greater ability? Who has obtained the advantage of Heaven and Earth? Whose laws and orders are more effectively implemented? Whose forces are stronger? Whose officers and troops are better trained? Whose system of rewards and punishments is clearer?' By considering these factors, one can discern the path to victory or defeat:[113] '*One who, fully prepared, awaits the unprepared will be victorious*'.[114]

The military classics that form the core texts of the *Seven Military Classics of Ancient China* strongly emphasise a competitor-orientated mindset. This is evident in various passages, such as the following illustrative examples:

1.  *Wei Liao-Tzu* highlights different approaches to achieving victory in warfare. It states that there are those who achieve victory through the application of *Tao*, those who achieve victory through awe-inspiring tactics, and those who achieve victory through sheer strength. By engaging in careful military discussions and thoroughly evaluating the enemy, one can disrupt their spirit (*qi*) and disperse their forces. Even if the

enemy's disposition is intact, they will be unable to effectively utilise it. This is referred to as victory through *Tao*.[115]

2. According to *Wu Tzu,* when deploying an army, it is crucial to identify the weaknesses and strengths of the enemy. The key is to swiftly seize opportunities by targeting their vulnerable points. By exploiting these vulnerable areas, one can gain a significant advantage in warfare.[116]

3. *The Methods of Ssu-ma*, also known as *Ssu-ma Fa*, presents a perspective on warfare that emphasises the importance of tactical observation. It suggests employing both large and small numbers of forces to study and understand the variations in enemy tactics. It advocates for strategic manoeuvres of advancing and retreating to assess the strength of their defences. By putting the enemy in a precarious situation, their fears can be observed. The text advises maintaining a calm and composed demeanour to gauge if the enemy becomes complacent. It also recommends making movements to test if the enemy harbours doubts. Finally, it suggests launching surprise attacks to evaluate the discipline of the enemy.[117]

Chinese literature, spanning ancient and contemporary works, encompasses military, history, philosophy, and literary genres, and has long explored strategies for confronting adversaries and attaining victory through the principles of *Tao*, often without resorting to large-scale conflicts. This distinctive tradition has shaped the worldview of Chinese decision-makers, rooted in a culture-based approach to understanding and addressing the enemy, holding profound implications for Western politicians and business leaders when developing their strategies towards China.

In a company that has embraced a competitor orientation, the organisation typically focuses on closely monitoring, imitating, manoeuvring, and strategically outperforming its competitors in terms of their products and business strategies.

It is worth noting that, while this imitation trend can have negative implications, there have been instances where successful commercial players started by imitating others and eventually attained a strong competitive position through subsequent improvement and innovation.[118] Here are two notable cases that exemplify this trajectory.

- Founded in 1995, BYD has emerged as the global leader in rechargeable batteries, solidifying its position as the largest supplier in the industry. Initially gaining recognition as a mimic of a highly popular automobile model, the company has since transformed into the foremost market leader in electric vehicles. Today, BYD proudly boasts the world's best and most extensively sold brands within the electric vehicle sector.

- Established in 2006, eHi Car Services is a prominent Chinese auto rental company headquartered in Shanghai. Drawing inspiration from renowned international car rental firms like Hertz and Avis, eHi Car Services initiated its operations. Given China's bustling traffic and rapidly expanding road networks, the conventional Western models were ill-suited for the needs of local executives striving for stress-free self-driving experiences. Consequently, eHi Car Services devised its unique operational approach, focusing on chauffeur-driven services. Today, it has emerged as the largest rental company in China, boasting a vast network of over 10 000 service locations spread across more than 500 cities. With a diverse fleet comprising over 200 vehicle types, eHi Car Services caters to customers nationwide.

Companies that embrace Chinese tradition and prioritise their competitors often adopt a cooperative approach, seeking coexistence or collaboration for mutual growth and harmony instead of seeking to eliminate or destroy their rivals, even when they have surpassed them. This strategic mindset reflects the fundamental principles of *yin* and *yang* found in the *I Ching* and is deeply intertwined with Confucianism, particularly the Middle Way.

Influenced by the Middle-Way philosophy, enlightened Chinese individuals tend to shy away from assuming the top position in an industry or drawing excessive attention to themselves. The principles of Taoism, as exemplified by Lao Tzu and Zhuang Tzu, have played a vital role in shaping the mindset of the Chinese people. Joseph Needham once posited that: 'A Chinese thought without Taoism is like a tree without roots'. The impact of Taoist philosophy in China has been acknowledged and underscored by various Chinese philosophers.[119]

The cultural inclination to avoid reaching the pinnacle or attracting undue attention has been encapsulated by various Chinese proverbs:

- The outstanding often bears the brunt of an attack.
- Fame portends trouble for men, just as fattening does for pigs.
- A tall tree catches the wind.
- The protruding beam is the first to decay.
- Contentment is true happiness.

Consequently, Chinese organisations often adopt a follower's strategy, akin to long-distance athletic competitions where most runners prefer to trail behind the leader until the final sprint. This seemingly uncontentious or unaggressive stance serves as a foundation for eventually assuming a leading position.

Huawei officially gained recognition as the world's largest telecommunication equipment manufacturer in 2012, surpassing Ericsson.[120] However, it had already surpassed Ericsson, but deliberately presented itself as the second, not the first, until it had to stand out. Interestingly, when Huawei initially entered the ranks of the Global 500 companies, as determined by the *Fortune* magazine, the announcement was made during a meeting by several members of Huawei's executive team in a rather 'dramatic' manner. The statement went as follows: 'I am delivering a piece of foreboding news: Huawei has now officially joined the Global 500 companies'. Notably, this news did not elicit a sense of joy within the company, nor did any celebration take place. In fact, Huawei's top management had actively endeavoured to postpone their inclusion in the Global 500.[121]

Furthermore, of particular interest, once Huawei garnered recognition as a global leader in 5G technology, the revolutionary fifth generation of mobile communications that facilitates worldwide connectivity, it became a prime target singled out by the US government for containment, restriction, and even attempts to ban its progress. This aligns with the foresight embedded in Chinese philosophy, as if it had foretold such a scenario.

China's Suntech Power serves as a prime example of the challenges faced by a company when it attains the leading position in its industry. Established in January 2001, Suntech Power focused on the development, manufacturing, and delivery of solar energy solutions. Remarkably, within a short span of time, the company gained recognition as one of the world's top 10 solar panel manufacturers, according to Photon International in 2004. The following year, in 2005, Suntech Power achieved another milestone by becoming the first Chinese privately-owned company to be listed on the New York Stock Exchange.

By 2011, Suntech Power had ascended to the pinnacle of the industry, securing its position as the largest solar panel manufacturer worldwide. However, despite its initial success, the company's reign at the top was short-lived. In 2013, Suntech Power was compelled to file for bankruptcy, facing significant financial difficulties and operational challenges.

Huawei and Haier have established themselves as prominent Chinese companies in their respective industries, and have successfully maintained their leading positions by avoiding swift competitive erosion. These companies attribute their sustained success to the astute management at the helm, which is well aware of the perils associated with being at the top. They understand that resting on one's laurels is not a secure strategy and are acutely mindful of the impending competitive threats that loom over them.

For example, Haier's top management acknowledges that the utmost challenge arises not from external rivals but from internal inertia and a lack of awareness regarding the company's vulnerability. They firmly believe that Haier's triumph hinges on their commitment to innovation and its ability to break free from complacency. In the eyes of the company's decision-makers, crises serve as catalysts for survival and growth, propelling the company forward.[122]

Ren Zhengfei shares a deep ideological connection with Mao Zedong, drawing inspiration from Mao's principles and embracing history as a reflective tool. When the People's Republic of China was founded in September 1949, Mao included the following poignant words in the Chinese National Anthem: 'The Chinese nation has reached a point where its very existence is at stake'. Ren Zhengfei frequently invokes these words to caution his executive team about impending crisis that may befall Huawei.

Moreover, Ren often reminds Huawei's top management of a crucial historical lesson: the downfall of the Qin Empire was not orchestrated by formidable external foes but rather by two 'farmers'[123] who led rebellions to overthrow the empire.[124] This tale serves as a constant reminder that even seemingly invincible empires can be brought to their knees by unexpected forces.

Research has indicated that being the first to enter the market can provide certain advantages. However, later entrants may also gain an edge through various factors such as lower costs, benefiting from free-rider gains, leveraging scope economies, and learning from the mistakes of the pioneers.[125] The success of a later entrant is generally influenced by three key factors at the time of entry: market opportunity, organisational resources, and product competitiveness compared to existing offerings.[126]

Interestingly, even in developed Western market economies, there tend to be more companies entering markets as later entrants rather than pioneers. Since it is not possible for a single firm to always be a pioneer all the time, many firms are encouraged to develop strategies that support a systematic approach to imitative strategies and later entry. This approach complements continued innovation and pioneering efforts.[127]

Chinese companies frequently capitalise on China's vast markets, gaining advantages from lower costs of imitating products and a deep understanding of local markets dynamics. This enables various companies to not only survive but to flourish using their initial resources, rapidly ascending to become global powerhouses. A notable example of such a company is Xiaomi, which managed to achieve remarkable success despite entering the market relatively late.

Xiaomi is an exemplary manufacturer of consumer electronics and smart devices, with a primary focus on smartphones and smart hardware interconnected through an IoT platform. The name 'Xiaomi' translates to 'millet' or 'rice' in English. Its founder, Lei Jun, associates the term 'Xiao' with a Buddhist concept that emphasises the significance of a single grain of rice being as majestic as a mountain, symbolising the company's endurance and resilience. The 'MI' in Xiaomi's logo represents 'Mobile Internet', while also alluding to the phrase 'Mission Impossible'. This acknowledges the seemingly insurmountable challenges faced by the company during its early days.

In 2010, Xiaomi made a bold entry into the intensely competitive smartphone market, but surprisingly, it did so without even having an actual phone to offer. Instead, the company initially provided a free operating system (OS) based on Android. However, in a remarkable turn of events, Xiaomi swiftly rose to become one of the leading smartphone manufacturers globally within a span of seven years, generating $15 billion in revenue. Over time, Xiaomi's growth rate gained momentum, propelling the company to transform into the world's largest consumer internet of things (IoT) firm by 2020.[128]

Initially, Xiaomi focused on selling its products exclusively online. However, it later expanded its business model by opening physical retail stores. By 2015, Xiaomi had diversified its offerings and developed an extensive range of consumer electronics. The company's growth trajectory continued. In 2020 alone, it achieved a remarkable feat of selling 146.3 million smartphones. Xiaomi's success extended beyond hardware sales, as its MIUI mobile user interface garnered a massive user base of over 500 million monthly active users.

In terms of smartphone shipments, Xiaomi secured the impressive position of being the third-largest player in the market during the second quarter of 2022. Additionally, Xiaomi has established itself as the leader in the consumer AIoT (AI+IoT) domain. As of 30 June 2022, the company boasted 526.9 million smart devices connected to its platform, excluding smartphones, tablets, and laptops. With its widespread reach, Xiaomi's products are available in over100 countries and regions worldwide.

Furthermore, Xiaomi's achievements have been recognised globally. As of August 2022, the company made its fourth appearance on the prestigious Fortune Global 500 list, securing the 266th position. This marked a significant jump of 72 places compared to the previous year's ranking, underscoring the company's sustained growth and success.[129]

Later entrants in the market may choose to adopt a resource substitution strategy as a competitive approach. This strategy involves the implementation of alternative management practices, technologies, or business models.[130] Huawei, for instance, initially faced challenges in competing with major rivals like Cisco in international markets due to technological disparities. However, Huawei consistently managed to overcome these limitations by adopting a distinct and more competitive approach. By leveraging this resource substitution strategy, Huawei successfully positioned itself in the market and competed with established players, despite having initially inferior technology.

In Western traditional strategic thinking, while a competitive analysis is commonly conducted before strategy formation, the analytical data primarily serve as an input for a customer-orientated strategy rather than actively guiding the organisation. A significant outcome of competitive analysis is the development of a product that distinguishes itself from competitors or surpasses them in quality.[131] The purpose of a company adopting a competitor orientation is to enhance its market orientation and better serve customers compared to existing and potential competitors.

In China, a competitor-orientated firm typically focuses on a specific target competitor's operation, encompassing aspects such as product functionality, design, manufacturing, and marketing. They may even engage in tactics like attracting key personnel from the competitor's organisation. The objective is to offer a product that is similar or comparable to competitors', but at a more competitive price or representing superior value. Occasionally, the firm may strive to develop a distinct yet superior variation of the product compared to its competitors.

A business adopting a competitor orientation in China often exhibits behaviours that are less conducive to becoming a technology originator, market leader, or significant investor in technology. The excessive emphasis on competitors has the potential to hinder original technological advancement in contemporary times. Chinese firms incline to prioritise the practice of reverse engineering competitor's products, wherein the competitors' products are systematically dismantled and reassembled. This process enables them to acquire knowledge about the structures and features of competitor's products, facilitating the development of similar 'copycat' variants. This orientation implicitly banks on gaining a competitive advantage as a later entrant in the market.

## AGILITY

Over the past decade, the significance of agility in attaining competitive advantages has been increasingly acknowledged by Western scholars and professionals.[132] In Western contexts, substantial efforts have been made to thoroughly study and comprehend this subject. However, only a limited number of Western scholars and practitioners have been aware of the fact that agility is deeply ingrained within Chinese culture. It is an inherent element of the *yin–yang* doctrine and Taoist dialectic, providing Chinese entities with an innate advantage.

Throughout the course of Chinese history, the ability to demonstrate exceptional agility has often been a determining factor in achieving victory. This was particularly evident during the Chinese Civil War, when Mao Zedong orchestrated a pivotal event that altered the fate of the CPC in the 1930s. In September 1933, the CPC faced the fifth encirclement and suppression campaign launched by their adversaries, the KMT army. Guided by the doctrinal leadership of Bo Gu and Li De, the CPC army pursued rigid strategies focused on defending territorial positions and capturing major cities. Unfortunately, this approach led to significant casualties among the CPC forces.

In response to the KMT's mobilisation of over 500 000 troops to continue their relentless attacks on the CPC, the latter found themselves on the verge of annihilation, compelling them to undertake the momentous Long March. It was during the notable Zunyi CPC meeting in January 1935 that Mao Zedong emerged as a vital figure within the CPC leadership, playing a crucial role in shaping military decisions.

Taking charge, Mao led the remaining CPC forces in adopting a strategy of mobile warfare, exemplified by his remarkable four-times crossing of the Red River. These audacious manoeuvres not only allowed the CPC to elude the encirclement imposed by the formidable KMT forces but also inflict significant casualties on the KMT. Consequently, these manoeuvres have come to be regarded as one of the greatest demonstrations of the art of war in modern China, forever altering the course of the CPC's destiny.[133]

Chinese agility can be understood as an outgrowth of Chinese dialectic, but it has been stretched to the point that it warrants recognition as a distinct category within Chinese strategic thinking. Chinese agility encompasses key aspects:

Firstly, it emphasises the triumph of the 'soft' over the 'hard' and the 'weak' over the 'strong'. By embracing this philosophy, a combatant gains self-confidence and courage to confront more powerful adversaries while maintaining a constant state of alertness and unwavering fighting spirit, avoiding complacency.

Lao Tzu explicates and advises that the most flexible and yielding entities in the world can overcome the most rigid and inflexible counterparts.[134] At the beginning of life, we are gentle and vulnerable. At the end of life, we become rigid and unyielding. All things, including grass and trees, are pliable and soft during life but become dry and brittle in death. Therefore, the soft and adaptable are companions of life, while the stiff and unyielding are companions of death. An army that refuses to yield will be defeated, just as a tree that cannot bend will snap in the face of the wind.[135]

Secondly, it refers to the ability to adapt swiftly and adeptly, to navigate, guide, or control a rapidly evolving situation, staying one step ahead of opponents. This aspect highlights the conduct a combatant should exhibit in combat, demonstrating their capacity to respond quickly and effectively.

An illustration of notable military prowess is showcased by the Chinese army during the Korean War, where they exhibited swiftness and agility. Within the initial phase of the conflict, the 113 Division of the esteemed 38th Corps achieved an extraordinary feat. They accomplished a stunning journey of 72.5 kilometres in a mere 14 hours, effectively cutting off the retreat route of UN forces. Notably, this remarkable achievement took place on treacherous mountainous terrain, navigating narrow lanes instead of the smooth asphalt surfaces typically encountered on roads. It stands as an unparalleled infantry record in the annals of military history, remaining unchallenged to this day.

In contrast, during the globally significant Iraqi war in 1990, the allied forces led by the United States possessed advanced heavy armoured vehicles. As they pursued a retreating Iraqi army, they managed to achieve speeds ranging from 50 to 60 kilometres per night, with their superior mobility and technology.[136]

Sun Tzu compares an army to water, noting that just as flowing water naturally seeks the lowlands and avoids high terrain, an army should avoid direct confrontation with strength and instead target weaknesses. Furthermore, water adapts its course based on the contours of the ground it traverses, and similarly, an army should adapt its strategies and tactics to exploit the circumstances and vulnerabilities of the enemy.[137]

As per Lao Tzu, nothing in this world is as gentle and adaptable as water. Yet, when it comes to confronting the hard and strong, nothing can surpass water in its ability to gradually triumph. Water is weak, but none can match its power. It is soft, yet none can damage it. It is yielding, yet nothing can erode it over time.[138]

In light of the wisdom imparted by ancient sages, it might be tempting to believe that their teachings only pertain to combatants who are weaker or smaller. Nevertheless, even if an individual has already attained a position of leadership within a specific field, it remains, if not more so, imperative to embrace this philosophy. This is because those at the pinnacle of power are most susceptible to attacks from all directions.

According to Liu An, those who achieve the Way possess a remarkable balance: their will is flexible, yet their actions are resolute. Their minds are empty, yet their responses are precise and accurate. When we speak of a supple will, it refers to their ability to be adaptable and gentle, maintaining a sense of calm and tranquillity. They conceal themselves when others hesitate, act when others are unable, remain composed and free from worry, and seize the opportune moment without delay. They flow harmoniously with the ever-changing world around them, without preconceptions or initiating actions, but rather responding to stimuli with perfect timing.[139]

The above teaching by ancient Chinese philosophers is rooted in the concept of *Tao*, which represents the natural order of things. It emphasises the principle that the soft can overcome the hard, and the weak can overpower the strong. Huang Shih-kung, in the book *Three Strategies of Huang Shih-kung*, elaborates on this idea.

According to the teachings, the softness symbolises virtue, while the hardness represents aggression. The weak refers to the aspect that garners support from the people, whereas the strong incites resentment. Each of these elements possesses specific situations in which they are established, applied, employed, or augmented. By harmoniously combining these four elements and exerting appropriate control over them, one can navigate the complexities of life effectively.[140]

A significant element of Chinese agility is commonly referred to as 'strategic detour'. It involves adopting a circuitous or indirect approach to accomplish strategic objectives, rather than opting for a direct path. Sun Tzu emphasises that the greatest challenge lies in transforming a circuitous route into a straight one and turning adversity into an advantage. By strategically manipulating the situation, one can entice the enemy onto a circuitous path, luring them with the promise of profit. Consequently, even if you pursue them, you will reach your destination ahead of them. This achievement is a result of comprehending both the tactics of the circuitous and the direct approaches.[141]

Between 1936 and 1939, Mao Zedong formulated the strategic theory of 'encircling cities from the countryside', which played a crucial role in the ultimate triumph of the CPC. Mao's ideas were expounded in publications like *Problems of Strategy in China's Revolutionary War*[142] and *Problems of War and Strategy*.[143] This strategic approach has since been adapted by Chinese companies in their internationalisation strategies, albeit with a slight modification known as 'encircling developed countries from developing countries', which has proven to be highly effective.

An additional aspect of the concept of Chinese agility is the principle of *wu wei*, which can be translated as 'non-interference', 'non-action', or 'effortless action'. This principle, like the flowing nature of water, emphasises allowing things to unfold naturally without unnecessary intervention. It is closely related to the concept of 'riding along with *Shi*'.

In the philosophy of Taoism, it is believed that individuals should lead their lives according to the principles of *Tao*, which involve practising humility, cultivating inner calmness, and embodying the spirit of *wu wei*. Taoism also advocates for the application of the *wu wei* approach in matters of governance and state affairs. Lao Tzu explained that, although *Tao* itself does not actively engage in action, it serves as the foundation of for all forms of action. It does not initiate movement, yet it is the wellspring of all creation. If princes and kings could embody the essence of *Tao*, their subjects would naturally flourish under their rule.[144]

Lao Tzu further suggested that the sages of Taoism advise that by acting with a pure heart, people can inspire transformation in others. By cherishing and nurturing one's own life, individuals can uplift those around them. By giving selflessly and without conditions, people can contribute to the prosperity of society; and by relinquishing personal desires and wants, individuals can help others find fulfilment and abundance.[145]

In essence, the principle of *wu wei* teaches us to align ourselves with the natural flow of events, to act in harmony with the underlying principles of existence, and to embrace a mindset of non-interference and effortless action.

By embodying these principles, individuals can cultivate a sense of balance, wisdom, and harmony, both within themselves and in their interactions with others.

The *wu wei* approach to business has been embraced by numerous successful Chinese businesspeople, including those at Huawei and Haier. Within this management philosophy, leaders of companies adhere to principles of *Tao*, which are embodied in the concept of *Shi*. Once strategies and organisational structures are established, management operations are entrusted to those who are assigned to the respective tasks, with minimum interference. This approach allows the organisation to function autonomously. Lao Tzu advises against impulsive actions, as they lead to ruin, and urges against grasping too tightly, as this causes things to slip away. Individuals who are on the brink of success often lose patience and fail in their endeavours. Therefore, it is crucial to be prepared and committed from the beginning to the end in order to avoid failure.[146]

## INFLUENCES

The upper section of the framework includes a subtitle of 'Influences', which plays a crucial role in determining the extent to which Chinese decision-makers embrace and practise different components of strategic thinking. These influences encompass various forms of media, including radio, television, and the internet, as well as literary and philosophical works, historical accounts, theatrical arts, and military classics. Each of these influences, to varying degrees, contributes to the dissemination of different aspects of Chinese strategic thinking.

Currently, there is no systematic teaching or formal dissemination of knowledge of Chinese strategic thinking. Instead, this knowledge is embedded within a wide range of various mass media and publications. The impact of each influential element on individuals and organisations is influenced by personal interests and the availability of media tools. In other words, individuals and organisations may be affected by these influences based on their own preferences and the extent to which they can access and engage with the media sources.

Haier, renowned as one of the world's leading and most valuable brands, owes much of its success to its founder, Zhang Ruimin. Notably, Zhang Ruimin is recognised for his voracious reading habits, which have greatly contributed to the company's achievements. During the early stages of Haier's development, Zhang Ruimin immersed himself in various subjects, including Chinese history and philosophy. He read notable works such as '*The Hundred Schools of Thought*', a classic philosophical book that encompasses a wide range of schools of thought from the pre-Qin era to the early Han Dynasty.

This comprehensive collection features the writings of ancient Chinese leading thinkers, including Lao Tzu, Zhuang Tzu, Confucius, Meng Tzu, Sun Tzu, Mozi, Liezi, Gui Guzi, Han Feizi, and many others.

In addition to his deep exploration of Chinese philosophy, Zhang Ruimin actively engaged with Western management masterpieces. He devoted time to studying the works of Joseph Schumpeter, an influential figure known for world-renowned theories on innovation. Likewise, Zhang Ruimin absorbed the insights of Peter Drucker, a distinguished management guru whose writings centred on management and innovation. Later in his career, he has continued his habit of reading, more than a hundred books each year.

Zhang Ruimin's broad range of reading materials, spanning from Chinese philosophical classics to Western management literature, has undoubtedly shaped his perspective and contributed to Haier's success as a company driven by innovation and effective management practices.

Another notable example is Jack Ma, the founder of Alibaba. His primary source of inspiration comes from Chinese historical literature, particularly the works authored by Louis Cha Leung-yung, better known by his pen name, Jin Yong. Jack Ma's deep admiration for Jin Yong's novels has even led him to encourage, and in some cases, enforce, the adoption of nicknames from these literary works among his colleagues and employees. This practice aims to foster a cohesive corporate culture within Alibaba.

Within Alibaba and throughout his online persona, Jack Ma is known as Feng Qingyang, a fictional swordsman created by Jing Yong. Drawing inspiration from one of Jin Yong's novels, Jack Ma has codified the company's values as 'Six Vein Spirit Sword'. Symbolically, this sword represents not an actual weapon but the concept of harnessing internal strengths to overcome any challenges or adversaries.

In the context of Alibaba, the strengths embodied by the Six Vein Spirit Sword align with the principles outlined in the company's 'Mission, Vision, and Values', which draw inspiration from Jack Ma's esteemed corporate mentor, Jack Welch, the former CEO of General Electric.[147]

By embracing Jin Yong's literary world, Jack Ma has instilled a sense of shared identity and purpose within Alibaba. This integration of characters and values from martial arts fiction demonstrates his creative approach to shaping the company's culture and ethos.

Many individuals who have limited access to formal education or a lack of inclination to read literal, philosophical, and historical publications are often influenced by mass media in shaping their thinking and worldview. In general, mass media, such as television, has a greater impact on the general Chinese population compared to books or literary sources. This is partly because many literary, philosophical, and military classics have been adapted into television drama series or films, which reach a wider audience. Through artistic creativity, these programmes can resonate with the hearts and minds of the general public, thus leaving a significant imprint on their perspectives and beliefs.

## AN INTEGRATED VIEW

The recent events surrounding the launch of Huawei's latest smartphone, the Mate 60 Pro, between late August and early September 2023, serve as a compelling example that illustrate the effectiveness of Chinese strategic thinking. This incident has not only puzzled decision-makers and citizens in Western countries, but has also sparked intense speculation worldwide, capturing the attention of people from different walks of life, including those in China.

Originally, Huawei had planned to hold a product launch conference on 12 September 2023, coinciding with Apple's unveiling of the iPhone 15, to officially introduce their new product into the market. However, on 29 August 2023, in an unexpected move, Huawei proceeded with the product launch quietly and without any formalities. Typically, prior to releasing a new product, Huawei would organise a large-scale event to showcase and publicise the product's specific features. This time, the launch took place discreetly within Huawei's specialty shops, without providing any official information about the product.

While Huawei had chosen not to release any official information regarding the product features, many interested individuals and enthusiasts had managed to uncover key details through a tear-down process. Here are some of the notable findings:

- The Mate 60 Pro boasts Huawei's proprietary Kirin 9000s chip, crafted by China's prominent contract manufacturer, SMIC. This chip offers remarkable support for 5G connectivity and artificial intelligence functionality. Notably, the Kirin 9000s chip leverages advanced 7-nanometre (nm) technology, highlighting Huawei's commitment to technological innovation.
- One standout feature of this product is its satellite calling capabilities, which represents a significant advancement in satellite connectivity for conventional smartphones. In contrast, the rest of the industry primarily focuses on emergency SOS and text messaging features, making Huawei's inclusion of satellite calling a noteworthy development.

Huawei's actions, from the perspective of Chinese strategic thinking, reveal the unfolding of the Chinese strategic mindset in this recent incident.

To begin with, Huawei's decision to launch its new product ahead of schedule, defying conventional expectations, exemplifies the application of stratagem as a fundamental aspect of Chinese strategic thinking. This strategic manoeuvre is characterised by its unconventional and surprising nature, catching primary competitors off guard. Simultaneously, it generates a substantial sensational impact on both the industry, which is accustomed to traditional business approaches, and the market, which becomes curious and intrigued as a result. This approach leads to significant marketing effectiveness.

Secondly, the timing of its release coinciding with the visit by Gina M. Raimondo, the Commerce Secretary of the United States, to China held significance. As the senior leader of the United States has led US efforts to restrict Beijing's access to advanced chips, her visit was likely to have played a role in Huawei's decision-making process, resulting in the earlier launch of Mate 60 Pro. This factor aligns with the '*Shi*' component of Chinese strategic thinking, which involves considering the timing and circumstances to gain an advantage.

The chip found within Mate 60 Pro represents a significant milestone in China's domestic technological advancement, surpassing previous iterations. This achievement is notable given the United States' efforts to impede China's progress in this area. The launch of the Mate 60 Pro can be seen as a testament to Huawei's resilience and resurgence, suggesting that the US containment strategy has not achieved its desired outcome. It is now crucial for the US government to re-evaluate its containment policies in light of these developments.

Huawei cleverly leveraged the presence of Gina Raimondo to promote its new product on a global scale, effectively turning her into an unofficial 'ambassador' for Huawei. Raimondo's influential status was also reflected online, with creative images featuring her holding the new phone accompanied by captions such as 'I am Raimondo, this time I endorse Huawei' and 'Huawei mobile phone ambassador Raimondo'. This demonstrates Huawei's strategic use of Raimondo's reputation to enhance its own brand visibility and credibility.

Thirdly, Huawei's decision to launch its new product ahead of schedule demonstrates the company's strategic agility, enabling it to adapt and adjust its strategy when opportune moments arise. This level of flexibility and responsiveness is akin to the flowing nature of water, allowing Huawei to seize opportunities as they emerge. Unlike Western companies, which often rely on meticulous long-term planning, Huawei's ability to make swift and decisive moves is a distinctive characteristic of its strategic approach.

In Western companies, implementing such rapid changes is often challenging due to the bureaucratic procedures involved. Even when the need for urgent change is recognised, the time to navigate through various administrative processes can be considerable. This contrast highlights the unique agility that Huawei possesses, allowing it to swiftly adapt to the evolving landscape of the industry and capitalise on emerging opportunities.

Fourthly, by launching its product ahead of schedule, effectively pre-empting the release of Apple's iPhone 15, Huawei has strategically positioned itself to gain an earlier mover advantage. This move aligns with a key aspect of Chinese strategic thinking known as competitor orientation.

By proactively entering the market before its leading competitor, Huawei has seized the opportunity to capture the attention and interest of consumers before they are exposed to Apple's offering. This strategic manoeuvre allows Huawei to establish a strong presence and potentially attract customers who may have otherwise opted for the competing iPhone 15.

This competitor-orientated approach demonstrates Huawei's astute understanding of the importance of timing and market dynamics. By gaining an early foothold, Huawei can potentially shape consumer perceptions and preferences, leveraging this advantage to solidify its position in the market.

Fifthly, this strategic move by Huawei is a manifestation of Chinese dialect from a perspective of Chinese strategic thinking. In the Western context, many companies facing the kind of restrictions, curbing, and containment that Huawei has endured for three years would likely succumb to the pressure and surrender their advanced technologies, such as Huawei's 5G, to the control of the powerful entities, such as the US government, that seek to dominate the technological landscape.

However, Huawei has chosen a different path. Rather than succumbing to the threats and restrictive policies imposed upon it, the company has transformed these challenges into opportunities. Instead of relinquishing its technological advancements, Huawei has responded by investing even more in new technologies and products. This proactive approach has led to the development and release of substitute technologies, such as Huawei's HarmonyOS4, which has reached a mature stage of development.

Huawei's ability to navigate and adapt in the face of adversity showcases its resilience and determination. By leveraging these circumstances, the company has not only preserved its technological prowess but has also managed to create viable alternatives to the dominant US technologies. This demonstrates Huawei's commitment to innovation and its capacity to turn challenges into driving forces for progress.

Finally, Huawei firmly holds the belief that it possesses the moral high ground, the *Tao*, for conducting business, rooted in its commitment to developing cutting-edge technologies, such as 5G, for the betterment of humanity. The company strives to make these advanced technologies accessible to a wide range of customers at affordable prices. Unfortunately, Huawei has found itself targeted by the US government, which has exerted pressure on the company to surrender the technology under its jurisdiction. Nevertheless, Huawei's unswerving determination to resist these pressures and restrictions, no matter how challenging they may be, stems from its firm grasp on the principles and values associated with its mission.

## NOTES

1.  Tzu, L. (2003). *Tao Te Ching* (J. Star, Trans. and Comm.). Penguin, p. 34.
2.  Te means moral principles or character.
3.  Tzu (n 1) p. 64.
4.  Mott, W.H. and Kim, J.C. (2006). *The Philosophy of Chinese Military Culture*. Palgrave Macmillan, p. 16.
5.  Ibid., p. 17.
6.  Tzu (n 1) p. 55.
7.  Mott and Kim (n 4) p. 17.
8.  Tzu (n 1) p. 4.
9.  Liu, A. (2010). *The Huainanzi* (J.S. Major, S.A. Queen, A.S. Meyer and H.D. Roth, Trans. and Ed.). New York: Columbia University Press, p. 584.
10. Sawyer, R.D. (1993). *The Seven Military Classics of Ancient China*. Westview Press, Inc, p. 158.
11. Hong, B. (2011). *Tian Jian (Heavenly Sword)*. Chinese Social Science Publisher, pp. 101–3.
12. Tzu (n 1) p. 38.
13. Ren, Z.G. (2013). *Wei Shen Mo Shi Mao Zedong? (Why Is Mao Zedong?)*. Guang Ming Daily Publisher, p. 3.
14. Clark, D. (2016). *Alibaba: The House that Jack Ma Built*, HarperCollins Publishers, p. 212.
15. Ibid., p. xiv.
16  Tzu (n 1) p. 54.
17. Schwartz, B. (1985). *The World of Thought in Ancient China*. Harvard University Press, pp. 350–82.
18. Fung, Y.L. (1962). *The Spirit of Chinese Philosophy* (E.R. Hughes, Trans.). Routledge, p. 4.
19. Ibid.
20. *Tao Te Ching* consists of two sections: Section One including Chapters 1–37 is known as the 'Tao *Classic*' and Section Two comprising Chapters 38–81 is termed the 'Te *Classic*'.
21. Fung (n 18) p. 11.
22. Tzu (n 1) p. 51.
23. Wee, C.H. (1993). 'Application of Military Strategies to Business: Why They Are More Relevant to Japanese than to American Companies', *The International Executives*, 35 (2), pp. 95–124.
24. Peffer, N. (1968). *The Far East: A Modern History*. The University of Michigan Press, p. 399.
25. Yu, X., Zhang, P. and Zheng, Y. (2015). Corporate Governance, Political Connections, and Intra-Industry Effects: Evidence from Corporate Scandals in China. *Financial Management*, 44(1), pp. 49–80.
26. People's Daily Online (2022). Chinese Securities Regulatory Commission (CSRC): In 2021, A Total of 609 Cases Were Processed, with Frequent

Occurrences of Major Fraud and Falsification. *People's Daily Online*, www
.finance.people.com.cn, 21 February 2022. Retrieved on 25 August 2023.

27.   Thomas, T.L. (2007). The Chinese Military's Strategic Mind-Set. *Military Review*, 87(6), pp. 47–55.
28.   Liu (n 9) p. 612.
29.   Sawyer, R.D. (2012). *Strategies for the Human Realm: Crux of the T'ai-pai Yin-ching*. Amazon.co.uk Ltd., Marston Gate, p. 50.
30.   Freedman, L. (2013). *Strategy: A History.* Oxford University Press, pp. 43–4.
31.   Wheeler, E.L. (1988). *Stratagem and the Vocabulary of Military Trickery*. E.J. Brill, p. 3.
32.   Ibid., pp. 5–10.
33.   Freedman (n 30) p. 43.
34.   Han Feizi, also known as Master Han, is a distinguished appellation bestowed upon Han Fei, an eminent Chinese philosopher who made significant contribution to the School of Legalism. The profound insights and teachings of Han Fei have been meticulously compiled by Burton Watson, resulting in the renowned work: *Han Feizi: Basic Writings*, B. Watson (Trans., 2003). New York: Columbia University Press.
35.   *Guiguzi* (鬼谷子), which translates to 'The Sage of Ghost Valley', is an ancient Chinese treatise that originated during the late Warring States period (475–221 BC) and extended until the end of the Han Dynasty (221 BC). Comprising approximately 6000 to 7000 Chinese characters, this work delves into the art of political manoeuvring, showcasing the principles of Taoist thinking. It is widely believed that the Guiguzi is an amalgamate of writings contributed by multiple authors, curated under the name of Master Guiguzi. Throughout history, this enigmatic figure has been revered as the mentor to numerous renowned political lobbyists and strategists.
36.   Griffith, S.B. (1963). *Sun Tzu: The Art of War*, Translated and with an Introduction by Samuel B. Griffith and a Foreword by B.H. Liddell Hart. Oxford University Press, p. 115.
37.   Jullien, F. (2004). *A Treatise on Efficacy: Between Western and Chinese Thinking* (J. Lloyd, Trans.). Honolulu: University of Hawaii Press, p. 17.
38.   Ibid., p. 165.
39.   Sawyer, R.D. (2007). *The Tao of Deception: Unorthodox Warfare in Historic and Modern China*. New York: Basic Books.
40.   Sawyer (n 10) p. 161.
41.   Sawyer (n 39) p. 57.
42.   Halberstam, D. (2007). *The Coldest Winter: America and the Korean War*. Macmillan, pp. 401–2.
43.   Jacob Stokes (2015). China's Road Rules: Beijing Looks West Toward Eurasian Integration. *Foreign Affairs*, April 19, 2015.
44.   Griffith (n 36) p. 152.
45.   Sawyer (n 39) pp. 58–9.

46. Cordesman, A.H. (2014). *Chinese Strategy and Military Power in 2014: Chinese, Japanese, Korean, Taiwanese and the US Perspectives*. Rowman & Littlefield, p. 119.
47. Griffith (n 36) pp. 96–7.
48. Ibid., p. 161.
49. Sawyer, R.D. (2004). *The Essence of War*. Westview Press, Inc., p. 220.
50. Sawyer (n 39) p. 58.
51. Daniel, D.C. and Herbig, K.L. (1981). *Strategic Military Deception*. Pergamon Press Inc.
    Lloyd, M. (1996). *The Art of Military Deception*. Pen and Sword.
52. Sawyer (n 10) p. 161.
53. Johansson, J.K. and Nonaka, I. (1996). *Relentless: The Japanese Way of Marketing*. Butterworth Heinemann, pp. 93–4.
54. Deshpande, R., Farley, J.U. and Webster, F.E. (1993). Corporate Culture, Customer Orientation, and Innovativeness in Japanese Firms: A Quadrad Analysis. *Journal of Marketing*, 57(1), pp. 23–37.
55. Pye, L.W. and Leites, N. (1982). Nuances in Chinese Political Culture. *Asian Survey*, 22(12), pp. 1147–65.
56. Sawyer (n 39) p. 59.
57. Sawyer (n 10) p. 167.
58. Christensen, C. M., Ojomo, E., and Dillon, K. (2021). Cracking Frontier Markets. *Harvard Business Review*, January/February, p. 90. https://hbr.org/2019/01/cracking-frontier-markets. Retrieved on 27 August 2023.
59. Griffith (n 36) p. 100.
60. Nixon, R.M. (1983). *Leaders.* Simon & Schuster, p. 226.
61. Yang, S.L. (2013). *Huawei Kao Shenme* (*On What Huawei Relies*). China CITIC Press, pp. 14–15.
62. Jullien (n 37) p. 1.
63. Ibid., pp. 4–5.
64. Ibid., p. 15.
65. Ames, R.T. (1994). *The Art of Rulership*. State University of New York Press, p. 68.
66. Griffith (n 36) p. 140.
67. Sawyer (n 10) p. 70.
68. Xue, Juzheng (2013). *Shi Sheng Xue* (*Studies on Achieving Victory through Shi*) (translated and commented by Ma Shuquan). Modern Publishing Media Ltd Inc.
69. Jullien, F. (1995). *The Propensity of Things: Toward a History of Efficacy in China* (J. Lloyd, Trans.). Cambridge, MA: Zone Books. Distributed by MIT Press, p. 10.
70. Ibid., p. 2.
71. Ames (n 65) p. 68.
72. Mott and Kim (n 4) p. 17.
73. Ibid., p. 18.
74. Griffith (n 36) p. 96.

75.   Jullien (n 37) pp. 17–18.
76.   Griffith (n 36) p. 138.
77.   Ibid., p. 142.
78.   Kissinger, H.A. (2011). *On China*. Penguin Press, p. 30.
79.   Ibid.
80.   Liu (n 9) p. 597.
81.   Mott and Kim (n 4) p. 107.
82.   Nolan, Peter (1994). The China Puzzle: 'Touching Stones to Cross the River'. *Challenge*, 37(1), pp. 25–31.
83.   Naughton, Barry (1993). Deng Xiaoping: The Economist. *The China Quarterly*, 135 (Special Issue: Deng Xiaoping: An Assessment), pp. 491–514.
84.   Liu (n 9) p. 575.
85.   Kissinger (n 78) p. 30.
86.   Hong, B. (2011). *Tian Jian (Heavenly Sword)*. Chinese Social Science Publisher, p. 136.
87.   Kissinger (n 78) pp. 367–71.
88.   Clark (n 14) p. 173.
89.   Nakamura, H. (1988). *The Ways of Thinking of Eastern Peoples*. New York: Greenwood Press.
      Peng, K. and Nisbett, R.E. (1999). Culture, Dialectics, and Reasoning About Contradiction. *American Psychologist*, 54, pp. 741–54.
      Norenzayan, A. and Nisbett, R.E. (2000). Culture and Causal Cognition. *Current Directions in Psychological Science*, 9(4), pp. 132–5.
      Liu, S.H. (1974). The Use of Analogy and Symbolism in Traditional Chinese Philosophy. *Journal of Chinese Philosophy*, 1, pp. 313–38.
90.   Wong, W.C. (2006). Understanding Dialectical Thinking from a Cultural–Historical Perspective. *Philosophical Psychology*, 19(2), pp. 239–60.
91.   Wilhelm, Richard (2003). *I Ching or Book of Changes*, translated by Richard Wilhelm with a forward by C.G. Jung. Penguin Books, p. xlvii.
92.   *Yinyang jia* is also rendered into English as 'School of Naturalists', 'Interrelation of Heaven and Man', or 'Correlative Cosmology'.
93.   Fung (n 18) p. 82.
94.   Wong (n 90) pp. 239–60.
95.   Fung (n 18) p. 89.
96.   Peng and Nisbett (n 89) pp. 741–54.
97.   Spencer-Rodgers, J., Williams, M.J., and Peng, K. (2010). Cultural Differences in Expectations of Change and Tolerance for Contradiction: A Decade of Empirical Research. *Personality and Social Psychology Review*, 14(3), pp. 296–312.
98.   Peng and Nisbett (n 96) pp. 741–54.
99.   Ibid.
100.  Tzu (n 1) p. 55.
101.  Nisbett, R.E. (2003). *The Geography of Thought: How Asians and Westerners Think Differently ... and Why*. New York: Free Press, p. 27.
102.  Ibid.

103. Rothkopf, David (2015). The Middle East's Pivot to Asia. *Foreign Policy*, April 24, 2015.
104. Mao Z., (1937). On Practice. *Selected Works of Mao Tse-tung: Volumes I*, 1965, Peking: Foreign Languages Press, p. 297.
105. Ibid., p. 58.
106. Spencer-Rodgers et al. (n 97) pp. 296–312.
107. Varnum, M., Grossmann, I., Kitayama, S., and Nisbett, R. (2010). The Origin of Cultural Differences in Cognition: The Social Orientation Hypothesis. *Current Directions in Psychological Science*, 19(1), pp. 9–13.
108. Nisbett, R.E., Peng, K., Choi, I. and Norenzayan, A. (2001). Culture and Systems of Thought: Holistic Versus Analytic Cognition. *Psychological Review*, 108(2), pp. 291–310.
109. Peng and Nisbett (n 96) pp. 741–54.
110. Spencer-Rodgers et al. (n 97) pp. 296–312.
111. Nisbett et al. (n 108) pp. 291–310.
112. Lin, Y.T. (1976). *The Wisdom of Taotse*. Edited and with an Introduction by Lin Yutang, New York: The Modern Library, p. 191.
113. Sawyer (n 10) pp. 157–8.
114. Ibid., p. 162.
115. Sawyer, R.D. (2004). *The Essence of War*. Westview Press, Inc., p. 113.
116. Ibid., p. 213.
117. Ibid., p. 226.
118. Tse, E., Ma, K. and Huang, Y. (2009). *Shan Zhai*: A Chinese Phenomenon. *Perspective*, Booz & Co.
119. Peng, K., Spencer-Rogers, J. and Nian, Z. (2006). Naïve Dialecticism and the Tao of Chinese Thought. In Kim, U., Yang, K. and Hwang, K. (ed), *Indigenous and Cultural Psychology: Understanding People in Context*, New York, NY: Springer, pp. 247–62.
120. De Cremer, David and Zhang, Jess (2014). Huawei to the Future. *Business Strategy Review*, 25(1), pp. 26–9.
121. Tian, T. and Wu, C.B. (2012). *Xia yi ge dao xia de hui bu hui shi Huawei? (Is Huawei Falling down next?)*. China CITIC Press, p. 73.
122. Yan, J.J. and Hu, Y. (2000). *Haier: Zhong Guo Zao (Haier: Made in China)*. Hainan Publisher, p. 112.
123. Several factors have been attributed to the untimely downfall of the Qin Dynasty. One significant factor was the uprising spearheaded by two commoners, Chen Sheng and Wu Guang, who were peasants or farmers. Their uprising dealt a severe blow to the military forces of the Qin Dynasty and ignited a fervent rebellion that rapidly spread throughout the nation. This event played a pivotal role in the demise of the Qin Dynasty, leaving an indelible mark on Chinese history.
124. Tian and Wu (n 121) pp. 163–4.
125. Lieberman, M.B. and Montgomery, D.B. (1988). First-Mover Advantages. *Strategic Management Journal*, 9(5), pp. 41–8.

Kerin, R.A, Varadarajan, P.R. and Peterson, R.A. (1992). First-Mover Advantage: A Synthesis, Conceptual Framework, and Research Propositions. *Journal of Marketing*, 56(4), pp. 33–52.

Robinson, W.T. and Chiang, J. (2002). Product Development Strategies for Established Market Pioneers, Early Followers, and Late Entrants. *Strategic Management Journal*, 23, pp. 855–66.

126. Shamsie, J., Phelps, C. and Kuperman, J. (2004). Better Late Than Never: A Study of Late Entrants in Household Electrical Equipment. *Strategic Management Journal*, 25(1), pp. 69–84.

127. Kerin et al. (n 125) pp. 33–52.

128. Yang, H.Y., Ma, J.J. and Chattopadhyay, A. (2021). How Xiaomi Became an Internet-of-Things Powerhouse. *Harvard Business Review*, April 26. https:// hbr.org/2021/04/how-xiaomi-became-an-internet-of-things-powerhouse. Retrieved on 5 September 2023.

129. Company's website: https://www.mi.com/global/about/. Retrieved on 5 September 2023.

130. Yoo, J. W., Choi, Y. (2005). Resource Substitution: Why an Effective Late-Mover Strategy? *Journal of Management Research*, 5(2), pp. 91–100.

McEvily, S.K., Das, S. and McCabe, K. (2000). Avoiding Competence Substitution through Knowledge Sharing. *Academy of Management Review*, 25, pp. 294–311.

131. Narver, J.C. and Slater, S.F. (1990). The Effect of a Market Orientation on Business Profitability. *Journal of Marketing*, (October), pp. 20–35.

132. Doz, Y. and Kosonen, M. (2008). The Dynamics of Strategic Agility: Nokia's Rollercoaster Experience. *California Management Review*, 50(3), pp. 95–118.

Doz, Y. and Kosonen, M. (2010). Embedding Strategic Agility: A Leadership Agenda for Accelerating Business Model Renewal. *Long Range Planning*, 43(2–3), pp. 370–82.

Lewis, M.W., Andriopoulos, C. and Smith, W.K. (2014). Paradoxical Leadership to Enable Strategic Agility. *California Management Review*, 56(3), pp. 58–77.

Sull, D. (2009). Competing Through Organizational Agility. *McKinsey Quarterly*, December, pp. 1–9.

133. American journalist and writer, Harrison Salisbury, has described and praised the Long March and the 'crossing the Red River four times'. Salisbury, H. (1985). *The Long March: The Untold Story*. Macmillan.

134. Tzu (n 1) p. 43.

135. Ibid., p. 76.

136. Li, Feng (2020), *Jue zhan chao xian* (*Showdown in Korea*), Contemporary Publishing House, p. 220.

137. Griffith (n 36) p. 153.

138. Ibid., p. 78.

139. Liu (n 9) p. 60.

140. Sawyer (n 10) p. 292.

141. Ibid., p. 169.
142. Mao, Z. (1936). Problems of Strategy in China's Revolutionary War. *Selected Military Writings of Mao Tse-tung*. Peking: Foreign Languages Press, pp. 71–150.
143. Mao, Z. (1938). Problems of War and Strategy. *Selected Military Writings of Mao Tse-tung*. Peking: Foreign Languages Press, pp. 267–83.
144. Tzu (n 1) p. 37.
145. Ibid., p. 57.
146. Ibid., p. 77.
147. Clark (n 14) pp. 29–32.

# 4.   Chinese stratagem culture

*Love and war are the same thing, and stratagems and policy are as allowable in the one as in the other.*
– Miguel de Cervantes

*It aren't what you don't know that gets you into trouble. It's what you know for sure that just aren't so.*
– Mark Twain

*Although deceit is detestable in all other things, yet in the conduct of war it is laudable and honourable; and a commander who vanquishes an enemy by stratagem is equally praised with one who gains victory by force.*
– Niccolò Machiavelli

## STRATAGEM AS A CULTURAL PHENOMENON

In China, there is a widespread understanding that the Chinese populace, throughout history, has demonstrated certain cultural characteristics in their thinking and behaviour that closely resemble those observed in military personnel when it comes to strategising for warfare. This phenomenon is commonly referred to as stratagem culture.[1] Chinese individuals, for instance, are often inclined to be wary of others[2] and tend to adopt an indirect method of communication, and employing strategies like 'strategic detours'[3] and 'misdirecting competitors'[4] in their social and business interactions.

In 1894, Arthur Smith, an American missionary, made an observation regarding people's lack of trust in one another:

> There are said to be two reasons why people do not trust one another: first, because they do not know one another, and second, because they do. The Chinese think that they have each of these reasons for mistrust, and they act accordingly.[5]

Throughout Chinese imperial history, a recurring pattern emerged where one dynasty would replace another in a cyclical fashion.[6] This process often involved stratagem battles, with the victorious party ultimately claiming the Chinese throne. Harrison Salisbury, a distinguished American journalist renowned for documenting China's Long March, summarises the events that unfolded between 16 October 1934 and 1 October 1949, when the People's Republic of China was established.

> China's stage was filled with heroism, tragedy, intrigue, bloodletting, treachery, cheap opera, military genius, political guile, moral goals, spiritual objectives, and human hatred. Shakespeare could not have written such a story. It is not yet finished. Perhaps it never will be.[7]

It has also been observed that, historically, individuals or groups who emerged victorious in military, political, and commercial arenas were often those who displayed adeptness in employing strategic tactics and manoeuvres. The utilisation of stratagems played a significant role in their success.[8]

Recognised as the progenitor of military strategy,[9] Sun Tzu's *Art of War* has left an indelible mark on the historical landscape of China[10] and has exerted a substantial influence on numerous Asian countries.[11] Central to this treatise are the discourses on stratagem, which have shaped the cultural phenomenon of utilising strategic deception within Chinese society. However, this phenomenon has often been overlooked or misunderstood by Western academics and practitioners.

Ralph Sawyer, a renowned American expert in Chinese warfare, presents an insightful exploration of Chinese stratagem in his seminal work, *The Tao of Deception: Unorthodox Warfare in Historic and Modern China*. In the book, Sawyer highlights, documents, analyses, and offers commentary on Chinese stratagems. Drawing from his extensive knowledge and expertise, he unravels the intricate web of strategic techniques employed throughout China's rich history, elucidating their underlying principles and applications. By examining historic and modern instances of unorthodox warfare, Sawyer unveils the timeless wisdom encapsulated within Chinese stratagems.

The illumination provided by Sawyer's analysis of Sun Tzu's perspective on stratagem is insightful. He delineates a topic that has mystified many who have grappled with Sun Tzu's monumental definition. The concept of unorthodox warfare, according to Sawyer, has often appeared shrouded in tactical opacity and conceptual obscurity deliberately cloaked in fog and darkness. However, he astutely points out that some individuals have mistakenly perceived it as mere simplicity, reducing it to do the notion of 'doing the opposite of what is expected'.[12]

Sawyer goes on to remark on the deep effect of the unorthodox on the realm of military affairs. While ordinary commanders may have been satisfied with a basic understanding or application of conventional tactics, he highlights the distinction found in extraordinary generals. These exceptional leaders, driven by imagination and inspiration, embrace the unorthodox with steady determination. They fearlessly employ unconventional strategies and unexpected methods, defying conventional wisdom and prevailing against all odds to secure resounding victories in seemingly impossible circumstances.[13]

In Western societies, there has been a growing recognition of the relevance of game theory, a branch of social science that deals with strategic decision making, not only in business but also in social interactions.[14] However, it differs from Chinese stratagem in certain aspects. In the West, the practice of strategic thinking based on game theory has evolved into a scientific discipline or profession that has witnessed substantial impact on various fields, including in industrial organisations, accounting, finance, marketing, law, and political sciences.[15] The knowledge and application of game theory is principally limited to a relatively small group of professionals or specialists.

In contrast, Chinese stratagem has undergone a notable evolution spanning four millennia, establishing itself as a cultural phenomenon deeply ingrained in all aspects of life. The practice of stratagems dates back 4000 years to the era of the legendary Yellow Emperor, and its legacy has been preserved through documented works such as the *Questions and Replies between T'ang T'ai-tsung and Li Wei-kung*, which is one of the *Seven Military Classics of Ancient China*. This text affirms that the study of the art of war had been examined and refined from the time of the Yellow Emperor, prior to 2070 BC, and onwards. It emphasises the importance of adhering to conventional principles before employing unconventional strategies, and prioritises virtues such as benevolence and righteousness, while also recognising the significance of power balance and craftiness in later stages.[16]

Ralph Sawyer has observed the existence of a variant form of stratagem culture known as 'martial culture' during the Warring States period around 475 BC.[17]

The widespread adoption of stratagem as a cultural phenomenon indicates its extensive use among the general population.[18] Chinese strategic thinking, which revolves around a competitor-orientated mindset, views the practice of stratagem as a form of game-playing within the realms of warfare or social interactions. It involves the utilisation of tactics such as deceptions, surprises, detours, risk-taking, and the potential outcomes of victory or defeat. In many instances, individuals involved in these strategic endeavours derive pleasure or become deeply engrossed in the act of playing and strategising.

In the Chinese literary masterpiece *Romance of the Three Kingdoms*, we witness the application of various stratagems by ancient Chinese generals. These stratagems often involved elements of deception, risk-taking, and surprise, with potential consequences that could be advantageous or detrimental. A prominent example from the story is the renowned strategist Zhuge Liang, who employed a clever tactic of capturing and releasing the barbarian tribal leader Meng Huo seven times. This strategy aimed to soften Meng Huo's heart and ultimately transform him into a friendly ally.

However, unlike the scientific approach of game theory in the West, the utilisation of stratagem in China is rooted in the art of war and the notion of game-playing. It relies on a wealth of experience-based principles and proven stratagems rather than a strict scientific framework. One well-known compilation of such stratagems is *The Thirty-Six Stratagems*, an ancient treatise that exemplifies stratagems successfully employed in the realms of warfare, politics, and civil relations.

Over the centuries, the Chinese game-playing mindset has evolved alongside stratagem culture. From antiquity, originally viewed as pastimes, games have become deeply ingrained in Chinese society, serving as both a source of entertainment and a platform for strategic contemplation. Two notable board games, *Wei Qi* (or Go) and Chinese chess, have been invented by the Chinese people, capturing their fascination and ingenuity.

*Wei Qi,* in particular, possesses a design that resonates with Chinese holistic thinking. Those who embrace a holistic mindset can fully appreciate the underlying principles and complexities of the game. Conversely, individuals who lack this holistic thinking or are unfamiliar with its principles are more prone to falling into traps and making strategic errors.[19]

In line with the perspective of Sun Tzu, Liu Bowen, a prominent Chinese strategist from the Ming Dynasty (1368–1644), synthesised ancient strategies and concluded that the utilisation of stratagem should prioritise considering all available options as the optimal approach to conducting warfare.[20] This echoes the belief that a comprehensive understanding of the battlefield, along with a flexible and adaptable mindset, is crucial for success in military endeavours.

## FORMATION OF CHINESE STRATAGEM CULTURE

The term 'culture' has been a subject of intense debate and defies easy definition.[21] As early as 1871, a definition of culture for social science emerged,[22] but its elusive nature has made it a challenging concept to grasp, known as 'one of the spongiest words in social science'.[23] In fact, the term 'culture' has been described as one of the most complex and ambiguous words in the English language.[24]

Throughout history, numerous definitions of culture have been proposed. In 1952, two American anthropologists, Kroeber and Kluckhohn, compiled a collection of as many as 164 definitions of culture.[25] This demonstrates the difficulty in pinning down a precise and universally accepted understanding of culture.

Similarly, the term 'subculture' has been the subject of ongoing debate and critique.[26] While it has been in use for a significant period of time, its various definitions have sparked heated discussions among scholars.[27] However, the aim of this chapter is not to scrutinise the intricacies of defining culture or subculture. Instead, it seeks to incorporate relevant concepts and apply them to explore the existence and pervasive nature of stratagem culture within Chinese society, which can be considered a subculture of Chinese culture. Furthermore, it aims to discuss the strategic implications that this subculture holds for decision-makers in the Western world.

The initial definition of culture can be rephrased as following: Culture encompasses a set of fundamental elements, including norms, values, beliefs, and expressive symbols.[28] It can be further described as the transmission and interconnectedness of meaningful systems such as values, ideas, and other symbolic representations, which influence human behaviour and the creation of artefacts resulting from that behaviour.[29]

Hofstede's perspective on culture characterises it as the collective programming of the mind that distinguishes one group or category of people from another.[30] In the context of business, culture contains shared values, shared understanding, shared assumptions, and shared goals that are acquired from previous generations, enforced by current society members, and passed on to future generations.[31] It provides individuals with a sense of identity, belonging, guidance for behaviour, and a framework for determining their actions.[32]

A previous definition of subculture can be reworded as follows: Subculture refers to distinctive culture expressions exhibited by specific segments of the population. These subcultures exist as distinct realms within the broader context of our national culture.[33]

According to Fine and Kleinman, subculture can be defined as a collection of shared understandings, behaviours, and artefacts that are utilised by specific groups and disseminated through interconnected group networks. This concept serves to (1) elucidate how cultural elements can permeate a population at large, (2) account for localised variations in cultural content resulting from interactive negotiations within group settings, and (3) facilitate an understanding of the dynamics involved in subcultural evolution and transformation.[34]

Clark has provided a critique of the existing research on subculture. In many instances, where sociologists have extensively utilised the concept of subculture, they have either assumed, implied, or elaborated on a theoretical framework that explains the origins and dynamics of the subculture. These theories can generally be classified into two categories based on whether the development is considered to be endogenous or exogenous. However, only a limited number of authors have attempted to offer a comprehensive explanation as to why subcultures, in general, emerge and endure.[35]

This section aims to explore the nature of stratagem culture in China by probing its origins, continuity, and evolution.

Figure 4.1 illustrates a model depicting the development of Chinese stratagem culture. It highlights three fundamental components: historical drivers and the crystallisation of stratagem concepts, the dissemination of these con-

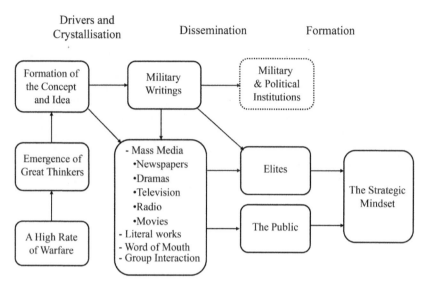

*Figure 4.1    A model of the formation of Chinese stratagem culture*

cepts, and the subsequent diffusion and formation of the culture. The historical drivers give rise to the stratagem ideas, which are then refined and solidified by notable thinkers into military writings. These writings, recognised for their practicality and value, are subsequently disseminated and diffused through multiple channels, initially reaching Chinese elites and then gradually permeating the general public through mass media, popular literature, and the theatrical performances. Ultimately, this widespread exposure leads to the establishment and flourishing of stratagem culture.

## DRIVERS AND CRYSTALLISATION

The extensive practice of stratagem in China has its roots in ancient times. The emergence of strategic thinking and writings relies on two crucial factors: a substantial prevalence of warfare and the presence of exceptional thinkers and writers capable of distilling, summarising, and crystallising the ideas born from these conflicts. A Chinese proverb vividly captures this phenomenon, stating that a person who endures a prolonged illness becomes an expert in medicine. Similarly, a significant frequency of warfare incidents creates a fertile environment for the development of strategic thinking.

Chinese history provides evidence of these conditions, with 1109 noteworthy military conflicts occurring between the Chinese and northern nomadic tribes from 215 BC to 1684 AD. Furthermore, between 210 BC and 1900 AD, there were 225 887 recorded instances of armed rebellions.[36] Another source indicates the presence of as many as 3790 wars, encompassing conflicts with foreign invaders and domestic rebels, spanning from 1100 BC to 1911 AD.[37]

Ralph Sawyer observes that 'virtually every year witnessed a major battle somewhere in China, significant conflicts erupted nearly every decade, and the nation was consumed by inescapable warfare at least once a century'.[38]

The era of substantial warfare in China coincided with the emergence of numerous influential military and philosophical thinkers who have indelibly shaped Chinese history. Among them, notable figures include Lu Shang (789–859 BC), Sun Wu (545–470 BC), Wu Qi (440–381 BC), Bai Qi (221–206 BC), Han Xin (206 BC–25 AD), Ban Chao (32–102 AD), Zhuge Liang (220–280), Liu Yu (420–581), Li Shiming (598–649), Yue Fei (1103–1142), Genghis Khan (1162–1227), Liu Bowen (1311–1375), Yuan Chonghuan (1584–1630), and many others.

Simultaneously, the Spring and Autumn (770–476 BC), as well as Warring States Periods (476–221 BC), witnessed a flourishing of great philosophical thinkers such as Lao Tzu, Confucius, Mencius, Guan Tzu, Mo Tzu, and many more. Consequently, these periods are commonly referred to as the era of the 'hundred schools of thought'. It is important to note that these thinkers also made significant contributions to military thinking and writings.

The philosophers of that time were inevitably compelled to grapple with military matters for two primary reasons. Firstly, the prevailing conflicts between different states manifested in the form of warfare. As all philosophies engaged in discussions concerning rulers' *Tao* (the Way or strategy) as a central philosophical concern, they could not evade contemplating and philosophising about the military affairs, politics, and economics, since these topics were intricately interconnected and inseparable.

Secondly, battles and wars themselves encompassed a wealth of dialectical phenomena that often provided relevant materials for making philosophical arguments.[39] These philosophers recognised the philosophical implications inherent in the complexities of warfare and sought to draw insights and lessons from these experiences to support and develop their philosophical viewpoints. Thus, military events and strategies became integral components of their philosophical discourse, enriching the overall philosophical landscape of the time.

Lao Tzu's *Tao Te Ching* contains substantial military insights, evident in numerous chapters of the classic. More than 10 chapters directly address military matters, while over 20 chapters possess indirect implications that can inform military decision-making. Lao Tzu's approach to military teachings differs from, or at times complements, the perspectives presented by Sun Tzu.[40]

The contributions of these thinkers extend beyond their own eras, shaping Chinese military thinking and written works. Subsequent dynastic periods witnessed the development of military writings and practices, accumulating and enhancing knowledge that enabled organisations and individuals to effectively pursue their strategic objectives. This valuable knowledge and belief system has been transmitted from generation to generation, preserving their relevance and applicability to the present day.

Ancient China gave rise to a substantial collection of Chinese literature from political and military thinkers who probed strategies and tactics. These writings, spanning over two millennia, have left a lasting impact. One of the earliest known works is the *Zuo Zhuan*, also referred to as *Tso Chuan* in traditional spelling (左传). Serving as both a narrative history and a literary masterpiece, this remarkable piece covers the period from 722 BC to 468 BC. During the West Zhou Dynasty (1046–771 BC), texts such as the *Military Annals* (军志) and the *Military Administration* (军政) existed, but unfortunately, they were lost during subsequent turbulent dynastic transitions.[41]

The periods known as the Spring and Autumn and the Warring States were marked by a surge in military writings in ancient China. However, during the Qin Dynasty, Emperor Qin Shi Huang issued a decree to burn most 'unorthodox' publications. This act was intended to suppress dissenting thought and voices, famously known in history as 'burning Confucian books and burying Confucian scholars'. Despite this tragic event, a considerable number of military books managed to escape destruction and were preserved.

During the reign of Emperor Cheng of Han (51–7 BC), a book titled the '*Seven Strategies*' was published, containing a volume called '*On the Art of War*'. This volume provided detailed insights into 63 schools of military methods.[42] In a study conducted in 2002, it was discovered that a total of 3380 books, comprising 23 503 recorded volumes, were published in ancient China, covering various aspects of military strategy, tactics, and organisation.[43]

From this extensive body of military literature, two emperors of the Song Dynasty (960–1279) ordered the compilation and selection of seven books to serve as standard military textbooks. These seven selected works came to be known as the *Seven Military Classics of Ancient China*, or *Wu Jing Qi Shu* ( 武经七书) in Chinese. They became mandatory reading materials at military academies and constituted essential knowledge for aspiring to senior military positions in ancient China.

Among all the classics, Sun Tzu's work stands out as the most comprehensive and influential in the realm of Chinese military literature. However, it is important to note that other thinkers and classics have also made significant contributions in this field. In Andrew Meyer's commentary on *The Dao of the Military: Liu An's Art of War*, he illuminates this subject.

While Sun Tzu remains the most exceptional surviving work, it is just a part of a vast collection of military texts from that era. The *Wuzi, Weiliaozi, Sima fa, Taigong liutao*, and *Huangshigong lüe* are some of the other surviving texts that explore military strategies and tactics. Additionally, composite texts like the *Lüshi Chunqiu* and *Guanzi* offer valuable examples of this genre.

Moreover, beyond these known texts, the bibliographical treatises found in the imperial histories provide references to numerous military writings that have unfortunately been lost over time. This highlights the extensive body of literature on military affairs that existed in ancient China.[44]

Lü Shang, also known by the honorific title T'ai Kung, holds a prominent position among the esteemed contributors to Chinese military literature. Renowned as both ancient statesman and strategist, he is highly regarded for his exceptional abilities. Sima Qian, in his monumental work *Records of the Grand Historian*, which covers the period from prehistory (around 3000 BC) to the early Western Han Dynasty (206 BC–25 AD), states that Lü Shang's influence was significant in the political landscape of his time.

According to Sima Qian, the Chou dynasty had garnered the allegiance of two thirds of the realm. In this context, the plan and strategies devised by T'ai Kung played a pivotal role in this achievement. His outstanding insights and schemes occupied a major part in the success of the Chou dynasty's political and military endeavours.[45]

During ancient times in China, the general population faced significant barriers when it came to accessing military classics. The possession of these works carried a risk of being perceived as an intent for rebellion or overthrowing the ruling authority. One such example is T'ai Kung's *Six Secret Teachings*, which belonged to the Seven Classics. This particular text contained revolutionary advocacy and instructions, making its possession highly perilous in the eyes of rulers. Consequently, these works were exclusively available to individuals of high status, including emperors, feudal lords, dukes, princesses, officials, army officers, nobility, and affluent individuals and families.[46]

Initially, the principles of stratagem thinking and behaviour were primarily confined to an elite subculture. However, as time progressed, the notions of effectiveness and utility inherent in stratagem started to permeate major non-military spheres and written works. The influence of stratagem thinking extended to anyone who possessed literacy skills, gradually spreading its impact. This phenomenon led to the emergence of a stratagem-orientated culture during the Spring and Autumn period (770–476 BC), as observed in *The Analects,* a collection of teachings attributed to Confucius.

As Confucius conveys his observations:

> In ancient times, the common people had three weaknesses, but even those weaknesses cannot be reliably found in them today. In antiquity, people's untamed nature made them impatient with restrictions, whereas now their untamed nature leads them astray from the correct path. In ancient times, when people were conceited, they were resolute and unyielding, but nowadays, their conceit merely manifests

as a bad temper. In antiquity, when people were foolish, they were straightforward and honest, but now, in their foolishness, they have become cunning and deceitful.[47]

Han Feizi (c. 280–233 BC), an esteemed philosopher of ancient China, holds a prominent position as a key contributor to the Legalist doctrine. He perceptively observed that, during the closing stages of the Warring States period (221 BC), the citizens of various states engaged in extensive discussions on military matters. It is noteworthy that every household possessed copies of works authored by Sun Wu (Sun Tzu) and Wu Qi, reflecting the widespread importance attached to their teachings.[48]

A subcultural phenomenon encompasses several critical aspects that demand demarcation: size, specificity of boundaries, inclusiveness or identity, and the dynamics of boundary specificity.[49] When considering size, it is crucial for a subculture to maintain a balance where it wields influence without becoming large enough to dominate. The proportion of elites within the subculture remains a minority, even though they may possess significant control over power and wealth. Within the subculture, members commonly employed strategic manoeuvres, known as stratagems, to attain power, accumulate wealth, advance their careers, and navigate military and political conflicts.

In ancient China, key industries such as bronze, porcelain, china, iron- and copper-making, salt, and silk production were predominantly controlled by government officials, key subcultural group members.[50]

The specificity of boundaries within a subculture refers to the degree of clarity in distinguishing its distinct identity. In the context of ancient China, the elites were easily discernible from the 'ordinary' people due to notable characteristics such as their education and knowledge of ancient history and literature, as well as their possession of power and wealth. Education and knowledge formed the foundation, while power and wealth serve as motivations for the utilisation of stratagem. Inclusiveness or identity plays a significant role, as membership in the elite class is a defining aspect of their identity.

In ancient times, elite group members such as emperors, feudal lords, princesses, and officials, continuously contemplated and applied stratagems as an integral part of their lives. These activities served both defensive purposes, safeguarding against potential attacks, and offensive objectives, aiming to achieve specific positions of power or political and military influence.

The dynamics of boundary specificity denote the rigidity of identity boundaries and involve the origin and potential evolution of a subculture. In its early stages, access to military classics was restricted, primarily limited to a distinct group with privileged accessibility. However, with advancement of communication technologies and the relaxation of access restrictions, literary works containing stratagem ideas began to disseminate, expanding, and popularising stratagem concepts among the Chinese populace.

## DISSEMINATION AND FORMATION

In ancient times, mass media comprised various forms such as bamboo books, cloth scrolls, and paper manuscripts. Paper emerged after the Eastern Han period, spanning from 25 to 230 AD. Theatres also played a significant role by showcasing performances primarily based on historical narratives derived from sources like the *Tso Chuan* and *Records of the Great Historian (Shiji)*.[51] Additionally, the dissemination of information occurred through word of mouth.

As communication technologies advanced and literacy improved, the influence of ideas regarding stratagems gradually expanded among the public. Chinese culture, characterised by holistic thinking, seamlessly integrated military, philosophical, historical, and literary writings, making them indistinguishable from one another. Chinese military thought and writings not only reflected but also crystallised Chinese political, philosophical, and ethical perspectives, and vice versa.

Chinese military classics prominently showcase the principles of Confucian benevolence. The concept of leadership by benevolence is also espoused by *T'ai Kung*, one of ancient China's renowned strategists.[52] Numerous Chinese historical, literary, and philosophical classics encompass stratagem ideas, principles, and stories. Examples of such works include the *Tso Chuan*, *The Analects*, *Lao Tzu's Tao Te Ching*, *Twenty-four Histories*, *Romance of the Three Kingdoms*, *The Water Margin*, *Journey to the West*, *A Dream of Red Mansions*, and many more. These texts serve as repositories of strategic wisdom and ethical teachings, reflecting the multifaceted nature of Chinese culture and philosophy.

Chinese histories have played a momentous part in disseminating and popularising stratagem culture among a wide segment of the population. This is largely attributed to the extensive documentation and influence of Chinese historical accounts and lessons regarding the strategic use of tactics in political and military contexts. In contrast to their Western counterparts, the Chinese people place a greater emphasis on history and its significance.[53] Throughout the ages, history has served as a fundamental wellspring of literary works, contributing significantly to the development and shaping of Chinese culture.

Chinese history has been methodically recorded in meticulous detail through a combination of official annals and private historical records. In ancient China, a system was established wherein dedicated officials were appointed to capture and document significant speeches, statements, and events associated with the ruler and their dynasty. Initially, there were two distinct positions: the 'Left Historian' and the 'Right Historian'.

The role of the Left Historian involved recording the important speeches and utterances made by emperors, while the Right Historian was responsible for documenting significant events. This division of labour ensured a comprehensive record of both the words and actions of the ruling authority. However, as time went on, these two positions were consolidated into a single role known as the Grand Historian.

The *Twenty-four Histories*, an esteemed compilation of official Chinese annals, stands as the most authoritative and comprehensive source of traditional Chinese history and culture. Encompassing a vast timespan, from prehistory around 3000 BC to the conclusion of the Ming Dynasty in 1644, this collection offers invaluable insights into the development of Chinese civilisation. Following the end of imperial China in 1911, an additional work documenting the Qing Dynasty was included, completing the compilation known as the *Twenty-five Histories*.

These annals provide a meticulous account of the major events, principal historical figures and families, political systems, and cultural transformations that shaped China over the millennia. They serve as a vital resource for scholars, historians, political and military leaders, and enthusiasts and aspirational individuals seeking to understand the nation's rich historical legacy.

Apart from the official historical annals, a wide array of influential private sources of historical documentation and writings also exist. These texts include the *Spring and Autumn Annals* by Confucius, the *Tso Chuan*, the *Strategies of the Warring States*, the *Discourses of the States*, and the *Bamboo Annals*. These private sources offer unique perspectives and valuable details that complement the official records, contributing to a more comprehensive understanding of China's past.

The writing of history has played a considerable role in the development of Chinese culture, serving as a primary source of literature. Throughout China's history, both official and private historical writings have meticulously documented the application of stratagems in battles, wars, and political power struggles.

One example of a private historical and literary masterpiece is the *Tso Chuan*. This exceptional work provides a detailed account of battles and wars between different states, spanning from 722 to 468 BC. The *Tso Chuan* vividly portrays the people and events involved, capturing the essence of intrigues, treachery, and heroism that unfolded during this period.[54] Within its pages, more than 400 battles and wars are meticulously described, with a particular emphasis on the vital role played by stratagem in determining victories.

The *Tso Chuan*'s enduring value is evident in its recognition as an excellent book on military strategy and tactics. Many generals in later dynastic periods have praised its insights, utilising its lessons to inform their own military endeavours. By chronicling historical conflicts and strategic thinking employed, the Tso Chuan has preserved past events, offering invaluable information to understand and study historical political and military wisdom.

*The Analects,* one of the revered Confucian classics and among the world's best-selling books, was composed during the Spring and Autumn period (770–476 BC). Since 206 BC, it has exerted an immeasurable influence on Chinese history and culture, serving as mandatory reading for all the scholars and officials of China for over two millennia. Within its pages, Confucius places great emphasis on the importance of stratagem in leading an army. A dialogue between Confucius and one of his disciples, Tzu-lu, is recorded in *The Analects.* Tzu-lu posed a question to his master, asking whom he would choose to accompany him if he were to lead the Three Armies.

Confucius responded by stating that he would not select anyone who foolishly attempted to confront a tiger with bare hands or recklessly crossed treacherous rivers, risking their life without remorse. Rather, his choice would be a person who, when faced with a task, harboured a healthy fear of failure, yet possessed the ability to effectively execute plans. This individual would not only possess a fondness for devising strategies but also demonstrate the competence to bring them to fruition.[55] From Confucius's viewpoint, possessing the ability to apply stratagem was deemed more crucial than valour in order to qualify as a military commander.

A group of Chinese researchers conducted a research project, leading to the publication of a comprehensive book spanning 893 pages. This book focuses on the application of stratagem throughout Chinese history, specifically drawing from the *Twenty-five Histories.* Titled the *Complete Works of Stratagem from the Extraction of Twenty-five Histories,*[56] the book explores a wide range of historical events, encompassing a timeline from 3000 BC to 1911. Through their diligent efforts, the researchers extracted 94 stratagems from the recorded 1560 historical events within these esteemed classics. This noteworthy outcome underscores the influential nature of these historical works, as they contain a wealth of inspiring accounts that effectively demonstrate the utilisation of stratagem. Moreover, it highlights their significant role in disseminating and advocating the ideas of stratagem among non-military populations.

In the era known as the Three Kingdoms, the renowned epic known as the *Romance of the Three Kingdoms* showcases a plethora of strategic manoeuvres that are depicted with artistic and mystical flair, highlighting their pivotal role in battles, wars, and power struggles. This literary masterpiece stands as a comprehensive compendium of political and military stratagems, earning it well-deserved acclaim. Among the numerous examples that exemplify the dramatic implementation of these stratagems, one particular incident stands out, warranting high praise.

During a tumultuous conflict between the states of Wei and Shu, a detachment from the Wei army managed to infiltrate the Shu defence line, exploiting a strategic error made by a Shu general. This unexpected turn of events led Wei forces to the very gates of the Shu city, where the revered Shu general, Zhuge Liang, resided. Caught off guard and ill-prepared, Zhuge Liang found himself in a precarious situation, with only a handful of soldiers stationed around the city walls, and the impending threat of capture looming over him.

Exercising his cunning intellect, Zhuge Liang issued an order for the city gate to be left wide open and unguarded, save for a few elderly men who were tasked with the simple duty of clearing away fallen leaves. Perched atop the city gate, Zhuge Liang exuded an air of serenity as his nimble fingers danced across the strings of his zither, producing a soothing melody that resonated through the air. His composed demeanour in the face of perilous circumstances left the enemy's general with a lingering sense of unease. The conspicuous absence of visible military preparations led the enemy to harbour suspicions of a concealed ambush. Thus, the Wei army, erring on the side of caution, chose to retreat of its own accord. This renowned historical event is known as the illustrious demonstration of the 'empty-city stratagem'.

Renowned statesman Henry Kissinger has drawn a parallel between Mao Zedong and Zhuge Liang, praising Mao as an embodiment of the masterful manoeuvring exhibited by the ancient strategist. Kissinger recognised Mao's adeptness in employing strategic tactics, akin to the brilliance demonstrated by Zhuge Liang himself.[57]

Mao Zedong, a pivotal figure in the establishment of the People's Republic of China, is widely acknowledged for his remarkable intellect, strategic acumen, and revolutionary prowess. Under his visionary leadership, the communist army achieved a string of resounding victories during the Chinese civil war, ultimately culminating in the Communist Party of China's triumph and assumption of power. Mao's firm determination and astute guidance successfully withstood formidable challenges posed by Western powers, exemplified by China's active involvement in the Korean War.

Despite not having received formal military education, Mao Zedong's vast reservoir of knowledge and wisdom on military affairs was largely derived from his deep immersion in Chinese histories, literary classics, and personal experiences. While he did not pursue a formal career as a historian or publish academic papers on history, his understanding of Chinese history and literary classics was unparalleled.[58] From the tender age of 13, Mao devoted himself to voracious reading, acquiring an extensive familiarity with renowned Chinese literary works such as the *Water Margin* and the *Romance of the Three Kingdoms*, the latter of which remained a constant companion throughout his 70-year journey.[59]

In contemporary Chinese society, the realm of stratagem culture has expanded to encompass a substantial portion of the population who have attained a relatively high level of literacy. However, the individuals within this group are still commonly regarded as 'elites', as the majority of stratagem practitioners are either already occupying or aspire to hold managerial positions in commercial, public, or government organisations. Their pursuit of career advancement is often driven by employing strategic manoeuvres. On the other hand, Chinese peasants and rural farmers, due to limited access to education and exposure to stratagem contexts, are less likely to have stratagem thinking or behaviour. Consequently, they are often characterised as 'simple and unpretentious', due to their circumstances.

The content of stratagem ideas is extensively incorporated within most Chinese historical, philosophical, and literary classics. This integration has played a fundamental role in the formation of stratagem culture in China.

The perspective of symbolic interactionism places significant importance on face-to-face interactions in the origin and activation of cultural ideas.[60] Observing the practical implementation of stratagems, both in achieving personal and organisational objectives, serves as a constant reminder and reinforcement of individuals' comprehension of the literature they have studied. Thus, personal experiences and word of mouth constitute crucial channels for the diffusion and transmission of stratagem culture.

The emergence of new media technology has greatly accelerated cultural diffusion. Cai Lun, an esteemed Chinese eunuch and official during the East Han Dynasty (25–230 AD), is widely credited as the inventor of paper and paper-making techniques.[61] These innovations are regarded as significant milestones in the history of human civilisation.[62] Additionally, movable printing technology was pioneered by Bi Sheng, a Chinese inventor during the Northern Song Dynasty (1041–1048).[63] Both paper and movable printing have played instrumental roles in facilitating the transmission of ideas and the advancement of culture.

During the Northern Song era, the pioneering use of printed books in society coincided with the compilation of the *Seven Military Classics of Ancient China*. In contrast, Europe fell behind in the advancement of paper and printing technologies. In China, paper made of plant fibres was more cost-effective than the rag-based paper in Europe, and wood-block printing, which was simpler, cheaper, and better suited for Chinese characters, prevailed over movable type. Printed materials became essential for the flourishing educated elite,[64] fostering the evolution of China's stratagem culture.

The advent of radio and television has brought about revolutionary change in the realm of communication media. In the past three decades, historical and literary television dramas have gained immense popularity in Greater China, comprising mainland China, Hong Kong, and Taiwan, and have garnered a high viewership rate. Furthermore, a multitude of movies based on literary classics, featuring intricate strategies and intrigues, have been produced, subsequently promoting the widespread adoption of stratagem thinking.

A plethora of television drama series and movies have been produced, showcasing the rise and fall of historical imperial families from the Spring and Autumn period (770–476 BC) to the last Qing Dynasty (1616–1911). These intriguing programmes depict intricate deceptions and strategic manoeuvring in political and military conflicts, captivating the audience and making them highly popular. In addition, television shows and movies based on renowned literary classics such as the *Romance of the Three Kingdoms*, *Water Margin*, *Journey to the West*, and Sun Tzu's *Art of War* have become favoured pastimes among the general public. Furthermore, contemporary programmes tackling themes of anticorruption, antidrug initiatives, civil wars, economic reforms, and business competition are interwoven with various plots, intrigues, and strategies, further promoting the diffusion of stratagem culture.

Chinese society continues to be influenced by mass media-based entertainment dramas and movies that actively promote and reinforce a culture of stratagem. Just as Christianity is often propagated through biblical storytelling, Chinese stratagem culture is also disseminated through various forms of media, including literary and historical dramas as well as dramatised narratives.

Ralph Sawyer has observed a notable prevalence of stratagem as a cultural phenomenon. In China, there has been a persistent pursuit of understanding and exploring stratagem. Sawyer noted that this interest began in the late 1980s but particularly intensified in 1991. This surge in interest coincided with the renewed recognition of classical military writings as valuable subjects for study. The exploration of strategy and stratagem in China encompasses a wide spectrum of intentions, ranging from the exploitation of the popular fascination with clever tactics and unconventional methods to more profound contemplations of theoretical aspects and the concept of unorthodoxy.[65]

Sawyer goes on to emphasise the significance of history in shaping Chinese stratagem culture, asserting that historical narratives play a pivotal role in instilling and perpetuating stratagem in China. He explores historical materials that have intensely influenced the collective mindset, become deliberate subjects of contemplation, and constitute an integral part of modern strategic culture. Notably, two renowned heroic novels, namely the *Three Kingdoms* and *Water Margin*, have long been acknowledged for their substantial contributions to the formation of both popular and defence-orientated strategic culture.[66]

## STRATAGEM CULTURE AND IMPLICATIONS

Stratagem culture can be described as the prevailing belief system and corresponding behaviours within a social group, influenced by past generations and mass media. It revolves around the notion that, when faced with conflicts or competition, the preferred approach is to strategically employ stratagems as tactics in order to gain a competitive advantage. China serves as a prime example of a society where a significant portion of the population, particularly those in positions of responsibility and authority, embraces the use of stratagems in various contexts such as business, social interactions, and politics.

In the realm of international business, particularly during the earlier stages when Chinese companies were comparatively weaker than their Western counterparts in terms of technological expertise and managerial skills, the utilisation of stratagems based on Sun Tzu's teachings became crucial for Chinese enterprises. By employing these tactics, Chinese companies aimed to level the playing field and enhance their competitive position.

Given the cultural phenomenon at hand, it is advisable for Western decision-makers to adopt a mindset that acknowledges the natural inclination of Chinese players to employ stratagems when engaging in competition or collaboration. It is crucial to thoroughly consider all potential outcomes and contingencies. Even if the Chinese player may initially appear significantly weaker, it is important to refrain from underestimating their capabilities and instead approach the situation with caution while actively seeking to uncover the truth.

The stratagem culture fosters a mentality centred around game-playing. In situations where the rules of a game are ambiguous, Chinese players may engage in what can be described as 'edge ball' tactics, pushing the boundaries but still operating within the confines of the rules. Conversely, in the West, where a more straightforward either/or mentality prevails, such 'edge ball' strategies may be considered unacceptable or unethical. In China, where the marketplace is often viewed as a battlefield, the principles of business are separated from personal considerations. Many Chinese business executives possess a natural inclination or adeptness in strategic thinking, excelling in employing these edge ball tactics. Individuals unfamiliar with this mindset may find themselves susceptible to falling into traps or disadvantageous situations.

Using the badminton match in the 2012 Olympic Games as an illustration, the coach of the Chinese women's team instructed his players to deliberately lose the games, believing that he was still operating within the 'rules', which were not specifically defined at the time. This tactic was employed to increase the Chinese players' chances of securing the gold medal. However, from a Western perspective and in terms of values, this approach was deemed to be contrary to the 'Olympic spirit', leading to the disqualification of the players involved. Nevertheless, the Chinese coach maintained that he had not engaged in any wrongful conduct.

The strategies employed by Chinese individuals when interacting with fellow countrymen or entities often differ from those used with individuals from Western cultures. In Chinese culture, there exists a shared understanding of logic and potential tactics. When Chinese individuals engage with each other, it can be likened to a game of chess, where both parties are well versed in the 'rules' and established winning strategies based on past experiences. The ultimate outcome of such encounters depends on the knowledge, experience, and intelligence of the participants. Appropriate remarks within this context might include phrases like 'I understand the nature of your approach' or 'while one side makes a move, the other is already ten steps ahead'.

However, employing stratagems becomes considerably easier when dealing with individuals who are unfamiliar with this particular way of thinking. It can be likened to watching a magic show, where if the audience is unaware of the 'answer' or 'the secret behind the trick', they are more likely to be surprised or confused. When a Western businessman or woman first arrives in China, Chinese colleagues may make comments such as 'they are quite naïve' or 'they have little understanding of the complexity of the situation'. Consequently, it is advisable for a Western company entering the Chinese market for the first time to have a native Chinese employee, on either a short- or long-term basis, who can act as a bridge between Chinese and Western parties, facilitating communication and understanding. Once a business deal is reached, it becomes crucial to localise the management by granting sufficient autonomy to local management, enabling them to make strategic decisions regarding local operations.

MNCs have recognised the value of employing individuals with Chinese backgrounds to facilitate local business management. Interestingly, there is a notable difference in localisation efforts between US MNCs and their European counterparts. Additionally, Japanese and Korean MNCs have experienced relative ease in conducting business in China compared to their European and American counterparts. This can be attributed to the Japanese and Korean understanding of Chinese thinking.

The Japanese are familiar with stratagem ideas and even share part of strata that were shaped by the profound influence of Chinese culture on Japan between 552 and 794.[67] Notably, the renowned *Sun Tzu's Art of War* was introduced to Japan in the 8th century,[68] remaining highly recommended reading for Japanese CEOs.[69] Therefore, it is advisable for decision-makers in European and American MNCs involved in Chinese business to familiarise themselves with select Chinese literary works such as the *Seven Classic Military Strategies of Ancient China*, *Tso Chuan*, *Tao Te Ching*, and the

*Romance of the Three Kingdoms*. Learning to play *Wei Qi* is also conducive to training themselves with Chinese thinking.

The successful implementation of stratagems relies on the swift realisation of unexpected or unorthodox ideas. In general, organisations with a centralised decision-making structure are more likely to achieve this, and this is particularly evident in Chinese organisations, both governmental and private. Chinese organisations are characterised by a centralised structure, wherein a strong leader, often referred to as 'Chairman' or 'CEO', stands out as the driving force behind the organisation. Many Chinese private businesses resemble mini-kingdoms in which the owner assumes the role of a 'quasi-emperor' who makes all strategic decisions.[70] This structure proves highly effective in materialising stratagems, especially when they are genuinely ingenious or extraordinary.

Behind the success of numerous Chinese companies lies a true leader or founder who issues what can be considered as 'imperial edicts'. For example, Wang Chuanfu of BYD Co. Ltd, Cao Dewang of Fuyao Glass Industry Group (one of the world's largest auto glass producers), Zhang Ruimin of Haier, Ren Zhengfei of Huawei, Jack Ma of Alibaba, Li Shufu of Geely Holding Group, and many others exemplify this leadership approach.

In addition to its advantages, a centralised organisational structure also has its drawbacks, particularly when it comes to the leadership capabilities of private business founders. Not all founders possess the acumen and capabilities required to effectively lead their organisations. Unfortunately, there are numerous cases where founders' unwise decisions have led to disastrous consequences.

State-owned organisations often face the issue of power concentration in the hands of a few individuals, which unfortunately gives rise to corruption. This is evident from the significant number of high-ranking officials and directors who have been arrested and incarcerated in the past decade due to their involvement in corrupt practices or embezzlement.[71]

These cases shed light on the scale of the issue, with the amount of financial assets implicated in corruption reaching billions of US dollars in various instances. It is worth noting that, as of June 2017, China has taken punitive measures against approximately 1.343 million street-level party cadres over the past five years.[72]

Chinese private firms face a significant challenge in their pursuit of competent middle management. This issue can be traced back to the country's stratagem culture, which makes it difficult for founders to identify and employ trustworthy individuals to fill the crucial role of implementing the firm's strategic plans. The founder is confronted with two key problems: assessing whether potential middle managers possess the necessary capabilities and competence required by the firm, as well as determining their trustworthiness.

The task of finding a suitable match between a private firm's requirements and a candidate's capabilities is a complex one. In numerous instances, founders have found that foreign-trained returnees, who are expected to possess 'modern' management skills, often fail to meet the expectations set by the founders. This mismatch further compounds the challenges faced by private firms in their search for qualified middle management.

When it comes to trustworthiness, some middle managers, despite their capabilities and competence, may not fully dedicate themselves to the company's strategy or mission. This can be attributed to two reasons. Firstly, there are instances where a manager's arrogance and excessive self-confidence lead them to make decisions that are not aligned with company strategy. However, such occurrences are uncommon in Western cultures, where subordinates typically adhere to orders and execute strategies faithfully. Secondly, middle managers may implement the company's strategic decisions, but not wholeheartedly in the best interest of the company's strategy. In many cases, these managers prioritise personal rewards, such as reputation or financial gain, which influences their choices and actions. These situations are often observed in the areas of purchasing, logistics, marketing, and construction.

To put it differently, in a culture where the practice of stratagem is prevalent, the founder of a private business has valid reasons for not fully trusting middle managers unless they have consistently demonstrated their trustworthiness. Entrusting decision-making authority becomes a persistent challenge for founders of Chinese private companies due to the inherent difficulties in establishing trust.

In a society characterised by a stratagem culture, there exists a natural inclination among individuals to harbour distrust towards others, particularly those who could potentially be perceived as competitors. This observation was made by an American missionary during the nineteenth century.[73]

In addition, an ancient philosopher, Han Feizi, who was a prominent Legalist philosopher in the 3rd century BC, advised against placing trust in others. Han Feizi cautioned that even one's own friends, relatives, spouse, and children should not be trusted, as each individual, for various reasons, may stand to benefit from one's demise. Consequently, Han Feizi emphasised the importance of remaining vigilant and being constantly on guard against deception from all directions, refraining from placing trust in others, and keeping one's inner thoughts and desires concealed.[74]

Throughout Chinese history, a recurring pattern emerged as a result of ancient Chinese emperors harbouring a low level of trust. Countless capable, loyal, and heroic generals found themselves executed after aiding their masters in ascending the throne. The newly crowned rulers exhibited a tendency to be excessively suspicious of those around them, suspecting hidden motives to overthrow either themselves or their successors. This unfortunate trend persisted across various dynastic empires following the unification of China under the Qin Dynasty, with one notable exception – the Yuan Dynasty, which was governed by the Mongols and embraced a nomadic culture. Remarkably, the Yuan Dynasty managed to evade the execution of its own generals.

In the Northern Song Dynasty, Emperor Zhao Kuangyi adopted a different approach by relieving his generals of their commands instead of resorting to execution. This decision, which transpired during a feast, became a legendary incident known as 'relieving the generals of their commands at a feast'.[75] Its uniqueness has ensured that it remains remembered to this day.

In a stratagem culture environment, social relationships are characterised by caution. In general, congenial teamwork is more of an exception than the norm in Chinese organisations. When two corporate entities or individuals enter into a business partnership or collaboration, the process of building trust takes precedence over other activities. It is crucial for them to establish a strong relationship based on trust before finalising any deals. Consequently, people generally adopt an indirect approach in their communications to avoid the potential disclosure of unfavourable information and to explore the possibility of gaining useful insights. Due to the necessity of cultivating *guanxi*, a term referring to the establishment of relationships, and the cautious communication style prevalent in Chinese business culture, negotiations between Chinese and Western organisations tend to be significantly lengthier than those between Western organisations.[76]

Establishing trust and securing full support from Chinese partners would demand significant efforts, such as strategic personnel selection, for Western companies engaged in partnership with Chinese counterparts. Conducting social research in China presents distinct challenges in gathering empirical data, especially when compared to Western societies, due to widespread scepticism among the populace regarding the true intentions of social researchers.

Due to the deep-rooted influence of *yin–yang* principles in Chinese culture, change is an integral part of the Chinese mindset. Chinese decision-makers are naturally inclined to constantly contemplate 'change' as a concept, much like water flowing towards opportunities and areas of strength, known as *Shi*. However, the *yin–yang* philosophy reminds us that everything possesses two facets, *yin* and *yang*. Consequently, while Chinese organisations excel in their agility and adaptability, they also face a significant challenge in terms of sustainable growth for private companies.

Chinese tradition dictates that a strong leader should guide an organisation, akin to a quasi-emperor. However, a Chinese proverb wisely implies that 'there cannot be two tigers in one territory' or 'if two men ride on a horse, one must ride behind'. The intense competition for the throne of the emperor often leads to internal conflicts, ultimately resulting in the division of the company among family members.

Han Feizi highlights three key factors that contribute to the strength of a leader's position.

The first factor is *Shi,* which refers to the disposition of authority or power. This type of power is not contingent upon the ruler's personal initiative or moral qualities. Han Feizi argues that, in the Legalist system, authority should be based on established and institutionalised power rather than relying on 'charismatic' authority. This is because placing too much emphasis on charisma can leads to a harmful emphasis on the elevated status of individuals.[77]

The second factor identified by Han Feizi is *Fa*, which pertains to laws. Han Feizi describes *Fa* as an intricate set of laws that are formulated by the ruler, disseminated to government officials, and then taught and elucidated to the illiterate population. The purpose of this comprehensive system of laws, supported by inevitable punishments, is to establish order within the nation. Han Feizi emphasises that this system leaves no room for chance, personal judgment, or the exploitation of privileges.

The third factor outlined by Han Feizi is *Shu*, which encompasses the arts of governing, administrative techniques, and statecraft. Han Feizi asserts that, while laws can guide and regulate the behaviour of officials and the general populace, the ruler, who is the originator of those laws and stands beyond them, must adhere to a distinct set of principles. These principles form the ruler's *Shu*, comprising the policies and strategies employed to exercise authority and maintain control over those under their governance.[78]

Han Feizi drew inspiration from the *Book of Lord Shang* to formulate his concept of *Fa*, and while Shen Pu-hai's doctrine influenced the development of *Shu*, Lord Shang's *Fa* offered a comprehensive framework for societal control, outlining a programme that encompassed various aspects of governance. On the other hand, Shen Pu-hi's *Shu* provided the organisational structure necessary for the effective implementation of the ruler's enlightened policies.[79] It is worth noting that this style of organisation, characterised by the integration of *Fa* and *Shu*, has persisted since the establishment of the Qin Dynasty in 221 BC. Barring an unimaginable revolution, it is likely to continue shaping China's governance in the foreseeable future.

A centralised power structure, by its very nature, can be prone to instability. However, the United States has established a stable government through its system of checks and balances. This system ensures that the Legislative, Executive, and Judicial branches of the government remain separate, thereby preventing the abuse of power. In metaphorical terms, one can envision a government or an organisation as an object lifted in the air. The US government has three supporting poles, symbolising the three branches of power, which distribute the weight and provide a solid foundation for stability. Conversely, the Chinese government's power structure is more centralised, akin to having only one supporting pole. This concentration of power can inherently introduce instability, as it increases the risk of abuses and corruption.

Lord Acton's famous remark, 'Power tends to corrupt, and absolute power corrupts absolutely',[80] serves as a poignant reminder of the dangers associated with unchecked authority. Systems that incorporate checks and balances aim to limit the accumulation of absolute power, maintain stability, and safeguard against corruption.

The Chinese centralised organisational structure, when combined with a stratagem culture, presents a significant drawback as it leads to internal friction within the organisation. In a Chinese organisation, cohesion is typically achieved through the leader's authority, corporate culture, or familial connections.[81] In the absence of these factors, teamwork within the organisation is prone to falter, giving the illusion of unity and cooperation while multiple factions may actually be at odds with each other.

As Chinese organisations grow in size and strength, most business partnerships are likely to disintegrate. The inability to effectively organise and sustain the organisational structure is a major hindrance in Chinese culture, preventing organisations and initiatives from attaining strong, large, and sustainable growth. Western scholars have recognised that excessively 'pliable' or 'bendable' Chinese organisations, labelled as suffering 'weak management', significantly impede China's competitiveness.[82]

Numerous instances in Chinese history serve as poignant examples of the failure of many organisations or initiatives due to their inherent organisational weaknesses.

Throughout Chinese history, spanning from the Qin Dynasty (221–206 BC) to the Qing Dynasty (1616–1911), there were numerous peasant rebellions or revolutionary wars that ultimately proved unsuccessful. The failures of these rebellions and revolutions were often attributed to a lack of effective leadership or organisational capabilities among the rebels.[83] One notable example is the Dazexiang Uprising (July–December 209 BC), led by Chen Sheng and Wu Guang, which marked the first uprising launched against Qin power after the death of the first Emperor, Qin Shi Huang. Tragically, both Chen Sheng and Wu Guang were assassinated by their own followers due to a lack of trust and unity within their ranks.[84]

Among various revolutions in Chinese history, the Huang Chao rebellion (878–884) stands out as the most enduring, influential, and far-reaching. The revolution resulted in the establishment of the Empire of Qi, with Huang Chao assuming the role of emperor. However, the eventual downfall of the empire can be ascribed to Huang Chao's inability to effectively control his followers or 'subjects'.[85]

During the 1930s, the CPC experienced a number of purges due to the prevailing stratagem culture. These purgative movements involved the arrests and execution of CPC members who were suspected of being 'disloyal' or 'treacherous'. Among those arrested and executed were individuals who were merely suspected of having affiliations with the AB, a relatively insignificant pro-KMT organisation that was established in 1926 during a period of collaboration between the CPC and KMT.

Although the AB had quickly faded away, a series of paranoid assumptions led CPC security agents to believe that the AB members were actually operatives sent by the KMT to infiltrate Communist ranks. They further speculated that the initials 'AB' stood for 'anti-Bolshevik'. As this unfounded paranoia persisted, thousands of individuals suspected of being AB members, approximately three to four thousand, were arrested in what became known as the Futian Incident. Tragically, many of them were executed as a result of these baseless accusations.[86]

Throughout the development of the CPC, there were significant power struggles and internal 'clique' conflicts that posed a severe threat to the party's existence. These struggles came close to causing the downfall of the CPC. However, whether by accident or inevitability, history ultimately bestowed upon Mao Zedong the role of shaping China's landscape, starting from the mid-1930s.[87]

Research indicates that none of the world's hundred oldest companies are Chinese. The absence of long-lasting Chinese companies can be attributed to several key factors, including a lack of trust among the founders, descendants, and professional managers. Internal conflicts or power struggles within families are also common, leading to challenges in sustaining the unity and continuity of the family business.[88] This phenomenon aligns with the opening line of the renowned Chinese literary work, the *Romance of the Three Kingdoms*, which vividly portrays the nature of change in empires, states, families, or businesses: 'Empires wax and wane; states cleave asunder and coalesce'.[89] Particularly after the demise of the founder, maintaining the cohesion of the family business becomes exceedingly difficult, often resulting in internal power battles among the sons and a subsequent breakdown or division of the business.

Figuratively speaking, the management styles of American and Chinese can be compared to playing bridge and mahjong, respectively. Playing bridge successfully requires close cooperation between partners who establish an alliance based on agreed-upon conventions. On the other hand, mahjong is an individualistic activity where each player primarily focuses on their own interests. To triumph in mahjong, a player must be cautious of the preceding player's moves and be vigilant against the next player's actions.

In essence, the stratagem culture in China leads to a significant weakness in Chinese organisations – namely, a lack of solidarity or a centripetal force. Any

Chinese organisation or team that has grown large and powerful would need to overcome the potential weaknesses stemming from the Chinese subculture.

In Chinese organisations and among elite individuals, the use of stratagem is widely embraced as a valuable approach. Surprisingly, this phenomenon has received little attention from Western academics and practitioners. Some Western countries still vividly remember how Japanese companies success-fully dominated their industries, including motorcycles, automobiles, cameras, electronics, printers, and more, utilising strategies that contained significant elements of stratagem, which were not well understood at the time.

Regardless of the strong political and ideological pressures in the West advocating for disengagement from Chinese organisations, the reality is that competing or cooperating with them has become a necessity. Western compa-nies must acknowledge this fact and reshape their mindsets accordingly. They need to prepare themselves to engage with Chinese counterparts, carefully considering the advantages and disadvantages involved in such interactions.

## NOTES

1.  In China, it is known as *bingjia wenhua* (兵家文化) in Chinese and it may also be translated as 'militarist culture'.
2.  Smith, A.H. (1894). *Chinese Characteristics*. Fleming H. Revell Company, pp. 242–65.
    Redding, G.S. (1993). *The Spirit of Chinese Capitalism*. De Gruyter Studies in Organization, pp. 66–8.
3.  Jullien, F. (2000). *Detour and Access: Strategies of Meaning in China and Greece* (S. Hawkes, Trans.). Cambridge, MA: Zone Books. Distributed by MIT Press.
4.  Chen, M.J. (2001). *Inside Chinese Business: A Guide for Managers Worldwide*. Harvard Business School Press, pp. 114–15.
5.  Smith (n 2) p. 246.
6.  Hucker, C.O. (1975). *China's Imperial Past: An Introduction to Chinese History and Culture*. London: Duckworth, p. 17.
    Watson, B. (1989). *The Tso Chuan: Selections from China's Oldest Narrative History* (B. Watson, Trans.). Columbia University Press.
7.  Salisbury, H. (1985). *The Long March: The Untold Story*. Macmillan, p. 2.
8.  Watson (n 6).
    He, J.J. (2003). *Ershiwu Shi Jimou Da Quan (Complete Works of Stratagem from Twenty-five Histories)*. Changsa: Yuelu Publishing House.
9.  Collins, J.M. (1973). *Grand Strategy: Principles and Practices*. Naval Institute Press.
10. McNeilly, M.R. (1996). *Sun Tzu and The Art of Business*. Oxford University Press, pp. 3–4.
11. Sawyer, R.D. (1993). *The Seven Military Classics of Ancient China*. Westview Press, Inc, p. 149.

12. Sawyer, R.D. (2007). *The Tao of Deception: Unorthodox Warfare in Historic and Modern China*. New York: Basic Books, p. 3.

13. Ibid.

14. Dixit, A.K. and Nalebuff, B. (1991). *Thinking Strategically: The Competitive Edge in Business, Politics, and Everyday Life*. New York: W.W. Norton & Company.
Dixit, A.K. and Nalebuff, B. (2008). *The Art of Strategy: A Game Theorist's Guide to Success in Business and Life*. New York: W.W. Norton & Company.

15. Camerer, C.F. (1991). Does Strategy Research Need Game Theory? *Strategic Management Journal*, 12, pp. 137-152.

16. Sawyer (n 11) p. 322.

17. Sawyer (n 12) pp. 124–5.

18. Swidler, A. (1986). Culture in Action: Symbols and Strategies. *American Sociological Review*, 51(2), pp. 273–86.

19. Nisbett, R.E., Peng, K., Choi, I. and Norenzayan, A. (2001). Culture and Systems of Thought: Holistic Versus Analytic Cognition. *Psychological Review*, 108(2), pp. 291–310.

20. Liu, B.W. (1996). *One Hundred Unorthodox Strategies: Battle and Tactics of Chinese Warfare* (R.D. Sawyer, Trans.). Westview Press, Inc, p. 19.

21. Zaman, R.U. (2009). Strategic Culture: A 'Cultural' Understanding of War. *Comparative Strategy*, 28, pp. 68–88.
Apte, M. (1994). Language in Sociocultural Context. In: R.E. Asher (Ed.), *The Encyclopedia of Language and Linguistics*. 4 (pp. 2000–10). Oxford: Pergamon Press.

22. Peterson, R.A. (1979). Revitalizing the Culture. *Annual Review of Sociology*, 5, pp. 137–66.

23. Clarke, M. (1974). On the Concept of 'Sub-Culture'. *British Journal of Sociology*, 25(4), pp. 428–41.

24. Eagleton, T. (2000). *The Idea of Culture*. Oxford and Malden, MA: Blackwell, p. 1.

25. MacWhite, E. (1954). Review. Reviewed Work: *Culture. A Critical Review of Concepts and Definitions* by A. L. Kroeber & Clyde Kluckhohn (1952). Cambridge, MA: Peabody Museum. *Anthropos*, 49(3/4), pp. 718–20.

26. Clark (n 23) pp. 428–41.

27. Fine, G.A. and Kleinman, S. (1979). Rethinking Subculture: An Interactionist Analysis. *The American Journal of Sociology*, 85(1), pp. 1–20.

28. Peterson (n 22) pp. 137–66.

29. Kroeber, A. and Parsons. T. (1958). The Concepts of Culture and of Social System. *American Sociological Review*, 23(5), pp. 582–3.

30. Hofstede, G. (2001). *Culture's Consequences: Comparing Values, Behaviors, Institutions, and Organizations Across Nations*. Sage Publications, p. 9.

31. Deresky, H. (2006). *International Management: Managing Across Borders and Cultures*. Pearson-Prentice Hall, p. 38.

32.  Moran, R.T., Harris, P.R. and Moran, S.V. (2007). *Managing Cultural Differences: Global Leadership Strategies for the 21st Century*. Butterworth-Heinemann, p. 6.

33.  Komarovsky, M. and Sargent, S.S. (1949). Research into Subcultural Influences upon Personality. In S.S. Sargent and M.W. Smith (Eds.), *Culture and Personality*. New York: The Viking Fund, p. 143.

34.  Fine (n 27) pp. 1–20.

35.  Clarke (n 23) pp. 428–41.

36.  Deng, K.G. (2000). A Critical Survey of Recent Research in Chinese Economic History. *Economic History Review*, 53(1), pp. 1–28.

37.  Zhang, S.G. (1999). China: Traditional and Revolutionary Heritage. In K. Booth and R. Trood (Eds.), *Strategic Culture in the Asia-Pacific Region*. Palgrave.

38.  Sawyer has made the comment in the Introduction to Liu Bowen's treatise: Liu (n 20) p. 1.

39.  Lu, T. (1999). *Zhonghua wenming xianqin shi* (*Chinese Civilisation: History of Pre-Qin Period*). Hebei Education Publishing House, p. 120.

40.  Yao, J.M. (2012). *Laozi zhihui* (*Lao Tzu's Wisdom*). Shandong People's Publishing House, pp. 171–4.

41.  In Chapter 7 of *Sun Tzu's Art of War*, a reference is made to 'Military Administration': Griffith, S.B. (1963). *Sun Tzu: The Art of War*, Translated and with an Introduction by Samuel B. Griffith and a Foreword by B.H. Liddell Hart. Oxford University Press, p. 161.
     Lu, T. (1999). *Zhonghua wenming xianqin shi* (*Chinese Civilisation: History of Pre-Qin Period*). Hebei Education Publishing House, p. 118.

42.  Ibid., p. 120.

43.  Xu, B.L. (2002). *Zhong guo bing shu tong lan* (*An Overview of Chinese Military Books*). PLA Publishing House, pp. 20–1.

44.  Liu, An (2012). *The Dao of the Military, Liu An's Art of War* (trans. with an Introduction, by Andrew Seth Meyer), Columbia University Press, p. 2.

45.  Sawyer (n 11) p. 29.

46.  Ibid., p. 16.

47.  Confucius (1979). *The Analects* (D.C. Lau, Trans. and Intro.). Penguin Books, p. 146.

48.  Han, F. (2003). *Han Feizi: Basic Writings* (B. Watson, Trans.). New York: Columbia University Press, p. 111.
     Here 'a copy of the works Sun Wu and Wu Qi' means 'Sun Tzu's Art of War' and 'Wu Qi', both of which are among the Seven Military Classics of Ancient China.

49.  Clarke (n 23) pp. 428–41.

50.  Jian, B.Z. (2006). *Zhongguo tongshi gangyao* (*The Essentials of Chinese General History*). Peking University Press.

51.  Feng, G.C. (2004). *Zhong Guo Wen Hua Su Cheng Du Ben* (*Chinese Culture: Quick Reader*). Beijing: Chinese Literature and History Press, pp. 404–12.

52.  Sawyer (n 11) p. 41.

53. Liu, S.H. (1974). Time and Temporality: The Chinese Perspective. *Philosophy East and West*, 24(2), pp. 145–53.
54. Ebrey, P.B. (1993). *Chinese Civilization: A Sourcebook.* New York: The Free Press, p. 14.
55. Confucius (n 47) p. 87.
56. He (n 8).
57. Ferguson, N. (2011). Henry Kissinger's Prescription for China. *Newsweek*, 15 May 2011.
58. Lu, Z.D. (2009). *Mao Zedong Ping Guoxue* (*Mao Zedong's Comments on Chinese Classics*). New World Press, pp. 57–66.
59. Sheng, X.C. and Li, Z.C. (2011). *Mao Zedong PinPing SiDa MingZhu* (*Mao Zedong's Commentaries on the Four Classics*). Central Compilation & Translation Press, p. 2.
60. Fine (n 27) p. 1–20.
61. Chen, J.L. (2004). *Zhongguo Lishi Yu Wenhua* (*Chinese History and Culture*). Hefei Industrial University Press, pp. 342–3.
62. Jian (n 50) p. 157.
    Keay, J. (2008). *China: A History*. London: Harper Press, p. 174.
63. Chen (n 61) pp. 343–4.
64. Fairbank, J.K. and Goldman, M. (1998). *China: A New History*. The Belknap Press of Harvard University Press, pp. 93–4.
65. Sawyer (n 12) p. 329.
66. Ibid.
67. Morton, W.S. and Olenik, J.K. (2005). *Japan: Its History and Culture*. McGraw-Hill, Inc., pp. 16–35.
68. Wee, C.H., Lee, K.S. and Bambang, W.H. (1991). *Sun Tzu: War & Management*. Addison-Wesley Publishing Company, p. 3.
    McNeilly (n 10) p. 4.
69. Wee et al. (n 68) p. 4.
70. This can generally include those that are really 'important', but many like to involve themselves in detailed administrative affairs with a hands-on approach.
71. Xinhua (2014). Anti-corruption Campaign Forcing Change in SOEs. *China Daily* (US ed.) [New York, N.Y] 03 July 2014, p. 4.
    Gong, T. (2014). Managing Government Integrity under Hierarchy: anti-corruption efforts in local China. *Journal of Contemporary China*, 26 November, pp. 1–17.
72. Tang, N., Ding, Z. and Xu, Y. (2018). Corruption and Anti-Corruption Research in China: A Critical Review of Chinese Top Journal Publications (1989–2017). *Chinese Public Administration Review*, 9(2), 79–149.
73. Smith (n 2) pp. 242–65.
74. Burton Watson's introduction to Han Feizi's treatise. Han (n 48) p. 11.
75. The emperor hosted a feast for his generals, during which he took over control of the armed forces. As part of his plan, he appointed the generals as local government officials and bestowed upon them land and gold as a sign

of recognition. However, the emperor's excessive vigilance in safeguarding his throne from potential usurpation inadvertently compromised the preparedness of the Song armies for combat. The unintended consequence significantly weakened their military strength, leaving openings for smaller Northern nomadic forces, including the Liao, Jin, and Yuan, to launch invasions into China.

76.   Tung, R. (1994). Strategic Management Thought in East Asia, *Organizational Dynamics*, 22(4), pp. 55–65.
77.   Schwartz, B. (1985). *The World of Thought in Ancient China*. Harvard University Press, p. 340.
78.   Ibid., pp. 339–41.
      Burton Watson's introduction to Han Feizi's treatise. Han (n 48) pp. 7–12.
79.   Schwartz (n 77) p. 339.
80.   Acton, J. (1887). Letter to Bishop Mandell Creighton, April 5, 1887. *Historical Essays and Studies*, (1907), J.N. Figgis and R.V. Laurence (Ed.). London: Macmillan.
81.   Some family ties are also considered as unreliable.
82.   Lieberthal, K. and Lieberthal, G. (2003). The Great Transition. *Harvard Business Review*, 81(10), pp. 70–81.
83.   Mao, Z. (1939). The Chinese Revolution and The Chinese Communist Party. *Selected Works of Mao Tse-tung: Volume II* (1965 edition). Peking: Foreign Languages Press, pp. 305–34.
84.   Feng, G.C. (2005). *Zhongguo Tongshi: Shang Juan (The General History of China: Book One)*. The Guangming Daily Publishing House, p. 106.
85.   Keay (n 62) pp. 289–90.
86.   Salisbury (n 7) p. 139.
87.   Ibid., pp. 127–35.
88.   Zhou, X.B. (2014). *Zhongguo jiazhu qiye weishenme jiaobuliaoban? (Why Chinese Family Enterprises Cannot Pass on their Businesses to their Next Generations?)*. The Eastern Publisher.
89.   Lo, K.C. (1959; 2002). *Romance of the Three Kingdoms* (C.H. Brewitt-Taylor, Trans.; R.E. Hegel, Intro.). Tuttle Publishing, p. 3.

# 5.  The Chinese strategic mind at work: the case of Mao Zedong

*Mao Zedong Thought is a treasure of the Chinese nation and a valuable asset of the international communist movement.*
– Xi Jinping

*Mao Zedong was a visionary leader with a deep belief in the transformative power of revolution. His character was marked by an unyielding commitment to his ideals and unwavering confidence in his own abilities.*
– Edgar Snow

## MAO ZEDONG AND MAO ZEDONG THOUGHT

Mao Zedong, the former leader of the Communist Party of China (CPC) and the founding father of People's Republic of China, is widely recognised as a significant strategist on the global stage. A plethora of books, journal articles, doctoral dissertations, and various publications have emerged both in China and internationally, exploring different facets of Mao Zedong's ideology and leadership. Over the past decade, there has been a resurgence of interest in re-evaluating Mao's historical presence within the context of China.[1]

In terms of research on Mao Zedong, one can metaphorically view it through a marketing lens. Some researchers can be likened to 'mass marketers', who delve into the entirety of Mao's life and work. Others engage in 'differentiated marketing', focusing on specific aspects of Mao's contributions, such as his poetry, dialectics, or philosophy. Lastly, there are those who pursue 'concentrated marketing', attending to particular elements of Mao's thoughts or actions. Examples of this include Mao's policies during the Great Leap Forward, the Cultural Revolution, or his military strategies during the Chinese Civil War.

This chapter adopts a concentrated marketing approach to delve into Mao's strategic acumen, specifically exploring how his strategic thinking was developed and effectively implemented. It is worth noting that this particular area of research has been relatively unexplored in a comprehensive and systematic manner by previous scholars.

I have chosen Mao Zedong's mindset as a case study for Chinese strategic thinking due to several compelling reasons. Firstly, Mao Zedong embodies the epitome of indigenous Chinese strategic brilliance. His approach encompasses the principles of *Tao*, skilfully employing stratagems, adeptly manipulating adversaries, showcasing Chinese dialectics, and harnessing the power of *Shi* through creation and adaptation. In addition, Mao's leadership style exhibits exceptional agility, allowing him to navigate complex situations effectively.

Furthermore, Mao's strategic thought not only led to a remarkable victory against the formidable Chiang Kai-shek-led Kuomintang (KMT) forces during the Chinese Civil War but also left a lasting impact beyond China's borders, influencing other nations as well.[2] Even today, Mao's strategic philosophy continues to be highly regarded and embraced by numerous Chinese leaders and government officials, as well as business executives and entrepreneurs.[3]

Mao Zedong's significant influence on Chinese business can be exemplified by the remarkable growth and viability of Huawei, a formidable Chinese multinational high-tech company. The strategies employed by Huawei, to a large extent, have been shaped by Mao's strategic mindset and approaches, particularly through the guidance of his 'disciple', Ren Zhengfei, the founder of Huawei.[4]

For Western decision-makers engaged in business interactions with Chinese officials or companies, a thorough understanding of Mao's strategic thought would be highly beneficial. Such knowledge not only enables them to gain clearer insights into the strategic intentions of their Chinese counterparts but also provides inspiration from Mao's thoughts and approaches for their own strategy development.

It is widely acknowledged that Mao Zedong possessed exceptional qualities and capabilities as a military strategist, philosopher, historian, and poet. His profound thinking and revolutionary spirit, coupled with an extensive historical knowledge, are undeniable. However, when it comes to his role as a nation-builder, doubts may arise, and some individuals may question his effectiveness in this regard.

There are those who hold reservations about certain aspects of Mao's action following the establishment of the People's Republic of China. The initiation of the Cultural Revolution, in particular, is seen by many as a period of significant devastation for China. This perspective, perceptively expressed by Richard Nixon, suggests that, while Mao played a crucial role in attracting intensely fanatical supporters and inspiring millions worldwide, he struggled in the realm of constructive nation-building, a common challenge faced by many revolutionary leaders.[5]

In certain aspects, Mao Zedong shares similarities with leaders like Winston Churchill and Charles de Gaulle, who were considered 'wartime' leaders but faced rejection by their countrymen once the World War concluded in democratic nations. One reason for this shift in public sentiment is that the qualities that make a leader great during times of war may not necessarily align with what people desire during times of peace.[6]

Mao Zedong, much like Churchill and de Gaulle, possessed the natural instincts of a combatant and strategist. While his mission should have been accomplished after the establishment of the People's Republic of China, Chinese tradition dictated that he remain in power, following the pattern of previous rulers. Mao applied his wartime thinking to the task of nation-building, yielding mixed results. Considering the challenging conditions under which he assumed leadership in China, it could be argued that the achievements attained during his tenure should not be dismissed as a failure.

Furthermore, Mao's strategic thinking and action-orientated spirit serve as an exemplary and inspirational model for those engaged in competition, conflict, or warfare. While his legacy as a nation-builder may be subject to scrutiny, his leadership style and strategic mindset continue to resonate with individuals involved in commercial, political, and military endeavours.

It is important to acknowledge that in the 1980s, a vigorous debate took place within the CPC regarding the assessment of Mao Zedong. During this period, there was a tendency among some party members to completely negate Mao's role in China's history, largely due to the mistakes he made during the 1950s and 1970s. The denunciation of the Cultural Revolution by the official party line was particularly forceful, and it seemed to have garnered significant public support, leading to a widespread condemnation of Mao Zedong.[7]

During this time, a considerable number of individuals emerged who portrayed Mao in an extremely negative light, even demonising him.[8] Many leaders within the CPC, at various levels, were driven by a strong desire for both political and personal revenge as a result of the setbacks they had experienced during the Cultural Revolution.[9]

In 1980, when there was an attempt to completely dismiss Mao Zedong's contribution to China, Deng Xiaoping, who was the de facto leader of the CPC at that time, adopted a resolute stance in objectively assessing Mao Zedong's legacy.

Deng Xiaoping's approach involved several key elements. Firstly, he made a clear distinction between Mao Zedong as an individual and Mao Zedong Thought as an ideological framework. This allowed for a more nuanced evaluation that separated the man from the ideas he espoused. Secondly, Deng emphasised that the essence of Mao Zedong Thought lay in the principle of 'seeking truth from fact'. This principle served as a guiding force that could be extracted and applied in a broader context. Lastly, Deng acknowledged Mao's contributions while also recognising his mistakes. Through this selective approach, specific principles from Mao Zedong Thought were emphasised, providing a foundation upon which the current generation of leaders could both uphold and develop these principles.[10]

This chapter deliberately avoids delving into convoluted debates regarding the morality or image of Mao Zedong. Instead, it primarily centres around two key aspects.

Firstly, the focus is on Mao Zedong Thought, specifically his strategic mindset, which continues to exert a significant influence on Chinese political, military, and business leaders. This aspect explores the enduring impact of Mao's strategic thinking and its relevance in shaping various facets of Chinese leadership.

Secondly, the chapter examines the period of Mao's leadership prior to 1957. During this time, Mao's leadership displayed notable qualities and achievements. However, it acknowledges that, after this period, Mao became increasingly preoccupied with successive political campaigns, leading to a series of grave mistakes and resulting in devastating consequences for the nation.

## A FRAMEWORK FOR MAO ZEDONG'S STRATEGIC MIND

Figure 5.1 outlines a framework that provides a comprehensive understanding of Mao Zedong's strategic mindset. The framework is composed of four interconnected sections that work in tandem to create the foundation of Mao's leadership power. These sections include:

Section 1: Influencing factors – This section examines the various micro or internal factors that shape Mao's strategic thinking, such as upbringing, personal experiences, knowledge development, and the historical context in which he lived.

Section 2: Personality and qualities – This section delves into Mao's unique qualities and characteristics as a leader, including intelligence, determination, decisiveness, perseverance, and self-confidence.

Second 3: Thought components – This section analyses the key elements of Mao's strategic thought, in line with those specified in the framework for Chinese strategic mind, such as his alignment with *Tao*, his utilisation of stratagem and *Shi*, his understanding of dialectics, and his exhibition of a holistic approach and agility.

Section 4: Implementation system – This section explores the practical applications of Mao's strategic thought, including the mobilisation of masses, utilisation of ideology, disciplines, alliances, and control of factions.

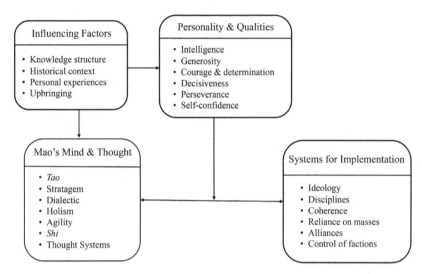

*Figure 5.1    A framework for Mao Zedong's strategic mind*

Despite the abundance of theories and models on leadership effectiveness, it can be challenging to put them into practice. Often, those who develop theories lack the power or ability to implement them, while those who hold power may struggle to truly embrace effective theories. Mao Zedong was one of the few leaders who was able to develop theories and implement them, resulting in his lasting impact on Chinese history.

Warren Bennis has garnered widespread recognition as the quintessential contemporary management thinker,[11] firmly establishing himself among the most influential minds in the world when it comes to leadership.[12] Despite his prowess as a theorist on the subject, Bennis had the opportunity to put his theories into practice as a senior member of a university's leadership team; however, he discovered that implementing his theories in managerial practices proved to be arduous and disheartening. Reflecting on his experience, Bennis candidly expressed his sentiment of feeling utmost powerlessness precisely when he possessed the greatest amount of power.[13] This serves as a poignant reminder that even a globally renowned expert in leadership theory can face formidable challenges in bridging the gap between theory and practice.

Richard Nixon emphasised the importance of a leader possessing not only knowledge of what is right but also the ability to act accordingly. In his view, a leader who lacks the judgement and perception to make correction decisions will fail due to a lack of vision. Similarly, a leader who understands what is right but cannot effectively implement it will fail due to their ineffectiveness.

Therefore, a truly exceptional leader requires both vision and the capability to accomplish what is morally and ethically correct.[14]

Mao Zedong stands as a noteworthy example of a leader who possessed a deep understanding of what was right and had the capacity to enact his vision. His legacy demonstrates his exceptional abilities as both a political and military thinker. His ability to translate his ideas into action showcased his effectiveness as a leader.

## PERSONALITY AND QUALITIES AND INFLUENCES

As seen in Figure 5.1, Mao Zedong's personality and qualities were marked by a combination of generosity, benevolence, open-mindedness, courage, determination, ambition, and decisiveness. The foundation of these traits can be traced back to his upbringing and background, which played a crucial role in shaping his character. From an early age, Mao immersed himself in the study of Chinese classics, which greatly influenced his learning and knowledge.

Growing up in a particular environment can shape one's values, beliefs, and behaviour. In Mao's case, his formative years were influenced by his family's values and cultural traditions, which instilled in him a sense of generosity and benevolence. These qualities contributed to his desire to improve the lives of the Chinese people and his commitment to social equality.

Moreover, Mao's exposure to Chinese classics from a young age provided him with a solid foundation of knowledge and wisdom. By probing the works of renowned philosophers and scholars, Mao cultivated an open-mindedness that allowed him to explore different perspectives and ideas. This intellectual curiosity combined with his inherent courage enabled him to challenge established norms and envision a new future for China.

Mao's upbringing fostered his determination, ambition, and decisiveness. Growing up in a society marked by political unrest and social inequality, he developed a strong drive to effect change and improve the conditions of the Chinese people. These qualities fuelled his revolutionary spirit and propelled him to become a prominent figure in Chinese history.

Mao Zedong was born on 26 December 1893, into a family of farmers in Shaoshan village in Hunan Province. His grandfather, Mao Enpu, led a modest and honourable life as a farmer but faced difficulties in preserving the inherited assets, resulting in a gradual decline in the family's wealth. Mao's father, Mao Yichang, assumed the responsibility of managing the family business at the tender age of 17. Through his father's competence and hard work, the family's fortunes were revived, eventually making them one of the most affluent households in the region.

A study conducted in the West has highlighted the enormous influence of Mao's family on his subsequent development. Mao was fortunate to grow up in a 'suburban' environment that provided him with opportunities to gradually move towards higher education and engage with an urban intellectual-political milieu. This alone distinguished him from the millions of rural youths residing in more isolated regions. Additionally, Mao grew up in a financially secure and prosperous family, by the standards of the time. This advantageous circumstance allowed him to receive a secondary school education, placing him in a highly privileged category among his contemporaries.[15]

Mao Zedong's father assuming responsibility for the entire family at a young age indicates an extraordinary bond and trust within the family. As a result, Mao Zedong never had to concern himself with his livelihood and experienced a harmonious family environment. During an interview with Edgar Snow, Mao emphasised the significant influence of his family in shaping his character. He described his mother as a compassionate and benevolent woman, always willing to share whatever she had. She expressed empathy for the less fortunate and frequently provided rice to those who sought help during times of famine.[16]

Harrison Salisbury asserted that Mao's mother was the primary influence during his early years. Mao held her in high esteem and repeatedly expressed his devotion to her. She was a diligent, compassionate, and considerate woman, always willing to assist those in need. On occasion, she provided rice to impoverished peasants, although she did so discreetly, ensuring that her stern husband remained unaware. She was a devout Buddhist, and it was through her influence that Mao himself became a believer in Buddhism.[17]

The family environment in which Mao Zedong was raised played a significant role in shaping his personality. When Mao's mother passed away at the age of 52, Mao travelled back to Shaoshan village from Changsha, the capital city of Hunan province, without hesitation, likely on foot, to be by her side during her final moments and the subsequent burial. In a poignant display of his emotions, Mao composed a heartfelt eulogy encompassing the ancient Chinese style known as *pian ti*. This touching tribute was translated into English by Harrison Salisbury:

> In reasoning and judgment her mind was clear and accurate
> Everything she did was done with planning and with care . . .
> When we were sick she held our hands, her heart full of sorrow
> Yet she admonished us saying: 'You should strive to be good.'[18]

The eulogy serves as a profound testament to Mao's deep affection and respect for his mother, highlighting her influential role in shaping his character. Her nurturing presence instilled in him qualities of kindness, generosity, selflessness, and open-mindedness, all of which formed the foundation of his leadership capabilities. Throughout Mao's life, it was widely recognised that he seldom handled two particular items personally: firearms and money, both of which were entrusted to his secretary. This practice further exemplifies Mao's focus on higher ideals and his delegation of practical matters, allowing him to concentrate on his broader vision and responsibilities as a leader.

Edgar Snow's observations and records elucidate Mao's character and personality during his youth. According to Snow, Mao Zedong exhibited marked liberal and humanistic inclinations in his early years. It appears that his transition from idealism to a more pragmatic mindset occurred primarily on a philosophical level. Despite being born into a peasant family, Mao did not personally experience significant oppression from landlords during his youth. From this, it can be deduced that his class hatred was likely an intellectually acquired mechanism deeply embedded within his philosophical framework, rather than an instinctive impulse for immediate action.[19]

With his skills and business acumen, Mao's father diversified his ventures beyond farming and ventured into selling rice and pigs. This expansion proved fruitful, leading to a significant increase in the Mao family's revenues and established them as relatively affluent within the Shaoshan village. Mao recounted to Snow that his father continued to accumulate wealth, amassing what was considered a substantial fortune within the small village. Rather than purchasing additional land, he invested in numerous mortgages on other people's properties. Over time, his capital grew to a noteworthy sum of two to three thousand Chinese dollars.[20]

Although Mao's family maintained a modest social status and financial wealth, they experienced a gradual process of growth and prosperity, steadily progressing on an upward trajectory development. Looking at it from a psychological perspective, Mao's family's favourable financial and social circumstances had a positive influence on his psyche, fostering a healthy and confident mindset.

In contrast, Chiang Kai-shek's family achieved greater wealth and higher social status, yet experienced a decline over time. Thus, this environment shaped Chiang Kai-shek to develop feelings of insecurity, selfishness, cruelty, and narrow-mindedness,[21] in contrast to Mao's disposition characterised by generosity, kindness, confidence, and open-mindedness.

Robert Scalapino has observed and discussed the influence of Mao's family circumstances on his psychological development. Mao, in many ways, embodied the spirit of his era, but he was fortunate to hold certain advantages that were not accessible to millions of his contemporaries. He possessed an extraordinary and a commanding presence. Furthermore, he was born during a time of significant transformation for China and the world, in a region that facilitated some exposure to the outside world, and into a family that allowed for upward social mobility.[22]

The enduring influence of Confucian doctrines on Chinese thought and behaviour over the two millennia is noteworthy. These doctrines, characterised by principles such as the Middle Way, moderation, humility, and obedience to rulers and fathers, conflict with the revolutionary and innovative spirit required for effective leadership. However, Mao Zedong's personal journey of education, self-education, and maturation allowed him to escape the Confucian influence. From an early age, around eight years old, Mao demonstrated an inherent and natural aversion, and perhaps even animosity, towards Confucian teachings. Consequently, he rebelled against his father and teachers, ultimately evolving into a perpetual and genuine 'revolutionary'. These rebellious tendencies, deeply rooted in his formative years, gradually moulded Mao into a decisive, courageous, rebellious, and fearless individual.

Mao's personal journey of growth and maturation stands in sharp contrast to the background of Zhou Enlai, a prominent revolutionary and core member of the CPC's leadership. Unlike Mao, Zhou was often described as a 'Confucian gentleman'.[23] A notable observation and comment on Zhou Enlai was made by Richard Nixon: Zhou's family lineage was deeply rooted in the traditions and customs of ancient China. For centuries, they maintained their social status by imparting education in Chinese classics to their children and securing positions within the imperial bureaucracy. Zhou, influenced by his family's cultural heritage, never sought to rid himself of their imprint. In fact, he harboured a deep respect for China's history, valuing the preservation of certain elements of the 'old society'.[24]

In the early history of the CPC, Zhou Enlai was one of the three key decision-makers within the party, while Mao Zedong did not hold such a position initially. Zhou held a superior position to Mao until the mid-1930s when Mao was elected to join the core decision-making group. Following this, Mao's leadership became firmly established within the party and persisted until his death in 1976.

Drawing upon his Confucian beliefs, Zhou Enlai demonstrated unswerving loyalty to Mao once a clear hierarchy was established between them. Throughout their association, Zhou remained steadily supportive of Mao. He did not make any attempts to challenge Mao's authority and maintained his loyalty until the very end of his life.

Harrison Salisbury provided insights on the dynamic between Mao Zedong and Zhou Enlai. Zhou wholeheartedly supported Mao and never, even in the critical year of 1976, did he question Mao's leadership. The intricacies that influenced Zhou's decision cannot be fully examined as his inner sentiments remain relatively unknown. However, from the Zunyi meeting onwards, where Mao's leadership was solidified, Zhou assumed the role of Mao Zedong's de facto chief of staff, regardless of his official title. This partnership between Zhou and Mao was unprecedented in Chinese political history.[25]

Mao's unparalleled knowledge of Chinese history is widely acknowledged, as he was well-versed in all the classics on history.[26] Mao once shared with Edgar Snow how he acquired some of his knowledge, even though these Chinese classics were banned from his school. While still a young student, Mao Zedong managed to read those outlawed books despite the vigilant disapproval of his teacher who considered them wicked. Whenever the teacher passed by, Mao would conceal them with a classic book and read secretly. Many of his classmates did the same. They absorbed the stories almost by heart, engaging in countless discussions and debates. Undoubtedly reading these books at an impressionable age had a deep influence on him.[27]

Stuart Schram has observed the notable influence that certain books had on Mao, asserting that there is no doubt that these novels left a lasting impact on him, particularly the historical works *Romance of the Three Kingdoms* and *Water Margin*.[28] Mao Zedong was an avid reader and prolific writer,[29] with an extensive knowledge of Chinese history, as evidenced by the volumes of his *Selected Works of Mao Zedong*, which encompass a wide range of historical figures, including sages, emperors, chancellors, politicians, strategists, scholars, poets, rebels, historians, traitors, and notorious eunuchs.[30] Despite Mao's claim of 'disliking' the classics, he displayed a deep understanding of them in his subsequent writings, frequently incorporating classical references.[31] For instance, he had thoroughly studied the *Twenty-four Histories*, the *Four Books and the Five Classics*,[32] and *Zizhi Tongjian (History as a Mirror)*.[33]

Harrison Salisbury also offers his insights into how Chinese classics influenced Mao. He explains that even though Mao attended a village school, he managed to study significant classics such as *the Analects of Confucius*, *Mencius*, and *Tso Chuan*, which is the commentary by Zuo Qiuming on *the Spring and Autumn Annals*. Many years later, Mao downplayed his study of the Chinese classics, claiming to have despised Confucius since the age of eight. However, the truth is that he internalised the teachings of the Five Classics and incorporated them into his intellectual frameworks. He frequently enriched his writings with quotes from Confucius and Mencius, demonstrating their influence on his thinking.[34]

Mao Zedong's intellectual development can be attributed more to Chinese historical and literary classics rather than formal or 'orthodox' education. His insatiable appetite for reading exposed him to a wide range of ideas that proved invaluable in navigating conflicts and revolutions. For instance, the *Yue Fei Chronicles*,[35] the *Water Margin*, the *Romance of Sui-Tang Dynasties*, the *Romance of the Three Kingdoms*, the *History as Mirror*, and the *Journey to the West*,[36] had provided ideas about rebellions, stratagems, agility, and political strategies and wisdom, serving as a guiding light and a source of inspiration for his action and decision making.

Taking the *Journey to the West* as an example, Mao was deeply influenced by its rebellious spirit and the agility displayed in battle. The Monkey King, a prominent character in this classic novel, exemplified exceptional skill and fearlessness. He dared to defy the Jade Emperor in Heaven and engaged in combat against the formidable warriors of Heaven. Notably, the Monkey King possessed a remarkable ability – each of his individual hairs held magical properties, enabling them to transform into clones of himself, as well as into various weapons, animals, and objects. This astonishing power allowed for 72 different types of transformations.

Mao drew inspiration from the Monkey King's versatility and employed this character to illustrate his own arguments in his writing titled *On Contradiction*. Mao utilised the Monkey King as a symbolic representation, emphasising the concrete and genuine nature of opposing forces and their dynamic transformation into one another under specific circumstances. Mythology itself offers countless examples of such transformations, with the Monkey King's 72 metamorphoses in *Hsi Yu Chi* being a prime illustration.[37]

In another article by Mao titled '*A Most Important Policy*', he makes reference to the Monkey King's tactics as a means of addressing the challenge posed by the enemy's apparatus. Mao draws inspiration from the episode in which the Monkey King faces off against Princess Iron Fan. Despite her formidable powers as a demon, Monkey King ingeniously transforms himself into a tiny insect, allowing him to infiltrate her stomach and ultimately overpower her.[38]

Another notable example of the Chinese classics' impact on Mao's thinking can be found in the renowned novel *Water Margin*. This literary masterpiece played a significant role in shaping Mao's worldview, particularly in regard to the importance of solidarity within organisations. Inspired by the novel, Mao adopted the slogan 'we are all brothers and sisters of the planet', reflecting his belief in the collective unity of humanity.

Stuart Schram has elucidated this particular influence. In the novel *Water Margin*, there existed a fortress called Liangshan, nestled within the mountains where the valiant bandit heroes fought tirelessly for justice and order in a world plagued by injustice and chaos. Fascinated by the characters and their struggle, Mao drew inspiration from their firm commitment to their cause. Marvellously, exactly a decade later, Mao embarked on a comparable adventure when he ascended the Chingkanshan (mountain). This mountainous journey mirrored the exploits of the heroes in *Water Margin* and symbolised Mao's own pursuit of justice and revolution in a world that desperately needed change.[39]

In line with the spirit of brotherhood exemplified in Liangshan, Mao continued to uphold principles of equality during the Yanan period (1935–1947). During this time, Mao advocated for a policy that fostered equal treatment between officers and soldiers. Even after the establishment of the People's Republic of China, Mao took steps to dismantle the existing military rank system and reinstated a policy of unity and equality between officer and soldier.

Mao's commitment to this principle extended beyond the revolutionary period, as he recognised the importance of maintaining a sense of camaraderie and shared purpose within the military. By abolishing the hierarchical structure, Mao aimed to cultivate an environment where every individual, regardless of their rank, felt valued and had an equal opportunity to contribute to the collective goals of the nation. This policy of equality and unity played a significant role in shaping the ethos of the Chinese military under Mao's leadership.

Mao Zedong drew valuable insights into Chinese dialectics from his reading of *Water Margin*, which he skilfully applied to expound upon the concept of 'contradiction' in his renowned article *On Contradiction*. Within this article, he ingeniously employed a tale from the classic novel to illustrate his point. In *Water Margin*, Song Jiang undertook three attacks on Chu Village. Initially, he suffered defeat twice due to his lack of understanding of the local conditions and the employment of an inappropriate strategy. However, he later adapted his approach. Firstly, he thoroughly investigated the situation and familiarised himself with the intricate road network. Subsequently, he dismantled the alliance between the Li, Huang, and Chu villages and cleverly dispatched his men in disguise to lie in wait within the enemy camp, employing a stratagem akin to the legendary Trojan Horse. As a result of these strategic adjustments, Song Jiang emerged triumphant on the third occasion.[40]

Mao Zedong held *The Romance of the Three Kingdoms* in high regard, considering it one of his most cherished books. Its influence on him was profound, as he kept it by his side until his last breath. This timeless masterpiece not only captivated him with its riveting narrative but also provided him with a wealth of strategic wisdom, effectively serving as a guidebook for military tactics and manoeuvres.

According to Stuart Schram, Mao gleaned valuable insights into the art of deception in warfare from his beloved novels, which included *The Romance of the Three Kingdoms* and *Water Margin*.[41] These literary works played a significant role in shaping Mao's strategic thinking.

Harrison Salisbury further emphasised the impact of Chinese classics on Mao Zedong's mindset and approach. Mao meticulously memorised the tales of the Three Kingdoms and the 'Outlaws' of *Water Margin*, immersing himself in the collections of slightly fictionalised historical episodes until his dying days. He repeatedly commented on these works and regarded them as textbooks for guerrilla warfare. Accused by his adversaries of employing tactics learned from the Outlaws in his military campaigns in Chingkanshan and during the Long March, Mao found in these accusations a practical acknowledgement of his capabilities. In truth, his enemies unwittingly paid him a compliment by recognising his adept application of strategies derived from these classical texts.[42]

Due to his in-depth understanding of ancient court intrigues, plots, and stratagems derived from Chinese historical records, both official and unofficial, Mao possessed a remarkable intellectual acumen. Skilfully blending this wealth of knowledge, he emerged as a master of deploying stratagems, surpassing adversaries both external and internal, including those within the party. This enabled him to cultivate a distinct and refined form of Chinese thought, characterised by its novelty and ingenuity.

Mao Zedong's strategic thought deviated from Karl Marx's emphasis on the proletariat as the driving force of revolution. Instead, Mao recognised the crucial role of the peasantry in China's revolution and mobilised them to become the primary forces of the CPC.

This insight originated from Mao's exploration of Chinese literary works, as he shared with Edgar Snow. Mao himself stated that he studied the old romances and tales of Chinese literature. It was during this process that he noticed a peculiar absence of peasants who toiled on the land. The stories mostly revolved around warriors, officials, or scholars, with no peasant heroes in sight. Mao realised that these narratives glorified individuals who possessed power, ruled over the people, and owned the land without having to work on it themselves. Instead, they relied on peasants to cultivate and labour on the land on their behalf.[43]

Mao's deep empathy for the peasantry was nurtured through his engagement with Chinese classics, which ultimately shaped his conviction that they would serve as the driving force behind the Chinese revolution. In a 1939 article, Mao elaborated on this belief, highlighting the relentless economic exploitation and political oppression that Chinese peasants endured, which drove them to revolt against landlord dominance. The magnitude of peasant uprising and wars throughout Chinese history was unparalleled elsewhere. Mao emphasised that the class struggles of the peasants, peasant uprisings, and peasant conflicts were the true impetus behind historical advancements within Chinese feudal society.[44]

While the academic consensus remains inconclusive regarding the extent to which a leader's personality determines their historic position of leadership, Mao Zedong's personality undeniably played an important part in establishing him as the prominent leader of the CPC.

Notably, Richard Nixon held Zhou Enlai, the Chinese Premier from 1949 to 1976, in high regard and considered him to be one of the world's outstanding leaders and statesmen. Nixon believed that Zhou lived in the shadow of a towering figure, Mao Zedong, and purposefully allowed Mao to bask in the limelight.[45] However, it is important to acknowledge that Zhou Enlai was unquestionably a remarkable leader and statesman. Nevertheless, Mao surpassed him as a leader of greater magnitude. To be more precise, Mao embodied the essence of true leadership, while Zhou excelled as a skilled and effective 'manager' on a national scale.[46]

Until 1935, Zhou Enlai held a position of authority over Mao, but following the Zunyi meeting of the CPC in early 1935, Mao gradually solidified his leadership role within the party.[47] According to Salisbury, the significance of Zunyi was that it marked a turning point, but the Long March persisted, with Mao assuming control and shaping China's trajectory for the next 50 years.[48] While leadership necessitates establishing direction and strategy for an organisation, Zhou Enlai struggled to fulfil the role during his tenure with the CPC. Conversely, Mao demonstrated his ability to guide the party in the right direction.

The contrasting capabilities of Mao and Zhou can largely be attributed to their distinct personalities and strategic knowledge. Mao possessed a strategic mind that was characterised by being attuned to strategic thinking, resolute, decisive, and adaptable. As described by Nixon, Mao's strength of will was instrumental in shaping his charismatic leadership.[49]

Moreover, Mao's strategic acumen was deeply ingrained in his Chinese heritage, as noted by Robert Scalapino. His continuous identification with Chinese culture influenced not only his way of expressing himself but also his thought processes and belief system. Despite his rebellious tendencies, Mao never completely disregarded the traditional Chinese elements that had a significant influence on his multifaceted persona.[50]

In contrast, Zhou Enlai displayed a more 'international' perspective in both his thinking and behaviour, as observed and documented by Harrison Salisbury. Unlike many others in the leadership group, Zhou had a background that made him somewhat of a 'foreigner'. He had spent significant years in France and Germany, and his time in Moscow exceeded what most people were aware of. Zhou possessed a cosmopolitan nature, finding cultural affinity in Paris more than any other place.[51]

Nevertheless, both Mao and Zhou relied on and supported each other throughout the Chinese Revolution and the subsequent socialist development of China. Nixon provides a vivid depiction of the significance of their relationship for China. Without Mao, the Chinese Revolution would never gained momentum, and without Zhou, it would have eventually extinguished, leaving behind only ashes.[52]

Since its inception, the CPC has embraced 'Marxism' and later 'Marxism-Leninism' as its guiding ideologies, which have formed an integral part of the CPC constitution. However, the early history of the CPC's revolutionary activities revealed that certain fundamental principles of

Marxism-Leninism failed to produce the desired outcome, resulting in numerous unsuccessful uprisings. Overall, China's adoption of foreign doctrines and methodologies has proved to be ineffective.

The connection between Marxism-Leninism and the CPC lies in the fact that Marxism-Leninism was the primary ideology that initially recognised and defined the 'classes' and advocated for the liberation of the exploited, urging the proletariat, or the working class in the Western context, to unite and engage in class struggles. Lenin played a crucial role in implementing Marxism and relied on uprisings of urban industrial workers to establish a socialist system of governance. Undoubtedly, Marxism-Leninism served as a source of inspiration for the formation of the CPC, as both ideologies have historically aligned themselves with the majority that experience exploitation.

The CPC has consistently acknowledged and celebrated Mao Zedong as a Marxist. This recognition is fitting, as both Mao and Marxism share common goals of socialism and communism, aiming to free the majority of society from exploitation and uplift the underprivileged. However, Mao astutely observed that, in China, the largest population of the victims of exploitation were not factory workers but rather the peasantry, who suffered under the oppression of landlords and the nobility. As a result, Mao developed his own theories and principles regarding the Chinese Revolution, distinct from foreign doctrines and ideologies, in order to address the specific conditions and needs of China.

Richard Nixon has recognised the differentiation between Mao and traditional Marxism, offering his observation on this matter. As a key figure in the Chinese Revolution, Mao left a lasting impact on history through his strategic acumen, tactical flexibility, and the utilisation of harsh violence. He departed from traditional Marxism by emphasising the peasantry as the revolutionary class instead of industrial workers. Additionally, he deviated from Leninism by conducting revolution with an organised army rather than relying on loosely organised insurrectionary groups.[53] Nixon's insights shed light on Mao's unique approach and contribution to revolutionary theory and practice.

## MAO'S MIND AND THOUGHT AND INFLUENCES

Mao Zedong was widely recognised as erudite and well-read, renowned for his exceptional knowledge of Chinese classics, both literary and historical. Drawing upon his intellect and wisdom, he skilfully synthesised the accumulated the wisdom of Chinese tradition, crafting a distinct strategic ideology that proved to be an indomitable force. The effectiveness of his strategic acumen manifested in the successful accomplishment of numerous military campaigns under his command and the profound impact of his influential works. The following examples serve to illustrate the remarkable depth and astute execution of the essence of Chinese strategic thinking.

## *Tao*

Mao Zedong's embrace of *Tao* is evident in his ambitious vision, which manifested at a young age. In 1971, Mao played a pivotal role in establishing the *Xin Min Xue Hui* or New People's Study Society (NPSS). In 1918, during a momentous gathering, Mao directed all members to adopt the society's objective as the 'transformation of China and the world'.[54] This objective exemplified Mao's extraordinary ambition. Mao aspired not only to govern China but also to revolutionise the very essence of Chinese society and culture, aiming to eradicate the country's weaknesses and garner respect on the global stage.[55]

In 1919, Mao was actively involved in coordinating an overseas work-study programme in which many of his close associates and best friends took part. Despite the opportunity, Mao made a conscious decision not to go abroad himself, driven by his personal convictions. He firmly believed that his friends should immerse themselves in Western culture and acquire knowledge and ideas that could benefit China. Mao saw a pressing need for the reform and reconstruction of China, and he strongly believed that he was the one best suited for this important task. Driven by a sense of responsibility, Mao felt compelled to remain in China and assume a leadership role in bringing about the necessary changes.[56]

Mao Zedong is recognised as one of the Chinese leaders who embraced the idea of 'equality'. While Western democratic governments have embraced equality as a fundamental principle since the promulgation of the American Declaration of Independence in 1776, China has had a long history of governance dominated by dictatorship, deeply rooted in Chinese tradition. Mao's embrace of equality, both in principle and practice, can be seen as a transformative departure aligned with *Tao* principles.

Mao's sensitivity to and adherence to *Tao* notions became evident in his strategic shift during the late 1930s and early 1940s. Initially, Mao employed a confrontational approach towards the KMT forces. However, influenced by the *Tao* ethos, he recognised the need for a more inclusive and cooperative strategy to counter the Japanese invitation.

Mao's transformation involved the formation of strategic alliances with all parties and classes, including the KMT. He understood that unity among various factions was crucial in the face of external aggression. Mao believed that the Chinese Civil War should be subordinated to the larger national war against imperialism aligning with the Tao principles.

According to Mao, when China faced armed attacks from imperialist powers, the Communist Party should unite all classes and social strata within the country. This unity would be directed against the foreign aggressors, as exemplified by the ongoing war of resistance against Japan.[57] By emphasising a national war against the common enemy, Mao sought to transcend ideological and partisan divisions for the greater good of the Chinese nation.

## Dialectic

Dialectic plays a distinctive role in Chinese strategic thinking, setting it apart from its Western counterpart. Mao Zedong's thorough understanding of dialectic is prominently reflected in his thought and works. Notable among these are his January 1930 piece, *A Single Spark Can Start a Prairie Fire*,[58] his 1937 piece, *On Contradiction*,[59] which, along with his theories on *The Strategic Defensive*, including concepts like, *Active and Passive Defence*, *Strategic Retreat*, *Strategic Counter-Offensive*, and *Mobile Warfare*,[60] as well as his framework of warfare known as the *Three Stages of the Protracted War*,[61] exemplify Mao's application of dialectic.

The significance of Mao' paper *On Contradiction*[62] cannot be overstated, as it stands as one of his most crucial philosophical essays. Within this work, Mao specifically delves into the nature of Chinese dialectic. Together with his other influential writing, *On Practice*,[63] these two works form the philosophical bedrock of his political ideology, ultimately giving rise to Maoism. This further underscores the indispensable role of that dialectic played in Mao's strategic mind.

## Holism

The essence of Chinese cognition lies in a holistic worldview deeply rooted in Chinese culture. This perspective, evident in Mao Zedong's leadership and decision-making, encompasses a comprehensive understanding of various aspects, be they military or civil affairs. This holistic approach is prominently reflected in his writings, speeches, strategic choices, and strategic actions.

For instance, Mao Zedong emphasised the significance of a holistic outlook when formulating military strategies in one of his articles. He recognised that the science of strategy entails studying the laws governing an entire war situation. Dismissing the notion that strategic victory solely hinges on tactical successes, Mao Zedong astutely acknowledged that the outcome of a war primarily depends on whether the overall situation and its different stages are adequately considered. He famously remarked, '*One careless move loses the whole game*', underscoring the importance of holistic thinking in both chess and warfare.[64]

Another instance involves his discussion on the 'agrarian revolution' within the context of China's revolutionary war.[65] Elliot-Bateman has pointed out that Mao Zedong considered the examination of war to be essentially an examination of society.[66]

## Stratagem

Stratagem, which is at the heart of Chinese strategic thinking, has consistently garnered great emphasis from Chinese strategists throughout the country's history. In the past, particularly in antiquity, it has been essentially synonymous with the concept of strategy. Mao Zedong, too, placed significant emphasis on the utilisation of stratagem as a crucial component of his strategic philosophy. His deep embrace and widespread implementation of stratagem can be discerned from his writings and theories. Notably, Mao was well-versed in works such as the *Twenty-four Histories*, *Tso Chuan*, and the *Romance of the Three Kingdoms*,[67] which are regarded as classic Chinese stratagem manuals.

Salisbury has acknowledged Mao Zedong's mastery of stratagem, highlighting the effectiveness of Mao's grand deception. This deception left Chiang Kai-shek and his generals in a state of bewilderment, unable to discern the movement of the Red Army. Mao's strategy resembled the elusive Scarlet Pimpernel, appearing here, there, and seemingly everywhere, further exacerbating the confusion and uncertainty among his adversaries. The Red Army's presence was indeed ubiquitous. It is unlikely that at any other point in time, before or after, the Red Army had ever been as extensively dispersed, simultaneously moving in numerous directions.[68]

Mao's theory on *Guerrilla War*[69] is a notable example of stratagem utilisation. Like an artist, Mao demonstrated mastery in employing various tactics and techniques. Through his succinct deployment of sixteen Chinese characters, which crystallised Chinese stratagems in poetic form during the Chinese civil war, he provided invaluable guidance to the CPC army, contributing to their years of success:

> The enemy approaches, we retreat.
> The enemy halts, we move in.
> The enemy tires, we attack.
> The enemy retreats, we pursue.[70]

The significance of the poetic form of stratagems has been noted by Salisbury, who emphasised that the poem served as the essence of guerrilla warfare, empowering the Zhu-Mao-led[71] army to achieve strength and resilience. It safeguarded the army from extermination.[72]

Henry Kissinger held great admiration for Mao Zedong's consummate ability to employ stratagem in his leadership. According to Kissinger, Mao was a proficient practitioner of the ancient Empty City Stratagem, a tactic that involves disguising weakness through a display of confidence, or even aggression.[73] Mao Zedong is often likened to Zhuge Liang, a revered symbol of wisdom in China.

Jonathan Fenby offers a vibrant portrayal of Zhuge Liang. Just as Machiavelli embodies European statecraft, Zhuge Liang, a general and strategist from 3rd-century China, holds a comparable significance in his nation's historical context. Zhuge Liang is regarded as a symbol of intelligence, embodying exceptional skills as a devoted commander statesman, scholar, and notably an astrologer, which held great importance in Chinese cosmology. In addition, Zhuge Liang is credited with being a master of cunning and deception.[74]

Harrison Salisbury placed great emphasis on the historical significance and enduring legacy of Zhuge Liang. Zhuge Liang, immortalised in the epic novel the *Romance of the Three Kingdoms*, held a prominent position in Mao's personal development, serving as a crucial influence throughout his life. Mao regarded the novel as a guiding text, not only in terms of his political ideology but also as a military strategy manual during the arduous Long March.

One notable example of Zhuge Liang's influence on Mao's military thinking was reflected in the intricate and cunning campaign conducted in Guizhou. The strategic manoeuvre of driving south into Yunnan, thereby opening a pathway to proceed northward, bore striking similarities to tactics employed by Zhuge Liang. It is even speculated that some of these tactics, attributed to Mao, might have been directly inspired by Zhuge Liang himself. The amazing resemblance between their approaches led to numerous instances where Mao was referred to by his comrades in the Red Army as 'Zhuge Liang', drawing a parallel between the two revered military strategists.[75]

## Agility

Chinese strategic thinking incorporates the concept of agility, which finds its foundation in the *yin–yang* principles. This distinctive aspect is exemplified by Mao Zedong, who placed significant importance on agility, as evident in his writing and actions. Mao's notable works emphasise the utilisation of initiative, flexibility, and planning in offensive operations,[76] as well as the flexible employment of forces.[77] The Long March, a monumental undertaking led by Mao Zedong following the Zunyi meeting, serves as triumphant ode to his strategic genius, embodying qualities such as *Tao*, stratagem, agility, bravery, indomitableness, and sacrifice.

According to Harrison Salisbury, the significance of China's Long March in 1934 goes beyond being a mere symbol. It stands as a remarkable human saga that tested the determination, courage, and resilience of the men and women comprising the Chinese Red Army.[78]

In his account, Edgar Snow provides detailed insight into the formidable hardship endured during the Long March, which served as a true test of human will. The arduous journey was marked by a skirmish nearly every day at various points along the route. In addition, a significant portion of the march involved engaging in major pitched battles, with a total of 15 whole days dedicated to such encounters.

Out of the 368 days spent en route, a staggering 235 days were consumed by marches during daylight hours, while 18 days were spent marching through the night. Among the 100 days of halts, many were punctuated by skirmishes. Notably, 56 of these halting days were spent in the northwest region of Szechuan, which is incredible considering the treacherous nature of the terrain. It is truly astonishing that a large army, along with its logistical support, managed to maintain such a phenomenal pace across some of the most hazardous terrain on Earth.[79]

Mao Zedong demonstrated remarkable leadership during the Long March as he guided the CPC armies in evading the encirclement of the KMT forces. Despite being outnumbered 10 to one and facing superior firepower and modern weaponry, the CPC employed agility and speed to manoeuvre around the KMT's formidable defences.

The situation can be likened to a vast fishing net cast by the KMT, with Mao Zedong embodying the fish that skilfully swam through the gaps in the net. With exceptional agility and speed, Mao and the CPC forces navigated through the openings in the KMT's encirclement. Their ability to exploit these gaps and swiftly adapt to the changing circumstances played a crucial role in their successful circumvention during the Long March.

Salisbury observed and described this marked phenomenon. According to his account, the Red Army's march and counter-march unfolded in a bewildering manner, leaving Chiang Kai-shek and his commanders perplexed. The KMT often struggled to accurately locate the Communist forces, with their reports sometimes being nearly a week late. Even Mao Zedong's own generals, including his protégé Li Biao, occasionally found themselves bewildered by the rapidity and intensity of the troop movements. Lin Biao voiced concerns about the need for rest, as he believed the troops were being pushed too hard and moved too rapidly. However, despite these objections, Mao's decisions prevailed, overriding the reservations expressed by his generals.[80]

### *Shi*

As a master of leveraging the principles of Chinese strategic thinking, Mao possessed extensive knowledge of *Shi* and adeptly capitalised on it to advance personally and professionally.

Mao's utilisation of *Shi* commenced during his youth, when he secured a position as a librarian at Beijing (or Peking) University through his father-in-law, Yang Changji, a Philosophy Professor. It was at this institution where Mao crossed paths with Chen Duxiu and Li Dazhao, two pivotal founders of the CPC. Through his interaction with these founders, Mao gradually matured in grasping communist ideology and gained access to literature on communism, as well to as other early members of the CPC. While it is challenging to precisely measure the extent to which Mao Zedong was influenced by these two key CPC figures, their influence on him was undoubtedly significant.[81]

During an interview with Edgar Snow, Mao Zedong acknowledged the pronounced impact of Chen Duxiu on his life. Mao revealed that his initial encounter with Chen Duxiu took place in Beijing while he was working at Peking National University, and he expressed that Chen's influence on him may have surpassed that of any other individual.[82] In essence, Mao leveraged Professor Yang's connection, a form of *Shi*, to pass through the gates of the CPC, ultimately ascending to the paramount leadership of the party.

Mao Zedong skilfully employed the *Shi* factor throughout various conflicts, such as the Chinese Civil War, the Korean War, the Sino-Indian War, and the Sino-Soviet War.[83] In the context of the Chinese Civil War, Mao's forces, led by him, faced off against Chiang Kai-shek's KMT forces. Initially, there was a significant disparity between the two sides, with Chiang's forces enjoying superior firepower and overall material strength. This contrast was observed and documented by Edgar Snow.

Chiang relied heavily on foreign equipment, training, and doctrines to bolster his forces, while Mao's armies had limited resources, primarily relying on locally produced grenades and the strength of the Chinese people. Mao recognised the need to address this asymmetry and devised a strategy of protracted warfare, targeting Chiang's weaknesses and vulnerabilities. Simultaneously, he sought to build up the *Shi* factor as a means to overcome the strengths of the Nationalist forces.[84]

The ultimate outcome of the warfare between the Red Army and the KMT force hinged on the clash between the strategic mindsets of Chiang and Mao. Chiang's strategic outlook had been heavily influenced by his education at the Tokyo Shinbu Gakko, an Imperial Japanese army academy. Furthermore, he had also received guidance from German military advisors, including General von Falkenhausen of the German Army, who served as Chiang's chief adviser,[85] as observed by Snow.

Richard Nixon, who had a long acquaintance with Chiang, provided his insights on the matter. Chiang was undoubtedly a skilled political and military tactician, but his rigid adherence to established principles limited his effectiveness as a strategist. Chiang's mind operated swiftly and decisively when working within a predefined framework of strategic assumption. As long as these assumptions remained unchanged, few could rival him. However, he faced challenges when required to transcend these assumptions and introduce innovative approaches that questioned the prevailing norms of the time.[86]

In contrast, Mao Zedong's strategic acumen was deeply rooted in Chinese tradition, characterised by a remarkable blend of strategic thinking, visionary leadership, deception, agility, and an appreciation of the concept of *Shi*. A prime example of China's triumph was the historic Long March, undertaken by the CPC troops from October 1934 to September 1935. Spanning a stunning distance of 12 000 kilometres, the arduous journey traversed 11 provinces, crossed 18 mountains, and navigated 17 rivers.[87] This epic undertaking stands as a testament to Mao's exceptional leadership in guiding the CPC army to success.

Salisbury has remarked upon the intricacies, formidable nature, and profound significance of the Long March. This historic undertaking exemplified the triumph of human resilience as it entailed a perilous and endless retreat from the clutches of Chiang Kai-shek's forces. The Long March teetered upon the brink of defeat and disaster numerous times and narrowly escaping catastrophe on multiple occasions. It was conducted without a comprehensive plan, with Mao being excluded from the preparation and only informed at the last minute. Ultimately, this arduous journey paved the way for Mao Zedong and his communist forces to claim victory and secure China. The impact of the Long March cannot be overstated – the event captivated the world's imagination and exerted a substantial influence on its future. Few events in the 20th century have captured global attention and shaped the course of history to such a significant extent.[88]

From Mao's *Shi*-orientated viewpoint, the Long March served as an indirect strategy aimed at establishing a solid political and operational foundation. Its primary objective was to unify numerous disparate communist activities under Mao's leadership. Mao and the CPC strategically utilised the Long March as a means to promote their revolutionary cause and engage in an unprecedented armed propaganda tour. This tour played a pivotal role in disseminating their message and garnering support for their revolutionary efforts, making it a significant milestone in the history of communist propaganda.[89]

Although the Long March undeniably stemmed from a strategic retreat necessitated by significant regional setbacks, the Communist forces ultimately achieved their intended goal. Through adept rationalisation, the Communists transformed what could have been a demoralising retreat into an invigorating march towards victory. This astute propaganda manoeuvre deserves recognition as a remarkable display of political acumen. In one way this vast migration can be deemed the most extensive armed propaganda tour ever conducted.[90]

The genesis and operation of the Long March reflect the nature of Chinese strategy. It was not a meticulously crafted blueprint but rather a dynamic process that Mao Zedong skilfully transformed into a comprehensive strategy, which was ultimately executed with success. Notably, strategy and execution were intricately intertwined and mutually reinforcing. François Jullien offers valuable insights into this phenomenon.

Central to Chinese strategy is the reliance on the inherent potential of the unfolding situation, embracing its evolution and allowing it to carry them forward. From the very beginning, this approach dismisses the notion of predetermined events dictated by a more or less definitive preconceived plan. Instead, the focus lies on adapting to and leveraging the ever-changing circumstances, without rigidly adhering to an idealised plan that must be fulfilled.[91]

### Mao's Thought System

Mao Zedong stands out among esteemed national leaders, having produced a notable abundance of writings that probe profound philosophical, political, and military concepts and theories. Alongside these works, his eloquent poetry vividly portrays his grand ambitions and optimistic vision for the future. The extensive compilation of Mao Zedong's selected works, spanning five volumes, serves as a testament to the breadth and depth of his ideological and military contributions.[92] His political and military theorems and theories have exerted significant influence within both domestic and international spheres, and continue to do so to this day.

However, in contrast to other strategists and theorists, Mao Zedong surpassed expectations by excelling not only as a statesman, strategist, and theorist but also an outstanding practitioner who effectively applied his principles and theories to achieve extraordinary feats in reality. Mao's greatness shines through his unparalleled capacity to seamlessly integrate theory with practice, epitomising the essence of Chinese strategic thinking.

## MAO'S SYSTEM FOR IMPLEMENTATION

Historically, Chinese culture has been plagued by disorganisation, which has often acted as a hindrance to societal progress. This can be attributed to the Chinese emphasis on dexterity and stratagem, which, while valuable in certain contexts, has led to failures in military and commercial endeavours. The inept organisational structures embedded in Chinese culture have been examined and critiqued.

According to Mao Zedong, Chinese history has been marked by a plethora of uprisings, ranging from minor rebellions to full-fledged peasant evolutionary wars. The sheer magnitude of these uprisings and wars involving the peasantry is unparalleled in any other society. However, despite the scale of these movements, every peasant revolution ultimately met with failure. Furthermore, the peasantry often found themselves manipulated by the landlords and nobility, who exploited their struggles either during or after the revolution, utilising them as a means to bring about dynastic changes.[93]

The question arises: what factors contributed to the success of the CPC uprising, which can be seen as a form of peasant revolution, considering the historical failures of numerous peasant revolts and rebellions? According to Mao Zedong, the key to success lies in the correct leadership provided by the proletariat and the Communist Party.[94] However, the question remains: How exactly did this leadership ensure success?

The older generation of Chinese people often attributes the success to 'Mao Zedong Thought' or 'Mao's infinite wisdom'. Nevertheless, the question persists: How did Mao Zedong manage to unite and mobilise the largely disorganised and mostly illiterate peasantry? Even if the ideas of the CPC or 'Mao Zedong Thought' resonated with the peasants, how were they educated, convinced, and organised by the Communist Party? Finding answers to these questions would shed light on the nature of Chinese organisation in its 'primitive' or 'unsophisticated' form.

Mao Zedong's strategy for Chinese revolution revolved around the belief that control of power could be achieved through the possession of arms. This power then enabled him to implement his grand vision of transforming China and the world. Mao recognised that the peasantry would serve as the central force driving this transformation.

To effectively rally the peasants to join the Chinese revolution, Mao astutely considered their most pressing desires. It became evident that land, predominantly owned by landlords and the nobility, held immense significance for the peasants. Land was not only the source of their livelihood but also their only means of accumulating wealth, a desire they yearned for individually.[95]

Consequently, Mao understood that an 'agrarian revolution' had to precede the Chinese revolution, establishing itself as an integral part of China's revolutionary war.[96] By addressing the peasants' aspirations for land and the subsequent redistribution of wealth, Mao aimed to mobilise their support and gain their active participation in the revolution.

Nick Knight has astutely noted Mao's strategic approach, which involved relying on peasants as the principal driving force of his movement. In the mid-1920s, Mao's understanding of the class dynamics within the Chinese Revolution was based on the belief that the central issue of the revolution lay in addressing the challenges faced by the peasantry. He recognised that the poor peasants, in particular, constituted the primary force behind the revolution.[97]

It became evident that attempting to reason with or 'educate' peasants in order to persuade them to join the revolution was an arduous task. However, Mao's intellectual brilliance led him to adopt a straightforward approach. He presented the plain facts to the peasants, emphasising that the Chinese revolution aimed to 'expropriate local tyrants and landowners and distribute land'

– a slogan that resonated easily with the rural population. Consequently, they became willing to join forces with the Red Army and make sacrifices for the cause of the Chinese revolution. Through this simple ideological instillation, Mao successfully mobilised the masses of peasants, incorporating them into the fighting force of the CPC. Between 1927 and 1930, Mao Zedong employed specific revolutionary strategies that primarily relied on the large population of peasants residing in the rural areas.

Nick Knight has provided a perceptive analysis of the significance of peasants in the Chinese revolution. It was the peasants who voluntarily joined the fight driven by their desire for the seizure and redistribution of land, the abolition of debts owed to landlords, and the reduction of the heavy burden of rent and taxes. Mao's decision to harness the anger and discontent of the peasants through armed struggle and the establishment of rural soviets was not a mere opportunistic manoeuvre. Instead, Mao genuinely recognised the pivotal role of the peasants and their grievances as the heart of the Chinese Revolution during that period.[98]

In order to address the historical issue of disorganisation among peasants that had led to the downfall of previous revolutions, Mao implemented a disciplinary policy aimed at instilling order and unity. This policy was effectively communicated through a captivating and easily understandable song known as *The Three Main Rules of Discipline and the Eight Points for Attention.*

The Three Rules were as follows:

1.  Obey orders in all your actions.
2.  Don't take a needle or a piece of thread from the people.
3.  Turn in everything you capture.

Complementing these rules were the Eight Points of Attention, which further emphasised the desired conduct:

1.  Speak politely.
2.  Pay fairly for what you buy.
3.  Return everything you borrow.
4.  Pay for any damage.
5.  Don't strike or swear at people.
6.  Don't damage the crops.
7.  Don't take liberties with women.
8.  Don't mistreat captives.[99]

The impact of powerful and emotionally charged political songs, carefully crafted by a dedicated special CPC department within the Red Armies was observed by Hung.

Mao and his associates held the belief that music served a purpose beyond mere artistic expression or practical utility, perceiving it as a potent political instrument. In their perspective, music, drama, art, and literature – the four disciplines encompassed within Luyi – were deemed as the most powerful tools for arousing and mobilising the masses. This sentiment was explicitly conveyed in Mao's inaugural statement of Luyi where he and his followers proclaimed that these creative forms were indispensable in fermenting and organising the people, playing a pivotal role in the socialist revolution. Mao recognised the significance of harnessing popular art forms to advance the objectives of the revolution.[100]

In present-day management terminology, Mao Zedong's accomplishment can be understood as the establishment of a strong 'organisational culture' within the Red Armies, achieved through the use of political songs. This culture not only effectively organised and motivated the peasant soldiers, but also fostered a positive perception among the general population, which stood in contrast to the KMT forces known for their frequent pillaging and looting.

During the Chinese Civil War, a significant number of leaders emerged who were known as 'returnees' because they had received training or education in Russia or Continental Europe. These individuals considered themselves well-versed in Marxism and Leninism, often adhering rigidly to their theories and Russian practices.

In contrast, Mao Zedong can be characterised as a 'scholar leader' due to his reputation for erudition, which he acquired through self-education. However, he was not an academic in the traditional sense and did not rely on textbooks or established theories, including those from Marxist and Leninist sources. Mao developed a unique approach within the Red Armies known as 'seeking truth from fact'.[101] This approach involved conducting thorough investigation and basing decisions on empirical evidence. Mao adopted a less radical approach, allowing well-to-do or upper-class families, as well as small and medium-sized landowners, to maintain their livelihoods without resorting to rebellion. This pragmatic policy aimed to strike a balance between social stability and progressive change.

After Mao's official inclusion of the tripartite leadership group and the acquisition of decision-making power within the CPC following the Zunyi Conference in 1935, his colleagues frequently harboured doubts about his decisions. Consequently, they often hesitated to fully commit to implementing them, leading to significant losses. Furthermore, some individuals openly challenged Mao's leadership, exacerbating the situation. Harrison Salisbury, an observer of the event, has made his note of and commented on this phenomenon.

During that period, Zhou, along with the other members of the troika, consistently opposed Mao's strategies and dismissed his suggestions. There was a lack of collaboration, and while there is no evidence to suggest that Zhou actively supported Bo Gu and Braun in their attempts to remove Mao from power, there is also no evidence indicating that Zhou actively opposed such manoeuvres. Throughout the period spanning from the Ningdu meeting in October 1932 to the commencement of the Long March in October 1934, Zhou never once consulted with Mao.[102]

As a result, Mao found it necessary to strengthen his leadership position within the CPC in order to effectively implement 'Mao Zedong Thought'. This led to the initiation of the Yanan Rectification Movement, which took place from 1942 to 1944. The movement, the first of its kind in terms of political and ideological mass mobilisation, aimed to consolidate Mao's authority. It was launched in Yanan, Northern Shaanxi, following the CPC's Long March.

The significance of the Yanan Rectification Movement in the history of the CPC under Mao's leadership cannot be overstated. It played a crucial role in consolidating Mao's position within the party and resulted in the adoption of a party constitution that officially recognised Marxism-Leninism, and Mao Zedong Thought as guiding principles.[103] In a comprehensive book titled *How did the Sun Rise Over Yan'an? A History of the Rectification Movement*, Gao Hua provides a detailed analysis of Mao's motivations behind initiating the movement.

The Rectification Movement explicitly aimed at dismantling and eradicating two distinct forms of influence within the party. Firstly, it sought to challenge and dismantle the influence of Russian-trained intellectuals who adhered to a Stalinist style of thinking. This group had previously held significant sway within the party leadership. Secondly, the movement intended to counter the influence of Western democratic liberalism, particularly prevalent among the May Fourth generation. Although this group wielded less power it encompassed a much larger contingent, including thousands of students who had arrived in Yanan following the outbreak of war in 1937.[104]

The Movement achieved unity of thought and action while strengthening the CPC organisation, ensuring strict adherence to Mao's strategic decisions.

## NOTES

1.    Karl, R.E. (2010). *Mao Zedong and China in the Twentieth-Century World: A Concise History*. Duke University Press.
      Kissinger, H.A. (2011). *On China*. Allen Lane.
2.    Elliott-Bateman, M. (1967). *Defeat in The East: The Mark of Mao Tse-tung on War*. London: Oxford University Press.
      Nixon, R.M. (1983). *Leaders*. Simon & Schuster, pp. 247–8.
      Mohanty, M. (1995). Power of history: Mao Zedong Thought and Deng's China. *China Report*, 31(1), pp. 1–14.

3.    Li, S. and Yeh, K. (2007). Mao's Pervasive Influence on Chinese CEOs. *Harvard Business Review*, 85(12), pp. 16–17.
4.    Tian, T. and Wu, C.B. (2012). *Xia yi ge dao xia de hui bu hui shi Huawei?* (*Is Huawei Falling Down Next?*) China CITIC Press, pp. 66.
5.    Nixon (n 2) pp. 247–8.
6.    Ibid., p. 34.
7.    Russo, A. (2013). How Did the Cultural Revolution End? The Last Dispute between Mao Zedong and Deng Xiaoping, 1975. *Modern China*, 39(3), pp. 239–79.
8.    Benton, G. (2011). Book Review: *Mao Zedong and China in the Twentieth-Century World: A Concise History*, by Karl, R.E. (2010), Duke University Press. *The China Quarterly*, June, pp. 431–2.
      Chang, G.G. (2013). The Man Who Would Be Mao. *The National Interest*, December 23 2013.
9.    Russo (n 7) pp. 239–79.
10.   Mohanty (n 2) pp. 1–14.
11.   Crainer, S. (1995). *The Financial Times: Handbook of Management*. FT Pitman Publishing, p. 105.
12.   Ignatius, A. (2014). Remembering Warren Bennis. *Harvard Business Review*, 92(10). P. 12.
13.   Crainer (n 11) p. 107.
14.   Nixon (n 5) p. 5.
15.   Scalapino, R.A. (1982). The Evolution of a Young Revolutionary – Mao Zedong in 1919–1921. *The Journal of Asian Studies*, 42(1), p. 61.
16.   Snow, E. (1968). *Red Star Over China*. London: Victor Gollancz Ltd, p. 132.
17.   Salisbury, H. (1985). *The Long March: The Untold Story*. Macmillan, p. 73.
18.   Ibid., pp. 73–74.
19.   Snow (n 16) p. 95.
20.   Ibid., p. 132.
21.   Ren, Z.G. (2013). *Wei Shen Mo Shi Mao Zedong?* (*Why Is Mao Zedong?*). Guang Ming Daily Publisher, pp. 7–10.
22.   Scalapino (n 15) pp. 29–61.
23.   Nixon (n 5) p. 226.
24.   Ibid., pp. 226–7.
25.   Salisbury (n 17) p. 132.
26.   Lu, Z.D. (2009). *Mao Zedong Ping Guoxue* (*Mao Zedong's Comments on Chinese Classics*). New World Press.
      Sheng, X.C. and Li, Z.C. (2011). *Mao Zedong PinPing SiDa MingZhu* (*Mao Zedong's Commentaries on the Four Classics*). Central Compilation & Translation Press.
27.   Snow (n 16) p. 133.
28.   Schram, S. (1967). *Political Leaders of the Twentieth Century: Mao Tse-tung*. Penguin Books, p. 21.
29.   Lieberthal, K. (1995). *Governing China: From Revolution to Reform*. W.W. Norton & Co., p. 60.

30. Lu (n 26) p. 57.
31. Schram (n 28) p. 21.
32. They are the Confucian authoritative books written before 300 BC. The Four Books are Great Learning, Doctrine of the Mean, Analects, and Mencius; and the Five Classics are Book of Poetry, Book of Documents, Book of Rites, I Ching, and Spring and Autumn Annals.
33. Lu (n 26).
34. Salisbury (n 17) p. 72.
35. Yue Fei (1103–1142) was a military general of the Han Chinese during the period of the Southern Song dynasty. He has been widely acclaimed as a patriot and national hero in China, because he led Southern Song forces in the wars against the Jurchen Jin dynasty in northern China in the 12th century. He was put to death by a court politician, Qin Gui (1090–1155), who was pushing an appeasement policy towards the Jin. Yue Fei is regarded as a patriotic martyr in China, while Qin Gui is remembered as a traitor.
36. Lu (n 26).
    Sheng, X.C. and Li, Z.C. (2011). *Mao Zedong PinPing SiDa MingZhu* (*Mao Zedong's Commentaries on the Four Classics*). Central Compilation & Translation Press.
37. Zedong, M. (1937). On Contradiction. *Selected Works of Mao Tse-tung*: *Volume I*, 1965. Peking: Foreign Languages Press, p. 340.
38. Mao, Z. (1942). A Most Important Policy. *Selected Works of Mao Tse-tung: Volume III, 1965*. Peking: Foreign Languages Press, p. 101.
39. Schram (n 28) pp. 43–4.
40. Mao (n 37) p. 324.
41. Schram (n 28) p. 159.
42. Salisbury (n 17) p. 73.
43. Snow (n 16) p. 134.
44. Mao, Z. (1939). Chinese Society. *Selected Works of Mao Tse-tung: Volume II* (1965 edition). Peking: Foreign Languages Press, p. 308.
45. Ibid., p. 3.
46. John Kotter has outlined the differences between a leader and a manager in detail: Kotter, J.P. (1999). *John P. Kotter on What Leaders Really Do*. Harvard Business School Press.
47. Although Mao had been in the control seat in the CPC since 1934, it was in 1943 that he was officially elected as 'Chairman Mao' by the CPC Politburo.
48. Salisbury (n 17) p. 126.
49. Nixon (n 5) p. 240.
50. Scalapino (n 15) pp. 29–61.
51. Salisbury (n 17) p. 131.
52. Nixon (n 5) p. 248.
53. Ibid., p. 240.
54. Mao Zedong played a leading role in the formation of the Xin Min Xue Hui or New People's Study Society. At a meeting in 1918, all members stipulated the objective of the society as the 'transformation of China and the world'.

55. Lieberthal (n 29) p. 59.
56. Ibid.
57. Mao, Z. (1938). Problems of War and Strategy. *Selected Military Writings of Mao Tse-tung* (1965 edition). Peking: Foreign Languages Press, pp. 267–83.
58. Mao, Z. (1930). A Single Spark Can Start a Prairie Fire. *Selected Works of Mao Tse-tung: Volume I* (1965 edition). Peking: Foreign Languages Press, pp. 117–28.
59. Mao, Z. (1937). On Contradiction. *Selected Works of Mao Tse-tung: Volume I* (1965 edition). Peking: Foreign Languages Press, pp. 311–47.
60. Mao, Z. (1965). The Strategic Defensive. *Selected Works of Mao Tse-tung: Volume I*. Peking: Foreign Languages Press, pp. 205–54.
61. Mao, Z. (1938). On Protracted War and Strategy. *Selected Military Writings of Mao Tse-tung*. Peking: Foreign Languages Press, pp. 187–266.
62. Mao, Z. (1937). On Contradiction. *Selected Works of Mao Tse-tung: Volume I* (1965 edition). Peking: Foreign Languages Press, pp. 311–47.
63. Mao, Z. (1937). On Practice. *Selected Works of Mao Tse-tung: Volume I* (1965 edition). Peking: Foreign Languages Press, pp. 295–309.
64. Mao (n 57) pp. 79–80.
65. Mao, Z. (1936). Problems of Strategy in China's Revolutionary War. *Selected Military Writings of Mao Tse-tung*. Peking: Foreign Languages Press, pp. 94–5.
66. Elliott-Bateman (n 2) p. 6.
67. Liu (n 26).
68. Salisbury (n 17) p. 166.
69. Mao (n 61) pp. 151–85.
70. Salisbury (n 17) p. 129.
71. During the Chinese Civil War, the leadership structure of the Chinese Red Army consisted of Zhe De as the commander-in-chief and Mao as the CPC secretary. It is important to note that, in the CPC system, the army has traditionally been subordinated to the party, with the party secretary serving as the paramount leader. Consequently, the collective leadership of Zhu and Mao was commonly referred to as Zhu-Mao. This arrangement underscored the party's authority over the military and reflected their respective roles within the Chinese Communist Party.
72. Salisbury (n 17) p. 129.
73. Ferguson, N. (2011). Henry Kissinger's Prescription for China. *Newsweek*, 15 May 2011.
74. Fenby, J. (2011). Zhuge Liang: 181–234. *Great Commanders of the Ancient World: 1479BC–453AD* (A. Roberts, Ed.). Quercus, pp. 296–7.
75. Salisbury (n 17) p. 172.
76. Mao (n 61) p. 154.
77. Ibid., p. 155.
78. Salisbury (n 17) p. 1.
79. Snow (n 16) pp. 204–5.
80. Salisbury (n 17) p. 154.

81. Snow (n 16) pp. 151–4.
82. Ibid., p. 154.
83. Mott, W.H. and Kim, J.C. (2006). *The Philosophy of Chinese Military Culture*. Palgrave Macmillan.
84. Ibid., p. 78.
85. Snow (n 16) p. 187.
86. Nixon (n 5) p. 245.
87. Mott and Kim (n 83) pp. 84–5.
88. Salisbury (n 17) p. 1.
89. Mott and Kim (n 83) p. 85.
90. Snow (n 16) pp. 205–6.
91. Jullien, F. (2004). *A Treatise on Efficacy: Between Western and Chinese Thinking* (J. Lloyd, Trans.). Honolulu: University of Hawaii Press, p. 20.
92. Mao, Z. (1965). *Selected Works of Mao Tse-tung: Volumes I–IV*. Peking: Foreign Languages Press.
Mao, Z. (1977). *Selected Works of Mao Tse-tung: Volume V*. Peking: Foreign Languages Press.
93. Mao (n 44) pp. 308–9.
94. Ibid., p. 309.
95. Ren (n 21) pp. 141–2.
96. Mao (n 65) pp. 94–5.
97. Knight, Nick (2007). *Rethinking Mao: Explorations in Mao Zedong's Thought*, Lexington Books, p. 79.
98. Ibid., p. 81.
99. Salisbury (n 17) p. 117.
100. Hung, C.T. (1996). The Politics of Songs: Myths and Symbols in the Chinese Communist War Music, 1937–1949. *Modern Asian Studies*, 30(4), Special Issue: War in Modern China, pp. 901–29.
101. This tradition of 'seeking truth from fact' was later embraced by Deng Xiaoping during the implementation of his reform policy in the 1980s.
102. Salisbury (n 17) p. 130.
103. Lieberthal, K. (2003). *Governing China: From Revolution to Reform* (second edition). W.W. Norton & Co, pp. 45–8.
104. Liang, K. (2004). The Rise of Mao and His Cultural Legacy: The Yan'an Rectification Movement. *Journal of Contemporary China*, 12(34), pp. 225–8.

# 6.	The Chinese strategic mind at work: the case of Huawei

*The human spirit must prevail over technology.*
*– Albert Einstein*

*Whenever an individual or a business decides that success has been attained,*
*progress stops.*
*– Thomas J. Watson*

*Innovation distinguishes between a leader and a follower.*
*– Steve Jobs*

## REN ZHENGFEI AND HUAWEI

Huawei has been chosen as the representative case to illustrate the applicability of the Chinese strategic mind due to several compelling reasons. In the previous edition of the book, the case involving Huawei was undoubtedly an excellent choice. Ren Zhengfei, the founder of Huawei, can be considered a disciple of Mao Zedong in every sense. Despite having limited financial resources, Ren Zhengfei successfully propelled the company onto the global stage by applying Mao's principles and strategies. This led to rapid growth and the establishment of a worldwide notable company within a short span of time.

While there are numerous world-class Chinese companies, Huawei stands out as a prime example due to its exceptional achievements and global recognition. The company's success is attributed to not only its technological prowess but also to its strategic mindset, which draws inspiration from Chinese principles and philosophies. By selecting Huawei as an illustrative case, the book highlights the effectiveness of the Chinese strategic mind in fostering the growth and success of a globally competitive company.

If Huawei had been considered as a potential case company one and a half years ago, I would have likely encountered challenges in providing a compelling rationale. At that time, Huawei had experienced a significant loss of revenue, amounting to one third, due to stringent technological sanctions imposed by the United States Government. The company had been on a rapid downward trend. For many, opting for a different case study might have been sensible and preferable.

However, with the benefit of hindsight, it is now abundantly clear that Huawei, as a Chinese company, has demonstrated actions and strategies that bear resemblance to those employed by the Red Army during the Chinese Civil War. Just like the Red Army, Huawei faced numerous challenges and 'encirclements' but exhibited great resilience, tenacity, and the ability to counterattack. Ultimately, Huawei emerged victorious and showcased remarkable vitality in the face of adversity.

In China, the technological conflict between Huawei and the United States Government is often compared to the intense battle that took place at 'Triangle Hill' during the Korean War. In this analogy, Huawei represents the target under heavy attack, facing an extraordinary amount of firepower in the form of severe sanctions and punitive actions imposed by the United States. These actions even included the detention of the founder's daughter in North America.

Despite being subjected to such immense pressure, Huawei did not surrender or lose hope. Instead, the company quietly resisted and fought back by dedicating itself to the development of technologies that had been sanctioned and banned. Through perseverance and hard work, Huawei managed to survive and even thrive in the face of adversity. It successfully developed a range of world-class new technologies and products that showcased its capabilities to the world.

Huawei's past and recent developmental processes reflect certain characteristics of Chinese strategic thinking, which can be likened to the strategies employed by Mao Zedong during his leadership of the Chinese armies. The underlying principles and approaches that have guided Huawei's policies and growth bear a resemblance to those employed by Mao Zedong.

Huawei, founded in 1987 by Ren Zhengfei, initially specialised in manufacturing telephone switches. However, the company's evolution into a global provider of information and communication technology (ICT) infrastructure and smart devices has showcased the characteristics that make it an ideal example of the effectiveness of Chinese strategic thinking within Chinese business.

From its humble beginnings, Huawei expanded its product portfolio to include various telecommunications equipment, networking solutions, and consumer electronics. This diversification allowed the company to cater to various market segments and capitalise on emerging technologies.

Key to Huawei's success has been its commitment to R&D investment. By dedicating substantial resources to technological innovation, Huawei has been able to stay at the forefront of the industry, introducing cutting-edge products and solutions. This commitment has been complemented by the company's competitive pricing, ensuring that its offerings remain attractive to customers worldwide.

Furthermore, Huawei's effective marketing philosophy has played a significant role in its rapid growth. The company has successfully positioned itself as a trusted and innovative brand leveraging strategic partnerships and global expansion to penetrate in over 170 countries and regions. With a vast workforce of 207 000 employees, Huawei has been able to serve more than three billion people around the world, solidifying its presence on a global scale.

Since 2019, the United States Government has imposed a ban on Huawei's access to chip-making tools, effectively crippling its smartphone business. As a result, the company experienced a significant decline in revenue during the first half of 2021, making its largest loss to date. Specifically, the company's revenue plummeted by 30%, reaching $35.5 billion, compared to its revenue of $107 billion in 2018.[1]

In a historical development, Huawei found itself at the centre of attention as it became the first ever target of the President of the United States, the world's most influential nation. On 15 May 2019, President Donald Trump invoked a national emergency, citing the need to safeguard American computer networks from potential threats posed by 'foreign adversaries'. To address this concern, he signed an executive order prohibiting US companies from utilising telecom equipment sourced from abroad. Although the executive order did not explicitly mention Huawei, it was widely believed to be directed towards the company.

Why has the United States specifically targeted and attacked Huawei instead of other prominent Chinese companies like Tencent, Alibaba, Didi, or Jingdong? The primary reason for this focused attention on Huawei is a combination of factors:

1.  Leadership position in 5G technology: Huawei has established itself as a global leader in 5G technology. Its advancements and dominance in the field have made the United States perceive Huawei as a significant threat. The strategic importance of 5G technology, which is considered a foundation for the Fourth Industrial Revolution, has intensified concerns regarding Huawei's influence and potential control over critical communications infrastructure.

2.  Independent technological development: Unlike other Chinese internet giants, Huawei has achieved astonishing success by independently developing its technology. For Western industrial powers, the technology domain has traditionally been their stronghold. However, a significant shift has occurred with the emergence of Huawei as the leader in a critical field like 5G technology. This marks the first time a Chinese company has accomplished such a position of prominence in the realm of technology.

    This self-reliance and ability to compete on a global scale have highlighted Huawei's capabilities and posed a challenge to the dominance of

US technology companies. This aspect, coupled with Huawei's strong leadership under a skilled Chinese business leader, has drawn additional attention and scrutiny from the United States.

3.  Limited dependency on US platforms: While other Chinese companies thrived and amassed significant wealth and size, they heavily rely on US platforms and technologies as foundations for their operations. In contrast, Huawei has managed to establish its own technology foundations, reducing its dependence on US platforms and technology. This independence has made it harder for the United States to exert control over Huawei's operations and has deepened concerns concerning potential national security risks.

4.  Geopolitical and trade dynamics: The targeting of Huawei may also be influenced by broader geopolitical and trade dynamics between the United States and China. As the two countries compete for technological and economic dominance, Huawei's prominence has become a focal point of their rivalry. The United States' actions against Huawei can be seen as part of a larger strategy to protect its own technological interests and maintain its competitive edge.

Despite the sanctions imposed on Huawei, the company has responded in a proactive and aggressive manner by heavily investing in R&D of alternative technologies. These counter strategies have yielded favourable outcomes. In 2022, Huawei began to show signs of recovery, with its revenue reaching $93.5 billion. Eric Xu, the rotating chair of the company, declared that 2023 would mark 'the first year of a return to business as usual', despite the ongoing presence of US export controls on high-end technology.

While Huawei's strategic thinking has been rooted in Chinese traditions, the company has actively learned from and incorporated Western management approaches at the operational and managerial levels. This includes adopting Western R&D processes and human resources systems. Huawei has recognised the benefits of integrating global best practice into its operations while maintaining its Chinese strategic mindset.

During the Cultural Revolution, Ren dedicated himself to studying the four volumes of the *Selected Works of Mao Zedong*. His comprehensive understanding of Mao's writings earned him the recognition of being an exemplary role model within the People's Liberation Army (PLA) after he joined it. Huawei's strategies bear a striking resemblance to Mao's works and actions. Furthermore, Huawei's implementation of the animated 'self-criticism' campaign reflects a similar approach to that found in Mao's actions.

Ren's strategic behaviour is strongly influenced by a military-style approach due to his military background. Understanding how the military aspect impacts business practices in China is significant, as Chinese holistic thinking emphasises the interconnectedness of mental activities in the military, business, and politics.

## A CONCEPTUAL FRAMEWORK FOR REN ZHENGFEI'S STRATEGIC MINDSET

Figure 6.1 illustrates a conceptual framework representing Ren Zhengfei's strategic mindset, which has played a pivotal role in Huawei's remarkable transformation into a leading high-tech company within a short span of time. The framework comprises four key components:

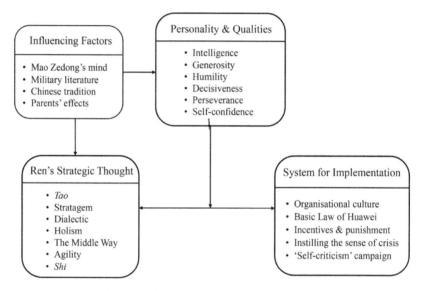

*Figure 6.1     A framework for Ren Zhengfei's strategic mindset*

1.  Ren's personal qualities: This segment encompasses a range of personal attributes and characteristics possessed by Ren Zhengfei, including intelligence, generosity, determination, decisiveness, perseverance, self-confidence, and ingenuity. These qualities are crucial in enabling Ren to effectively tackle challenges, attract and retain talented individuals, cultivate a strong and cohesive corporate culture, and maintain a vibrant and optimistic outlook.
2.  Ren's strategic thought: This section explores the distinctive strategic characteristics that set Ren apart from his Western counterparts. These characteristics encompass the embrace of *Tao* principles, holism, and

the application of dialectic thinking. Ren also demonstrates adeptness in utilising stratagems and leveraging the concept of *Shi*, while actively pursuing actions with agility.

3.  Influencing factors: In this section, we delve into the factors that significantly influenced the formation of Ren's strategic thinking. These factors include the strategic thought and actions of Mao Zedong, as well as the rich tapestry of Chinese traditions such as the *I Ching*, Lao Tzu, Buddhism, and Confucianism. Furthermore, Ren's upbringing, educational experiences, and family background have played a vital role in shaping his mindset.

4.  Ren's System for Strategy Implementation: This pivotal component of the framework focuses on the practical execution of Ren's strategic thought. It encompasses various elements, such as the development of an effective organisational culture, the establishment of a company 'constitution', the implementation of incentive and punishment schemes, and the adoption of Mao's style of 'self-criticism/reflection' campaigns.

## PERSONAL QUALITIES AND INFLUENCES

Ren Zhengfei is succinctly described by *The Economist*. He was born in 1944 to parents who worked as teachers. Ren pursued civil engineering studies before embarking on a career in the People's Liberation Army (PLA). In 1987, following the disbandment of the PLA's engineering corps, Ren utilised 21 000 yuan (equivalent to $4400 at the time) from his personal funds to establish Huawei. Initially, the company imported telephone switches from Hong Kong. However, Ren made the pivotal decision to develop Huawei's own products and allocate an average of 10% of revenues towards research and development.[2]

Ren Zhengfei's father, Ren Moxun, came from a village in Zhejiang province. He became the first young person to gain admission to a university and was among the earliest university students and graduates in China. He pursued a specialisation in economics and possessed lofty aspirations, extensive knowledge, and idealistic convictions.

Following his graduation, Ren Moxun embarked on a career as an accountant at a KMT ordnance factory. Despite his employment with the KMT, he remained supportive of the Communist Party. Consequently, he found himself evading an arrest warrant issued by the KMT and sought refuge in a secluded mountainous region in Guizhou.

During his time in Guizhou, Ren Moxun met Cheng Yuanzhao, whom he eventually married. It was in this union that Ren Zhengfei, their son, was born on 25 October 1944. Ren Moxun bestowed upon his son the name of 'Ren Zhengfei', symbolising the pursuit of justice. Ren Zhengfei's parents went on to have a total of seven children. Despite their large family and limited financial resources, they made every effort to make ends meet. Ren Zhengfei's parents prioritised his education and academic pursuits, ensuring that he received a proper schooling.

Before the onset of the Cultural Revolution in 1966, Ren Moxun assumed the position of headmaster at two schools in Guizhou. Following the Cultural Revolution's end in 1976, he became the headmaster of another school that achieved distinction and served as a shining example in the region. An impressive 90% of its graduates were able to secure admission into universities.

However, just as Ren Zhengfei's business began to see progress and overcome the initial challenges, tragedy struck in 1995. Ren Moxun passed away from food poisoning. This heart-breaking event brought immense sadness to Ren Zhengfei and drew him closer to his mother.[3]

Ren's mother, a senior mathematics teacher, accompanied her husband to work in Guizhou and made significant contributions to the school she served. She demonstrated immense care, love, and kindness towards students at the schools, while also displaying industriousness, frugality, and a devotion as a mother within the family.

During a business trip abroad in 2001, Ren Zhengfei received distressing news that his mother had been hospitalised following a car accident. While she was admitted into a hospital, she was registered under the name of 'unknown' and possessed a mere 20 yuan (equivalent to approximately two pounds sterling) in her pocket. Meanwhile, her son had recently paid over 2 billion yuan in taxes to the government. Such was the selfless nature of Ren's family, characterised by their altruism, generosity, care, diligence, and thriftiness. It is not surprising that Ren Zhengfei has inherited most of these qualities from his parents, which laid a solid foundation for his entrepreneurial success. Ren once remarked: 'I have learned to be unselfish from my parents', and he believes that Huawei's success today, to some extent, can be attributed to his own selflessness.[4]

Ren Zhengfei's notable characteristic is his humility. Despite Huawei's immense success in its early days, Ren chose to maintain a low profile and limited media exposure. Ren has even issued a directive to his senior management team, stating that unless it involves clients or business partners, all social invitations and activities should be declined, with consequences for any violations.

Ren firmly believes that Huawei's accomplishments are the result of the collective efforts of all employees and the management team. He understands that taking credit for the company's success would create a false impression and fail to reflect reality. Therefore, Ren prefers to remain behind the scenes and let the collective achievements of the company speak for themselves.

Despite Ren's intentional efforts to limit his public appearances, his achievements garnered notable recognition. In 2005, *Time*, a prestigious US magazine, honoured Ren Zhengfei as one of the world's most influential figures, making him the sole representative from China to receive such a recognition. The selection committee provided the following complimentary commentaries: Ren Zhengfei is an individual who rarely seeks public attention, yet he is the most respected Chinese entrepreneur.

In 2010, Ren Zhengfei secured the top spot on *Forbes* magazine's list of the most internationally respected Chinese entrepreneurs. Furthermore, in 2011, *Fortune* magazine published a list of the 50 most influential business leaders in China, with Ren Zhengfei claiming the coveted first position.[5] These recognitions further underscore Ren's significant contributions and impact within the business sphere.

Despite the severe sanctions imposed on Huawei by the US, Ren Zhengfei remained optimistic about Huawei's future, emphasising that the company was particularly energised by the challenges posed by the United States. He believed that the US attacks on Huawei had inadvertently served as highly effective 'advertisement'. These attacks conveyed the message that Huawei had become so strong that the United States felt threatened by its superior and highly competitive products. Consequently, several companies rushed to sign contracts without waiting for further product testing, leading to rapid growth in contractual agreements.[6]

Ren's upbringing and the influence of his parents served as a catalyst for instilling in him the qualities of industriousness, perseverance, and determination. One instance illuminates this matter. At the onset of his entrepreneurial journey, Ren Zhengfei directed all the company's resources and key personnel, including over 50 R&D staff, towards a crucial project – an HJD exchanger required by a customer. It was a 'life and death' battle for the company.

For several months, Ren and his team tirelessly toiled day and night, working, eating, and sleeping in a rented office building. Due to the lack of beds, many resorted to sleeping on polystyrene foam boards. This relentless dedication paid off, as they ultimately succeeded in developing and delivering the product as per the contractor's requirements.

The stakes were high during this endeavour, as Huawei's survival hinged on the success of this product development. Failure would have left the company drained of funds and at risk of bankruptcy. This kind of intense working and living style became a recurring occurrence at Huawei, leading to the establishment of a reputation known as the 'mattress culture'. Many newly-recruited researchers often extended their shifts, working and sleeping on mattresses in their offices,[7] mirroring the steadfast commitment and sacrifice demonstrated by Ren Zhengfei and his team.

Ren Zhengfei inherited certain qualities from his parents, including a strong work ethic and a thirst for knowledge. Ren once expressed the belief that, without valiant effort and hard work, one may fall behind in the competitive landscape. He also emphasised the importance of continuous learning, stating that three days without studying would result in being unable to catch up with industry leaders such as Cisco, Ericsson, and Alcatel.[8]

Ren possesses an amazing capacity for learning, immersing himself in both Chinese and Western literature, particularly in the fields of history, military affairs, and philosophy. However, he intentionally avoids reading Western strategy publications and encourages Huawei's senior executives to do the same. His rationale behind this approach is that relying on Western strategy works would limit their strategic thinking by confining them within predefined 'frameworks'. Ren believes that true innovation and strategic breakthroughs require a fresh perspective and an ability to think beyond established paradigms.

## REN ZHENGFEI'S STRATEGIC MIND

### *Tao*

*Tao* encompasses the supreme position among the components of the Chinese strategic mindset. A victor or pioneer in momentous endeavour embodies the essence of *Tao*, which is manifested through a visionary outlook, alignment of the natural order, pursuit of justice, and adherence to high ethical standards. Since the inception of Huawei's entrepreneurial journey, Ren Zhengfei has exemplified a grand vision and ambition for the future of his company. *The Economist* vividly portrays this as follows: Mr Ren's mission is to facilitate the development of China's indigenous telecommunications technology, with Huawei's name signifying both 'China can' and 'splendid act'.[9]

Huawei, founded in 1987, embarked on a transformative journey in 1994 when Ren Zhengfei envisioned a future where the telecommunication equipment market would be divided among Siemens, Alcatel, and Huawei.[10] This vision was articulated with great ambition in Huawei's 1997 Basic Law,[11] declaring the company's aspiration to become the world's leading telecoms enterprise.

Huawei's forward-looking vision ultimately saved the company from a potential catastrophic downfall. In 2012, as a dominant player in the telecommunications equipment industry, Ren Zhengfei recognised the need for Huawei to create its own terminal operating systems as part of a strategic plan. He emphasised the importance of developing backup foundational products, such as operating systems, to safeguard against potential disruptions.

Ren Zhengfei conveyed his perspective on the necessity of having contingency plans in place, highlighting the risks associated with relying solely on external suppliers for critical components like Android and Windows Phone 8. He compared this situation to being cut off from the supply of food, leaving Huawei stunned and immobilised. To mitigate such risks, he encouraged the development of advanced chips while acquiring US advanced chips, when possible, and also advocating for a thorough understanding of these products. In the event that suppliers ceased selling to Huawei, although the quality of company's own products might be slightly lower, they could navigate through the challenge.

Ren Zhengfei drew parallels between chip development and operating systems, emphasising their significance as vital components. By creating their own operating systems, Huawei could have a backup solution in case their suppliers stopped delivering. Although the need for these backup products might not arise for decades, it was crucial to invest in their development. Ren Zhengfei emphasised that leaving a strategic loophole open could result in losses amounting not just to millions, but billions of dollars.[12]

In May 2019, the Bureau of Industry and Security (BIS) of the US Department of Commerce made an announcement that had significant implications for Huawei and its non-US affiliates. The BIS added Huawei and 46 of its non-US affiliates to the Entity List, effective from 16 May 2019. This decision was based on information available to the BIS, which concluded that Huawei was engaged in activities contrary to US national security or foreign policy interests. As a result of this inclusion in the blacklist, suppliers were restricted from shipping goods and technology to Huawei, unless they obtained licences.

However, Ren Zhengfei demonstrated his visionary and farsighted approach by proactively preparing backup products. This strategic move proved crucial in saving Huawei from potential downfall. One such backup product was the Harmony OS, which quickly became a formal offering, providing Huawei with an alternative operating system. Ren Zhengfei's forward-looking mindset allowed him to face US severe sanctions without intimidation.

When confronted with assertive journalists, Ren confidently expressed his viewpoint, emphasising that Huawei's capability to produce chips of similar quality to those made in the United States did not imply a complete cessation of purchasing US chips. He advocated for a collaborative approach, stating that exclusion of US chips would be narrow-minded, and instead, he believed in the importance of mutual growth. However, Ren emphasised the need for backup products when faced with supply challenges.

Huawei's dedication and achievements became evident as it joined the prestigious *Fortune Global 500* list in 2010, marking a significant milestone for the company. As the sole Chinese private company on the list, Huawei secured the 397th position. Demonstrating remarkable growth, Huawei continued to ascend the ranks, breaking into the top 50 for the first time in 2020, landing at an impressive 49th place on the *Fortune 500* list.

However, the year 2022 brought challenges for Huawei due to the sanctions imposed by the United States. Consequently, the company's ranking on the *Fortune 500* list declined to the 96th position, reflecting the impact of these sanctions on its business operations. Despite this setback, Huawei remains a prominent player in the telecommunications industry, with a legacy of innovation and global reach.

In 2010, Huawei held the second position in the telecommunications industry, trailing behind Ericsson. The difference in revenue between the two companies amounted to $2.8 billion. However, a senior executive from Huawei acknowledged that Huawei actually preferred being in the number two position, until they had no choice but to head for the top position due to their exceptional performance.[13] This outcome and trend aligned with the vision set by Ren Zhengfei in 1994, where he aimed for Huawei to be among the top three industry players. This vision was realised by that time. Furthermore, in 1998, Huawei set a sales target of $70 billion for 2017,[14] and impressively, they surpassed this target by achieving actual sales of $78.51billion.

In the Western context, when a company reaches a comparative size to that of Huawei, it would typically result in the creation of numerous 'millionaires' and 'billionaires'. In particular, the founder would typically find a place in the world's richest list. However, many Western readers may be surprised to discover that Ren Zhengfei, the founder of China's prominent high-tech company and its largest shareholder, holds a relatively small percentage of Huawei's shares. As of 31 December 2019, Ren's ownership of Huawei amounted to only 1.04%, with the remaining shares being held by 104 572 employees. This is a notable occurrence in the history of global business, reflecting Ren's philosophy. Ren Zhengfei has explained his decision, stating:

> I played a crucial role in establishing Huawei, but why should I hoard the company shares among other employees? Huawei is a high-tech company that thrives on the talent and ambitions of its workforce. We need more capable and driven individuals to join us, collaborating for both the good and for the bad. Our veteran pioneers and senior managers should embrace sacrifice and dilute their shareholdings to encourage and inspire more talented people to join Huawei.[15]

This decision exemplifies Ren's embodiment of *Tao* principles such as sacrifice, self-discipline, unselfishness, and endurance. By implementing the shareholding structure, Ren aims to cultivate the values of diligence, ambition, teamwork, and passion within Huawei. This action by Ren resonates with the teachings of Confucianism, emphasising leadership through benevolence and serving as a role model.

Huawei's success has been built upon its commitment to delivering the best solution to its customers, rather than relying solely on providing the most advanced technology. It is often said that Huawei has entered top-tier markets with technology that may be considered less advanced, but this achievement can be attributed to the unique relationships the company has formed with its customers. These relationships are rooted in the credibility and integrity of Huawei's employees. Ren Zhengfei firmly believes that this distinctive and strong bond with clients is the company's core competence.

During the 1990s, China's telecommunications market was highly fragmented, with different countries' companies providing technologies. This situation was often referred to as 'seven nations and eight systems'. Large multinational corporations (MNCs) from America and Europe dominated the market with their superior technology, displaying a sense of complacency and arrogance, as they believed there were no worthy Chinese competitors. These MNCs, holding a monopoly on technology, primarily focused their attention on the headquarters or decision centres of Chinese telecom sectors in major cities.

Recognising the competitive landscape, Huawei took a different approach. The company deployed its sales teams to 270 small and medium-sized cities across China, establishing strong relationships with individuals at all levels of telecom organisations. This included senior managers and general technicians, even though immediate sales opportunities were not apparent. This strategy mirrored replica of Mao's 'encirclement of cities from the countryside' tactic and proved to be effective. Many of these relationships eventually developed into lucrative business contracts for Huawei.

During a speech delivered to marketing team leaders, Ren Zhengfei underscored the significance of fostering strong customer relationships. He urged the teams to avoid perceiving customers solely as transactional entities and to refrain from looking down upon those in lower positions solely for the purpose of closing deals. This, he asserted, is the fundamental principle of marketing within Huawei. Ren Zhengfei stressed that the cultivation of a 'universal customer relationship'[16] is not solely the responsibility of the marketing department, but rather a company-wide objective.[17]

Ren Zhengfei emphasises the utmost significance of upholding 'credibility and integrity'. Huawei's wellbeing is of utmost importance, as it ensures the continued trust and protection of its clients' valuable investments. To achieve this, Huawei should foster symbiotic growth and advancement alongside its clients, considering their success as its own. It is worth noting that, despite Huawei's exceptional global standing, Ren Zhengfei continues to live a modest and unassuming life. Nonetheless, whenever a collaborative venture with clients necessitates investment, he wholeheartedly and decisively commits to it.

In 1998, after a decade of development, Huawei achieved financial stability with a significant amount of cash in its accounts. In contrast to many other Chinese companies that favoured investing heavily in the lucrative property market, which became a prevailing trend among Chinese businesses, Ren Zhengfei made a bold decision. He chose to allocate the company's funds towards the construction of the world's largest telecom equipment plant and the establishment of a 'Huawei University' in Shenzhen. This university aimed to provide technical and technological training to both employees and clients.

Despite being a seemingly unprofitable non-commercial endeavour, the substantial investment in the university had an inordinate impact on the company's profits. Ren Zhengfei, however, regarded it as a reflection of Huawei's core values or the *Tao* that the company adhered to.

In 2003, during the internet bubble burst, the Huawei University attracted numerous potential clients who recognised the importance of establishing what appeared to be an unprofitable institution. Thus, many of these attendees signed significant investment contracts. By the end of 2012, millions of individuals from telecom operators and clients from over 100 countries had participated in training programmes at the university. This greatly enhanced Huawei's credibility and image while cultivating a vast pool of potential clients.[18]

Huawei's embrace of *Tao* is evident in its understanding of the determinants of success or failure in the high-tech industry. In its earlier days, Huawei was a latecomer to the game and, despite being among the top players in telecom equipment and services, it mainly followed technological trends rather than leading them. Huawei's technological advancement was not on a par with competitors like Cisco and Alcatel-Lucent.

However, Huawei managed to surpass its competitors through a strategic grasp of the 'rules' or success factors in the industry. Metaphorically, in high-tech sectors, those with basic core technology could participate in the high-end market game. But only those with long-term sustainability could remain and emerge victorious. This sustainability depended on 'stamina', which combined core technology with low operating costs, rather than solely relying on the absolute level of technology. Huawei achieved notable success in the international market by outperforming its formidable competitors through its unique advantage in 'stamina'.[19]

### *Shi*

Ren Zhengfei's foray into entrepreneurship in the 1980s showcased his astute recognition of the concept of '*Shi*' and his ability to adapt and seize opportunities. During this period, China was undergoing a wave of economic reforms spearheaded by Deng Xiaoping, ushering in a dynamic era of transformative change and societal upheaval. Ren's decision to immerse himself in this trend embodied both the potential for success and the inherent risks associated with it, aligning with the age-old Chinese proverb that states, 'a hero is born in times of turmoil'.

For Ren Zhengfei, the leap from being a highly respected army officer to a small trader represented a momentous and dramatic transition. In the 1980s, being a small trader was considered one of the lowest social strata in China. This shift demanded exceptional courage, visionary thinking, determination, a willingness to take risks, and perseverance.

At the time, Ren possessed no prior knowledge of telecommunications technology. However, what he did possess was impeccable timing and a favourable location – the presence of a Special Economic Zone. These zones offered a conducive environment for conducting business, characterised by significant freedom and quasi-market conditions. In essence, Ren found himself positioned in the midst of the economic winds, or *Shi*, which allowed him to harness the prevailing circumstances and propel himself forward.

With Huawei's Headquarters strategically located in Shenzhen, a designated Special Economic Zone established to experiment with capitalist practices under Deng Xiaoping's reform policies, Ren Zhengfei adeptly leveraged the prevailing *Shi* of economic reform. He recognised the unique opportunities presented by this environment and seized them with great acumen.

Established in 1984, Cisco Systems is a well-established multinational corporation based in the United States, specialising in digital communications technology. As a major player in the industry, Cisco develops, manufactures, and markets a wide range of networking hardware, software, telecom equipment and other advanced services and products.

During the early 2000s, Cisco held a dominant position as the pioneer of the multiple-protocol router and industry leader. At the time, the company's CEO, John Chambers, had significant concerns regarding the potential rise of Huawei Technologies, a Chinese network gear manufacturer. Chambers believed that Huawei posed a significant challenge to Cisco's market dominance, surpassing other competitors such as Juniper or HP.[20]

In a strategic move to safeguard its position and prevent Huawei Technologies from emerging as a formidable rival, Cisco Systems took legal action against Huawei on 23 January 2003. Cisco filed a lawsuit in the United States District Court for the Eastern District of Texas, alleging that Huawei had engaged in the unauthorised copying, misappropriation, and infringement of Cisco's software, as well as the violation of Cisco's patents.[21]

The choice of this particular court was deliberate, as it had a reputation for expediting legal proceedings and imposing severe penalties. The indictment against Huawei consisted of an extensive 77-page collection of documents, detailing 21 distinct violations that encompassed a wide range of charges related to patent infringement. The comprehensive nature of these allegations left no stone unturned in addressing potential infringement. Because of the lawsuit's initiation, Huawei's reputation suffered significant damage.

Cisco enjoyed a home-court advantage in this legal battle. At the time, the *Wall Street Journal* reported that the timing of the lawsuit was unfavourable for Huawei, which had been heavily investing in marketing efforts to enhance its brand recognition in developed markets, including Europe and North America.[22] A loss in the case would have resulted in Huawei facing substantial financial penalties, legal fees, and potential expulsion from the lucrative US market. Such an outcome would have inflicted substantial damage to Huawei's reputation and potentially caused psychological distress for the company.

The lawsuit presented a pivotal juncture for Huawei, representing a considerable peril to its aspirations and expansion within the global market. Cisco's selection of the lawsuit's filing date, 23 January 2003, was a meticulously calculated move. Strategically scheduled just over a week before the Chinese New Year, which holds a similar significance as Christmas in Western cultures, the intention was to catch Huawei off guard and hinder their case preparation. It created a crisis that Huawei had been dreading.

The clash between Cisco and Huawei can be viewed as a clash of personalities embodied by John Chambers and Ren Zhengfei. Both of whom shared certain traits such as strong determination, self-confidence, and assertiveness. However, they also differed in their social demeanour. Chambers was known for his diplomatic skills, eloquence in speech and manner, while Ren Zhengfei was often described as socially awkward but possessing penetrating eyes that seemed to read one's thoughts.[23] Furthermore, their approaches represented two distinct styles of strategic thinking: the 'Clausewitz' approach and the 'Chinese mind'.

Chambers adopted a Clausewitzian perspective, perceiving the battles as a means to compel the opponent to fulfil his own will. According to this thinking, the objective of war is to disarm the enemy completely, making disarmament the immediate goal of hostilities in theory.[24] Chambers, in line with this mindset, aimed at bringing Huawei to its demise through the lawsuit battle. As a senior executive from Cisco revealed, the ultimate objective was to bring Huawei to ruin.[25]

On the other hand, Ren Zhengfei pursued a different approach, seeking a middle ground or compromise rather than aiming to 'defeat' Cisco outright. His intention was to achieve a mutually beneficial outcome, avoiding a total victory or defeat scenario.

In pursuit of its objective, Cisco intended to execute a swift and decisive strike against Huawei, displaying resolute confidence in its ability to emerge victorious from the battle. This approach was aligned with Chambers' personal style, characterised by aggression, offensive tactics, and a willingness to spare no expense. Cisco set aside a substantial advertising budget of $150 million and prepared to publicise any news that could potentially undermine Huawei's reputation.[26]

In contrast, Huawei adopted a '*Taiji*' approach in response, employing a seemingly slow and gentle demeanour while possessing strong resilience and counter power. This strategic approach involved leveraging the opponent's own force to mount a counterattack or utilising the opponent's momentum against them, akin to borrowing the opponent's energy (*Shi*) in the practice of *Taiji*.

In their pursuit of legal representation, Huawei reached out to Heller Ehrman, an esteemed international law firm with rich history dating back to 1890, specialising in laws on Intellectual Property Rights (IPR). To familiarise the lawyers with Huawei's operations, the legal firm was invited to visit Huawei's impressive manufacturing and R&D facilities, which were developed in collaboration with IBM. This visit allowed the lawyers to gain insights into Huawei's organisational structure, rigorous R&D processes, and established procedures. After conducting a comprehensive examination of Huawei's integrated R&D systems, and core competencies, Heller Ehrman made the decision to accept the case, bringing some of the world's top IPR lawyers to Huawei's defence.

With the support of this highly capable legal team, Huawei began to witness a shift in its defence position. In a strategic move, the lawyers representing Huawei filed an anti-trust litigation against Cisco,[27] further shaping the dynamics of the legal battle.

During the legal proceedings, an esteemed professor specialising in digital communications from Stanford University was called up to present a report that would have a profound impact on the case. The professor's report emphasised that the disputed products at the centre of the lawsuit belonged to different categories or natures, absolving Huawei from any infringement of IPR. This revelation came as a shock to both the judge and the jury, significantly altering the course of the trial.

In a timely move, Huawei established a joint venture with an American digital electronic manufacturer, 3Com Corporation, on 19 March 2003. This joint venture played a crucial role in Huawei's defence strategy. Bruce Claflin, the President and CEO of 3Com, took a stand in court and attested to Huawei's credibility. Claflin disclosed that he had made numerous visits to Huawei and had spent eight months meticulously evaluating and certifying Huawei's technologies. Based on his extensive experience and career, he believed Huawei to be a trustworthy company. Claflin also highlighted that if Huawei had indeed been involved in any infringement of IPR, 3Com would not have taken the risk to enter the joint venture.[28]

The legal battle between Cisco and Huawei reached its conclusion after a suspenseful one-and-a-half-month period. The resolution had a dramatic effect. The case was settled through reconciliation, with no penalties, apologies, or compensation awarded to either party. Both companies were permitted to continue selling their respective products as usual. Additionally, Cisco agreed to refrain from initiating any further legal action against Huawei concerning the same matter. While no explicit victory or defeat was declared, the media portrayed it as a significant win for Huawei.

A senior executive from Huawei elucidated the implications of the legal battle. From Huawei's perspective, the outcome held substantial strategic value. By settling the case, Cisco inadvertently promoted Huawei on a global scale through extensive media coverage. This exposure effectively brought attention to Huawei as a formidable competitor capable of challenging and competing with Cisco. Such a result provided Huawei with an opportunity to gain worldwide recognition and establish itself as a prominent player in the industry. This level of exposure and recognition would have been difficult to achieve even with billions of dollars spent on marketing efforts alone.[29]

In essence, the attention garnered through media coverage and Cisco's inadvertent promotion contributed to Huawei's rise in prominence, cementing its position as a worthy opponent in the global market. To some extent, this incident resembles the Long March, wherein a crisis transformed into a catalyst for tremendous momentum within the organisation. Chapter 3 details how the CPC army embarked on the Long March due to the imminent threat of annihilation by the KMT army. Despite facing a dire situation, the CPC skilfully transformed their potential defeat into a powerful propaganda tool that astounded the world. Likewise, when Cisco initiated legal action against Huawei, the latter found itself in a precarious predicament akin to the Long March. However, Huawei managed to navigate this challenging circumstance and ultimately transformed from a relatively obscure entity into a globally recognised company.

In 1996, while most telecom equipment manufacturers were focused on developing fixed-line-based digital telephone exchanges, Huawei realised that the market for fixed-line telephony would soon reach saturation point. Thus, the company made a bold move and directed substantial investments towards R&D in the field of internet protocol (IP), which underpins internet networking and essentially establishes the foundation of the internet.

While other companies adopted a 'wait and see' approach, Huawei took the risk of venturing into the development of broadband access network products. When the internet market emerged and gained momentum in China, Huawei, along with ZTC, had already established dominance in China's market.

By 2006, Huawei and ZTC were the only two Chinese companies to have secured positions among the world's top eight telecom equipment providers. Numerous MNCs with greater R&D capabilities and financial resources missed the opportunity to become leading telecom equipment and service providers because they lagged behind the prevailing trend.[30]

## Holism

Huawei's strategic development reflects its embrace of a holistic perspective, which sets it apart from the Western approach that tends to prioritise analytical cognition. Unlike many companies in the West that focus on specific industries, Huawei has successfully diversified its operations across multiple industrial sectors and competes with global companies from different industries.

When it comes to its prime rivals, Huawei faces competition from renowned companies such as Apple and HP in the computer and office equipment sector, Amazon and eBay in Internet services and retailing, IBM in information technological services, and Intel, NAVIDIA, Broadcom, Texas Instruments, and QCOM in semiconductors and electronic components. In addition, Cisco poses a challenge in the networking and telecom equipment and services domain, while VMWare is a competitor in computer software.[31]

This phenomenon of a single Chinese company like Huawei competing against an array of US corporate giants is not commonly seen in the West. It is a uniquely Chinese occurrence and has become a principal reason why politicians in the United States fear Huawei. Consequently, there have been attempts to undermine Huawei's growth, as they perceive it as a threat to the dominance of US corporations.

Huawei has conducted research and discovered that companies that are excessively innovative and ahead of the market often face challenges similar to those that lack innovation altogether. This observation is exemplified by the experiences of Fujitsu and NEC, two Japanese companies. During the era of analogue phones, these companies established a significant advantage over their competitors with their technology. However, when digital phones emerged as the new standard, Fujitsu and NEC slowed down their pace of innovation, allowing Lucent, Siemens, and Alcatel to surpass them.

To reverse their declining position, Fujitsu and NEC introduced a model that boasted more advanced technology than most digital phone offerings in the market. However, due to the technology being far ahead of what customers desired, they failed to gain traction in the market. This case serves as a lesson for Huawei, shaping its innovation strategy. The company strives to differentiate itself from competitors by being 'better' but only by a small margin, or what Ren Zhengfei refers to as 'a half step'. By adopting this approach, Huawei ensures that its innovations align closely with customer needs and preferences, avoiding the pitfalls of being too far ahead of the market.[32]

In the Global Innovation Index released by the WIPO In 2022, Huawei's corporate R&D expenditure ranked 8th, after Nvidia, SK Hynix, MediaTek,

Apple, Intel, Siemens, and Qualcomm.[33] Despite this, Huawei's innovative endeavours have yielded impressive and impactful results.

Huawei's decision-making principles embrace a comprehensive outlook, reflecting the distinctive characteristics of the company. The strategic decision-making process adheres to the principle of 'democratic decision but authoritative management'. This approach entails that strategic decisions are formulated by a select group of accomplished individuals within the organisation known as the 'Executive Management Team' or EMT. Ren Zhengfei firmly believes that the essence of truth often eludes superficial appearances and is concealed from immediate observation. Unveiling the truth necessitates deep contemplation, exploration, and practical application, which can only be accomplished by a limited number of individuals possessing in-depth knowledge and extensive hands-on experience. The responsibility of unearthing truth lies in the hands of the few.

Huawei has embraced a policy that offers generous rewards for small-scale advancements in terms of proposals, while encouraging suggestions for significant innovations without providing financial incentives. According to Ren Zhengfei, ordinary employees are primarily expected to excel in their assigned roles. However, if they propose improvements or innovations directly related to their job responsibilities, they have the opportunity to receive substantial rewards. On the other hand, they are discouraged from making suggestions on matters outside their job descriptions.[34] Typically, proposals for major innovations are expected to originate from EMT members. As developing viable proposals is an integral part of their jobs, they are not eligible for additional rewards in this regard.

In Western strategic thinking, companies typically develop a plan that outlines a clear and explicit strategy. This plan serves as a roadmap, providing direction, objectives, and the means to achieve those objectives. Western corporations are often likened to ocean liners, steadily navigating towards a predetermined destination set by the captain. Apple, in its early days, exemplified this approach, acting as a formidable liner sailing towards a specific direction as envisioned by Steve Jobs.

On the other hand, Huawei, considering itself as a medium-sized liner, has charted a different course in the vast ocean of business. Huawei's guidance system is based on Ren Zhengfei's 'theory of grayscale'.[35] This theory acknowledges the rapid and unpredictable changes in the business environment, making it difficult to accurately predict the future direction. Since it is impossible to envision the exact nature of the future information society, designing a flawless business model becomes an elusive task. Consequently, Ren Zhengfei advocates for an alternative approach to dealing with this uncertainty.

According to Ren Zhengfei, the best way forward is to foster internal unity and seek external cooperation. By doing so, the company can navigate the turbulent waters of the industry together with others, collectively identifying the future direction. In the past, Huawei may have considered many of its counterparts as 'enemies', but now, 20 years later, the company aims to transform those 'enemies' into friends.[36] Ren believes that, by embracing this collaborative mindset, the entire industry can thrive and grow progressively brighter over time.

Ren Zhengfei holds the belief that human nature is inherently grayscale and perceiving it in terms of black or white would result in misleading conclusions. To lead employees of a company in the right direction, it is necessary to adopt grayscale perspective that encompasses compromise and forgiveness. Chinese people tend to adopt extreme positions, whether in public or private organisations. Once an organisation becomes entrenched in extremism, it would be challenging to return to a balanced grayscale approach. While it may be easier to make decisions in terms of absolutes – either white or black – blending the two faces great difficulty. For instance, being excessively innovative can be just as perilous as lacking innovation altogether for a high-tech firm.

Huawei's approach to Human Resources Management is rooted in the grayscale principle. It places value on respecting individuals while emphasising teamwork. The company consciously avoids extremes, recognising that adhering to grayscale principles leads to greater harmony and success.[37]

In response to a question raised by a senior politician from the United States regarding the factors that have contributed to Huawei's growth and success, Ren Zhengfei identified three key elements: openness, compromise, and grayscale. These factors have been instrumental in Huawei's evolution from a humble beginning to its current stature as a large and powerful company.

Ren Zhengfei emphasised the significance of 'openness' as a fundamental principle for Huawei's success. He highlighted the importance of constantly learning from others, including companies from the United States, and continuously upgrading their goals while maintaining a sense of crisis. Ren Zhengfei cautioned that if Huawei were to adopt a closed-loop system, it would face the risk of rapid bankruptcy.

Furthermore, Ren Zhengfei stressed the essential role of a leader in providing direction and setting the pace for an organisation's development. He described the achievement of balance between direction and the pace of growth as the art of leadership.

Finding the right balance between direction and pace necessitates embracing compromise and grayscale. Chinese organisations, by their nature, are characterised by instability, consequently needing the pursuit of harmony. This pursuit is encapsulated in the concept of 'compromise', which leads to the outcome of 'grayscale'.

For example, young employees at Huawei often exhibit great enthusiasm and energy, approaching their work with aggression. However, they may lack an understanding of how to compromise, resulting in unintended consequences. Throughout Chinese history, there have been numerous instances where reformers and revolutionaries adopted extreme or aggressive approaches only to face failure as a result.[38]

On one occasion, Ren Zhengfei asked a colleague if they knew what had contributed to Huawei's success. Upon realising that the colleague was unable to provide an answer, Ren himself interjected with his response: 'the middle way'.[39]

## Dialectic

Ren Zhengfei possesses multiple roles and interests beyond being an entrepreneur or practitioner. He is an avid reader and thinker who has observed a common phenomenon known as 'organisational fatigue' within various types of organisations, particularly in the commercial sector. It becomes evident that commercial organisations tend to age rapidly, often exhibiting inertia and resistance to change within a decade or even less. This phenomenon is primarily rooted in the very factors that contributed to their initial success.

Ren Zhengfei highlights several noteworthy companies, including Bell Laboratories, Motorola, Nortel, NEC, and Sony, which were once at the forefront of their industries. However, these companies eventually became ensnared in a multitude challenges, leading to their decline and loss of former glory.

The phenomenon of organisational fatigue stems from a combination of external and internal factors. Among the internal factors, one significant contributor is the attachment to a company's 'glorious history'. Such companies tend to rely on past achievements, leading to limited ambition and a lack of innovative thinking, making it challenging for them to adapt to rapidly changing environments. The weight of 'history' becomes a formidable obstacle in combating organisational fatigue.

Numerous leaders and politicians from different countries have visited Huawei and have expressed admiration for its success. Many have proposed the idea of establishing a museum to showcase Huawei's history. However, Ren Zhengfei's response to this suggestion was quite different. He stated that Huawei does not require a focus on its history. On the contrary, he believes that Huawei should let go of its past and move forward without being entangled in its own history.[40]

Ren Zhengfei consistently emphasises the significance of Chinese traditional wisdom, particularly the concept of 'thinking of danger in times of peace', in his writings such as 'Huawei's Winter' and 'How Long Can

Huawei's Flag Fly?' He firmly believes that acknowledging and discussing failures is more crucial than focusing solely on success. In the fiercely competitive and ever-evolving business landscape, Ren Zhengfei recognises that it is imprudent to wait until a crisis arises to address it. Therefore, he advocates for Huawei to maintain a constant state of vigilance, proactively identify potential signs of crisis, and resolve them before they escalate. Ren Zhengfei's approach to navigating the smokeless battlefield of commerce underscores the importance of being proactive and prepared in order to thrive and sustain success.

During one of Ren Zhengfei's visits to Panasonic, a prominent Japanese multinational corporation, he was deeply impressed by what he observed. Everywhere he looked within the company's premises, whether it was conference rooms, offices, or walls, he encountered a captivating painting depicting a massive ocean liner on a collision course with an iceberg. Beneath the artwork, a caption read: 'Only you can save this liner'. This striking scene resonated overwhelmingly with Ren's thought and concerns.

When Huawei has experienced rapid growth and international expansion, others may have perceived only prosperity and glory. However, Ren, in contrast, constantly contemplated the potential crises that could be lurking nearby. He pondered the challenges of high costs, inefficiency, and quality issues that could arise as the company continued to expand. Moreover, he had a persistent worry about the gradual accumulation of bureaucracies within the organisation, which might cause the fading of indomitable spirit and industriousness.

In response to these pressing issues, Ren took measures to address them. He recognised the importance of safeguarding the company's core values and maintaining its competitive edge. With proactive mindset, he implemented strategies to streamline processes that enhance efficiency and ensure the preservation of Huawei's commitment to excellence. Ren's visit to Panasonic and the powerful imagery of the ocean liner served as a constant reminder of the need to remain vigilant and proactive in the face of potential challenges.

The Bureau of Industry and Security of the United States Government decided to include Huawei on the Entity List on 16 May 2019. Initially, it seemed that this action would severely impact Huawei, potentially resulting in psychological and financial losses for the company. However, Huawei, being a company deeply rooted in Chinese culture and values, has demonstrated a contrasting response to sanctions and restrictions. Like Newton's Third Law of Motion, which states that every action has an equal and opposite reaction, Huawei has reacted in an optimistic and positive manner to the actions taken by the United States.

Rather than succumbing to despair, Ren Zhengfei has chosen to interpret the US action in a favourable light. During an interview with a journalist in August 2019, he shared his perspective on the matter. Considering the political climate within the United States government at the time, Ren Zhengfei expressed his doubt that the sanctions and restrictions would be lifted soon. However, he highlighted an interesting viewpoint, stating that the US 'entity list' had presented a favourable opportunity for Huawei. It compelled the company to reassess its strategy and adopt a more focused strategy.

Ren Zhengfei emphasised that the imposed restrictions helped Huawei streamline its product portfolio by eliminating less significant products and concentrating on a core set of offerings. Prior to the actions taken by Trump's administration, Huawei's organisational structure was relatively loose and lacked agility. However, in response to the attack, the company underwent a process of revitalisation and reactivation. Ren Zhengfei expressed gratitude for the impact of these events, as they served to reenergise Huawei as a whole.

## Stratagem and Agility

On a particular occasion, Ren Zhengfei was queried about why Huawei had not yet been listed on the stock market. In response, he promptly expressed his intention to avoid the proliferation of billionaires and millionaires within the company. He believed that, by doing so, Huawei would maintain its dynamic, energetic, and innovative nature, while also attracting more talented individuals to join its ranks. One of the reasons was that, as a private company, Huawei had the privilege of not having to disclose its financial details, enabling it to keep its strategic plans closely guarded.

Ren Zhengfei's thinking and approaches have been influenced, whether directly, indirectly, or unconsciously, by the strategic mindset of Mao Zedong. Ren Zhengfei has embraced Mao's renowned 1938 speech delivered to a group of Chinese cadres. This embrace includes adopting a firm and unwavering political direction, cultivating a work style characterised by arduous struggle, and employing responsive and flexible strategy and tactics.[41]

To maintain nimbleness within the company, Huawei implemented a unique system where three of its executives take turns serving as the chief executive for six-month intervals. This approach, as reported by *The Economist*, aims to ensure the company's agility and adaptability in the ever-changing business landscape.[42]

During the initial decade of Huawei's growth, the company relied on strategic manoeuvring and adaptability to ensure its survival and progress. In terms of technology and resources, Huawei was not on par with multinational competitors like Alcatel, Ericsson, and Siemens. Consequently, it faced difficulties establishing a presence in urban areas, which were predominantly controlled by state-owned enterprises and foreign multinationals.

Taking inspirations from Mao's military strategy of the 'encirclement of cities from the countryside', Huawei decided to adopt a similar approach. This astute strategy was acknowledged and commented upon by *The Economist*:

One of Mr Ren's business strategies involves 'using the countryside to encircle and finally capture the cities.' Due to the challenges encountered in selling their products to carriers in China's major coastal cities, where state-owned equipment manufacturers and foreign vendors held sway, Huawei initially focused on provincial rural areas. By offering technically advanced yet more affordable equipment and deploying large sales teams, the firm swiftly convinced local operators to purchase its products. From there, Huawei expanded its reach gradually.[43]

Established in 1984, Alcatel-Lucent Shanghai Bell emerged as the pioneering Sino-foreign joint venture in China's telecommunications industry. The venture's shares were directly overseen by the State Asset Supervision and Administration Commission (SASAC). In the 1990s, China's telecom market experienced a surge in demand. During this period, multiple suppliers from different countries with varying systems, collectively referred to as the 'seven nations with eight systems', resulted in a perplexing array of systems accompanied by exorbitant prices. Consequently, Chinese buyers displayed a strong inclination toward Shanghai Bell and eagerly sought its PBX products. In a span of three years, Shanghai Bell's S1240 model captured an impressive 50% of market share in China.

In the mid and late 1990s, the emergence of new internet access technology created a demand that Shanghai Bell's telecom equipment could not adequately meet. Unfortunately, the company's top management failed to recognise the significance of this issue. Identifying it as a valuable opportunity, Huawei decided to apply Mao's strategy of 'concentrating a superior force to destroy the enemy forces one by one' to address this situation. Leveraging its technological and financial resources, Huawei swiftly developed competitive internet access products.

By entering the market with these internet access products, Huawei gradually made inroads into the telecom industry. Building on its initial success in internet access technology, Huawei expanded its product offerings to include fibre optic, digital communication, and intelligent networking solutions. As a result, the company surpassed Shanghai Bell in sales by 1998.

By 1999, broadband technology had emerged as the predominant method of internet access, providing Huawei with a further edge over Shanghai Bell. This allowed Huawei to expand its presence into urban markets and challenge the monopoly held by the 'seven countries with eight systems'. During this period, Huawei's products exhibited technical features and performance that were on par with multinational competitors like Cisco, Alcatel-Lucent, Nokia-Siemens

Networks, and Juniper Networks. Not only were Huawei's offerings competitively priced, but also boasted superior service capabilities.

Through these advantages, Huawei successfully executed its strategic transition from rural areas to urban centres by 2003.[44] This marked a significant milestone in the company's growth as it established a strong foothold in the city market, effectively breaking the hegemony of the established multinational players.

During its internationalisation process, Huawei employed a strategy similar to 'encircling cities from the countryside'. This involved initially entering developing or less-developed markets before moving into more developed markets.

Huawei embarked on its internationalisation journey by making its entry into the Russian market. This strategic move was motivated by the changing political landscape, which presented a favourable opportunity. In 1996, the then Russian President Yeltsin paid a visit to China, establishing a strategic alliance based on equality and mutual trust between the nations. Recognising the potential business prospects arising from the evolving Russia-China relationship, Ren Zhengfei promptly made a decision to venture into the Russian market.

However, Huawei's international team encountered a series of challenges as they set their foot in the Russian market. At the time, Western multinational companies like Ericsson, Alcatel, and Siemens dominated the Russian market, while Huawei remained relatively unknown in Russia, despite its strong reputation in China. In addition to the difficulties, there was an abundance of low-quality, inexpensive Chinese products in Russia, which had contributed to a general perception of scepticism towards Chinese goods among the Russian population.

In 1996, a vice president of Huawei embarked on a journey in Russia. At the time, many Russians held a condescending belief that Chinese companies, including Huawei, were incapable of producing PBX products. However, Huawei's sales team managed to change this perception by showcasing their sample products to Russians, revealing the company's far more advanced technological development.

The year 1997 brought about an economic depression in Russia with no sign of recovery. Consequently, numerous Western multinational companies like NEC, Siemens, and Alcatel swiftly withdrew from the Russian market. In contrast, Huawei chose to remain and patiently waited in Russia. The persistence paid off three years later when Huawei successfully secured a contract with Ural for PBX systems and with Moscow for mobile network systems.

In 2001, Huawei achieved another milestone by signing a significant contract worth tens of millions of US dollars with Russian National Telecom. The contract involved the supply of GSM equipment. The following year brought even more success as Huawei secured a larger contract to provide long-distance optical fibre transmission, specifically the DWDM system, between St. Petersburg and Moscow. As a result of these achievements, Huawei emerged as the largest foreign investor in Russia and attained a dominant market share of over 50% in the Russian broadband network market.

In the early stage of Huawei's international strategy, prioritising the African market was crucial. Ren Zhengfei recognised the importance of the African market, explained it as follows:

> As we embarked on our international expansion and surveyed the global landscape, we observed that Western MNCs had already occupied all the fertile fields and productive farmlands. Consequently, only the remote, tumultuous, abominable, and challenging countries and regions are for us to explore due to MNCs' hesitancy and limited investment. Nonetheless, these circumstances presented potential opportunities for Huawei.[45]

The initial opportunity arose in the Republic of Kenya, when a senior official briefly visited the Huawei desk during an international information and communication exhibition and left a name card for a Huawei senior engineer. Known for its proactive 'wolf-culture', Huawei's sales team took swift action by actively following up with the potential client. They provided detailed and impressive information packs, ultimately capturing the interest of the potential client, whose senior management subsequently agreed to visit Huawei in China to further explore the possibility of Huawei becoming their supplier.

Upon arriving in China, the group of executives was taken on a tour of Beijing and Shanghai, where they witnessed highly developed infrastructure and modern architectures. This experience positively influenced their perception of China as the supplier's country. Subsequently, they visited Huawei's corporate base in Shenzhen, where they were impressed by impressive high-rise buildings, the large number of R&D personnel, sophisticated research processes and facilities, as well as advanced operations management and automatic production lines. As a result, Huawei was accepted as the supplier company.

Furthermore, Huawei's sales team presented the executives with meticulously prepared information packs and demonstrated successful cases. This comprehensive approach, known as 'three axes' – country, company, and product – contributed to the executives' acceptance of Huawei's products.

The Kenyan government made the decision to implement a wireless ETS system in Naivasha, a small town near Nairobi, the capital of the Republic of Kenya. Huawei was chosen as the supplier for the project. Despite facing various challenges such as differing technological standards and working traditions during the installation process, Huawei successfully completed the project. This achievement led to Huawei becoming the primary supplier in the

Kenya telecom equipment market. The success of the Kenya project marked the beginning of Huawei's expansion into other African markets.

In March 2019, a well-known US magazine called *Foreign Policy* published a report revealing that Huawei had 70% of market share in 4G networks across the African continent, surpassing its European counterparts by a significant margin. Among all the existing suppliers of telecom equipment, Huawei stood out in terms of cost-effectiveness and capabilities, making it unrivalled in the eyes of various African countries. The Huawei brand had deeply resonated with and become indispensable to these nations.[46]

Latin America was considered an important part of Huawei's internationalisation strategy, despite being seen as a relatively underdeveloped market compared with its neighbours, the United States and Canada. Most countries in Latin America were characterised by limited economic resources and wealth. In addition, the dominant languages in the region, Spanish and Portuguese, posed communication challenges for Huawei. Furthermore, during the 1990s, Latin America faced economic depression, and the telecom sectors were largely controlled by European and American companies, which had significant influence over purchasing decisions. Moreover, many Latin American countries lacked diplomatic relations with China. The challenges in the Latin American business environment could not be overstated.

As part of its market entry strategy, Huawei selected Brazil as a strategic gateway to the Latin American market. Despite Brazil's moderate level of economic development, the country's open-door policy presented Huawei with an equal opportunity compared to other international competitors.

In 1999, Huawei established a representative office in Brazil, marking its initial foray into the Latin American region. This milestone was accompanied by an initial investment of $3 million towards its marketing efforts. However, Brazilian companies predominantly placed their trust in European and American products, paying little attention to the relatively unfamiliar Chinese company, Huawei. In addition, the Brazilian economy was facing significant challenges, proving a difficult business environment.

Meanwhile, Huawei's marketing endeavours in other Latin American nations faced various challenges and yielded little success. Nonetheless, Huawei persisted and patiently sought out potential opportunities. After five years of unswerving dedication, in 2004, Huawei finally secured a partnership with a prominent Brazilian telecom operator, CTBC, to develop a state-of-the-art telecommunications network. This marked Huawei's inaugural contract in Latin America.

Following the successful completion of the project, Huawei swiftly gained traction in the Brazilian market, thanks to its exceptional technology, competitive pricing, and outstanding services. Accordingly, the company was able to penetrate and thrive in other Latin American markets. In 2011, Huawei invested $300 million to establish a research centre in Brazil, and in 2012, its sales reached $2 billion. Concurrently, Huawei rapidly expanded its presence in other Latin American countries. It became the primary supplier in Argentina and formed partnerships with all major Chilean telecom operators. In addition, Huawei ventured into the markets of other Latin American countries, such as Venezuela, Peru, Bolivia, Dominica Republic, and Ecuador. In fact, by 2012, Huawei had employed over 1400 Venezuelan workers alone, exemplifying its growing influence in the region.

As of 2013, Latin America had emerged as Huawei's most rapidly expanding market abroad, boasting the highest number of overseas employees, exceeding 10 000 individuals. Huawei fostered strong business relationships with 14 Latin American countries, establishing 19 workstations, three software development centres, and three training centres within the region. Huawei had established itself as the top provider of telecom technology and infrastructure in Latin America.[47]

In the year 2000, Huawei successfully expanded its presence in various Asian markets, including India, Indonesia, Thailand, Bangladesh, Cambodia, Nepal, Singapore, Malaysia, and the United Arab Emirates. This expansion allowed Huawei to emerge as the leading provider of GSM/CDMA systems within these countries.

In Huawei's strategic approach of 'encircling cities from countryside', previous national markets symbolised 'countryside', while Europe held immense significance as one of the key 'cities' to be encompassed. Europe has long been recognised as one of the world's largest and most advanced markets, housing the headquarters of prominent European telecom operators like Vodafone, British Telecom (BT), Deutsch Telekom (Germany), Telefonica (Spain), Orange (France), and Telecom Italia (Italy).

Within Europe, numerous telecom equipment suppliers can be found, including Ericsson from Sweden, Siemens from Germany, Alcatel-Lucent from France, and Marconi from Britain. If Huawei were to enter the European market and secure contracts, it would serve as a notable achievement and a demonstration of their capabilities to other developed markets.

In 2004, Huawei entered a contract valued at €200–400 million with Telfort, a German mobile telecom company. The following year, Huawei achieved the status of a qualified supplier for the BT 21 Century Network (21CN) and formed an alliance with Vodafone, the world's largest mobile phone operator.[48]

In February 2005, Huawei underwent a rigorous scrutiny and examination process and was selected as the exclusive provider for the Next Generation Network (NGN) project of Deutsch Telekom (DT), surpassing other global NGN providers. This led to DT announcing a strategic partnership with Huawei. By 2017, Huawei's sales in Germany had reached $2 billion.

Europe boasted strong competitors like Ericsson and Nokia in the European market; however, these companies had intricate and time-consuming R&D procedures. Consequently, it often took them over a year to deliver solutions to their clients. In contrast, Huawei's diligent work ethic and business agility allowed them to penetrate the European market by swiftly responding to client demands.

For example, Vodafone was the telecommunication operator for a specific region in Spain, covering the area between Madrid and Seville. In this region, there was a high-speed train service connecting the two cities, with an average speed of 250 miles per hour. However, passengers frequently complained about the poor-quality sound of mobile reception during the journey, which lasted approximately four hours.

While this issue affected Vodafone's customers in this particular region, it was not a widespread problem throughout Europe due to the limited coverage of high-speed railways. Consequently, European telecom equipment suppliers considered it a low priority and estimated that it would take more than two years to address the issue. Faced with this timeline, Vodafone sought a solution from Huawei, although they did not have high hopes for a quick resolution.

To their surprise, Vodafone was informed that a solution had been found just three months after reaching out to Huawei. Upon receiving Vodafone's requirements, Huawei's research institute in Shanghai formed a dedicated project group. They secured a 24-kilometre stretch of the high-speed railway for testing purposes, aiming to address the problem of poor sound quality on the trains. The institute installed more than 20 base stations specifically for this project and conducted rigorous testing to improve the sound quality.

After months of hard work involving over 100 R&D staff, Huawei successfully resolved the problem. Following the completion of the project, representatives from Vodafone were invited to experience the improved sound quality on the high-speed train and review the test data. They were thoroughly impressed by the results and found Huawei's accomplishment to be surprising. Vodafone's representatives praised Huawei repeatedly, acknowledging the significant achievement in resolving the sound quality issue. As a result, Huawei gained the trust and confidence of European telecom operators.

Huawei's ability to respond swiftly to client requirements became a fundamental value for the company. This successful project positioned Huawei as a preferred provider of telecom equipment and services in the European market. The company's commitment to meeting customer needs promptly and effectively solidified its position in the industry.[49]

# SYSTEMS FOR IMPLEMENTATION

## The Basic Law of Huawei

Huawei's initial approach during the first stage of development, which focused on rural and provincial markets within the country, was characterised by a certain level of 'roughness' compared to a more professional or refined method of tapping into these markets. However, as Huawei progressed into the second stage of development, with a strategic focus on urban areas and international markets, it found itself in direct competition with MNCs like Alcatel-Lucent and Siemens. In order to compete with and even surpass these MNCs, Huawei recognised the need to manage the company in a similarly professional manner.

Ren Zhengfei observed that, in the Western business landscape, there are numerous companies with long and storied histories, many of which have been operating for over a century. In contrast, China had relatively few such companies with extensive histories. This led Ren Zhengfei to ponder the reasons behind the sustainability of these Western companies and to consider what Huawei could do to achieve similar sustainability.

Driven by a desire to find answers to these pressing questions, Ren Zhengfei embarked on a journey to engage with these MNCs. Through extensive travel and inspections around the globe, he arrived at a significant realisation: the disparities between Huawei and these exceptional MNCs were not primarily attributed to differences in resources, talent, or technology. Instead, the underlying factor lay in corporate culture. Ren Zhengfei recognised that all successful MNCs had developed a robust and profound corporate culture that played a pivotal role in shaping their sustainability.

During Huawei's rapid growth, Ren Zhengfei became aware of several emerging challenges. He observed that the drive and enthusiasm of employees were diminishing, and internal communication between senior management, middle management, and employees was seriously disrupted. Ren identified the root cause of these problems as stemming from the companies' policies of 'three highs': high salary, high efficiency, and high pressure, as well as strict disciplinary measures imposed on employees. These factors had inadvertently dampened employee enthusiasm and motivation due to inadequate management practice and the underdevelopment of a strong corporate culture, which could have otherwise effectively addressed these emerging challenges.

Ren Zhengfei recognised the crucial need for Huawei to establish a set of 'strategic guidelines' in order to cultivate effective management and organisational systems. Coincidentally, during this time in 1996, the Basic Law of Hong Kong was being drafted, which outlined the fundamental policy of

'One Country and Two Systems' and provided a clear strategic direction for the future development of Hong Kong. Inspired by the role of the Basic Law of Hong Kong, Ren Zhengfei contemplated the creation of a similar guiding document for Huawei, which he referred to as the Basic Law of Huawei. However, the question arose as to who would be responsible for drafting such a strategic document.

In 1995, with China's economy showing signs of growth, major multinational consulting firms like McKinsey, BCG, A.T. Kearney, and PricewaterhouseCoopers established offices in China. Ren Zhengfei engaged in discussions with the senior management of these firms to explore what they could offer to Huawei. However, Ren and his senior management team acknowledged that the concepts and approaches put forth by these firms were predominantly rooted in Western traditions and systems. They realised that integrating these concepts and approaches into Huawei without incorporating core elements of Chinese culture could potentially lead to Huawei losing its identity through excessive Westernisation.

During this time, Ren Zhengfei had a fortuitous encounter with five professors from the renowned People's University of China, known for its expertise in humanities. Recognising their extensive experience studying and working in developed countries including deep understanding of advanced management practices in North America and Europe, as well as the internationalisation processes undertaken by Japanese companies, Ren saw an opportunity. He engaged in discussions with these professors about the nature of the strategic document he envisioned.

Impressed by their comprehensive knowledge of both Western and Chinese cultures, Ren Zhengfei announced during a senior management meeting that the five professors from the People's University of China would be invited to draft the Basic Law of Huawei. Their unique understanding of both cultures would enable them to leverage Western concepts to enhance Chinese culture, aligning perfectly with Huawei's requirements.[50] With this decision, the drafting group for the Basic Law of Huawei was formed.

During the document drafting process, the working group amalgamated Sun Tzu's teachings with the corporate culture, mission, and responsibility of world-renowned multinationals such as IBM, HP, and Intel. The Basic Law laid out the core values and fundamental policies that would govern the company's organisational and management systems.[51] The document had six chapters: corporate mission, business policy, organisational policy, human resource policy, control policy, the successor, and further revision of the Basic Law.

The inception of Huawei's Basic Law can be traced back to 1995. Throughout the drafting process in 1996, it was initially referred to as the 'Huawei Managerial Guidelines' until its finalisation and approval in March 1998. Since its creation, the Basic Law garnered significant acclaim within the industry, earning the moniker of 'Huawei's Bible' within the company itself. Essentially, it represented the first comprehensive document that expounded upon Huawei's core values, drawing from the perspective of Ren Zhengfei and company's managerial experiences. This foundational document provided strategic guidance for Huawei's second phase of entrepreneurship.

Ren Zhengfei aptly captured the essence of the Basic Law by emphasising that, over the course of 10 years, Huawei had amassed a wealth of lessons through both successes and failures. Through these experiences, the company discovered the beacon of progress amidst the darkness of setbacks, exhibiting indomitable determination during its initial entrepreneurial stage. The valuable lessons derived from these failures, along with the practical experiences gained served as nourishment for Huawei's second entrepreneurship.

During this second phase, Huawei sought to refine and formalise its management practices while contending with formidable international competitors who possessed invaluable managerial experiences and theories. Huawei endeavoured to amalgamate its hard-learned lessons from a decade of operations with the best industry's thinking and practices. This strategic approach aimed to enhance the company's competitiveness and steer it away from relying solely on empirical methods. These are the fundamental rationales for the formulation of the Basic Law of Huawei.[52]

## Culture and its Evolution

In the Western context, extensive research was conducted on the role of corporate culture in shaping organisational performance during the 1980s to the 1990s. The findings from the research consistently indicate that a strong organisational culture, particularly one that is market-orientated, tends to have a positive impact on organisational performance.[53] It is widely recognised that corporate culture is primarily influenced by the top management of an organisation.[54]

In contrast, research on corporate culture in China started much later than in the West and has been heavily influenced by Western studies. Similarly, in Chinese organisations, the CEOs or founders typically play a significant role in shaping the organisational culture. This culture can be consciously or unconsciously formed, depending on the leadership style. In well-run organisations, leaders are often astute and mindful, actively observing and contemplating strategic and managerial issues. They consciously foster and nurture a viable culture within the organisation. Zhang Ruimin of Haier and Ren Zhengfei of Huawei are noteworthy examples of such business leaders who have successfully shaped organisational culture in this manner.

To foster a sustainable culture, it is essential for a leader not only to design and nurture the culture but also to bring colleagues and employees together in embracing its core values. In China, a distinctive aspect of cultural cultivation and implementation, unlike in Western businesses, is the attachment of personal feelings and emotions to the organisation. This emotional connection makes the culture more influential due to the leader's charisma or power of influence.

Ren Zhengfei presents his distinctive viewpoint on the role of corporate culture in the management and development of Huawei, as outlined below.

In the context of Huawei being a commercial and utilitarian group, the focal point of every aspect within the organisation is centred around business interests. Consequently, the culture fostered at Huawei is referred to as 'corporate culture', emphasising its alignment with the specific objectives of the company.

According to Ren Zhengfei, culture is not merely a byproduct but a form of management itself, representing an advanced and elevated form of management practice. The distinctive characteristic of Huawei's culture lies in its service-oriented nature, recognising that it is through exceptional services that tangible business benefits can be obtained. While material resources may deplete over time, culture has the capacity to thrive continuously.

Ren Zhengfei draws a parallel between the relationship of culture and management and that of soil and crops. Culture serves as the nurturing soil for Huawei's development. Its fundamental mission is to enrich and loosen the soil, creating an environment conducive to the growth of crops. Management, in this analogy, is likened to the crop itself, with its mission being the generation of more crops, symbolising the organisation's ongoing growth and prosperity.

If executive management can be likened to dictatorship and 'rule by man', and institutional management represents 'rule of law', then cultural management embodies democratic management. When an enterprise reaches a point where it can be effectively governed through culture alone, it approaches the concept of 'governing by doing nothing',[55] a fundamental principle of Taoism.

In 2008, Ren Zhengfei officially introduced the core values of Huawei as 'centre on customers, respect for strivers (hard-working employees), and strenuously and persistently strive'. This core value was later solidified as the standardised version of Huawei's core value on 20 January 2010, after a comprehensive examination of the successes and failures of global multinational corporations. Ren Zhengfei's 30 years of hard-learned lessons and experiences played a significant role in this process, embodying profound insights and a forward-looking perspective.[56]

Ren Zhengfei conveys the essence of Huawei's core values, which have been shaped and refined over the past two decades, embodying the true nature of Huawei's culture:

> Our fundamental objective is to offer customers timely, precise, high-quality, and cost-effective services. Undoubtedly, we place the customer at the centre of everything we do, recognising that without customers, our existence would be jeopardised. Embracing a mindset of striving for excellence aligns with our customer-centric approach. We hold great regard for employees who excel in serving customers, acknowledging them as the backbone of our company, and celebrating their contributions to fostering strong customer relationships.
>
> Moreover, our employees' steadfast dedication also demonstrates their commitment to put the customer first. It is vital to remember that everything we consume ultimately originates from our customers. Engaging in wasteful practices not only increases costs for our customers but also becomes unacceptable to them. If one shies away from demanding roles, avoids confronting challenging circumstances, and lacks a customer-orientated mindset, customers will not embrace or acknowledge such individuals, leading to an unfulfilling professional life.[57]

Huawei's strategic direction was outlined in The Basic Law, serving as a roadmap for the company. However, to make progress as a unified entity, Huawei also needed the impetus or driving force to propel them forward. In the early stages of their development, Huawei's sales force had to venture into remote rural areas and foreign countries to secure business opportunities. In addition, they had to act swiftly in Chinese cities, where dominant multinational companies controlled the market, capitalising on brief windows of opportunity. Huawei likened this situation to 'treading in the narrow alleys', engaging in fierce battles to survive and thrive.

Consequently, a distinct organisational culture known as 'wolf culture' emerged within Huawei, shaped by the challenging business environment. Ren Zhengfei provides an explanation for this wolf culture. He believes that an enterprise should cultivate a group of 'wolves' who possess three key characteristics:

1.  Acute Sensibility: These 'wolves' possess a keen sense of smell, enabling them to detect potential opportunities or targets.
2.  Offensive Spirit: They exhibit an unswerving and indomitable offensive spirit willing to make sacrifices and overcome obstacles.
3.  Teamwork: Collaboration and teamwork are essential qualities for these 'wolves' as they work towards expanding the business. Huawei's marketing department, for example, adopts an organisational plan that combines the aggressiveness of a wolf with the strategic management skills of a jackal.[58]

Huawei's team building and cultural cultivation are guided by a set of principles that have shaped the company's strategic thinking. This is evident in their
distinctive 'wolf-like' corporate culture, which is reinforced and promoted by
its reward and punishment systems. Hardworking individuals are duly recognised and rewarded, while those who display a lack of diligence are encouraged
to leave the company. From the very beginning, Huawei has been steadfast in
implementing this policy, resulting in a workforce composed of individuals
who have proven their resilience and determination through a rigorous process
of natural selection. These employees not only receive substantial financial
benefits, but also embody a strong sense of viability and fighting spirit.[59]

The wolf-like culture of Huawei, together with its complementary reward
and punishment system, is characterised by what is known as the 'three
heights': high pressure, high performance, and high return/reward. The significance of this culture-driven system in Huawei's earlier development cannot
be overstated.

However, starting from mid-2006 onwards, the number of employees
exceeded 60 000, including a diverse range of both foreign nations and
foreign-resident Chinese employees. By 30 October 2019, the company had
expanded its workforce to over 194 000 employees worldwide, serving customers in more than 170 countries. Furthermore, the localisation of employment had reached a commendable 75% mark.[60]

Under the new multicultural management approach, Huawei has encountered a series of challenges in its organisational culture. One notable issue
is the potential conflict between individual performance and the company's
overall performance and customer value, which are fundamental to its mission.
In the current stage of development, the company's long-term viability and
profitability take precedence over mere growth. Recognising these challenges,
Ren Zhengfei sought a solution and found inspiration in an unexpected source
– the performance of a traditional Chinese dance during a nationally televised
CCTV event celebrating the Chinese New Year in 2005.

The dance, known as '*Qian Shou Guan Ying*' or 'the goddess of mercy
with thousand-hands and thousand-eyes;, deeply moved billions of Chinese
viewers. However, what truly amazed Ren Zhengfei was not the narrative of
the dance itself, but rather the fact that the dancers were deaf individuals who
captivated the audience within a mere six minutes. This revelation sparked
inspiration within Ren Zhengfei.

The dancers and director embodied the spirit of relentless pursuit of excellence, displaying firm determination and seamless teamwork. Their motivation
stemmed not from the allure of accolades or reputation, as they could not
hear the resounding and ceaseless applause. This unique perspective deeply
impacted Ren Zhengfei, leading him to adopt the concept of *Qian Shou Guan
Ying* as Huawei's new corporate culture for the evolving era.

From 2006 to 2012, Huawei experienced remarkable growth, with its employee count surging from 60 000 to 150 000 and sales skyrocketing from $100 billion to $300 billion. This successful cultural transition stands as a testament to the enduring effectiveness of the chosen approach.[61]

## Mao-Style Movements

Ren Zhengfei has incorporated certain aspects of Mao's approach into Huawei, drawing attention from publications like *The Economist*. One notable tactic Ren Zhengfei has emulated from Mao Zedong is ideological education. In the early years, he had employees engaging in activities such as singing revolutionary songs. Even today, the company continues this tradition by providing a six-month course for the thousands of new recruits hired annually. This programme includes two weeks of cultural immersion at the Shenzhen campus and an internship where they contribute to setting up base stations. This phase is intended to instil the 'wolf spirit' that is said to drive the firm forward.[62]

Similar to Mao Zedong's Yanan Rectification Movement, which took place from 1942 to 1944 and proved successful in unifying the thoughts of the CPC and consolidating Mao's leadership within the party, Ren Zhengfei has employed a comparable approach. Mao later repeated this tactic in subsequent years for various political purposes, further demonstrating its efficacy.

Drawing from extensive knowledge and intellectual acumen, Mao Zedong astutely observed the cyclical nature of nations and political parties, noting patterns of rise and fall. In contemplating how to prevent the exhaustion of both the nation and the party, Mao developed the concept of the political 'movement'. These movements aimed to achieve social transformation by eliminating organisational inertia and unhealthy elements while revitalising the nation and the party. Mao described his approach as a dialectical process seeking to transition from a state of chaos and turmoil to one of stability, unity, and order.

With his background in the military and his exposure to Mao's ideologies and practices, Ren Zhengfei naturally absorbed the influence of Mao's thoughts. Consequently, Ren Zhengfei has incorporated a similar style of movement within Huawei, aiming to 'extract the essence and discard the dross' to invigorate the organisation.

Huawei has adopted one of Mao's notable styles of 'movement' known as 'criticism and self-criticism', which was extensively employed within the CPC. In line with this concept borrowed from the CPC, Huawei has placed significant emphasis on self-criticism while minimising mutual criticism, as the latter could potentially create friction within the company. Self-criticism has become an integral part of the Huawei's core values, as defined by Ren Zhengfei, in order to maintain a motivated and energetic workforce within the highly competitive environment. Ren has expressed the belief that the long-term stability and sustainability of Huawei hinge upon the company's ability to engage in self-criticism and embrace shades of grey.

Ren Zhengfei highlights the significance and necessity of practising self-criticism. Despite Huawei's youthful vigour and passion, it also exhibits noticeable naivety and arrogance. The standardisation of Huawei's management is still a work in progress. The quickest path for the company's staff members to mature is through consistent self-reflection. It is important to understand that self-criticism should not be pursued solely for the purpose of criticising or completely negating the past. Rather, it should be undertaken with the explicit aim of promoting company development and optimising operations, ultimately enhancing the overall core competence of the organisation.

The marketing system within the company demands self-criticism due to its position at the forefront, characterised by heightened sensitivity and dynamism. Without self-criticism and prompt adjustments to rectify past mistakes, the company would have faced the risk of being driven out of business long ago. The fact that the R&D system has undergone a comprehensive process of self-analysis and self-criticism can be regarded as a significant milestone and turning point in the history of the company's corporate development.

Nevertheless, it is important to note that excessive self-criticism has the potential to undermine a mature and stable operating order, and therefore, it should be avoided. The frequency and extent of self-criticism should be determined based on its alignment with the prevailing operating environment. It is crucial to reject metaphysics, mechanical dogma, and idealism. The management process should be grounded in seeking truth from facts, avoiding the appearance of being left-winged while actually being right-winged.[63]

For over two decades, Huawei practised the movement of self-criticism. Regular 'democratic live meetings' are held once a month, where everyone, from top management to ordinary employees, is required to attend and openly discuss their own shortcomings and inadequacies. During these meetings, individuals analyse the underlying causes of their inadequacies, with the assistance of their colleagues in a constructive manner. The focus is on identifying causes without resorting to exaggeration, personal attacks, or engaging in politics and emotional outbursts.

Chinese culture, including its organisational culture, has historically exhibited a susceptibility to internal friction and factionalism, which can undermine the stability of an organisation. Recognising this challenging, both Mao Zedong and Ren Zhengfei implemented measures to address it. While it may seem straightforward to tackle this issue, overcoming it proves to be a significant challenge. Huawei's success in this regard can be attributed to Ren Zhengfei's personal involvement as the top leader in driving the movement, without being concerned about losing face. Additionally, the application of a nuanced understanding of diverse perspective, without resorting to extreme actions, has played a crucial role. It is precisely due to these factors that only a few companies have been able to achieve the level of success that Huawei has attained.[64]

Huawei stands out as a premier 'homegrown' Chinese company from which Western companies can draw valuable lessons:

1. When engaging with a competitive Chinese company, it is advisable to avoid a confrontational approach. Western companies should seek mutually beneficial solutions to resolve conflicts whenever possible.
2. If sanction becomes necessary, Western companies must carefully assess their own vulnerabilities to potentially retaliatory action from the sanctioned party.
3. Western companies should recognise their natural inclination toward analytical strategic thinking in strategic development, while acknowledging that a holistic strategic approach may be far more advantageous. Understandably, it is simple to recognise it, but it is challenging to implement it in reality.
4. When considering customer solutions, prioritising 'best technology' may not always be the most effective approach; instead, companies should strive for cost-effective solutions.
5. During a phase of growth or success, the company should anticipate future challenges by considering the following questions: (1) What should the company do if key supplies of components or technology are suddenly cut off? (2) How should the company respond if its core product faces sudden competition from a new rival?

## NOTES

1. Chen, P.F. (2020). *Huawei Quan Qiu Hua (Huawei Globalization)*, Zhejiang University Press, p. 9.
2. The Economist (2011). The Long March of the Invisible Mr Ren. *The Economist*, June 2, 2011.
3. Sun, L.K. (2021). *Huawei Zhuan (The Legend of Huawei)*. China Friendship Publishing Company, pp. 6–7.
4. Yang, S.L. (2013). *Huawei Kao Shenme (On What Huawei Relies)*. China CITIC Press, p. 8.
5. Chen (n 1) pp. 277–8.
6. Ibid.
7. Tian, T. and Wu, C.B. (2012). *Xia yige dao xia de hui bu hui shi Huawei? (Is Huawei the Next One to Fall?)*. China CITIC Press, pp. 29–35.
8. Ibid., p. 029.
9. The Economist (n 2).

10.  Yang (n 4) p. 20.
11.  The nature of the document will be discussed in detail later in this chapter.
12.  Chen (n 1) p. 22.
13.  Tain and Wu (n 7) p. xxx.
14.  Ibid.
15.  Ibid., pp. 46–8.
16.  It is concerned with all those relevant individuals, regardless of their positions, within a client organisation.
17.  Yang (n 4) pp. 25–7.
18.  Ibid., pp. 25–30.
19.  Yang (n 4) pp. 42–3.
20.  Bort, J. (2012). Cisco CEO John Chambers Slams His Chinese Competitor, Hints It Steals Stuff. *Business Insider*, April 9, 2012.
21.  Thurm, S. (2003). Cisco Files Patent Suit in U.S. Against Huawei. *Asian Wall Street Journal* (Hong Kong), 24 January, 2003.
22.  Bolande, H.A. (2003). Cisco's Lawsuit Against Huawei is Test for Beijing. *Wall Street Journal*, Eastern Edition (New York), 29 January 2003.
23.  Tian and Wu (n 7) p. 104.
24.  Clausewitz, C. von (1997). *On War* (J.J. Graham, Trans.). Wordsworth Editions, pp. 5–6.
25.  Tian and Wu (n 7) p. 105.
26.  Ibid., pp. 104–5.
27.  Yang (n 4) pp. 203–6.
28.  Ibid., p. 205.
29.  Tian and Wu (n 7) p. 70.
30.  Yang (n 4) pp. 42–3.
31.  Chen (n 1) pp. 9–10.
32.  Ibid., pp. 38–9.
33.  Dutta, S., Lanvin, B., León, L.R. and Wunsch-Vincent, S. (2023). *Global Innovation Index 2023 Innovation in the face of uncertainty*. World Intellectual Property Organization. https://www.wipo.int/edocs/pubdocs/en/wipo-pub-2000-2023-en-main-report-global-innovation-index-2023-16th-edition.pdf. Retrieved on 14 October 2023. p. 31.
34.  Wu, C.B. (2014). *Huawei meiyou mimi* (*Huawei has no Secrets*). China CITIC Press, p. 33.
35.  Ren Zhengfei's grayscale theory is another way of interpreting and applying the Confucian *Middle Way*.
36.  Tian and Wu (n 7) pp. 124–5.
37.  Wu (n 34) p. 27.
38.  Tian and Wu (n 7) p. 126.
39.  Ibid., p. 102.
40.  Ibid., pp. 154–5.
41.  Ibid., p. 137.
42.  The Economist (2014). The Great Disrupter's New Targets: Huawei. *The Economist*, September 20, 2014, pp. 61–2.

43. The Economist (n 2).
44. Yang (n 4) pp. 23–5.
45. Chen (n 1) p. 60.
46. Ibid., pp. 65–8
47. Sun (n 3) pp. 127–8.
48. Sun, J. and Wang, D. (2011). *Zhonguo shi guanli de sitangke* (*Four Lectures of Chinese-style Management*). Enterprise Management Publishing House, pp. 284–5.
49. Chen (n 1) pp. 71–2.
50. Yang (n 4) p. 91.
51. Ibid., pp. 90–92.
52. Sun (n 3) pp. 186–8.
53. Byles, C.M. and Keating, J.R. (1989). Strength of Organization Culture and Performance: Strategic Implications. *Journal of Business Strategies*, 6, pp. 42–54.
    Sorensen, J.B. (2002). The Strength of Corporate Culture and the Reliability of Firm Performance. *Administrative Science Quarterly*, 47, pp. 70–91.
    Kohli, A.K. and Jaworski, B.J. (1990). Market Orientation: The Construct, Research Propositions, and Managerial Implications. *Journal of Marketing*, 54 (1), pp. 1–18.
54. McDaniel, S.W. and R.T. Hise (1983). Have CEOs Adopted the Marketing Concept. In P. Varadarajan (ed.). The Marketing Concept: Perspectives and Viewpoints. *Proceedings of Workshop*, Texas A&M University, College Station.
    Webster, F.E., Jr. (1981). Top Management's Concerns about Marketing: Issues for the 1980's. *Journal of Marketing*, 45 (Summer), pp. 9–16.
55. Cheng, D.S. and Liu, L.L. (2017). *Huawei Shanshi Nian* (*Thirty Years of Huawei*), Guizhou Publishing Group, pp. 17–18.
56. Chen (n 1) p. 86.
57. Chen (n 55) 397–8.
58. Sun and Wang (n 48) pp. 293–4.
59. Tian and Wu (n 7) p. 126.
60. Chen (n 1) p. 17.
61. Yang (n 4) pp. 222–3.
62. The Economist (n 2).
63. Cheng and Liu (n 55) pp. 466–8.
64. Tian and Wu (n 7) pp. 170–71.

# 7.  Chinese vs. Western strategic systems: theory and practice

*In theory, theory and practice are the same. In practice, they are not.*
– Albert Einstein

*The chess player aims for total victory. The wei qi player seeks relative advantage.*
– Henry Kissinger

The preceding chapters have examined the unique characteristics that distinguish Chinese strategic thinking. This chapter aims to further scrutinise the crucial questions: What sets the Chinese strategic mindset apart from Western counterpart, and how does this disparity hold significance for Western leaders across different global arenas? To address these questions, a comparative analysis of the Chinese and Western strategic systems will be conducted, drawing from both theoretical and practical perspectives.

## CHINESE VS. WESTERN STRATEGIC SYSTEMS: A THEORETICAL PERSPECTIVE

### (I)

Considerable literature has explored the contributions of two distinguished strategists, Sun Tzu from the East and Carl von Clausewitz from the West. These comparisons sought to uncover disparities or similarities between the two military luminaries. While an extensive array of references exists on this subject in the West, two notable authorities who have weighed in on the matter are Professor Michael Handel and Sir Basil Liddell Hart.

Despite Handel and Liddell Hart's esteemed status as military experts, their perspectives may primarily represent Western viewpoints, potentially overlooking valuable insights from other cultural contexts, such as the Chinese perspective. In light of the growing recognition of cognitive disparities between Chinese and Western individuals, the reassessment and comparison of Sun Tzu and Clausewitz can be performed by incorporating a Chinese lens.

The contrasting evaluations of Sun Tzu's and Clausewitz's treatises by the two experts highlight their divergent perspectives. Liddell Hart, in contrast to Handel, holds a greater appreciation for the practicality and subtleties inherent in Sun Tzu's teachings, rooted in Chinese culture. According to Hart, Sun Tzu's insights possess a heightened clarity, profoundness, and an external freshness.

In contrast, Clausewitz's inclination towards emphasising logical ideals and 'the absolute' is seen by Liddell Hart as a departure from realism and moderation. This tendency, as observed by his followers, has led to the development of the theory and practice of 'total war' that surpasses sensible boundaries.[1]

Conversely, Michael Handel holds the belief that the two writers share more similarities than difference, taking into account time, geographic conditions, and cultural influences.[2] Handel argues that the disparities in emphasis and occasionally in substance between these two eminent strategists should not be overly magnified. In reality, these seemingly contrasting works on strategy possess as much common ground as they do apparent distinctions.[3]

Considering the extensive literature comparing the works of Clausewitz and Sun Tzu, the primary aim of this discussion here is to highlight the disparities in their fundamental thinking and reasoning.

Central to Clausewitz's doctrine is his understanding of the essence of war, which he defines as combat. Consequently, his doctrine emphasises key elements, such as the enduring spirit of conflict, the paramount importance of decisive battles, bolstered by the concentration of forces and aggressive tactics, all aimed at achieving the complete defeat of the enemy.[4] This perspective stems from his military and political worldview.[5]

Carl von Clausewitz witnessed the devastating Prussian defeat at Jena in 1806 and was subsequently taken prisoner by the French, until 1809. Following his release, he collaborated with Scharnhorst, Gneisenau, and Hermann von Boyen on the reform of the Prussian army. He then served as an instructor at the Military School in Berlin until 1812. He dedicated himself to the service of the Tsar of Russia out of Prussian patriotism, despite the King of Prussia's decision to safeguard his dynasty by accepting a compelled alliance with the emperor of France. Clausewitz participated in the Russian campaign and, despite being in disfavour, took part in the campaign of 1814–1815 in Prussian service. From 1818 to 1830, he led the Berlin Military School until he passed away in 1931.[6]

Clausewitz's worldview was deeply influenced by two major factors: the tumultuous events of the French Revolutionary and Napoleonic Wars, and the intellectual climate of his era, characterised by the transition from the Enlightenment to the age of Romanticism. The transformative nature of the wars with France provided Clausewitz with invaluable insights into the relationship between the military and the state, revealing that the structure and deployment of a nation's armed forces are intricately linked to its political, economic, and social conditions.

Furthermore, the prevailing intellectual currents of the time, particularly the German Counter-Enlightenment, shaped Clausewitz's thinking. He was convinced by the arguments put forth by the German Counter-Enlightenment that there were no universal, fixed rules that could comprehensively govern the conduct of war. This realisation led him to reject the notion that there existed a single, all-encompassing set of principles that could systematically master the art of warfare.

The convergence of Clausewitz's practical experiences as a military officer and his intellectual development resulted in his adoption of a historicist perspective. Central to this outlook was his rejection of absolute standards and his recognition of the significance of the 'spirit of the age' in shaping historical epochs. Clausewitz sought to capture the essence of war in his work, understanding that it was a multifaceted phenomenon deeply intertwined with the social, cultural, and political dynamics of each historical period.[7]

Clausewitz was inherently an outsider in his chosen profession, both by birth and by temperament. Additionally, despite participating in various military engagements, he never attained the coveted position of commanding troops on the battlefield to which he aspired. Furthermore, all his military encounters occurred in opposition to Revolutionary and Napoleonic France. He personally witnessed the immense destructive capabilities of the French armies that had conquered Europe in the years leading up to 1815.[8]

Clausewitz can be characterised as an 'academic' strategist, whose practical experience and direct knowledge of warfare or generalship were relatively limited. His renowned classic is characterised by a profound academic or philosophical exploration of warfare.

Notably, Clausewitz's understanding of the nature of war originated from both his military and political perspectives, which he integrated into his definition of war. Within the military realm, this perception was shaped by the dramatic collapse of traditional warfare when confronted with the Revolutionary and Napoleonic art of war. It was during this time that a single state, for the first time in modern European history, inflicted a decisive defeat upon all other powers on the continent, leaving a lasting impact on Clausewitz's conceptualisation of warfare.[9] His observation of 'destructive power' in shaping the outcome of battles during the Napoleonic era deeply influenced his strategic thinking.

Clausewitz's thinking was strongly influenced by the teachings of Immanuel Kant,[10] a German philosopher (1724–1804) who made significant contributions to various areas of philosophy, including metaphysics, ethics, and epistemology. Kant's philosophical framework emphasised the vital role of reasoning and concepts in understanding the nature of human behaviour, morality, and the limits of knowledge. Kant's influence shaped Clausewitz's mindset and aligned it with Kantian logic. For instance, Clausewitz sought to dissect and understand the dynamics of conflict and introduced various definitions and concepts related to warfare, defining war as 'an act of violence intended to compel our opponent to fulfil our will'.[11]

Despite recognising that previous approaches to understanding warfare fell short by attempting to create a model of something that could not inherently be modelled, Clausewitz still grappled with the theory–practice dichotomy.[12] Clausewitz's first type of war corresponds to a Kantian 'ideal type', representing an abstract notion of what war would be like if it could be waged in isolation. He refers to this concept as 'absolute war'. Applying logical reasoning, 'absolute war' would persist until it concludes with the total triumph of one side over the other.[13]

However, Clausewitz perceives warfare as series of discrete engagements, where time becomes a crucial factor introducing uncertainty. Consequently, Clausewitz arrives at the conclusion that achieving victory in war ultimately relies, to some extent, on luck.[14]

The title 'Sun Tzu', which means 'Master Sun', is an honorary name. His birth name was Sun Wu, also known as Chang Qing. As a contemporary of Confucius, Sun Tzu lived between 545 and 470 BC. His family lineage consisted of nobles and generals, which undoubtedly shaped his upbringing and influenced his strategic thinking. The era in which he lived was marked by frequent inter-state conflicts and the flourishing of various philosophical schools, like Confucianism, Taoism, Mohism, and others. These diverse influences played a significant role in the development of Sun Tzu's strategic mindset.

Sun Tzu led and won numerous crucial battles against the State of Chu. His military prowess greatly contributed to the rise of the State of Wu as a prominent power during his time. Through his direct participation in leading King Wu's armies, Sun Tzu gained invaluable practical experience in warfare. Sun Tzu's strategic philosophy is rooted in Chinese thought and logic.

Within Sun Tzu's teachings, there exists no dichotomy between theory and practice, and the Chinese perspective on warfare is continuous and process-orientated. Skilled Chinese generals would only engage in battles when victory was already assured, at least on paper.[15]

Clausewitz and Sun Tzu possess fundamentally distinct strategic mindsets due to their divergent cultural background, logics, philosophies, and experiences. Metaphorically, they can be likened to two artistic painters who have created two separate paintings – one depicting the landscape of a Western nation, such as France, and the other capturing ancient China. While both landscapes may share elements like mountains, rivers, forests, or deserts, the contours and topographies differ significantly. Moreover, the methods and approaches employed by the two painters are entirely dissimilar, influenced by their distinct training backgrounds.

Determined and dictated by his cultural background and mindset, Sun Tzu does not offer any definitions on the 'strategies' (indeed, he never employs this specific term in his writings, as found in Western literature) he preaches. Instead, his teachings are characterised by concise and practical guidance, devoid of abstractions, and focused on tangible applicability.

In 1772, *Sun Tzu's Art of War* made its way to Europe through French Jesuit Joseph Amyot and initially gained considerable popularity, only to later fade into obscurity. It was Mao Zedong's triumphs that reignited interest in this manual of indirect strategy.[16] Despite this resurgence, Western scholars continue to grapple with the intricate nuances of this ancient Chinese masterpiece, highlighting the considerable difficulties they encounter in grasping its principles.[17] Despite its global recognition as a renowned treatise on strategy, there is a paucity of publications in top academic journals that effectively illustrate the successful application of Sun Tzu's teachings in Western contexts.

A comprehensive understanding of Sun Tzu's treatise necessitates a deep familiarity with Chinese strategic thought, deeply embedded in Chinese culture. In essence, one must initially grasp the fundamentals of Chinese strategic thinking in order to fully comprehend *Sun Tzu's Art of War*.

Mao Zedong's ideas and leadership played a pivotal role in China's transformation from a backward and semi-colonial nation to an independent and globally respected power. Despite not having had an opportunity to read Sun Tzu's renowned work, *The Art of War*, Mao's strategic approaches during the Chinese civil war bore remarkable resemblance to the principles advocated by Sun Tzu.[18] This shared resemblance can be attributed to their common adherence to the strategic thinking deeply rooted in Chinese culture.

A study has investigated the connection between time and strategy, comparing the works of Clausewitz's *On War* and *Sun Tzu's Art of War*. The findings of the study reveal notable diversities between the two classic texts.

In Clausewitz's *On War*, strategic thinking is characterised by limited flexibility and preconceived knowledge. The emphasis is placed on tactical manoeuvres rather than overarching strategy, and surprise is considered an obstruction to successful strategy implementation.

On the contrary, *Sun Tzu's Art of War* portrays strategy as a long-term endeavour that necessitates continual adaptation. The attainment of advantage is achievable through the element of surprise, while flexibility and foreknowledge play crucial roles. Moreover, Sun Tzu's work places more emphasis on strategy itself. The concepts of time in each of these works also diverge significantly.[19]

By revisiting the Korean War through the lenses of philosophy and the backgrounds of US commanders, we may better comprehend how US commanders, particularly General MacArthur, pursued a strategy aimed at annihilating the North Korean Army. Matthew Ridgway, who succeeded General MacArthur during the Korean War, reflected on MacArthur's fervour to fulfil his assigned mission – the mission he had fervently advocated for: the complete eradication of all enemy armed forces on the Korean peninsula.[20]

The decision made by General MacArthur to cross the 38th parallel, which subsequently triggered China's intervention in the Korean War, can be understood within the framework of Clausewitz's concept of the 'imperative of destruction', which lies at the core of Clausewitz's principles.[21] Clausewitz's doctrines have long been an integral component of military education in the Western world, including institutions like West Point Military Academy, where General MacArthur received his education and served as a Superintendent.

The impact of Clausewitz's principles has been widely observed in both the military and literary realms in the United States.[22] An example of this influence can be seen in the book *Men at War*, edited by Ernest Hemingway.[23] It is recognised that this book played a role in popularising Clausewitz's ideas in the United States during World War II and the early Cold War period.[24]

After the daring and risky decision of General MacArthur that led to the triumphant Inchon landing, the question arose as to whether the UN forces should cross the 38th parallel. It is suggested that any US military commander would probably have arrived at the same strategic decision if MacArthur had not been the commander-in-chief at that moment. While it is true that most of General MacArthur's military staff may not have supported his decision regarding the Inchon landing, few of them opposed the subsequent decision to cross the 38th parallel. This can be attributed to the shared influence, thinking, or logic prevalent among them.

## (II)

Figure 7.1 highlights the inherent differences in strategic practices between China and the West, which can be attributed to distinct theories and frameworks underlain by strategic thinking. Western strategies are supported by theories that have been developed based on Western cognitive perspectives, while Chinese military practices are influenced by Chinese military classics that deeply are rooted in the Chinese strategic mind. Consequently, despite the availability of texts like *Sun Tzu's Art of War* and *Mao Zedong Selected Works* in the West for an extended period, only a limited number of Western military and political leaders have truly grasped them.

In Figure 7.1, it is important to observe a small, vertically overlapping rectangle. This signifies that, despite significant disparities between Chinese and Western strategic systems, there are certain aspects that both sides consider. These shared factors encompass elements such as terrain, weather, firepower, logistics, politics, and more. However, these similarities are limited to the

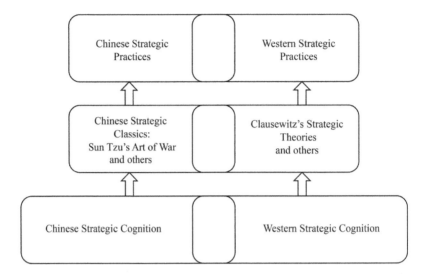

*Figure 7.1      A comparison of Chinese and Western strategic systems*

'what' nature, rather than the 'how' aspect, which holds greater determinism in the context of battles and wars.

François Jullien has noted that one of the most challenging aspects of Chinese thought lies in its inherent ability to convey and imply concepts without explicitly stating them.[25] This intriguing characteristic is deeply rooted in Chinese culture, where individuals who share the same cultural background are expected to comprehend the underlying messages. However, in contemporary times, this assumption no longer holds true, necessitating the expertise of specialists to elucidate the connotations for untrained individuals.

In his concise treatise, *Sun Tzu's Art of War*, which spans 6075 Chinese characters, Sun Tzu heuristically employs numerous key terms without offering explicit definitions. Consisting of 13 chapters, Sun Tzu's treatise can be viewed as a practical guide for military operations.

The subsequent section provides specific examples to point out fundamental theoretical differences in the works of Sun Tzu and Clausewitz and to demonstrate difficulties encountered by Western readers in comprehending and implementing the teachings of Sun Tzu, primarily due to the lack of understanding of the underlying Chinese strategic mindset.

**(1)**

The foundation of the two military theoretical systems of Sun Tzu and Clausewitz is fundamentally different, leading to distinct theoretical orientations.

Sun Tzu, at the beginning of his treatise, emphasises the significance of warfare as the paramount affair of the state, the essence of life and death, and the path to survival or extinction. He stresses the necessity of deep contemplation and thorough analysis of warfare, cautioning against launching it lightly.[26] Among the five key factors that Sun Tzu identifies as influencing the outcome of warfare, the foremost is the concept of the *Tao*, which entails achieving unity and harmony between the people and their leaders.[27]

The *Tao* factor holds a distinctive position within the Chinese strategic system, shaping the nature of conflict and its ultimate trajectory and outcome. This emphasis is aligned with that of Confucianism. It represents a crucial aspect that sets apart the Chinese strategic system from its Western counterpart.

Sun Tzu's teachings emphasise the significance of the *Tao* in aligning the people with the ruler. Fundamentally, it signifies that the ruler must possess moral integrity, uphold justice, and prioritise the welfare of the majority. Failure to do so would result in a lack of followship, thereby undermining the ruler's authority. The Chinese civil war serves as a fitting illustration of this principle.

In the aftermath of Japan's surrender in World War II on 15 August 1945, Chiang Kai-shek's KMT initiated preparations for a civil war against the CPC. Upon completing their military deployments, the KMT unilaterally abandoned the armistice pact with the CPC.

On 26 June 1946, the KMT forces launched an offensive against the CPC-controlled regions of the Central Plains, marking the commencement of the civil war. At that time, there existed a substantial power disparity between the two sides. The KMT army boasted over 4.3 million armed personnel, predominantly composed of well-trained regular troops equipped with modern weaponry provided by the United States. This arsenal included aeroplanes, warships, tanks, and armoured vehicles. The KMT governed a population exceeding 339 million individuals and controlled a land area surpassing 7 million square kilometres. The majority of transportation networks were under the jurisdiction of the KMT forces.

In contrast, the CPC held dominion over approximately one-third of the national population within the liberated regions under its control. The territorial expanse administered by the CPC accounted for less than one-quarter of the entire nation. The armed forces led by the CPC principally consisted of peasants, characterised by limited training and outdated weaponry.[28]

Due to the absence of the *Tao*, the KMT army faced a disconnect between their soldiers and their commanders and decision-makers. As clashes with the CPC PLA commenced, many KMT soldiers quickly surrendered, lacking the will to fight, and joined the ranks of the PLA, thereby bolstering its strength.

On the other hand, despite their inferior weaponry compared to the KMT forces, the CPC army received significant support from the general population.

During the military campaigns of Liaoshen, Huaihai, and Pingjin, which dealt devastating blows to the KMT troops, the CPC army was bolstered by the assistance of 5 million civilian personnel, who provided over 100 000 stretchers, 380 000 carts, 1 million livestock, and 8.5 billion catties of grain. The ratio of soldiers to civilian workers varied from 1:1 to 1:3. The substantial support from the populace played a crucial role in the CPC army's triumph over the KMT troops, as a result of the CPC's adherence to the principles of the *Tao*.

This swift transformation altered the power dynamics between the two sides in favour of the CPC armed forces. In 1949, the CPC achieved a definitive and comprehensive triumph over the KMT forces, prompting the remnants of the KMT to flee to the island of Taiwan.

It can be seen that, throughout Chinese history, the leaders of the nation have refrained from aggressive expansion of territories through military prowess. This approach is regarded as one of the fundamental reasons behind China's status as the only surviving civilisation since ancient times.

In contrast to Sun Tzu's cautious approach to warfare, Clausewitz offers a different perspective. He defines war as a violent act aimed at compelling the enemy to comply with one's desire. According to Clausewitz, violence equips itself with the tools of art and science to confront and overcome opposing violence. War operates within self-imposed restraints, often subtle and easily overlooked, such as the application of international law, which do not significantly diminish its efficacy. Thus, violence – specifically physical force – becomes the means, while the ultimate objective remains the enforced submission of the enemy to one's will.[29]

The United States, often influenced by Clausewitz, has been involved in numerous foreign interventions throughout its history. It can be observed that the United States has participated in nearly 400 such interventions, based on a broad definition of military intervention, between 1776 and 2023. Approximately half of these operations occurred after 1950, with over 25% taking place in the post-Cold War era. The objectives for these interventions have encompassed various aspects, such as economic interests, territorial considerations, social protection, regime change, the safeguarding of US citizens and diplomats, policy reforms, the pursuit of empire, and the establishment of new regimes.[30]

A celebrated admonition from the ancient Chinese text, *The Methods of the Sima*, underscores the principle that, regardless of a state's vastness, those who have an affinity for warfare will ultimately face destruction. Even when tranquillity reigns throughout the land, those who neglect the art of warfare will undoubtedly find themselves in danger.[31] This timeless wisdom from Chinese tradition advises that a nation, regardless of its size, should avoid bellicosity, which leads to inevitable downfall, and also should not disregard the importance of war during times of peace, as it can expose the nation to perilous situations.

**(2)**

The warfare objectives of Sun Tzu and Clausewitz can be understood as representing two different approaches to conflict, each with its own desired outcomes. Sun Tzu's perspective can be characterised as promoting a cooperative or win-win game, where the goal is for both parties to thrive and prosper. In contrast, Clausewitz's viewpoint aligns with a more competitive or zero-sum game, where one side's victory comes at the expense of the other side's defeat.

Sun Tzu emphasises the importance of forward-thinking, cunning tactics, and understanding the enemy to achieve victory while minimising casualties and destruction. His objective is to secure advantageous positions and outcomes that benefit both sides, leading to a harmonious and prosperous coexistence. On the other hand, Clausewitz places greater emphasis on the use of force and the destruction of the enemy's capabilities. He argues that war is a violent clash between opposing forces, where victory is achieved through the complete defeat or destruction of the adversary.

Clausewitz argues that wars, including both military and political aspects, consist of numerous simultaneous or consecutive combats, both major and minor. The reason for this fragmentation of activity lies in the multitude of interrelated factors that give rise to wars: each strategic action can be traced back to a specific combat, since it involves the utilisation of military force, and the fundamental concept behind it is always the act of fighting. Consequently, any military activity within the realm of strategy can be broken down into individual combats, focusing on the objective and the causes that give rise to them. At this point, it can be recognised that every combat, regardless of its scale, serves its own distinct purpose in support of the overarching objective. In light of this understanding, the destruction and conquest of the enemy should be seen merely as a means to achieve this objective, which it undoubtedly is.[32]

The objectives pursued by Cisco and Huawei in their legal battles, as discussed in Chapter 6, can be understood through the lens of the contrasting philosophies of Sun Tzu and Clausewitz. In this context, Cisco's aim was to inflict severe damage on Huawei, leaving no chance for its survival. On the other hand, Huawei's founder, Ren Zhengfei, sought a compromise, a Middle Way, where both parties could derive benefits without causing harm to each other.

Cisco's objectives align more closely with the principles espoused by Clausewitz. Clausewitz emphasised the concept of total victory and the eradication of the enemy's capabilities. In line with this, Cisco sought to use legal battles as a means to cripple Huawei's operations, ensuring Cisco's dominance in the networking and telecommunications industry. Their objective was to eliminate Huawei as a significant competitor, thereby securing their own market position and preventing any future challenges.

Conversely, Huawei's approach, as driven by Ren Zhengfei, reflected a more conciliatory and compromising stance reminiscent of Sun Tzu's teachings. In this light, Huawei aimed to find a middle ground where both Cisco and Huawei could coexist and benefit from the situation. Ren Zhengfei's objective was to reach a mutually advantageous resolution that would allow Huawei to continue its operations and growth while minimising the potential harm inflicted by the legal battles.

Specifically, Sun Tzu states that 'Subjugating the enemy's army without fighting is the true pinnacle of excellence'.[33] This profound wisdom caught the attention of Liddell Hart, who initially became intrigued by Sun Tzu's work through a letter from Major General Sir John Duncan, a British Army officer who commanded the Shanghai Defence Force from 1927 to 1928. In his letter, Sir Duncan introduced Sun Tzu's treatise to Liddell Hart, emphasising a principle that fascinated him: 'the supreme art of war is to subdue the enemy without fighting'.[34]

Liddell Hart expressed his belief that when later translations of Sun Tzu's works reached the Western world, the military community was predominantly influenced by the extreme views of Clausewitz. Subsequently, the voice of the Chinese sage went largely unheard. Soldiers and statesmen failed to heed Sun Tzu's warning that 'there has never been a protracted war from which a country has benefited'.[35]

In truth, even if *Sun Tzu's Art of War* had been introduced into Europe simultaneously with the publication of Clausewitz's *On War*, it would not have been able to surpass the latter's influence. The primary reason for this is that few Europeans would have comprehended and embraced Sun Tzu's principles due to their varied strategic perspectives and understandings.

Despite the alluring concept and vast potential benefits, only a small number of Western readers have contemplated the systematic implementation of this idea. The question that lingers is: How can Western military leaders effectively translate this seemingly straightforward strategic advice into reality? If we approach this wisdom metaphorically, the logic can be understood as follows.

Sun Tzu, the esteemed Chinese sage, advises that when faced with a menacing tiger, one should endeavour to transform it into a docile domesticated pet. Sun Tzu's reputation as a renowned strategist leads us to believe that his teachings hold merit. In the Western world, this advice may be readily accepted, as it sounds appealing and implies no harm, while offering potential benefits from the tamed tiger. However, Western individuals should pause and consider a crucial question: How can we effectively accomplish this transformative process?

While Sun Tzu advocates for tiger-taming, it is essential to recognise that taming tigers is deeply ingrained in Chinese culture, and many individuals in China are trained in this practice from a young age. While the advice may appear straightforward, its successful implementation relies on understanding the unique cultural context in which it originated. What may be feasible and practical in one culture may prove challenging or even impossible in another.

If Western individuals genuinely wish to embrace and apply this philosophy, they must invest time and effort in probing Chinese culture to gain a comprehensive understanding of how tigers are tamed with relative ease. It requires a willingness to bridge the cultural gap and learn from the expertise and traditions of another society.

From the Western perspective, Clausewitz explicitly dismisses the possibility of conquering an enemy without engaging in combat. He argues that the notion of disarming and subduing an adversary while minimising bloodshed may seem plausible to some philanthropists, who perceive it as the ideal objective of the art of war. However, Clausewitz asserts that this belief is fundamentally flawed and should be eradicated. He contends that, in the realm of war, errors stemming from a spirit of benevolence are the most dangerous.[36]

The impact of Clausewitz's philosophy on the inevitability of bloodshed in warfare resonates strongly within the Western military community. This sentiment is exemplified by Matthew Ridgway, who assumed commander of the Eighth United States Army, or Commander of UN forces, succeeding General MacArthur, during the Korean War.

During Ridgway's initial major offensive in Korea, he designated it as 'Operation Killer'. However, a colleague raised concerns, suggesting that the name was excessively bloodthirsty and could pose challenges for the Army's public relations efforts.

Ridgway, perplexed by this objection, shared his view: he failed to comprehend why it was deemed objectionable to acknowledge the fundamental reality that war involves the act of killing the enemy. Naturally inclined against any attempt to portray war as a minimally disagreeable endeavour that necessitates little bloodshed, Ridgway expressed his bewilderment towards such perspectives.[37]

Occasionally, circumstances arise where the enemy is compelled to surrender without engaging in battle. This outcome typically occurs when the enemy is surrounded by overwhelmingly superior forces, effectively cutting off their access to vital supplies such as water, food, or ammunition. This dire situation often compels them to surrender. This kind of circumstances could be found on battlefields during World War II. A prime example of this occurred during the Anglo-American landings in North-West Africa in November 1942, where the Allied forces encircled several hundred thousand German and Italian troops in northern Tunisia, leading to their surrender in May 1943.

However, it should be noted that this Western approach does not necessarily embody the strategic wisdom emphasised in Sun Tzu's teachings. Rather, it can be attributed to instinctual or logical combat tactics. True strategic wisdom, according to Sun Tzu, lies in the ability to overcome formidable hostile opponents using limited resources, often inferior to those of the enemy. This is achieved through meticulously devised strategic or tactical manoeuvres, aligning with Sun Tzu's guidance on strategic wisdom.

In the renowned tale from the *Romance of the Three Kingdoms*, there is an illuminating example of achieving victory without resorting to devastating warfare. During the tumultuous period of the Three Kingdoms, Zhuge Liang, the esteemed Prime Minister of the Shu Kingdom, was given a crucial mission by Liu Bei, the late King of Shu. The mission was to fulfil Liu Bei's lifelong aspiration of conquering the Central Plains through a Northern Expedition, thereby restoring the glory of the Han Dynasty and establishing Shu's domination.

However, the rear of the Shu Kingdom, in the South, was plagued by numerous rebel factions, which posed a grave threat to the stability of the realm. This instability greatly hindered Zhuge Liang's Northern Expedition, making it imperative to address the rebel issue first.

To achieve a definitive and all-encompassing solution for the success of the Northern Expedition, Zhuge Liang recognised the imperative of winning the hearts and minds of the southerners. On his mission to pacify Meng Huo, Zhuge Liang employed a strategy that involved capturing and releasing the rebel leader multiple times.

The attainment of victory without confrontation often resorts to the utilisation of the *Shi* strategy, which lacks an exact equivalent in Western culture. Through the deployment of *Shi* strategies, the adversary may perceive, after careful calculation and contemplation, a limited chance of successfully resisting and may opt to surrender. In such cases, the victorious party may not possess superior resources or firepower; rather, they rely on strategic manoeuvring, the creation of advantageous circumstances, or the utilisation of existing opportunities, to convince the opponent of the potential dire consequences of continued fighting. It is crucial to reiterate that comprehending the Chinese strategic mind necessitates the adoption of a comprehensive perspective.

Another distinct element of Chinese strategy that supports the implementation of the 'winning without fighting' tactic is the artful utilisation of stratagems. Chinese society has long embraced a culture of employing stratagems, which has transformed the Chinese military into masters of deception. Through skilful application of stratagems, Chinese armed forces can effectively create illusions that magnify the perceived strength of a small army to the extent that it appears a hundred times more powerful. This strategic manipulation often overwhelms the enemy, instilling feelings of intimidation and hopelessness, ultimately leading them to surrender.

In a renowned historical battle between Sun Bin and Pang Juan, Pang Juan possessed a significant advantage in terms of armed forces and resources in his confrontation against Sun Bin. However, he ultimately suffered a decisive defeat because of falling into Sun Bin's cunning trap.

To deceive Pang Juan into believing that Sun Bin's army was significantly smaller than its actual strength, Sun Bin devised a strategic retreat. As part of this elaborate ruse, Sun Bin gradually reduced the number of field caul-drons, which allowed for an estimation of the number of soldiers being fed. Through this clever tactic, Pang Juan was led to believe that Sun Bin's forces were steadily dwindling due to heavy desertions. Consequently, Pang Juan personally led a small army in pursuit of Sun Bin, unaware that the latter was patiently lying in wait within a favourable terrain, prepared for an ambush. With a well-timed strike, Sun Bin delivered a fatal blow to Pang Juan, resulting in his demise on the battlefield.

A culture-related element exemplifying the notion of 'achieving victory without battles' is deeply rooted in Confucianism. Throughout and following World War II, China gained a reputation for its exceptional treatment of prisoners of war, marked by benevolence, generosity, and a lack of cruelty. Mao Zedong's policy for preferential treatment of prisoners had a great impact during the Chinese Civil War, anti-Japanese War, Sino-Indian War, and Korean War, effectively reducing resistance from adversaries.

Matthew Ridgway, a staunch believer in American power, expressed his admiration for the significant influence of the Chinese prisoner policy. According to Ridgeway, Chinese soldiers were known for their tenacity, ferocity, and resilience, but it was discovered that they exhibited a higher level of civility towards prisoners compared to their Korean counterparts. On numerous occasions, they willingly shared their limited food with prisoners and adopted friendly attitudes towards them.[38]

During the initial military campaign of the Korean War, the Chinese army took more than 1000 American and South Korean soldiers as prisoners. However, rather than retaining them for an extended period, the Chinese made a strategic decision to release them, for two specific reasons.

Firstly, this act served as a psychological manoeuvre aimed at dispelling the prevailing rumour that 'the Chinese kill all prisoners'. By releasing the prison-ers after a brief period of education, the Chinese sought to communicate their policy of preferential treatment towards prisoners to the UN force involved in the conflict.

Secondly, the release of prisoners was intended to deceive General McArthur into believing that it stemmed from the Chinese army's fear of engaging in direct confrontation with the UN, particularly the US forces.

Unfortunately, along with other deceptive tactics employed by the Chinese, General McArthur fell for the ruse, disregarding the presence and capabilities of the Chinese army in the war. The miscalculation resulted in heavy losses for the UN forces during the initial military campaign.[39]

Following the conclusion of the second military campaign, a significant shift in behaviour was observed among American soldiers who had become aware of the Chinese prisoner policy. When battlefield situation seemed bleak, a considerable number of American soldiers willingly surrendered without engaging in fierce combat.

According to a document from the Central Intelligence Agency (CIA), the Chinese prisoner policy had a notable impact on the captured American soldiers. The document revealed that approximately one-third of American prisoners developed suspicions regarding the American system, while another third committed various offences against the United States within the prison camps, ranging from minor infractions to more serious crimes. In addition, a small percentage of the prisoners, around one per cent, underwent a change in their religious beliefs.[40]

Furthermore, within a holistic culture, Sun Tzu's wisdom of 'winning without battles' can be achieved by building strategic alliances. By forging strategic alliance with like-minded nations or organisations, one can combine resources, knowledge, and influence, enabling the creation of a united and impactful entity. Robust alliances serve as a deterrent to potential adversaries and facilitate the achievement of goals through collaborative endeavours, thus avoiding direct confrontation.

In 354 BC, King Hui of Wei sought to avenge a previous defeat that resulted in the loss of Zhongshan, a small state originally belonging to Wei, located to the north. During Wei's national mourning, Zhongshan was captured by the kingdom of Zhao.

Perceiving Zhongshan as insignificant and in proximity to Zhao, Pang Juan proposed a bolder approach. He suggested launching an attack on Handan, the capital of Zhao, reasoning that Wei possessed a superior armed force. This strategy would serve the dual purposes of revenge and reclaiming Zhongshan. King Hui accepted the suggestion and dispatched General Pang Juan towards Handan.

In response to the imminent threat from the formidable Wei army, King Zhao pursued a defensive strategy by seeking a strategic alliance with Qi. He promised to reward King Qi with the territory of Zhongshan in exchange for their assistance. King Qi agreed to the proposal and sent General Tian Ji along with Sun Bin, Tian's military advisor, to undertake the rescue mission.

When the troops of the Qi kingdom, en route to rescue Zhao, reached the border between Wei and Zhao, General Tian Ji initially planned to swiftly advance to Handan and engage in direct combat with Pang Juan's army.

However, Sun Bin intervened, offering his strategic counsel. With most of Wei's elite troops deployed to Zhao, their homeland defences would be weakened. Sun Bin proposed an alternative approach: by directly threatening the Wei king and placing him in grave danger, Pang Juan would be compelled to return to protect his ruler. Consequently, the siege of Handan by Wei would be lifted without need for military confrontation. Qi could stage an ambush on Pang Juan's return journey, inflicting a heavy blow on his army.

General Tian Ji agreed to follow Sun Bin's strategic counsel. The subsequent events unfolded exactly as Sun Bin had planned and anticipated. On their way back to Wei, Pang Juan's forces fell into the Qi army's ambush. The weary Wei soldiers were defeated. This renowned event has been immortalised as one of the 'Thirty-Six Stratagems', known as 'surrounding Wei to rescue Zhao'.[41] It serves as a prime example of an indirect approach to pursuing victory without battles.

## (3)

According to Clausewitz, it is generally impossible to ensure victory in a war before it begins. This is because real warfare never conforms entirely to theoretical models and concepts. The application of strict mathematical principles is incompatible with the nature of war, and achieving logically necessary outcomes is not feasible. The intricate and uncertain nature of the relationships involved in warfare introduces numerous factors that cannot be precisely evaluated.

In war, the element of chance cannot be eliminated, which introduces an inherent unpredictable aspect. From a subjective standpoint, the commanding officer often encounters unforeseen challenges that deviate from their initial expectations. As a result, doubts may arise regarding the efficacy of the formulated plan, requiring the commander to rely on their willpower to adhere to it. In the best-case scenario, a general must operate based on probabilities, and in situations where certainty is absent, they must place trust in destiny or chance, regardless of the terminology used.[42]

In contrast, according to Sun Tzu, victory could be secured by meeting certain conditions. Sun Tzu highlights the importance of understanding the enemy and oneself: 'Know the enemy and know yourself; in a hundred battles, you will never be in peril'.[43]

From Sun Tzu's viewpoint, the triumph of a victorious combatant can be likened to the sudden release of a pent-up torrent hurtling down a deep gorge. This represents the strategic deployment of forces. If one attempts to win solely through brute strength, no matter how formidable, there will always be moments when defeat is possible. However, a skilled general takes proactive measures upstream in the process. They identify favourable factors before they fully materialise, shaping the situation to align with their interests. When the accumulated advantage becomes overwhelming in their favour, the general fearlessly engages in battle, ensuring success.[44]

# CHINESE VS. WESTERN STRATEGIC SYSTEMS: A PRACTICAL PERSPECTIVE

In the previous sections, theoretical aspects concerning distinctions between Chinese and Western strategic systems have been explored. The following sections will scrutinise the practical outcomes that have emerged because of these divergent approaches. The assessment of the effectiveness and competitiveness of the two strategic systems will involve an examination of three key factors: philosophical and political foundations, economic fundamentals, and strategic approaches. These factors are shaped by divergent strategic mindsets.

Philosophical and political foundations, along with economic fundamentals, form the basis of a nation's direction and momentum. These factors are inherently dynamic. Using the analogy of an ocean liner, the philosophical and political foundation sets the navigation course, while economic fundamentals serve as the engine propelling the liner forward. If these components malfunction, the liner may veer off course or lack the power to progress.

The nature of a strategic approach can be compared to the captain of an ocean liner. A visionary and far-sight outlook would enable the liner to reach its destination more efficiently and safely, avoiding undersea reefs, rocks, and icebergs. Conversely, a narrow-minded and inward-looking worldview is likely to steer the ship towards various obstacles, leading the liner astray.

## Philosophical and Political Foundations

### (1)

Enlightened Chinese leaders in politics, the military, and business recognise the value of adhering to Chinese traditional wisdom, which emphasises the importance of standing on higher moral ground to achieve ultimate success. This principle, known as following the *Tao*, is embraced by various Chinese philosophies, such as Confucianism, Taoism, and Mohism.

Throughout history, Chinese philosophical and military texts have offered numerous admonitions, aphorisms, and stories that serve as reminders to Chinese elites and those aspiring to noble causes. These teachings convey a fundamental message: 'goodness can never be suppressed by evil', and 'a cause rooted in justice garners ample support, while an unjust cause struggles to find it'.

However, the concepts of 'good and evil' and 'just and unjust' are not universally agreed upon or adhered to. This divergence is particularly evident in the international arena, where individuals may believe that their actions are driven by national interest and therefore represent 'justice'. Nonetheless, such actions may be perceived by others as 'unjust' or even 'brutal'.

The Chinese perspective places great importance on a distinct guiding principle, as exemplified by Mao Zedong and his policies. This principle revolves around the interests of the majority of the people, which formed the foundation for the CPC victory over the KMT led by Chiang Kai-shek. The KMT relied heavily on a select group of wealthy industrialists, landlords, nobles, and officials, while the CPC prioritised the wellbeing of the broader population.

Following the establishment of the People's Republic of China, Mao continued to uphold this principle by fostering alliances with smaller and economically disadvantaged countries in Africa, Asia, and Latin America. Through the support of these seemingly less influential nations, China gained prominence on the global stage and became a member of the United Nations in 1971. This principle has also been carried forward by China's current president Xi Jinping, as demonstrated by initiatives like One Belt and One Road, which align with this guiding principle.

This concept has roots that extend far back in history. Over two millennia ago, various schools of Chinese philosophy, such as Mohism, Taoism, and Confucianism, embraced the essence of this principle. One prominent figure who specifically articulated this notion was Mencius. Often referred to as the 'sub-sage', Mencius was considered second only to Confucius himself. Mencius's belief in the centrality of the populace is encapsulated in the statement that 'the populace is the most important, followed by the nation, while the ruler is the least important'. This idea had an impact on the development of Mao Zedong's ideology, particularly his emphasis on 'the populace as the driving force behind the creation of world history' and the principle of 'serving the people', which became Mao's guiding motto.[45]

Now, considering the United States as a highly developed capitalist country, one might question whether the *Tao* principle is applicable there. If something is indeed true, it should hold relevance universally.

**(2)**

World War II originated and spread from Europe, initially causing the United States to adopt a stance of distance from the conflict. However, the ill-advised actions of Japan, such as the bombardment of Pearl Harbor on 7 December 1941, compelled the United States to join the Allies. The United States' participation in the Allies positioned it as a formidable force combating the Axis powers of Nazi Germany, Imperial Japan, and the Kingdom of Italy. During this time, the United States represented justice and stood as a beacon of democracy, playing a decisive role in tilting the balance of power in favour of the Allied forces.

Over a span of three decades, the United States found itself engaged in two world wars, resulting in the loss of 522 000 American lives. These wars originated thousands of miles away from American shores. By the time Germany surrendered on 7 May 1945, there were 3 077 000 American troops stationed in Europe.[46] Throughout both conflicts, the United States not only embodied a formidable and righteous military presence but also advocated for the interests of the majority of the global population.

As Europe remained the centre of the conflict, many European nations were left shattered, experiencing economic hardships and devastation. Recognising the importance of Western European unity and recovery for global security and stability, the United States devised the Marshall Plan, with the aim of assisting in the post-war reconstruction of Western Europe.

The Marshall Plan, implemented between 1948 and 1951, allocated over $15 billion to support the reconstruction of war-torn European Countries. This four-year initiative, named after its architect, US Secretary of State George C. Marshall, aimed to facilitate the rebuilding of cities, industries, and infrastructure, while also promoting trade and economic cooperation among European nations by eliminating trade barriers and fostering commerce.[47]

The United States played a key role in establishing a new, integrated Western Europe, based on its own models. However, this involvement became a realisation of the very entanglement in European affairs that George Washington had warned against.[48] In his Farewell Address, Washington cautioned against entangling the United States in European affairs, questioning the wisdom of intertwining the nation's destiny with that of any part of Europe. He warned that such entanglement could jeopardise America's peace and prosperity by subjecting it to the ambitions, rivalries, interests, whims, and caprices prevalent in Europe.[49]

The Marshall Plan was effectively executed and made a significant impact on the rapid revival of industries such as chemicals, engineering, and steel, stabilising war-torn Europe. Essentially, the Marshall Plan was a mutually beneficial initiative: it helped revive the European economy while also strengthening the global standing of the US dollar and promoting American trade through increased sales of industrial goods to Europe.

The actions taken by the United States during and after World War II align with the concept of *Tao* and with Mao Zedong's strategic practices during and after the Chinese Civil War. After World War II, the United States deviated from George Washington's injunction of maintaining a distance from the rest of the world, particularly Europe.

During this period, a growing awareness and determination emerged in the White House that a framework needed to be established to prevent future wars. This led to the creation of the United Nations, which included a Security Council to deter military aggression. Additionally, institutions such as the

International Monetary Fund (IMF) and International Trade Organisation (ITO), later succeeded by the World Trade Organisation (WTO), were established to prevent 'economic aggression', a term coined by US Treasury Secretary Henry Morgenthau.[50] The United States played a pivotal role in the establishment of these organisations and spearheaded efforts to promote internationalisation in the 1960s and 1970s, greatly facilitating global trade and benefitting economies worldwide.

**(3)**

Over the past two decades, the United States has experienced stagnation and has faced great challenges, domestically and internationally, as noted by Friedman and Mandelbaum in 2011 when they stated that 'America today is not healthy – economically or politically'.[51] This situation can largely be attributed to the departure from the *Tao* principle. The United States began to disregard the importance of the United Nations and unilaterally initiated the Iraq war.[52] Its focus shifted away from prioritising global economic interests towards assuming the role of the world's police officer and becoming more inward-looking.[53]

Following the US victory in the Cold War, the celebration of national military strength became deeply ingrained in Washington's political culture. This trend culminated in 2001 with the convergence of arrogance and militarism in a vision for American dominance known as *pax americana*, championed by neoconservative advocates who came to influence US military and foreign policy during President George W. Bush's administration.

Under this leadership, the US embarked on a systematic campaign against multilateral institutions, withdrawing from the Anti-Ballistic Missile Treaty, attempting to undermine the International Criminal Court, resisting efforts to strengthen the enforcement of the conventions against chemical and biological weapons, and exploiting the events of 11 September 2001 as the pretext for the invasion of Iraq in 2003, a move that deliberately challenged the authority of the Security Council.[54]

When engaging in international conflicts, the United States has consistently faced challenges, often exceeding budgetary limits and prolonging the duration of wars. From the late 1940s to 2004, the United States spent 12 trillion dollars in military-related expenses. From the time of both the first Bush and Clinton administrations, the United States witnessed sustained military build-ups, a gradual militarisation of foreign policy, and an increased willingness to employ force in international affairs.[55]

In addition, the Afghanistan war, spanning from 2001 to 2021, incurred a cost of $2.3 trillion for the United States.[56] Nobel laureate Joseph Stiglitz and Linda Bilmes estimated the cost of the Iraqi war at $3 trillion.[57] When evaluating the outcomes of these wars, the expenditure may appear as a complete squandering of resources, leading to more problems than gains.

Undoubtedly, this aggressive stance would have a significant impact on the US economy. The country would be compelled to allocate substantial resources towards its armed forces, investing heavily in military hard- and software. Consequently, this would result in a drain on US funds, diverting resources away from infrastructure development and advanced scientific and technological projects. Notably, the military budget of the United States exceeds the combined military expenditures of nine other countries, including China, India, Russia, the United Kingdom, Saudi Arabia, Germany, France, Japan, and South Korea.

Interestingly, the current confrontation between the United States-led bloc and the China-linked bloc bears resemblance to the historical conflict between the KMT led by Chiang Kai-shek and the CPC led by Mao Zedong during the Chinese Civil War. During that time, the KMT relied primarily on nobles, landlords, industrialists, and merchants, representing a small and privileged group of individuals. On the other hand, the CPC had the backing of a larger number of less fortunate people, predominantly farmers or peasants, along with a limited number of intellectuals influenced by Karl Marx.

Currently, global power dynamics are characterised by the United States forming alliances primarily with industrialised nations, particularly those of Western Europe, Japan, and Australia. In contrast, China has been forging closer collaborative relationships with developing or less developed countries, as depicted in Figure 7.2. The United States exerts significant influence on its alliance partners, while China's engagements with developing nations primarily revolve around economic development, fostering mutually beneficial and complementary outcomes.

The industrialised nations have generally been inclined to follow the leadership or influence of the United States, largely due to the economic support they received from the United States in the aftermath of World War II and its economic and military influence.

China's connection with the developing world is epitomised by its extensive engagement in the B&R initiative. As of September 2023, China had established partnerships with 154 nations through the B&R, encompassing approximately 80% of the member countries of the United Nations.[58] It is evident that the majority of these countries fall into the category of developing or underdeveloped countries.

The current dynamic between the US-led bloc and China-linked bloc can be compared to a situation where the China-linked bloc is constructing a massive reservoir on higher ground, accumulating a significant amount of waterpower, known as *Shi*, which could be released at a later time. In this analogy, the US-led bloc finds itself situated in lower terrain, facing a significant threat

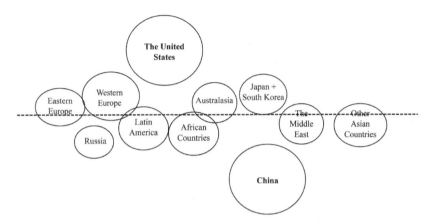

*Figure 7.2*      *US-led vs. China-linked blocs*

from the potential torrential floodwaters that could be released from the hilltop reservoir.

In response to this threat, the strategy of the US-led bloc is to construct a dam in order to block or control the potential deluge. However, this approach is unlikely to be effective. An alternative strategy that the United States could consider is to elevate the base terrain of its own bloc to higher ground, thereby reducing the potential impact of waterpower. Additionally, another approach could be to wait and observe, allowing the reservoir to develop additional water outlets. This would result in multiple streams of water, each with reduced power.

Rather than wasting resources on constructing a futile dam to control China's technological advancements, the United States should reconsider its approach. By attempting to control China's progress, the United States not only loses billions of dollars from the sale of its high-tech products, but it also relinquishes access to a critical market for its own high-tech products. Throughout the past three decades, the Western bloc has continuously attempted to impede the sale of crucial high technologies, without achieving any significant outcomes. Instead, these technologies have continued to emerge, filling gaps and even displacing Western technologies in international markets.

From a Chinese philosophical and political perspective that spans millennia, the divergent paths of economic development between the United States-led bloc and China can largely be attributed to the former's gradual departure from a morally elevated position to a lower one. The United States, once a leading advocate and facilitator of global trade, has undergone a transformation towards deglobalisation and anti-free trade. In contrast, China has emerged as a replacement, driving and promoting international trade.

The dynamic between the United States-led bloc, representing a minority of wealthy nations, and China-linked bloc, encompassing the majority of less affluent developing countries, has become increasingly evident. However, the latter possesses and controls a significant share of crucial natural resources and serves as an industrial powerhouse, despite the former commanding greater financial and technological resources. This calls for a time of reflection for the United States-led bloc to re-evaluate their policies and strategies.

It is important to highlight that the involvement of the United States in World War II, which shifted the balance of power between the Allies and the Axis Powers, was primarily driven by significant issues concerning China. Specifically, these issues were the protection of China's territorial integrity and safeguarding US interests in the region.

The United States' entry into WWII was prompted by a widespread public disapproval of Japan's actions, particularly their brutal treatment of defence-less Chinese cities, their discriminatory and contemptuous treatment of Europeans and Americans in China, and their alignment with the Axis Powers.

In mid-July 1939, the US government took a significant step by providing the required six months' notice of its intention to terminate the standard treaty of amity and commerce between the United States and Japan. This move granted the United States the ability to sever commercial relations with Japan at any time. The American public strongly demanded an end to the sale of supplies to Japan.

Recognising their vulnerability to a potential US embargo, the Japanese initiated negotiations with the United States in 1941, aiming to find a basis for agreement. Both parties expressed their desire for peace and a comprehensive solution of Far Eastern issues. However, translating these aspirations into concrete terms proved impossible. The primary point of contention between them was China.

The United States reiterated its principle of upholding China's territorial integrity and ensuring equal opportunities for all nations in the region. For the United States, this meant that Japan must abandon any attempts to bring China, or any part of it, under Japanese control. Consequently, Japan would need to withdraw its forces from China. The issue at hand was one that Japan could not effectively address, regardless of the length or skill of the negotiations.

Japan insisted that the United States cease its assistance to China, believing that this would leave China no choice but make peace on Japan's terms. Conversely, the United States insisted that Japan withdraw from China and relinquish any aspirations of ruling the country. Both sides had become irreversibly and irreconcilably committed to their respective positions.

Eventually, the Japanese bombing of Pearl Harbor occurred, awakening the sleeping giant and altering the course and outcome of World War II.[59]

From a historical point of view, the United States and China have shared significant experiences and common causes. For instance, in the late 19th century, approximately 15 000 Chinese workers assisted in the construction of US railways, making a substantial contribution to the US economy.[60] Additionally, in the late 1930s and early 1940s, the Sino-US joint air force known as the Flying Tigers led by Major General Claire Chennault played a crucial role in resisting the Japanese invasion of China.[61] It is worth noting that, throughout history, China has seldom embarked on overseas invasions despite possessing the potential capabilities to do so.

Considering these historical events, the United States may need to carefully contemplate whether China should be viewed as an adversary or as a partner with whom both nations can develop and prosper together.

**Economic Fundamentals**

By analysing the historical development of the world's two largest economies, namely the United States and China, we can uncover similarities in their growth patterns and gain insights into the dynamics of economic ascent and decline experienced by nations. Probing the evolution of these factors enables us to understand why the US economy has exhibited a downward trend in its national competitiveness, as described by Alan Greenspan, the former Chairman of the Federal Reserve Board, and Adrian Wooldridge who referred to it as 'America's fading dynamism'.[62] China's economy has consistently demonstrated a strengthening of its industrial and technological capabilities, exerting a positive influence on China's military prowess and political impact on the global stage.

**(1)**

Figure 7.3 provides a model of the economic evolution of the United States. The process begins with a surge of immigration from Europe, bringing a substantial influx of labour and skilled entrepreneurs to the nation. These entrepreneurs bring technology from their home countries and drive new innovations and inventions. Simultaneously, a thriving finance and banking sector provides strong support for entrepreneurship endeavours, leading to industrialisation. The establishment of an advanced railway system enhances efficient supply and distribution networks, further fuelling economic expansion and prosperity. This heightened economic development, in turn, fosters additional innovations and inventions, creating a positive economic feedback loop.

The initial phase commenced with the influx of immigrants from Europe, further facilitated by the Act to Encourage Immigration passed by the US Congress in 1864. During the late 19th century, the United States witnessed a significant surge in immigration, with 5.3 million individuals moving to

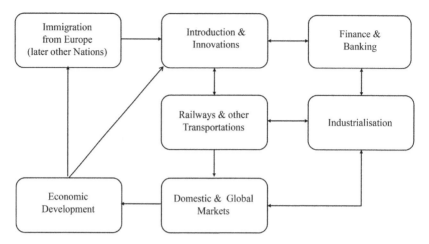

*Figure 7.3*     *A historical view of US economic development*

the country in 1880 alone. This constituted 10.5% of the total population of 50 million at the beginning of the decade. By 1914, the US population had reached 99 million, with a considerable portion of this growth attributed to immigration.

By 1920, immigrants and their children comprised over half of the manufacturing workforce in the United States, making significant contributions to the nation's industrial output. These immigrants brought with them valuable skills and expertise. For instance, skilled British immigrants continued the tradition of sharing Britain's industrial secrets in areas such as metallurgy, weaving, and chemicals across the Atlantic.[63]

The period between 1865 and 1914 witnessed a remarkable influx of fundamental innovations. These included the introduction of materials such as new types of steel, a novel fuel source in the form of oil, the emergence of electricity as a power source, the invention of the motorcar for personal mobility, the introduction of the telephone as a means of communication device, and countless other innovations that either built upon existing technologies or forged new paths independently.

From 1860 to 1890, the US Patent Office granted an incredible 500 000 patents for various inventions, surpassing the total issued in the preceding 70 years and eclipsing those awarded by any other country. The United States, once a fast follower, now boldly occupied a leading position, pioneering the technological frontier and paving the way for other nations to follow suit. This position has persisted to this day.[64]

The United States demonstrated superior prowess in harnessing steel-making technology, surpassing its rivals. During the first half of the 20th century, the

United States held the position of the world's leading steel producer, consistently contributing between 38% and 72% of the global output from 1913 to 1945.[65]

The 19th century witnessed a significant expansion of financial intermediation and banking, facilitating the rapid growth and industrialisation of the economy. In 1818, the country had 338 operating banks with total assets of $160 million, but by 1914, these numbers skyrocketed to 27 864 banks with total assets of $27.3 billion. This surge in financial institutions provided potential inventors with readily available capital to launch their business. Furthermore, the fierce competition among banks and financial institutions ensured capital accessibility at relatively low interest rates.[66]

Fundamentally, the United States predominantly comprised immigrants from Europe. Through the influx of both new and existing immigrants, the nation experienced a surge in technological development and innovation. The consequential outcome of this immigration and innovation was rapid industrialisation within the United States. From 1870 to 1910, the US share of global manufacturing rose from 23.3% to 35.3%,[67] solidifying its prominent position as the world's leading industrial power. It held this position until 2010, when China surpassed it.

The United States experienced an unprecedented expansion of its railway system from the mid-19th century. Railroad companies added more than 13 miles of track daily for 40 years, starting from 1870. This expansion resulted in a five-fold increase in total railway mileage, constituting 35% of the world's railway mileage by 1917.[68] Three significant inventions from the latter half of the 19th century – the railroad, steamships, and the telegraph – paved the way for accelerated progress after 1870.[69]

The introduction of railroads revolutionised the transportation of goods by significantly reducing costs. By 1890, the cost of shipping freight by rail was $0.875 per ton-mile, compared to $24.50 per ton-mile for wagon freight, representing a reduction of 96%. The construction of the transcontinental railroad reduced the time required to traverse the continent from six months to six days.

The advent of railways in the United States fundamentally reshaped the country's economic landscape. Prior to the railway age, the flow of goods predominantly followed a north–south (or vice versa) pattern, utilising coastal routes and the nation's extensive river systems. However, with the introduction of railways, there was a significant shift towards an east-west flow of goods.[70]

As depicted in Figure 7.3, three key factors played a crucial role in enhancing the economic growth and prosperity of the United States: technological advancements and innovations, industrialisation, and a highly developed railway system. The era spanning from 1870 to 1970 has been viewed as an economic revolution in the United States, one that was unparalleled in human history and unlikely to be replicated.[71]

However, since the 1970s, the United States has experienced economic decline and deindustrialisation.[72] The overall performance of the US economy indicates a significant deceleration in productivity growth, with a brief resurgence during 1996–2004 that many experts attribute to a surge in investment in information and communication technology equipment. Over the past decade, productivity growth has been even slower than the period between 1970 and 1996.[73]

Japanese and European companies have devastated US traditional industries such as automotive and steel, as well as high-tech business.[74] Two fundamental industries suffered significantly: motor vehicles and steel, impacting related industries as both suppliers and users. By 1979, Japanese automakers held a 20% share of the US car market, and the US global steel output share plummeted from 43% in 1953 to 11% in 1982.[75]

The growing industrial strength of foreign competitors has resulted in the contraction of US industrialisation, thereby weakening the nation's overall competitiveness. The US automotive industry offers a compelling example in this regard. In the aftermath of World War II, Japanese and European companies, driven by a desire to catch up, were able to achieve greater cost-effectiveness. Conversely, US companies experienced a waning drive for innovation, with the most significant innovation being automatic transmission in 1948. Furthermore, they neglected to recognise and adapt to shifting consumer preferences and overlooked product quality issues. Ultimately, US auto companies lagged their foreign counterparts in terms of cost-competitiveness, adaptability, quality, and productivity.

Following the active involvement of Japanese and European companies in US industries and markets, companies from China and other Asian economies, such as South Korea, Taiwan, and Singapore, gradually gained a foothold.[76] The trade imbalance in favour of China and the ascent of China's high-tech industry, which poses a threat to the dominant position of the US high-tech industry, have heightened tensions between the two nations.

Figure 7.4 illustrates the process of US deindustrialisation, initially instigated by Japanese and European companies and subsequently compounded by Chinese and other nations' companies. The level of industrialisation is pivotal to a nation's competitiveness. During the First and Second World Wars, the United States played a dominant role in tipping the balance of power, largely due to its unparalleled industrial capabilities, effectively serving as the primary global supplier of firearms and industrial supplies.

While the United States continues to maintain a leading role in specific domains of advanced technology, the realisation of the value of these technologies necessitates a reliance on industrialised countries like China, thereby closely intertwining the fortunes of US developers and Chinese users. The

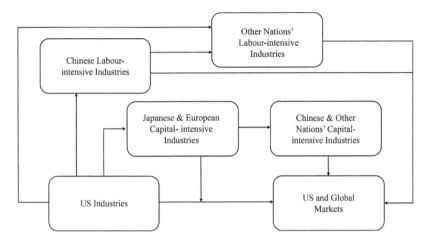

*Figure 7.4      Decline of US industrialisation*

robust industrial standing once enjoyed by the United States has now shifted to a more vulnerable position.

In 1960, the United States led the world in R&D expenditure, accounting for 69% of the global total, with two-thirds of this investment coming from state public finance. Much of this funding was focused on military R&D, driving the development of key emerging technologies like semiconductor integrated circuits, supercomputers, the internet, and aerospace through military budgets, government R&D contracts, and other support mechanisms.

However, 50 years later, the US share of global R&D expenditure had fallen to around 30%, and the proportion of state funding had decreased from two-thirds to about one-quarter. The share of R&D investment in national defence, which had played a significant role in advancing cutting-edge science and technology, had plummeted to one-tenth of its 1960 level. Even the remaining public funding increasingly favoured medical and pharmaceutical research with predictable returns, neglecting traditional basic sciences such as mathematics, physics, and chemistry, as well as fields like optomechanical and electrical engineering.[77]

As US industrialisation waned, its railway system underwent a rapid decline as well. Koll noted that the US rail network contracted by an average of 600 miles annually from 1945 to 1955.[78] This reduction may mirror the deindustrialisation of the United States and, in turn, reinforce the deindustrialisation trend.

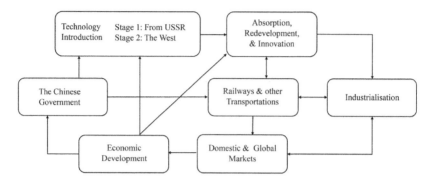

*Figure 7.5     A historical view of China's economic development*

**(2)**

Figure 7.5 illustrates a framework outlining China's distinctive path of economic development, which diverges significantly from that of Western nations. China's economy is ideologically 'socialist', with the government playing a vital role in its economic growth. The Chinese government has been pivotal in the assimilation of foreign technology, a process that unfolded in two distinctive stages.

The initial stage, beginning in the early 1950s, involved the introduction of 156 major industrial projects from the Soviet Union. The subsequent stage, commencing in the early 1990s, saw the acquisition of advanced technologies primarily from developed countries such as the United States, Japan, and European countries. Through absorption, adaptation, and further innovation, these technologies facilitated and expedited China's path to industrialisation, ultimately leading to its status as the only nation with comprehensive industrial categories and classifications recognised by the United Nations. Furthermore, China has established the world's largest high-speed railway network and highly developed highway systems, enabling efficient connections with suppliers and distributors.

Essentially, China's successful technological assimilation, adaptation, and innovation led to rapid industrialisation. This progress was supported by highly developed transportation systems that effectively managed the high volume of supply, production, and distribution, meeting the demands of a burgeoning industrial sector. Combined with global trade, China's economy has experienced a positive cycle over the past three decades.

On 1 October 1949, Mao Zedong proclaimed the establishment of the People's Republic of China. From 1950 to 1952, China prioritised the restoration of the nation's economy, which had been left in ruins by the previous government. All industrial and commercial establishments previously owned by the Nationalist government and bureaucratic capitalists were seized by the 'people's government', including all factories, plants, mines, railways, shipping, post offices, banks, shops, and other businesses. By the end of 1949, there were 2858 industrial enterprises with 750 000 employees under government control, and these state-owned enterprises contributed approximately 40% of the total industrial output.[79]

In 1954, Mao Zedong described the dire state of China's industrialisation, saying, 'At present, what can we produce? We can make tables and chairs, craft tea bowls and teapots, grow grain for flour, and produce paper. But we are unable to manufacture automobiles, airplanes, tanks, or tractors'.[80]

At the outset, China embraced the Soviet model of central planning as the foundation for its economic development. Between 1953 and 1957, China successfully implemented its first Five-Year Plan with the assistance of the Soviet Union. By 1956, a centrally planned economic system had been implemented. The number of enterprises under the control of the central government had reached 9300 in 1957, and their output accounted for 50% of the total state sector.[81]

The Five-Year Plan prioritised the development of heavy industry and focused on 694 large projects, including 156 key projects introduced from the Soviet Union. During this period, China's GDP experienced an average annual growth rate of 8.9%, as numerous new projects filled gaps in China's industrial landscape, such as aircraft, automotive manufacturing, high-alloy steel and nonferrous smelting, heavy and precision machinery, and metallurgical and mining equipment.[82]

By the end of 1952, China and the Soviet Union had agreed upon the initial phase of 50 major projects aimed at bolstering economic recovery and national development. These projects primarily focused on the energy sector, including coal and electricity, as well as raw material industries such as steel, nonferrous metals, and chemicals, in addition to national defence.

Following the eruption of the Korean War, China entered the second stage of the Sino-Soviet Agreement in May 1953. This agreement centred on the provision of complete sets of equipment targeting the defence and military industry, along with its related support sectors, encompassing a total of 91 projects.

In October 1954, the third phase of the Sino-Soviet Agreement was signed, encompassing a total of 15 projects within the energy and raw material industries. A decision was reached to broaden the scope of supply for the original 141 complete sets of equipment projects. This development brought the total number of aid projects between China and the Soviet Union to 156, subsequently known as the '156 Projects'.[83]

By 1969, all the '156 projects' had been successfully completed and were operating at full capacity. They stand as the cornerstone of modern China's industrialisation and represent a pivotal milestone in the nation's economic development. After over 60 years of advancement, some of the enterprises linked to the '156 projects' have undergone reorganisation or restructuring, while others have ceased operations. Presently, more than 100 of these enterprises remain operational, wielding a definitive influence across various industries.[84]

By 1978, several industries including energy, metallurgy, machinery, the chemical industry, national defence, and others had achieved significant scale. Aerospace, electronics, aircraft, automobiles, precision machine tools, the nuclear industry, and the petrochemical industry made substantial advancements, while light industries such as textiles, sugar, and paper-making experienced rapid development, collectively making industry the cornerstone of the national economy.[85]

In November 1977, the State Planning Commission reaffirmed the goals of realising 120 major projects by the year 2000. The primary strategy to achieve this ambitious plan involved increasing the scale of foreign investment and equipment introduction. In 1978, foreign investment contracts totalling $5.8 billion were signed, amounting to 89.2% of China's cumulative $6.5 billion foreign investment received from 1950 to 1977.[86]

As a result of the reform measures, China experienced substantial increase in exports, rising from $13.7 billion in 1979 to $52.5 billion in 1989, while imports grew from $15.7 billion to $59.1 billion during the same period. This shift was accompanied by a decline in the exports of primary commodities and a surge in the exports of manufactured goods. Furthermore, there was a significant increase in the imports of advanced technology and equipment, as well as a rise in the inflow of foreign capital.

Throughout the 1980s, China's agreed foreign investment totalled $33.7 billion, of which $15.4 billion was effectively utilised. The influx of foreign capital played a crucial role in driving China's economic development and accelerating the pace of economic reconstruction.[87]

China's effective utilisation of foreign direct investment (FDI) surged from $111.72 billion in 2012 to $173.48 billion in 2021, marking a growth rate of over 55%. The annual FDI inflow ranked second globally, maintaining the top position among developing countries for a continuous 30-year period. The cumulative FDI inflow exceeded $1.2 trillion. The proportion of FDI absorbed by high-tech industries escalated from 14.1% in 2012 to 30.2% in 2021, more than doubling.

Over the past two decades, FDI has played an indispensable role in propelling China's economic expansion, fostering industrialisation, enhancing corporate governance, and bolstering the international balance of payments. Foreign-invested enterprises have facilitated China's deep integration into global industrial and supply chains and value chains and have served as a driving force for innovation and economic structure upgrading, elevating the international competitiveness of China's economy.[88]

Similar to the historical pattern of rapid economic growth in the United States, China's swift economic expansion was accompanied by a substantial increase in steel production capacity. From 2002 to 2007, China achieved an annual GDP growth of 9.8%, while witnessing a 2.75-fold increase in crude steel output, with an annual growth rate of 22%. Additionally, from 2008 to 2013, China's GDP grew at an annual rate of 11.4%, while crude steel output increased by 1.81 times, with an annual growth rate of 12.6%. By 2018, China's crude steel production had reached 928.3 million tonnes, representing 51.3% of the global output.[89]

Following more than 70 years of rigorous advancement, China has emerged as the sole nation globally to boast a complete production chain encompassing all industrial categories outlined in the United Nations Industrial Classification. This includes 41 major industrial categories, 207 medium industrial classes, and 666 small industrial sectors. As such, it has gained the title of the 'World's Factory'.[90]

Following the establishment of the People's Republic of China, the government acknowledged the significance of railways in nation-building, economic distribution, and the facilitation of military, political, and technical activities. With the economic reforms of the early 1990s, which emphasised the development of an export-orientated economy, railways assumed a pivotal role in the government's strategies for fostering economic expansion. In line with the symbolism of railways in other national cultures, they have come to represent modernity within the context of China's economic development.[91]

By the close of 2020, China had established itself as a dominant force in the transportation sector, leading the world in high-speed rail, expressway, and railway infrastructure:

- The country's railway network spanned 146 000 kilometres, with 43 cities operating rail transit systems comprising 226 rail transit lines covering 7355 kilometres.
- China's expressway network extended to 161 000 kilometres, and its highways totalled 5.20 million kilometres.
- Civil aviation mileage reached 8.38 million kilometres, marking a 735-fold increase since 1949, with a total of 4,945 schedule routes, a 28-fold increase from three decades prior.
- In 2020, the total passenger traffic amounted to 9.67 billion trips, resulting in a turnover of 1.93 trillion passenger-kilometres, marking a 71-fold and 124-fold increase from 1949, respectively.

- China's waterway transportation had significantly advanced, with 22 142 production berths at ports, including 2592 in the over 10 000-ton class, representing 11.7% of the total and ranking first globally.
- The domestically-produced bullet trains, known as 'Rejuvenation', covered 5.8 kilometres per minute, and the Beijing Capital International Airport saw 1.5 flights arriving and departing per minute.
- China held the record for the largest numbers of bridges over highways and tunnels globally.[92]

A significant portion of the disparity in infrastructure quality between the United States and other industrialised nations can be attributed to varying levels of funding. According to the OECD, the United States has allocated a smaller percentage of its GDP to transportation infrastructure investment compared to countries such as France (0.9%), Germany (0.8%), Japan (1.1%), the United Kingdom (0.9%), and Australia (1.5%). Notably, China (4.8%) has invested ten times more than the United States (0.5%) as a percentage of GDP.[93]

The divergence in economic trajectories between the US and China in the past three decades can be attributed to their distinct strategic approach. Guided by analytical thinking, the United States has primarily prioritised sectors such as Wall Street, finance and banking, the military, high-tech, and services to maximise financial gains. This has involved relocating less profitable industries to other nations, including China, resulting in strategic industry vacuums in the US.

Conversely, directed by holistic thinking, China has focused on developing a broad range of industries. The evolution of China's machine tool industry illustrates this approach. Despite Western dominance in the high-end of the segment for three decades, particularly in the medium and high-end numerical machine tool market, China persevered in R&D efforts to overcome technological barriers and develop its own products, rather than solely relying on Western supplies. Consequently, by 2021, China had significantly narrowed the technological gap.[94]

In a global free-trade environment, the US economic development characterised by prioritising profitable sectors could maintain its industrial integrity. Nevertheless, in special scenarios like restricted trade policies, wartime emergencies, and a focus on national security, the United States may need to deviate from the free-trade system, potentially causing bottlenecks in critical industrial sectors.

## Strategic Approaches

This section explores the impact of strategic approaches on economic development. Strategies guided by analytical thinking have proven to be ineffective in maintaining national competitiveness and addressing international conflicts, often leading to prolonged conflicts and significant associated costs.

The US government has adopted a competitor-orientated philosophy in its approach to economic development and international relations. This philosophy holds that the continued global dominance of the United States depends on its ability to suppress potential competitors that may surpass it. Its primary focus is to employ political or military means to achieve its objectives. This approach has historically been successful in undermining the economies of former competitors like the Soviet Union and Japan when their GDPs approached around 70% of the United States' GDP.

However, this orientation has encountered challenges when dealing with the rise of China, which possesses a different strategic approach and system compared to that of the United States.

The United States maintains its global dominance through its unparalleled military expenditure and advancement of weaponry technology. This military power is often utilised to overwhelm potential competitors through coercive power, which initially seems cost-effective and efficient in preserving its global economic position. However, in the long run, this approach becomes prohibitively expensive, as it necessitates a large military budget to maintain a global presence. The combination of a bellicose culture[95] and a focus on competition leads to a tendency to resort to military means for resolving disputes and conflicts.

Notably, the United States has recently made efforts to draw China into its competition-driven approach with the goal of achieving victory in this rivalry. The Biden administration has emphasised the importance of establishing 'guardrails' to promote healthy competition and prevent harmful outcomes. Consequently, Washington has worked diligently to keep high-level military communication channels open.

Despite these efforts, China has repeatedly turned down US requests to reopen these channels. It has been suggested that US policymakers should comprehend the reasoning behind China's reluctance to establish guardrails, and to consider resetting Washington's competition strategy. China is primarily focused on advancing its economy, bolstering the confidence of its citizens, and maintaining social stability. On the international stage, China is intent on achieving the reunification of Taiwan as a strategic springboard for global expansion.

In contrast, the United States is focused on marshalling its national resources to tackle China's multifaceted challenges, maintain its influence in the Asia-Pacific region, and upholding its global supremacy. The distinct fundamental objectives of China and the US are evident, making it problematic for Washington to convince Beijing to establish guardrails based on a bilateral consensus within the international order and norms.[96]

The Western culture, characterised by analytical thinking, influences the decision-making process in the United States military. Thus, most strategic military decisions and implementations involve multiple stages, thereby prolonging the duration of conflicts and exponentially increasing military costs. Consequently, a vicious cycle emerges within US society, where a national bellicose culture[97] promotes the ready utilisation of coercive measures to resolve conflicts, while military actions tend to be protracted, leading to a significant escalation in military expenditure. Overspending on the military comes at the expense of economic development, including investments in infrastructure and innovation.

Particularly, from the 1980s onward, the US economy has been characterised by significant military expenditure alongside production reorganisation. This has led to the military and aerospace industries becoming the primary earners in manufacturing exports.[98] However, despite the potential profits from weapons sales, the effective channels for directing these funds towards supporting economic development are often lacking. Consequently, the United States has faced challenges due to its outdated infrastructure and diminished industrial capabilities, significantly impeding its national competitiveness.

It has been recognised that, in the United States, there is a deep-seated structural entrenchment of social inequality and political and corporate unaccountability, with limited public avenues for addressing these issues. The prominence of the military industrial complex in the American economy and politics serves as a major distraction. The preference for military contracts has led to decreased competitiveness in the US economy.[99]

In 2010, President Barak Obama expressed his disappointment over the insufficient investments in US infrastructure, highlighting that it was illogical for China to possess superior rail systems and Singapore to have better airports. He also noted that China had surpassed the United States in having the fastest supercomputer, emphasising the importance of strategic investments for long-term benefits.[100]

Recently, US economists and experts have emphasised the critical state of the country's infrastructure, noting that it is both severely overburdened and falling behind that of other leading economies, particularly China. The existing systems, such as roads, railways, electrical grids, and internet networks, were constructed decades ago and are struggling to meet current demands. This situation has led to delays and escalating maintenance expenses, which are impeding economic growth. Furthermore, civil engineers have raised concerns about safety risks posed by structurally deficient bridges and outdated water infrastructure.[101]

In contrast, China has embraced an economy-orientated approach as a cultural and policy matter, prioritising economic development over other considerations compared to the competition-orientation of the United States. In 1990, as the second generation of China's top leader, Deng Xiaoping was the first to articulate a specific policy as 'observing calmly, consolidating your foundation, working with aplomb, keeping a low profile, biding your time, staying humble skilfully, avoiding taking the lead, and making a difference'.[102] China's preference is to resort to military measures as a last resort, and unless forced into desperation, China strives to avoid military conflicts.

However, if China is perceived as being 'provoked' into military conflicts, its leaders primarily adopt a holistic perspective. Under the leadership of Mao Zedong, China was involved in the Korean War, the Sino-Indian War, and the Sino-USSR War, while under the guidance of Deng Xiaoping, China participated in the Sino-Vietnam War. These wars were characterised by being well-timed and of limited scope, taking advantage of favourable international conditions and minimising the potential for uncontrollable escalation of conflicts.

Notably, in early 2023, President Xi Jinping introduced a shift in policy that reflects China's evolving global position, demonstrating a greater assertiveness. The new policy, characterised by the principles of 'staying calm, standing firmly, striving for progress while maintaining stability, taking proactive actions, presenting as united front, and daring to fight',[103] has become evident in China's diplomatic engagements on the global stage of international relations.

The following examples illustrate how the United States allowed the conflicts to drift much longer than necessary, while how China managed to control the timing and limit the scale of military conflicts.

**(1)**

*The Afghanistan War*
The Afghanistan War spanned from 2001 to 2021 and pitted US-led forces against the Afghan Taliban. Despite an initially successful military campaign, the war ultimately ended in ignominy in August 2021, nearly two decades after it began, with the complete triumph of the Taliban following the withdrawal of US forces. With a cost of $2.3 trillion and the loss of 2488 American lives, it stands as a blatant testament to failure. It was the longest war in US military history.[104]

Extensive research has been conducted on the Afghanistan War and other conflicts within the realms of war, defence, and security studies, exploring various factors responsible for the failure of these endeavours.[105] However, the focus here will be on how Western strategic thinking contributed to the outcomes, as compared to Chinese strategic thinking in China's international conflicts.

In the context of Western strategic thinking, it becomes evident that there are common factors contributing to the ultimate outcomes of the Afghanistan War, as well as the Korean War, the Vietnam War, and Iraqi War. Primarily, the leadership of the United States lacked a holistic perspective in guiding these endeavours.

The lack of clearly defined objectives in the Afghanistan conflict led to a drifting and uncontrollable expansion of its goals. Initially, the political aims of the Afghanistan War were focused on seeking revenge for the 9/11 attacks, removing the Taliban from power, and capturing Osama bin Laden. While the Taliban were swiftly defeated and replaced, the capture of bin Laden proved a more elusive objective. Over time, additional political aims such as democratisation, counterterrorism, and nation-building were introduced.

As the conflict progressed, the mission evolved from a relatively straightforward one to a more complex and challenging endeavour. Aligning military operations with the shifting political aims became increasingly difficult for US forces. Ultimately, the United States and NATO were unable to contain the resurgence of the Taliban. Although bin Laden was eventually located and eliminated, it took a decade to accomplish, and groups like Al Qaeda continue to pose a threat not only in the region but also around the world.[106]

It was also evident that the war's objectives were overly ambitious, encompassing goals such as defeating or minimising the Taliban insurgency, preventing transnational terrorists from operations on Afghan soil, and establishing a viable Afghan state capable of safeguarding the human rights and civil liberties of its citizens. Additionally, political leaders struggled to clearly articulate a strategy to achieve these objectives and navigate the challenge of coordinating goals and resources among NATO members. Furthermore, the US involvement in the war in Iraq contributed to strategic diffusion by diverting resources and shifting political and bureaucratic focus away from Afghanistan.[107]

A report linked the US setback in the Afghanistan War to two key factors. Firstly, the Taliban effectively employed guerrilla warfare tactics reminiscent of those used by the Viet Cong against the United States in the 1960s. These tactics aimed to undermine the legitimacy of governments through widespread assassinations of key leaders, terrorise populations through kidnappings and bombings, infiltrate organisations, and procure weapons and supplies from their adversaries. The US military's failure to fully appreciate this type of warfare led to its defeat by the Taliban, much like its defeat by North Vietnam in 1975.

The second issue was a flawed strategic and tactical culture within the US military. American commanders hindered US-supported Afghan forces from adopting effective strategies to counter guerrilla warfare tactics. Senior leaders considered Afghanistan a distraction that diverted essential resources from their perceived primary mission of developing armed forces capable of decisively defeating enemies across all domains of warfare. It was highlighted that US nation-building efforts in Afghanistan were misguided, essentially indicating that the United States was fighting the wrong war.[108]

Based on these studies, the factors contributing to the US failure in Afghanistan, as viewed through Western strategic thinking, can be summarised as follows:

1. Lack of a comprehensive understanding of warfare led to poorly defined objectives that tended to drift and expand to additional unmanageable goals, resulting in a significant increase in military expenditure.
2. Overly ambitious and unrealistic objectives led to excessively expensive and unattainable military efforts.
3. Ignorance or failure to adapt to adversaries' tactics such as guerrilla warfare, which had been extensively utilised during the Vietnam War, indicating a repeated failure in addressing similar challenges.
4. The military pursued its own agenda to prepare for warfare without fully aligning with the nation's political objectives.

These factors ultimately point to a deficiency in the comprehensive understanding of warfare stemming from a Western-centric strategic perspective. Moreover, inadequate coordinated political and military decisions or a lack of harmonisation in civilian–military relations resulted in the ineffective identification and resolution of these issues. Additionally, Western strategic culture has overlooked the significance of garnering support from the local populace.[109]

Chinese theories and practice have compellingly illustrated the crucial importance of securing popular support for achieving ultimate military and political success. In both the Afghanistan War and Iraqi War, the US military achieved initial victories but ultimately experienced significant losses, largely attributable to the absence of support from the local populace, who aligned themselves with the insurgents.

*The Sino-Vietnam War*
The Sino-Vietnam War, also known in China as the self-defence counterattack against Vietnam, refers to the war that occurred between the People's Republic of China (PRC) and the Socialist Republic of Vietnam (SRV) on the Sino-Vietnam border from 17 February to 16 March 1979. The decision

to engage in this conflict was primarily driven by Deng Xiaoping, who had recently risen to become the de facto paramount leader of China.

Under the guidance of Deng Xiaoping, on 14 February 1979, the Central Committee of the Chinese Communist Party issued an official document to all Party and military organisations explaining its decision to launch a self-defence counterattack on Vietnam. It emphasised that the conflict would be limited in its geographical extent, duration, and magnitude. Referring to the Sino-Indian border conflict of 1962 and the Sino-Soviet border clash of 1969, the document insisted that China had no intention to seize any of Vietnam's territory and was committed to preventing the SRV from occupying any Chinese land.[110]

The SRV posed a significant challenge as a potential adversary. It signed the Soviet-Vietnamese Treaty of Peace and Friendship on 3 November 1978, exerted influence over Laos, and conducted an invasion of Cambodia. With a population of 50 million, Vietnam maintained a formidable army of one million soldiers. Drawing on 30 years of combat experience, including its conflict with the United States, the SRV demonstrated considerable military prowess and possessed advanced weaponry, including equipment received from China during wartime, as well as Soviet and surplus United States military technology left behind after the US withdrawal from Vietnam. Often referred to as the 'Cuba of the East', Vietnam's military capabilities surpassed those of Cuba in the West. The Soviet Union leveraged this alliance to pursue dominance in Southeast Asia, disrupt peace and stability in the region, and threaten the security of China's southern territory, thereby straining China's relationships with other Asian nations.[111]

Deng Xiaoping presented three compelling rationales for initiating punitive action against Vietnam:

1.  The ongoing international struggle against Soviet Union hegemony was faltering as the United States, Japan, and Europe hesitated to confront the USSR, despite its military build-up for war and rapid expansion. Given Vietnam's aggression in Cambodia and its persistent provocations along China's border, Deng argued that China must assume a leading role in this fight. The self-defence counterattack was not solely about border disputes, but rather about addressing the broader situation in Southeast Asia and even globally.
2.  In order to pursue its Four Modernisations, China required a secure and stable environment. China could not afford to be encircled by the Soviet Union from the north and Vietnam from the south. Deng believed that China should expose the hollowness of Vietnam's self-proclaimed status as 'the world's third strongest military power' and as 'ever victorious'. Failure to act would not only embolden Vietnam's aggression but potentially invite further Soviet Union intervention from the north. Thus,

China's pre-emptive counterattack would serve as a deterrent to the Soviet Union, cautioning it to restrain its own expansionist ambitions.

3. The PLA had not engaged in warfare for three decades. There was widespread scepticism globally regarding China's ability to prevail over Vietnam, and even within China, some leaders harboured doubts about military's continued effectiveness. Despite appearing as an unconventional rationale for military action against Vietnam, Deng Xiaoping believed that such a conflict would illustrate China's status as a formidable power. A successful war against Vietnam would serve to rejuvenate the military's standing and afford more officers with valuable combat experience. Additionally, battlefield experience was expected to drive the PLA to become more agile and effective in its operations.[112]

Deng's decision-making deeply considered Soviet military deployments and potential responses to the self-defence counterattack. Three potential Soviet intervention strategies were identified, each carrying different levels of risk: large-scale, medium-scale, and small-scale reactions.

A large-scale intervention would entail a full-scale assault by the Soviet army from the Sino-Soviet border, with substantial forces advancing into northern China, possibly reaching Beijing, the capital. Despite the Soviet claim of stationing one million military personnel along the border, US satellite sources indicated that this number was greatly exaggerated. It was revealed that, in 1979, there were 57 divisions of Soviet troops along the border, of which only 30% were fully equipped and 60% were capable of rapid mobilisation.

Strategically, the main Soviet troop deployments and crucial military installations were based in Europe, with the Western front as the strategic focus. The PLA estimated that it would take at least two months to shift adequate forces and logistics from Eastern Europe to the border, by which time the Chinese military could have achieved their objectives in Vietnam and redirected their forces northward.[113] Ultimately, dispatching troops from Europe to combat Chinese forces was not in the best interests of the Soviet Union.

The medium-scale intervention would involve the mobilisation of the 'brigade of revanche', which aimed to rally the people of Xinjiang and Inner Mongolia, who had earlier defected to the Soviet Union under duress, to infiltrate Xinjiang and Inner Mongolia. Meanwhile, the small-scale reaction would focus on border provocations. However, the Chinese military was well-prepared to effectively respond to these conflicts, rendering them inconsequential. Despite the remote likelihood of large-scale intervention from the Soviet Union, the Chinese military remained fully prepared for any potential events, ready to engage in warfare at any scale.[114]

After identifying and analysing potential Soviet interventions, Deng Xiaoping needed to devise a strategy for addressing these risks. While the Chinese military prepared for conflict with Vietnam, Deng Xiaoping embarked on a diplomatic journey to the United States, from 29 January to 5 February, 1979, with the hope of securing indirect US support for China's self-defence counterattack against Vietnam, ultimately aiming at the common adversary, the Soviet Union.

During a meeting with President Jimmy Carter, Deng conveyed to the president that, in response to escalating Soviet expansionism, the Chinese leadership deemed it necessary to restrain the ambitious actions of the Vietnamese and impart a measured, punitive response. Deng also discussed potential Soviet reactions and China's plans to address them. Carter's response seemed dismissive, as he argued that a limited penal war would not dissuade Vietnam's occupation of Cambodia and might entangle China in a protracted conflict. Despite Carter's apparently unsupportive stance, Deng did not believe that the United States would have a negative impact on China's military action against Vietnam.[115]

While the United States expressed disapproval of China's proposed action, it recognised that the meetings between the Chinese and US leaders would create an impression that the Chinese military 'hit Vietnam with the appearance of United States acquiescence'. Additionally, the United States aimed to assure China of its commitment to act as a counterbalance to Soviet military build-up in Asia and to support a 'strong, secure, and peaceful China' capable of deterring a Sino-Soviet conflict. In pursuit of this goal, the United States demonstrated a willingness to relax its control of arms sales to China by Western European nations.[116]

After the war, Deng's prediction that the Soviet Union would not intervene proved accurate. In the following months, China worked to further isolate Vietnam on the global stage while also seeking to improve relations with the Soviet Union. This resulted in China strengthening its position in Southeast Asia, asserting itself as the dominant regional power, willing to endure and inflict casualties to achieve its strategic goals. The Sino-Vietnam War served as a direct warning to other nations not to challenge China's influence in Southeast Asia lightly.[117]

The assessment of the outcome of the Sino-Vietnam War varies depending on different perspectives. However, in this context, the aim is to compare China's campaign from a holistic standpoint with the wars conducted by the United States, which typically adhere to a Western atomic strategic outlook.

An impartial evaluation, not aligned with China or Vietnam, highlighted the PLA's deficiencies in modern combat doctrine and tactics. Nonetheless, China controlled the conflict's tempo and initiative from start to finish. Beijing, rather than Hanoi, determined the war's pace, structure, battlefield, geostrategic engagement, and duration. Particularly surprising was Beijing's ability to launch massive attacks and then swiftly withdraw without becoming embroiled – a development that the overconfident Hanoi regime, drawing from its prior experience in a vastly different conflict against the Americans a decade earlier, had not foreseen.[118]

The Sino-Vietnam War, akin to the conflict along the Sino-Indian border, showcased the Chinese military's capacity to effectively restrict the scale, pace, and geographic scope of their operations, concluding them within a defined timeframe before swiftly withdrawing without becoming mired in prolonged engagements. It also demonstrated the capability of the Chinese political leadership in accurately assessing and anticipating external challenges, including potential Soviet intervention, and effectively managing them.

Fundamentally, from a strategic standpoint, Chinese political and military leadership has adeptly maintained control over their domain. However, operationally, there may be significant room for improvement and learning from Western practices within the Chinese military.

## (2)

Over the past two decades, China has experienced significant advancements in its naval capabilities and satellite navigation systems, known as Beidou. These advancements can largely be attributed to a particular action taken by the United States, which, rather than achieving its intended outcome, inadvertently fuelled China's determination and drive to address its vulnerabilities exposed by this action.

On 7 July 1993, a Chinese cargo ship, named Yinhe, meaning 'Galaxy' in English, embarked from Tianjin, carrying 628 containers, with its destination set for the Port of Dubai in the Persian Gulf by 3 August. However, on 23 July, the United States received intelligence suggesting that the Yinhe was transporting thiodiglycol and thionyl chloride – substances that could potentially be used in the production of chemical weapons. It was suspected that the ship was heading towards Iran's Bandar Abbas Port.

Consequently, when the Yinhe entered the Indian Ocean, it was intercepted by a US warship on the high seas. By disabling the ship's GPS system, the US effectively rendered the vessel immobile. Simultaneously, the United States issued a communication to the Chinese government, informing them that exporting hazardous chemicals to Iran was illegal. The Yinhe was presented with two options: either return home to its point of origin or permit an inspection by US personnel.

To the best of the Chinese government's knowledge, the cargo aboard the Yinhe consisted solely of stationery items, hardware, mechanical parts, dyes, and other goods intended for the Middle East, with no hazardous chemicals present. During the negotiations, the Yinhe received an order to temporarily halt in the deep sea at the east entrance of the Strait of Hormuz, where the crew remained and waited for 22 days.

Following the negotiations, China and the United States reached an agreement to allow a third party to board the ship and conduct an inspection. On 28 August, a team of seven personnel from Saudi Arabia was dispatched to inspect the Yinhe. China sent 15 representatives to assist in the process, while the United States had a significant number of personnel monitoring the proceedings.

The inspection continued until 4 September. Saudi personnel thoroughly examined all 628 containers, paying particular attention to eight containers holding liquids, and found no chemical raw materials. Eventually, the US government acknowledged that some of the intelligence about the Yinhe may have been incorrect, leading to the mistake.[119]

The Yinhe incident had a profound impact on the People's Liberation Army Navy (PLAN). Although the US warship intercepted the Yinhe on the high seas rather than in US territorial waters, the PLAN was unable to respond effectively to this challenge. Following this incident, the Chinese Navy placed great emphasis on enhancing its ocean combat capabilities and spared no effort in developing large ocean destroyers.

Since then, there has been a tremendous growth in both the number and tonnage of Chinese naval vessels. The *Economic Times* reported that, with the influx of new vessels each year, the PLAN has emerged as one of the most advanced and capable navies globally, surpassing all other Asian navies by a significant margin. In 2021 alone, China added 170 000 tons of total tonnage to its navy fleets, an amount that is nearly equivalent to rebuilding the navy of a medium-sized European country in just one year.[120]

During the time when the Yinhe was at sea, it experienced an unexpected loss of GPS signal. It later became apparent that the US military deliberately blocked the signal. The incident raised concerns about the vulnerability of Chinese warships in the event of a conflict with the United States, as they would be deprived of GPS services. The implications of such a scenario for Chinese warships were significant.

Initially, China had no plans to develop its own navigation guidance system, due to limited demand at the time. However, in 1994, just one year after the Yinhe incident, China officially initiated the development of the Beidou satellite navigation test system (Beidou-1 system). Over time, the Beidou System has progressed to its third generation and has emerged as the only serious competitor to the US GPS system, establishing China's independent navigation capabilities.[121]

Essentially, the United States often approach military actions with an analytical mindset, viewing each operation in isolation without fully weighing its potential consequences across various strategic domains. By engaging in seemingly insignificant aggressive manoeuvres to imposing US rules in international arenas and demonstrate US military strength, the United States inadvertently provoked a powerful response from China, leading to the rapid development of more balanced or even stronger military capabilities for counterattack readiness.

**(3)**

In its effort to shape its policy towards China, the United States government has adopted a strategic approach that has been rooted in Western cognition. This approach aims to exert control over and restrict Chinese access to Western high-tech products and technology, such as computer and AI chips, as well as electronic design automation (EDA) software.

However, prominent Western business leaders, including Bill Gates of Microsoft and CEOs of major US chipmakers like Intel, Qualcomm, and NVidia, have warned the US government that such controls would only serve to stimulate and facilitate China's development of its own high-tech products and technologies. Instead of impeding China's progress, these leaders believe that fostering collaboration and open access to technology would be more beneficial for both China and the Western world.

The strategic approach adopted by the US government is rooted in Western thinking, influenced by Clausewitz's principles of annihilating the enemy and achieving total victory. While this approach may have proven effective in the Western context, its applicability to the Chinese situation is questionable.

A historical example that illustrates the effectiveness of this approach in the Western world is the rise of Japanese semiconductor companies in the late 1980s. At that time, Japanese companies surpassed the United States, capturing over half of the global semiconductor market. In response, the US implemented containment measures to curb these Japanese companies. The intervention led to Japan ceding its dominance to companies in South Korea and Taiwan.[122]

The United States attempted to replicate its success against Japanese companies with Chinese companies, but this time the strategy has not yet yielded the desired results. The circumstances and dynamics at play in China differ significantly from those in Japan, rendering the same strategic approach less effective.

The US policy of controlling and blocking China can be seen as ineffective. To illustrate this, we can draw a metaphorical comparison of a rising China to a powerful flood surging towards the Western world. In response, the Western nations are attempting to construct embankments to halt the flood's progress. Interestingly, Chinese antiquity provides us with a story that depicts the challenges of containing such floods.

During the reign of Emperor Yao around 1953 BC, devastating floods plagued the Central Plains, causing immense suffering for the populace. To address this crisis, the emperor entrusted Gun, a tribe leader, with the task of controlling the flood.

Gun employed a strategy of building river embankments to contain and block the floodwaters. However, the water level of the flood often rose significantly higher than the embankments, leading to their eventual erosion and destruction under the force of powerful waves. After nine years of endeavour, the strategy proved unsuccessful in quelling the floodwaters.

Gun's failure to tame the floodwaters led to his replacement by his son, Yu. Having learned from his father's mistakes, Yu decided to adopt a different approach to tackling the issue. Instead of relying solely on barriers to block the floodwaters, Yu focused on dredging and diverting them to minimise their impact. For thirteen long years, he persevered and successfully brought the floodwaters under control, putting an end to the devastating scourge of flooding in the Central Plains.

If the US government had permitted Chinese companies to continue using their high-tech product and technologies, it is likely that many of these companies would have been satisfied with simply importing these products and technologies with limited efforts in developing their own products and technological advancement. Chinese companies have long admired Western products and technologies, considering them to be more advanced and of higher quality than their own early-developed counterparts.

However, the US government's policy of restricting access to these high-tech products and technologies has had unintended consequences. Rather than stifling this group of people, it has spurred and facilitated the development of Chinese products and technology. Faced with limited access to Western goods, Chinese companies and innovators have been compelled to invest in their own R&D efforts. This has led to a significant boost in the advancement and improvement of Chinese products and technologies. Therefore, China has made substantial progress in various industries, becoming a formidable player on the global stage.

To extend our analogy, the restriction imposed on the exports of Western products and technologies to China can be compared to the construction of embankments as a means of controlling floodwaters. This approach is destined to fail. On the other hand, allowing and facilitating the export of these products and technologies can be likened to the practice of dredging and diverting floodwaters, which leads to the desired outcomes.

Allowing American high-tech companies to export their products and generate profits would enable these companies to invest in the development of newer technologies, sustaining a competitive edge. On the contrary, if exports are blocked, these high-tech companies would lose substantial profits, limiting their resources for further research and development. This scenario could pave the way for the rise of Chinese high-tech companies. Once Chinese companies overcome the technological barriers, Western high-tech companies would not only lose the Chinese market but also face challenges in other international markets.

## NOTES

1. Griffith, S.B. (1963). *Sun Tzu: The Art of War*. Translated and with an Introduction by Samuel B. Griffith and Foreword by B.H. Liddell Hart. Oxford University Press, p. v.
2. Handel, M.I. (2012). *Masters of War: Classical Strategic Thought*. Routledge, p. 20.
3. Ibid.
4. Gat, A. (1989). *The Origins of Military Thought: From the Enlightenment to Clausewitz*. Oxford University Press, p. 199.
5. Ibid., p. 200.
6. Chaliand, G. (1994). *The Art of War in World History: From Antiquity to the Nuclear Age*. University of California Press, p. 671.
7. Kinross, S. (2008). *Clausewitz and America: Strategic Thought and Practice from Vietnam to Iraq*. Routledge, p. 7.
8. Graham's introductory note on Clausewitz's *On War*: Clausewitz, C. von (1997). *On War* (J.J. Graham, Trans.). Wordsworth Editions Limited, pp. xi–xii.
9. Gat (n 4) p. 200.
10. Graham (n 8) pp. ix–x.
11. Ibid., p. 5.
12. Jullien, F. (2004). *A Treatise on Efficacy: Between Western and Chinese Thinking* (J. Lloyd, Trans.). Honolulu: University of Hawaii Press, p. 11.
13. Graham (n 8) p. xiii.
14. Jullien (n 12).
    Henkel, J.E. (2006). A Treatise on Efficacy: Between Western and Chinese Thinking (review). *Philosophy East and West*, 56(2), pp. 347–451.
15. Jullien (n 12).
    Henkel (14) pp. 347–451.
16. Chaliand (n 6) p. 221.
17. Handel (n 2) p. 21.
    Yuen, M.C. (2008). Deciphering Sun Tzu. *Comparative Strategy*, 27(2), pp. 183–200.
18. Roberts, A. (2011). *The Art of War: Great Commanders of the Ancient World*. Quercus, p. 71.
19. Paquette, L. (1991). Strategy and Time in Clausewitz's On War and in Sun Tzu's The Art of War. *Comparative Strategy*, 10(1), pp. 37–51.
20. Ridgway, M.B. (1967). *The Korean War*. Da CAPO Press, p. 74.
21. Gat (n 4) pp. 199–214.

22.  Beaumont, R. (1996). Landmarks in Defense Literature (Book-Review). *Defense Analysis*, 12(3), pp. 381–2.
     Beaumont, R. (2010). Decoding Clausewitz: A New Approach to (Book-Review). *The American Historical Review*, 115(1), pp. 309–10.
23.  Hemingway, E. (Ed.) (1942). *Men at War*. New York: Crown Publishers.
24.  Beaumont (n 22) pp. 309–10.
25.  Jullien (n 12) p. 74.
26.  Sawyer, R.D. (1993). *The Seven Military Classics of Ancient China*. Westview Press, Inc., p. 157.
27.  Ibid.
28.  Zhang, Y. and Zhou, S.H. (2020). *Da Dang Mei Li (The Captivation of the Great Party)*. Red Flag Publishing House, pp. 59–60.
29.  Graham (n 8) p. 5.
30.  Kushi, S. and Duffy Toft, M. (2023). Introducing the Military Intervention Project: A New Dataset on US Military Interventions, 1776–2019. *Journal of Conflict Resolution*, 67(4), pp. 752–79.
31.  Sawyer (n 26) p. 126.
32.  Graham (n 8) p. 204.
33.  Sawyer (n 26) p. 161.
34.  Liddell Hart, B.H. (2005). Forward to the Translation of and Introduction to *Sun Tzu: The Art of War* by Samuel B. Griffith. Duncan Baird Publishers, Ltd, p. 6.
35.  Ibid., p. 7.
36.  Graham (n 8) p. 6.
37.  Halberstam, D. (2007). *The Coldest Winter: America and the Korean War*. Macmillan, p. 490.
     Ridgway (n 20) p. 110.
38.  Ibid., p. 59.
39.  Ibid., p. 593.
40.  Li, Feng (2020). *Jue zhan chao xian (Showdown in Korea)*, Contemporary Publishing House, pp. 206–7.
41.  Department of War Theory and Research, Academy of Military Sciences (2011). *Zhongguo Gudai Jingdian Zhanzheng Zhanli (Classic War Cases of Ancient China)*. Liberation Army Publishing House, pp. 51–3.
42.  Jullien, F. (2004). *A Treatise on Efficacy: Between Western and Chinese Thinking*, translated by Janet Lloyd, Honolulu: University of Hawaii Press, pp. 41–2.
     Graham, J.J. (1997). Clausewitz, C. von: *On War*. Translated by J.J. Graham and Abridged and with an Introduction by L. Willmot. Wordsworth Editions Limited, pp. 19-20.
43.  Griffith (n 1) p. 125.
44.  Jullien (n 42) p. 42.
45.  Lu, Z.D. (2009). *Mao Zedong Pin Guo Xue (Mao Zedong's Appreciation of Chinese Classics)*. New World Press, p. 31.

46. Steil, B. (2018). *The Marshall Plan: Dawn of the Cold War*. Oxford University Press, pp. 1–2.

47. Dale, I. (2021). *The Presidents: 250 Years of American Political Leadership*. Hodder & Stoughton, p. 339.

48. Ibid., pp. 12–13.

49. Stent, A. (2019). *Putin's World: Russia Against the West and with the Rest*. Twelve, pp. 110–11.

50. Steil (n 46) p. 2.

51. Friedman, T.L. and Mandelbaum, M. (2011). *That Used to Be US: What Went Wrong with America – and How It Can Come Back*. Little, Brown, p. xi.

52. MacAskill, E. and Borger, J. (2004). Iraq War was Illegal and Breached UN Charter, says Annan. *The Guardian*. https://www.theguardian.com/world/2004/sep/16/iraq.iraq. Retrieved on 15 November 2023.
    Soros, G. (2004). *The Bubble of American Supremacy*. Weidenfeld & Nicolson.

53. Biegon, R. (2019). A Populist Grand Strategy? Trump and the Framing of American Decline. *International Relations*, 33(4), pp. 517–39.

54. Dyer, G. (2021). *The Shortest History of War*. Old Street Publishing Ltd, p. 212.

55. Pieterse, J.N. (2004). Can the United States Correct Itself? *Cultural Studies – Critical Methodologies*, 4(3), pp. 281–411.

56. King, A. (2023). Why Did the Taliban Win? *Armed Forces & Society*, 49(4), pp. 923–38.

57. Stiglitz, Joseph and Bilmes, Linda (2008). *The Three Trillion Dollar War*. Allen Lane.

58. Tiezzi, Shannon (2023). How China's Belt and Road Took Over the World. *The Diplomat*, September 12, 2023. https://thediplomat.com/2023/09/how-chinas-belt-and-road-took-over-the-world/. Retrieved on 27 October 2023.

59. Peffer, N. (1968). *The Far East: A Modern History*. The University of Michigan Press, pp. 393–418.

60. Zraick, K. and Lee, C.W. (2019). Chinese Railroad Workers Were Almost Written Out of History. Now They're Getting Their Due. *The New York Times*, May 12, 2019. https://cn.nytimes.com/usa/20190521/golden-spike-utah-railroad-150th-annversary/dual/ Retrieved on 14 November 2023.

61. Schaller, M. (1976). American Air Strategy in China, 1939–1941: The Origins of Clandestine Air Warfare. *American Quarterly*, 28(1), pp. 3–19.
    Halberstam, D. (2007). *The Coldest Winter: America and the Korean War*. Macmillan, p. 225.

62. Greenspan, A. and Wooldridge, A. (2018). *Capitalism in America: A History*. Allen Lane, p. 26.

63. Ibid., pp. 94–5.

64. Ibid., pp. 98–9.

65. Greenspan and Wooldridge (n 62) p. 314.

66.  Acemoglu, D. and Robinson, J.A. (2012). *Why Nations Fail: The Origins of Power, Prosperity, and Poverty*. Profile Books, pp. 33–4.

67.  Greenspan and Wooldridge (n 62) p. 94.

68.  Ibid., pp. 96.

69.  Gorden, R.J. (2017). *Rise and Fall of American Growth*. Princeton University Press, p. 4.

70.  Greenspan and Wooldridge (n 62) pp. 96–8.

71.  Gorden (n 69) p. 1.

72.  Greenspan and Wooldridge (n 62) p. 310.

73.  Gorden (n 69) p. 523.

74.  Hayes, R.H. and Abernathy, W.J. (1980). Managing Our Way to Economic Decline. *Harvard Business Review*, 58(4), pp. 66–77.

75.  Greenspan and Wooldridge (n 62) pp. 312–14.

76.  Hayes, R.H. and Abernathy, W.J. (2007). Managing Our Way to Economic Decline. *Harvard Business Review*, 85 (7/8), pp. 138–49.

77.  Science and Engineering Programme Group of the Monitoring Network (2022). *Shiye Qiangguo: Zhongguo Zhizhao Ziqiang Zhilu* (*Bolstering National Competitiveness with Industry: China's Manufacturing Pathway to Self-Advancement*). People's University Press, pp. 29–35.

78.  Koll, E. (2019). *Railroads and the Transformation of China*, Harvard University Press, p. 223.

79.  Ma, H. (1982). *Zhongguo Xiandai Jingji Daquan* (*Encyclopaedia of China's Modern Economy*). China's Social Science Publishing House, pp. 46–7.

80.  Liu, J.L. (2019). Xin zhongguo liyong waizi 70 nian: Licheng, xiaoying yu zhuyao jingyan (70 Years of Foreign Investment Utilisation in New China: History, Efficacy, and Main Experiences). *Management World*, 10 December 2019. http://gjs.cssn.cn/kydt/kydt_kycg/201912/t20191210 _5056540.shtml. Retrieved on 12 December 2023.

81.  Qian, Y.Y. (2000). The Process of China's Market Transition (1978–98): The Evolutionary, Historical, and Comparative Perspectives. *Journal of Institutional and Theoretical Economics*, 156, pp. 151–71.

82.  Twitchett, Denis and Fairbank, J.K. (1987*). The Cambridge History of China: Volume 14, The People's Republic, Part 1: The Emergence of Revolutionary China 1949–1965*, Cambridge University Press, pp. 51–3.

83.  Li, Y. (2019). Di yi ge wunian jihua de '156 xiang' (The '156 Projects' of the First Five-year Plan). *Communist Party of China News Network*，www .cpcnews.cn. Retrieved on 12 December 2023.

84.  Zhao, X.J. (2021). 156 Xiang jianshe xiangmu dui zhongguo gongyehua de lishi gongxian (The Historical Contribution of 156 Construction Projects to China's Industrialization). *Research on Chinese Economic History*, 4, pp. 26–37.

85.  Liu, J.J and Sun, Q. (2021). Review and Prospect of the Centenary of China's Industrialisation: The Industrialisation Strategy of the Communist Party of China. *China Economist*, No.5, 4 November, 2021. http://gjs.cssn.cn/kydt/

kydt_kycg/202111/t20211104_5371661.shtml. Retrieved on 12 December 2023.

86. Chen, D.L. (2004). Zhongguo gaige kaifang qian de duiwai jingji yinjin (China's Introduction of Foreign Investment Before Reform and Opening-up). *China Social Sciences Network*, 14 September 2009. http://hprc.cssn.cn/gsyj/jjs/jjyxs/200909/t20090914_3958564.html. Retrieved on 12 December 2023.

87. Ma, J.L. (1991). Prospects of China's Economic Development. *China Report*, 27(3), pp. 255–6.

88. *Report on Foreign Investment in China 2022*. Ministry of Commerce of the People's Republic of China. http://images.mofcom.gov.cn/wzs/202301/20230104194942451.pdf. Retrieved on 14 December 2023.

89. Dong, H.B. et al. (2019). Roadmap of China Steel Industry in the Past 70 Years. *Ironmaking & Steelmaking: Process, Products and Applications*, 46(10), pp. 922–7.

90. Zhao (n 84) pp. 26–37.

91. Koll (n 78) pp. 293–4.

92. Zhao, S.Y. (2021). China's Transportation Development Turns Country into 'Strong Power'. *Chinadaily.com.cn*, 1 June, 2021. https://global.chinadaily.com.cn/a/202106/01/WS60b486fca31024ad0bac28e8.html. Retrieved on 15 December 2023.

93. McBride, J., Berman, N. and Siripurapu, A. (2023). The State of U.S. Infrastructure. *Council on Foreign Relations*, September 20, 2023. https://www .cfr .org/ backgrounder/ state -us -infrastructure. Retrieved on 12 December, 2023.

94. Science and Engineering Programme Group of the Monitoring Network (n 77) pp. 295–300.

95. Dyer (n 54) p. 173.

96. Zhou, J.H. (2023). Why Beijing isn't Interested in Setting Guardrails for China-US Competition. *The Diplomat*, August 03, 2023. https://thediplomat .com/2023/08/why-beijing-isnt-interested-in-setting-guardrails-for-china-us -competition/. Retrieved on 23 November 2023.

97. Dyer (n 54) p. 173.

98. Lovering, J. (1987). The Atlantic Arms Economy: Towards a Military Regime of Accumulation? *Capital & Class*, 11 (3), pp. 129–55.

99. Pieterse (n 55) pp. 281–411.

100. Obama, B. (2010). Press Conference by the President. https://obamawhitehouse .archives .gov/ the -press -office/ 2010/ 11/ 03/ press -conference -president. 03 November, 2010. Retrieved on 20 November 2023.

101. McBride et al. (n 93).

102. The Communist Network (2023). Deng Xiaoping's Diplomatic Thought will Shine Forever. https://www.12371.cn. 11 March 2023. Retrieved on 23 November 2023.

103. The Chinese Communist Party Network (2023). Put Down the Burden and Develop Dauntlessly. cpc.people.com.cn. 11 March 2023. Retrieved on 23 November 2023.
104. King (n 56) pp. 923–38.
105. Haigh, M.M. (2014). Afghanistan War Coverage More Negative Over Time. *Newspaper Research Journal*, 35(3), pp. 38–51.
     Honig, J.W. and Käihkö, I. (2023). An Exemplary Defeat: The West in Afghanistan, 2001–2021. *Armed Forces & Society*, 49(4), pp. 989–1000.
     Travis, D.S. (2023). Why the U.S. Military Lost Afghanistan. *Armed Forces & Society*, 49(4), pp. 939–952.
     Brooks, R. (2023). The Best They Could Do? Assessing U.S. Military Effectiveness in the Afghanistan War. *Armed Forces & Society*, 49 (4), pp. 913–22.
106. Inbody, D.S. and Shields, P.M. (2023). Perspectives on the Afghanistan War: Commentaries on a Misadventure. *Armed Forces & Society*, 49(4), pp. 883–92.
107. Brooks (n 105) pp. 913–22.
108. Travis (n 105) pp. 939–52.
109. Honig and Käihkö (n 105) pp. 989–1000.
     Svet, O. (2012). COIN's Failure in Afghanistan. *The National Interest*, 31 August, 2012. https:// nationalinterest .org/ commentary/ coins -failure -afghanistan-7409. Retrieved on 1 December 2023.
110. Zhang, X.M. (2015). *Deng Xiaoping's Long War: The Military Conflict between China and Vietnam, 1979–1991*. The University of North Carolina Press, p. 64.
111. Shi, H. (1979). Deng Xiaoping on Sino-Vietnam War. *China Report*, 15(3), pp. 53–7.
112. Zhang (n 110) pp. 54–5.
113. Gin, C. (2015). *The 1979 Sino-Vietnamese War: How China Wins*. U.S. Army Command and General Staff College, p. 75.
114. Shi (n 111) pp. 53–7.
115. Zhang (n 110) pp. 60–1.
116. Gin (n 113) pp. 60–61.
117. Ibid., pp. 81–2.
118. Zhang (n 110) pp. 120–21.
119. Kristof, N.D. (1993). China Says U.S. is Harassing Ship Suspected of Taking Arms to Iran. *The New York Times*, 3 September 1993. https://www .nytimes.com/1993/08/09/world/china-says-us-is-harassing-ship-suspected -of-taking-arms-to-iran.html. Retrieved on 20 December 2023.
120. The Economic Times (2022), 'A Powerful Chinese Navy Ready to Flex its Muscles', *The Economic Times*, 4 January 2022. https://economictimes .indiatimes.com/news/defence/a-powerful-chinese-navy-is-ready-to-flex-its -muscles/articleshow/88661655.cms. Retrieved on 20 October 2023.
121. Science and Engineering Group of the Monitoring Network (n 77) p. 283.

122. Sugiura, E. and Slodkowski, A. (2022). Japan's Biggest Chipmakers from Toshiba to Sony Brace for Engineer Shortage. *The Financial Times*, 26 June 2022. https:// www .ft .com/ content/ b90da329 -a2e5 -486a -860f -a20a3afc707a. Retrieved on 18 October 2023.

# Epilogue

*If you do not change direction, you may end up where you are heading.*
— Lao Tzu

*Trust your instinct to the end, though you can render no reason.*
— Ralph Waldo Emerson

In the West, strategic decisions across various domains are generally guided by analytical thinking deeply rooted in the culture. Conversely, decisions made by Chinese counterparts in these same areas are typically characterised by holistic thinking, leading to distinct strategic patterns and outcomes. Consequently, when international conflicts arise between China and Western nations, there is a significant risk of misunderstanding unless specific measures are taken to prevent this possibility.

The theoretical and practical strategic frameworks of China and Western nations have developed from distinct cultural roots, leading to different strategic priorities and implementation approaches. This contrast may elucidate why only a limited number of Western readers have truly grasped *Sun Tzu's Art of War*, which was introduced to Europe in the 18th century. While certain aspects of Sun Tzu's teachings, such as prioritising the avoidance of warfare and achieving victory without battle, have been widely admired and embraced, they have seldom been effectively executed by Western nations.

Western research on strategic management typically views the organisation as a decision unit, focusing on the collective roles and characteristics of senior executives. Although there is a considerable body of literature on leadership in the West, it is principally situated within the field of human resources management rather than strategy. In essence, applying Western group-based theories and frameworks of strategic management to understand or interpret Chinese strategic decisions and behaviour would be off the mark.

In most Chinese organisations, strategic decisions tend to be centralised and made by the top leader of the organisation, reflecting Chinese tradition. Therefore, to understand organisational strategic decision-making or 'thinking organisation' in China, attention should be directed to the organisational leader.

The strategic minds of different cultures vary, with the extent of difference depending on linguistic associations. People who speak Indo-European languages tend to think more similarly to each other than they do to those who speak languages from other language families, such as Chinese and Japanese. In certain Asian nations, such as China, Japan, and Korea, their languages have historical connections, and thus, people from these countries generally understand each other better than those from Western cultures, although there are still substantial differences among these countries. Essentially, it requires more effort for Western individuals to comprehend Chinese tradition and the Chinese mind.

A nation's global competitiveness and position are shaped by three factors: philosophical and political foundations, economic fundamentals, and strategic approaches.

Chinese theories and practices have illustrated the pivotal role of morality in shaping the outcomes of international cooperations and conflicts. The ascent of the United States to global dominance in various arenas has reflected the high moral standing of its earlier administrations. Similarly, China's appeal to developing nations is linked to its commitment to fair play, bolstered by its economic prowess. It is apparent that the United States has gradually relinquished its high moral ground, leading to an increasing distance from many of other nations.

The historical evolution of the United States and China illustrates that industrialisation, innovation, and transportation systems form the bedrock of a nation's competitiveness. The gradual decline of industrialisation in the United States has significantly hampered its capacity to uphold global dominance. Conversely, China's unswerving emphasis on industrialisation is elevating its global influence.

The United States' competitor-orientated strategy to sustain its global supremacy raises questions about its cost-effectiveness in achieving strategic objectives. In contrast, China's economy-centred strategy has progressively bolstered its economic strength, thereby enhancing its international influence.

These components are interconnected and reliant on each other. The philosophical and political foundations shape the spiritual and organisational dimensions, while economic fundamentals influence the material strength and resilience. Strategic approaches impact the effectiveness of utilising and mobilising spiritual and material factors.

Within academia, research on Chinese strategic thinking in the field of strategic management has been limited, as such endeavours require a holistic perspective that is at odds with the prevailing Western research culture. While there has been acknowledgement in the field of social psychology of cognitive differences between Chinese and Western individuals and efforts to study these disparities have been made, nevertheless, establishing effective mechanisms and incentives for cross-disciplinary research has remained a challenging pursuit.

The transformation of strategic thinking should commence within universities, where students' intellects are modelled. However, before educational initiatives can be implemented, the academic community must thoroughly understand the nature of the Chinese strategic mind and its distinctions from Western perspectives. It is anticipated that, in the coming years, there will be an increase in textbooks and scholarly works dedicated to the Chinese strategic mindset.

# Index